Service Science: Research and Innovations in the Service Economy

Series Editors:
Bill Hefley
Wendy Murphy

More information about this series at http://www.springer.com/series/8080

Jorge Cardoso • Hansjörg Fromm
Stefan Nickel • Gerhard Satzger
Rudi Studer • Christof Weinhardt
Editors

Fundamentals of Service Systems

Foreword by Jim Spohrer

 Springer

Editors
Jorge Cardoso
Department of Informatics Engineering
Universidade de Coimbra
Coimbra, Portugal

Huawei European Research Center (ERC)
Munich, Germany

Stefan Nickel
Karlsruhe Service Research Institute
Karlsruhe Institute of Technology
Karlsruhe, Germany

Rudi Studer
Karlsruhe Service Research Institute
Karlsruhe Institute of Technology
Karlsruhe, Germany

Hansjörg Fromm
Karlsruhe Service Research Institute
Karlsruhe Institute of Technology
Karlsruhe, Germany

Gerhard Satzger
Karlsruhe Service Research Institute
Karlsruhe Institute of Technology/
  IBM Deutschland GmbH
Karlsruhe, Germany

Christof Weinhardt
Karlsruhe Service Research Institute
Karlsruhe Institute of Technology
Karlsruhe, Germany

ISSN 1865-4924   ISSN 1865-4932   (electronic)
Service Science: Research and Innovations in the Service Economy
ISBN 978-3-319-79457-0   ISBN 978-3-319-23195-2   (eBook)
DOI 10.1007/978-3-319-23195-2

Springer International Publishing AG Switzerland is part of Springer Science+Business Media (www.springer.com)

Foreword

Writing a textbook about the world of service is a daunting task in part because the world of service is truly vast. Where to start? How best to guide students as they begin their journey? To become oriented quickly, students will need a good map.

In *Fundamentals of Service Systems*, Jorge Cardoso, Hansjörg Fromm, Stefan Nickel, Gerhard Satzger, Rudi Studer, and Christof Weinhardt all from the Karlsruhe Service Research Institute (KSRI)—provide a map with multiple entry points for students of service. Students who read this textbook learn that context matters. For example, economists have their definition of service, and computer scientists have a different definition. Compounding the learner's dilemma, service is a commonly used word in everyday conversations! From business to government to technology, every student has undoubtedly been a customer of an enormous range of types of service by the time they enter college, which is just one more type of service system with a focus on education.

Jorge Cardoso and Hansjoerg Fromm—together with their coeditors Rudi Studer, Stefan Nickel, Christof Weinhardt, and Gerhard Satzger,

One of the great strengths of this new college-level textbook is that it provides students with up-to-date examples in context. Of course, the world of service technologies is fast moving, and we can only hope that the excellent and finely tuned examples in this textbook will be refreshed regularly. In fact *textbooks as a service* is an area of service innovation that is evolving rapidly, in the age of MOOCs (Massively Open Online Courses), cognitive assistants, and crowdsourcing.

Scholars of service who are familiar with the daunting challenges posed by explaining service to students may be reminded as I was of Richard Normann's book *Reframing Business: When the Map Changes the Landscape*.[1] In that classic book, value-creating systems are presented as rapidly evolving, increasingly dense, and interconnected configurations of resources that shape us as we shape them. Consistent with Normann's view of service (value-creating systems with us inside), this textbook provides a clear map of the world of service for today's students and practitioners while also providing a sky crane for scholars and entrepreneurs actively engaged in reconstructing this constantly changing landscape.

---

[1]Richard Normann. *Reframing Business: When the Map Changes the Landscape*. Wiley, 2001.

In Chap. 1 Foundations, this textbook answers the question of why everyone should consider becoming a student of service. Simply put, we all live in a service-oriented society. The economic significance and technological sophistication of diverse types of service, which make up our service-oriented society, should be understood by students of management and engineering as well as those in the liberal arts and humanities, because together we co-create service systems. By the end of the chapter, students will arrive at a deeper understanding of service as transformation processes involving resources from both provider and customer.

Chapter 2 Electronic Services will appeal especially to students of computer science and information systems (informatics). Service progress is shaped by the desire of people to automate activities and evolve better programming paradigms that augment human intellect unlocking new levels of productivity and creativity. Web service technologies, cloud services, and the Internet of services enable the automation of activities (human labor outsourced to technology) and use of powerful programming paradigms (augmentation and amplification of human intellect with technology).

Chapter 3 Service Innovation is the chapter that entrepreneurial students and those interested in creating the next world-changing service may decide to use as an entry point. Also students of innovation and technology management can find concepts and tools in this chapter to systematically explore a variety of innovation frameworks. Context maps, Janus cones, value curves, business model canvas, and other techniques are introduced and clearly illustrated. This chapter also provides insights regarding servitization as an innovation process that manufacturing firms can use to shift from commodity products to higher-value service offerings and solutions.

Chapter 4 Service Design may be the chapter where liberal arts and humanities students want to begin their journey. Methods such as stakeholder maps, persona, customer journey maps, service blueprinting, and other design tools are introduced and clearly illustrated. Service design as a process that is human-centric, interactive, holistic, and iterative and makes use of prototypes is introduced.

Chapter 5 Service Semantics will resonate with students of computer science and information systems who wish to understand the cutting edge of technologies reshaping the service landscape today. Linked USDL is a service description language built with Semantic Web Technologies. APIs (Application Programming Interfaces) from Twitter, LinkedIn, Google, YouTube, Facebook, Dropbox, Instagram, Wordpress, and Lastfm are introduced as contributing to the rapidly growing API economy. The combinatorial possibilities for creating new service offerings continue to grow.

Chapter 6 Service Analytics may be the chapter where students interested in some of the hottest new jobs want to begin their service journey. Data as a resource is still largely untapped, even though it continues to grow exponentially. ITIL (Information Technology Infrastructure Library) is introduced, and analytics for extracting insights from incidence management reports can be used to improve service delivery. Cluster analysis and text mining techniques are also presented.

Chapter 7 Service Optimization will appeal especially to students of operations research and operations management. This is the most mathematically demanding of all the chapters and introduces students to tools and techniques for quantitatively modeling service systems and solving for optimal solutions. Classic problems such as bin packing (configuration planning) and the traveling salesman (route planning) are also presented, along with an introduction to queuing theory.

Chapter 8 Service Co-creation is a chapter well crafted for those interested in systems thinking and the way multiple entities interact in service ecosystems. Value propositions, service quality, service productivity, customer relationship management (CRM), business-to-business (B2B) engagements, customer lifetime value, and customer equity are key concepts introduced in this chapter.

Chapter 9 Service Markets brings the student almost full circle, back to where the textbook began examining the service-oriented society in which we all live. However, in this chapter, microeconomics and agent-based computational economics and other tools and techniques for market engineering are introduced. Pricing strategy and service network platforms are also covered.

Chapter 10 Service Research will appeal especially to students of social sciences and those interested in network theory, but also to today's social-media-savvy millennial generation as well as business practitioners interested in social network analysis. Service network analysis and service level engineering are introduced. The opening case cites a Nov. 7, 2013, article in Forbes that declares a Twitter user is worth $100, Facebook's $98, and LinkedIn's $93. Well-crafted cases like this one draw the students in and set the stage for learning about technical tools and methods.

Scholars can use this textbook to learn about other areas of service outside their core area expertise, and they will also appreciate the carefully selected additional readings and extensive references that accompany each of the chapters. By providing these detailed references, the textbook provides a map of the world of service to both students in college and students of service who may be practitioners in business or governments, as well as scholars who need to grasp fundamentals outside their home academic discipline. Furthermore, each chapter begins with a summary and set of learning objectives, as well as a case, that link clearly to the review section, key terms, exercises, and questions at the end, reinforcing the set of concepts and methods that each chapter covers.

In sum, this comprehensive new college-level textbook provides a clear and concise introduction to service-oriented ways of thinking for undergraduate students across the spectrum of academic disciplines. While appealing perhaps most strongly to computer science and information systems (informatics) students, the textbook makes clear that diverse teams will be needed to build and manage tomorrow's service systems. The cases and projects will likely be most useful when discussed and undertaken by multidisciplinary teams of students that include computer science and information systems (informatics) students, as well as students of management, engineering, operations, liberal arts, design, humanities, social sciences, and other areas of academic study. In this sense, the textbook provides a common ground to engage students across the academic spectrum, encouraging students to become more T-shaped with both depth in their academic major as well as boundary-spanning breadth to communicate with others, and all the while prepare them well for real-world teamwork in business, government, and society.

This textbook is one that I have been waiting for, and KSRI team is to be congratulated!

IBM Almaden Research Center   Jim Spohrer
San Jose, CA, USA
April 6, 2015

Preface

What Is This Book About?

In the last three decades, the world economic landscape has changed at a fast pace shifting from manufacturing to the provision of services. In fact, the service sector is the strongest economic industry of most modern nations, and it is also rapidly becoming an important sector in developing countries. As a result, the interest on services has grown and has originated an emerging and much needed field coined service science.

But what is service science? In very simple terms it is the study of service systems and services. This new field of science started in 2004 as a movement towards making services a first-class discipline. Service systems are structures configured with people, technology, organizations, and information. Services are instances of service systems which typically cause a transformation of the state of an entity resulting from the contractual agreement between a service provider and a service customer.

The typical example of this progression towards services is the concept and model known as *software as a service* such as Google Mail and Microsoft Office 365. The software (product) does not shift anymore in ownership. The provider has ownership and is responsible for its maintenance, upgrades, and repair. The customer has access to the leased product available as a service and pays a fee for its use. Since the service sector is amazingly varied, many other examples exist from transportation and distribution services, utilities and city planning services, and banking and insurance services to computer, legal, and consulting services.

The study of service systems is multidisciplinary and interdisciplinary and draws on concepts, theories, methods, and tools from a number of existing areas such as innovation, design, computer science, information systems, operations research, marketing and business, and economics with the main objective of creating an integrated, coherent, and consistent body of knowledge.

Why Is This Textbook Necessary?

One key element of service systems is their nature, focusing not merely on one particular characteristic of a service but rather considering a system of interacting elements (parts) which include:

- People skills and competencies
- Organizational structures encompassing business models
- Technologies supporting mobile and electronic services
- Information, knowledge, and analytics to deliver intelligent services

Studying these basic elements and the principles that interconnect them provides a body of knowledge underlying service systems. Furthermore, understanding how service systems can be created, designed, analyzed, and commercialized is yet another challenge for service experts. Nonetheless, current approaches for studying service systems—at an academic and professional levels—vary from organization to organization. In practice, *informal*, *ad hoc*, and *disconnected* methods are often used. For example, it is not uncommon to find professionals creating their own languages, techniques, architectures, and graphical representations.

Thus, the integrated knowledge provided by this textbook is indispensable to foster a new wave of future professionals to think in a service-focused way with the right balance of competencies in computer science, engineering, and management.

Who Should Read This Textbook?

The concepts presented in this textbook are precious for organizations, practitioners, researchers, and students who need to move towards new, innovative business models that rely on services as a source of new opportunities for generating value and driving a higher customer experience. The material explored, while not exhaustive, enables to train T-shaped professionals who must have a deeply developed specialty area (e.g., business management or computer science) as well as a broad set of skills and capabilities in the field of services (e.g., service design and optimization).

The intended audience of this book is twofold. For researchers, teachers, and students who want to learn about this new emerging science, this textbook provides an overview of the core disciplines underlying the study of service systems. It is aimed at students of information systems, information technology, and business and economics. It also targets business and IT practitioners, especially those who are looking for better ways of innovating, designing, modeling, analyzing, and optimizing service systems.

Book Content

This textbook is a centerpiece of a course syllabus on service systems. It provides a source of information and insights on a subject that was not properly covered by existing bibliography. It brings together in one place ten relevant subjects.

Chapter 1. Foundations   What are services? Why are they becoming increasingly important for society? What is a service system? How are they structured? How do they contrast with goods?

Chapter 2. Electronic Services   Which developments enabled the evolution of services into electronic services? What different types of electronic services exist? Which technologies are available for their implementation?

Chapter 3. Service Innovation   What is service innovation? Which available methods support projects for new services development?

Chapter 4. Service Design   How is service design related to service innovation? Which known methods and techniques are available to design services?

Chapter 5. Service Semantics   How to enrich the description of electronic services with semantic knowledge? What are the benefits for service providers?

Chapter 6. Service Analytics   How can the wealth of data generated by services be used for analysis? Which main tasks and methods are available?

Chapter 7. Service Optimization   Which mathematical models can be used to solve planning problems arising in the area of services? Which tools can be used to assist engineers?

Chapter 8. Service Co-creation   What is value co-creation, service encounters, service quality, and service productivity? Which methods can be used to manage them?

Chapter 9. Service Markets   How can service systems be commercialized? Which methods enable the creation of competitive service markets? Which frameworks exist to model markets?

Chapter 10. Service Research   What is the importance of recent research streams, such as service network analysis and service level engineering, for service systems? Why are service networks important for an interconnected world?

Each chapter includes a summary, a list of learning objectives, an opening case, and a review section with questions, a project description, a list of key terms, and a list of further reading bibliography. All these elements enable students to learn at a faster and more comfortable peace.

Suggested Course Structure

The guiding principle in writing this textbook was to make its content on service systems suitable for several contexts.

Service engineering   This textbook is a central reference for a degree on service engineering since it brings under one umbrella several fields which contribute in one way or the other to the development of services with a superior quality.

Computer science   will benefit from new insights from service innovation, design, semantics, analytics, and optimization to implement superiorly engineered electronic services such as Web or cloud services.

Industrial engineering   will benefit from principles and methods to design services and approaches to analyze and optimize services.

Operations management   can explore the fields of service design, service analytics, and service optimization for overseeing, controlling, and improving the process of production and redesign of services.

Service design   naturally benefit from service innovation and service design but can also benefit from service co-creation and service markets to understand the synergies between all the stakeholders involved in service provisioning.

Marketing engineering   can capitalize on service markets and co-creation chapters to understand organizational control systems such as sales force management systems and customer relationship management tools.

Table 1 shows how various degrees and courses benefit from the textbook.

Table 1 Coverage of the chapters (●, full; ◐, partial; ○, optional)

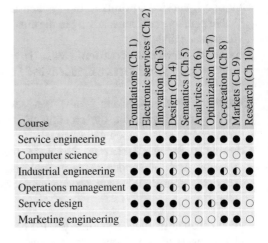

Course	Foundations (Ch 1)	Electronic services (Ch 2)	Innovation (Ch 3)	Design (Ch 4)	Semantics (Ch 5)	Analytics (Ch 6)	Optimization (Ch 7)	Co-creation (Ch 8)	Markets (Ch 9)	Research (Ch 10)
Service engineering	●	●	●	●	●	●	●	●	●	●
Computer science	●	●	◐	◐	●	●	●	○	○	●
Industrial engineering	●	●	◐	◐	○	●	●	◐	◐	●
Operations management	●	●	◐	◐	◐	●	●	●	●	●
Service design	●	●	●	●	○	◐	◐	●	●	○
Marketing engineering	●	●	◐	◐	○	○	○	●	●	○

Website Companion

This textbook has a companion website. It provides additional material to help lecturers use the text in their teaching and help students to deepen their understanding. The website is accessible at:

- http://www.fundamentals-of-service-systems.org

Acknowledgments

The writing of this manuscript has been an extensive and stimulating expedition and led to a new view on service systems. It was idealized by Jorge Cardoso during his research stay at the Karlsruhe Institute of Technology (KIT) in Germany and driven in close collaboration with Hansjörg Fromm, together with their coeditors Stefan Nickel, Gerhard Satzger, Rudi Studer, and Christof Weinhardt, all affiliated with the Karlsruhe Service Research Institute (KSRI) at KIT.

This textbook has involved an extensive collective effort of a group of professionals and researchers that spread over more than 20 months. Coordination, self-motivation, inspiration, knowledge, meetings, discussions, phone calls, e-mails, and many slides were all indispensable ingredients in its conception. Contributing experts are identified in each chapter.

While listing all the people with whom we had at some point interacted would be an almost impossible task without forgetting someone, we would like to thank the ones that were closer to us and that reviewed and provided valuable feedback for each chapter:

Paul P. Maglio   Chapter 1
University of California, Merced, USA

Eric Dubois   Chapter 2
Luxembourg Institute of Science and Technology, Luxembourg

Jan Marco Leimeister   Chapter 3
Universität Kassel, Germany, and *Universität St. Gallen, Switzerland*

Stefan Holmlid   Chapter 4
Linköping University, Sweden

Rama Akkiraju   Chapter 5
IBM Almaden Research Center, USA

Stephan Bloehdorn   Chapter 6
IBM Global Business Services, Germany

François Habryn   Chapter 6
IBM Global Technology Services, Switzerland

Boris Amberg   Chapter 7
FZI Forschungszentrum Informatik, Germany

Stephen K. Kwan   Chapter 8
San José State University, USA

Steven Kimbrough   Chapter 9
University of Pennsylvania, USA

Barbara Pernici   Chapter 10
Politecnico di Milano, Italy

About the Editors

Prof. Dr. Jorge Cardoso joined the Information System Group at the University of Coimbra in 2009. Since 2015, he is Lead Architect for Cloud Computing at Huawei's European Research Centre (ERC) in Munich. In 2013 and 2014, he was a Guest Professor at the Karlsruhe Institute of Technology (KIT) and a Fellow at the Technical University of Dresden (TU Dresden), respectively. Previously, he worked for major companies such as SAP Research (Germany) on the Internet of services and the Boeing Company in Seattle (USA) on Enterprise Application Integration. Since 2013, he is the Vice-Chair of the KEYSTONE COST Action, a EU research network bringing together more than 70 researchers from 26 countries. He has a Ph.D. in Computer Science from the University of Georgia (USA).

Prof. Dr.-Ing. Hansjörg Fromm studied computer science and mathematics and received his Ph.D. in 1982 from the University of Erlangen-Nürnberg. After a research assignment at the IBM Watson Research Center, Yorktown Heights, New York, he joined IBM Germany, where he had different management positions in Software Development, Manufacturing Research, and Business Consulting, and received the title of an IBM Distinguished Engineer. From 2006 to 2010 he was the European Director of the IBM Center for Business Optimization (CBO). From 2011 to 2014, Prof. Fromm was a director at the Karlsruhe Service Research Institute (KSRI). After his retirement, he is still active as an honorary professor at the Karlsruhe Institute of Technology and the University of Erlangen-Nürnberg.

Prof. Dr. Stefan Nickel obtained his Ph.D. in Mathematics at the Technical University of Kaiserslautern, Germany, in 1995. From 1995 to 2003 he was assistant and then Associate Professor in mathematics at the Technical University of Kaiserslautern. After a Full Professor position at Saarland University (Chair of Operations Research and Logistics) from 2003 to 2009, he became one of the directors of the Institute for Operations Research at the KIT in April 2009. In 2011, he became director at Forschungszentrum Informatik (FZI) and Karlsruhe Service Research Institute (KSRI). His research focuses on location planning, area planning, health care, and online optimization. He has coordinated the Health Care Working Group within the German OR society (GOR) and was president of the GOR.

Prof. Dr. Gerhard Satzger leads the research group "Service Innovation and Management" at KSRI focusing on designing novel data-based services and business models. He holds a diploma in Business Engineering from the University of Karlsruhe and an MBA from Oregon State University, as well as a Ph.D. in Information Systems (University of Gießen) and a postdoctoral lecturer qualification in business administration (University of Augsburg). Simultaneously, he has pursued an industry career with IBM since 1989 – among others serving as CFO for IBM's Global Technology Services business in Central Europe (2002–2007), and as Head of IBM Business Performance Services Europe (2011–2014). He built up the KSRI as an industry-on-campus concept 2008–2011 and returned to KSRI as a director in 2014.

Prof. Dr. Rudi Studer is Full Professor in Applied Informatics at the Karlsruhe Institute of Technology (KIT), Institute AIFB. In addition, he is director at the Karlsruhe Service Research Institute (KSRI) as well as at the FZI Research Center for Information Technology. His research interests include knowledge management,

Semantic Web technologies and applications, data and text mining, big data, and service science. He obtained a Diploma in Computer Science at the University of Stuttgart in 1975. In 1982 he was awarded a Doctor's Degree in Informatics at the University of Stuttgart, and in 1985 he obtained his Habilitation in Informatics at the University of Stuttgart. From 1985 to 1989 he was project leader and manager at the Scientific Center of IBM Germany.

Prof. Dr. Christof Weinhardt is heading the Institute of Information Management and Systems (IISM) at KIT. He is member of the board of directors at the Research Center for Information Technologies in Karlsruhe (FZI). Since its foundation, Prof. Weinhardt is director at KSRI, heading the research group Information and Market Engineering. Christof Weinhardt received his Diploma in Business Engineering and his Ph.D. in Economics in 1989 at Universität Karlsruhe. Until 1994, he was an Assistant Professor at the University of Giessen. He then was assigned chair of the Department for Quantitative Methods in Business Administration at the University of Bielefeld. In 1995, he became Full Professor and head of the Department for Information Systems, University of Giessen.

Contents

Foundations

1

Hansjörg Fromm and Jorge Cardoso

Summary

This chapter starts by providing evidence of the growing importance of services in our society which was reinforced by recent technological and economic developments. Thereafter, a service definition is presented and discussed in detail to explain the basic principles of services. Concepts from operations management are used to describe services as transformation processes involving resources from both customer and provider. The last section contrasts services with goods and investigates the differences in marketing and management of these distinct economic commodities.

Learning Objectives
1. Identify the recent developments that enabled the expansion of the service sector and its most predominant service industries.
2. Explain the concept of service and analyze the various types of interactions that can occur during service delivery.

(continued)

H. Fromm
Karlsruhe Service Research Institute (KSRI), Karlsruhe Institute of Technology (KIT), Karlsruhe, Germany
e-mail: hansjoerg.fromm@kit.edu

J. Cardoso (✉)
Department of Informatics Engineering, Universidade de Coimbra, Coimbra, Portugal

Huawei European Research Center (ERC), Munich, Germany
e-mail: jcardoso@dei.uc.pt; jorge.cardoso@huawei.com

© Springer International Publishing Switzerland 2015
J. Cardoso et al. (eds.), *Fundamentals of Service Systems*, Service Science: Research and Innovations in the Service Economy, DOI 10.1007/978-3-319-23195-2_1

3. Apply the I-T-O model from operations management to analyze and understand a service system.
4. Compare the main characteristics that make services and goods fundamentally different and explain how they can be bundled into one unique offering.

► **Opening Case** Services in the clothing industry

MAN-MADE CUSTOMIZATION TO MASS PRODUCTION ... TO MASS CUSTOMIZATION

In the pre-industrial era, getting a new dress was a personal experience. In a collaborative face-to-face process, the tailor and his assistant took measurement, while the customer formulated her wishes and desires. Together they selected fabrics, colors, and patterns. Then the tailor would start the cutting and sewing, possibly requiring additional fittings, until the final product could be delivered.

Nowadays, only few people can afford custom-tailored dresses or suits. Clothes are typically pre-fabricated in large quantities and are sold ready-to-wear in fashion boutiques or department stores. Even if occasionally assisted by the store personnel, the customer is largely in a self-service mode in looking for sizes, assessing qualities, trying clothes on, and finally making the choice.

Mass production resulted in affordable prices at the cost of standardized products of limited choice. With the advent of intelligent manufacturing and information technologies, mass production evolved in what is called mass customization—the production of individualized and personalized products in large volumes.

IT-enabled mass customization is the most recent evolution in the information age which provides innovative services to shoppers to enable them to customize their products with a range of options, for instance, when ordering clothing, a car, or a computer (Fig. 1.1c). The use of web-based configurators, which emerged in the late-2000s, made possible to deliver customized products manufactured by well-established production processes. Shoppers can use web-based configurators to indirectly and dynamically program robotic systems that can switch between clothing models and variants with little loss of efficiency and at a low cost.

For example, youtailor.de (Fig. 1.2) provides an effective online customizing tool—the Designer Studio, which allows shoppers to easily design their shirts according to exact preferences. It is possible to choose from more than ten configuration parameters (e.g., fabric, fit, buttons, color, style). The visual representation is 3D to enable customers to "see" the final product.

Why to study services?
An example from the clothing industry...

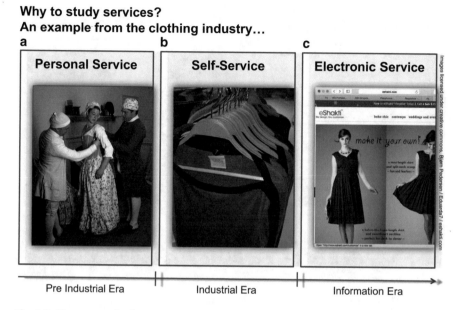

Fig. 1.1 From customization, to mass production, and to mass customization

The three situations depicted in Fig. 1.1 perfectly symbolize the historical development of services over the last centuries: all started with highly-individualized, face-to-face services, evolved into highly-standardized, customer-anonymous self-services, and has now reached a stage that can combine the advantages of the previous two: highly-individualized and personalized electronic services.

▶ **Opening Case**

1.1 Service-Oriented Societies

The intense competition of economies and the globalization of worldwide markets in conjunction with the generalization and expansion of information systems and information technologies have opened up significant opportunities for the conception of new specialized services. Providers are focusing on services for increased differentiation and creation of consumer value as a source of competitive advantage. In the age of information technology, traditional trading processes which involve a close and intense human interaction are often inadequate and can become a burden for companies competing in a globalized world.

Fig. 1.2 The Design Studio configurator of YouTailor

1.1.1 Recent Developments

The rapid dissemination of services in society is visible at various levels.

Service Economies   Agriculture and manufacturing used to be the major productive elements of the world's economies. Nowadays, services are the new fundamental element driving economies to grow. Services represent 80 % of the US economy and account for more than 50 % of the economies in countries such as Brazil, Germany, Japan, Russia, and the UK [1].

Service-Dominant (S-D) Logic   Recent theoretical contributions, such as S-D Logic [2], indicate that all markets are centered on the exchange of services, and all economies and societies are service based. It views service as the focus of economic and social exchange.

Electronic Services   Several governments have already made the decision to invest in strategies to provide public services online in a systematic manner. For example, the UK government launched the Government Digital Service (GDS) initiative. The "Digital by Default" strategy was implemented in April 2014. The New Zealand government has followed the same path and is also making their services online in a digital form (beta.govt.nz).

Mobile Services   There is an increasing use of services from mobile devices. From Facebook to Dropbox to Gmail and beyond, most people use one or more mobile services in their personal lives. Mobile services are also entering the agenda of companies to improve the efficiency of employees, as a new marketing and delivery channel, and as a form to create new disruptive business models.

Cloud Services Companies are using cloud services, which use the utility model, to outsource their applications, development platforms, and infrastructures. The main driving factors include cost reduction and the scalability offered. Important cloud computing companies include Amazon, IBM, Microsoft, Google, and Rackspace. Global Software as a Service revenues are forecasted to reach $106B in 2016, increasing 21 % over projected 2015 spending levels [3].

Service Marketplaces Several service marketplaces—such as ServiceMagic. com, Sears' ServiceLive.com, ServiceAlley.com, and RedBeacon.com—are growing very quickly to enable consumers to find local services through the internet. The value of this type of marketplaces is attracting the attention of large companies. For example, RedBeacon.com, a platform that lets users search, browse, and hire local home service providers such as painters and house cleaners, was acquired in 2012 by The Home Depot, the largest home improvement retailer in the US.

Although many of these developments are recent, they are already having a positive impact on society. Consequently, more progress are needed in developing new theories, systematic methods, and tools for service innovation, design, implementation, analysis, and optimization, just to name a few.

1.1.2 Services Sector Growth

In 2005, the concept of service acquired a renewed importance since after several years of public debate, the European Parliament approved the *service directive* [4]. This directive intended to enhance competition by removing restrictions on cross-border market access for services in Europe. The implications of this measure for businesses and the IT community are enormous since the service sector represents more than 70 % of the Gross National Product (GNP) of EU countries and the directive can amplify the consumption of services in the European Union by 0.6 % (€ 37 billion) [5].

Figure 1.3 shows a more statistical perspective given by The World Factbook published by the Central Intelligence Agency (CIA). In 2013, US, China, Japan, and Germany were the countries with the highest service revenues.[1]

Between 1997 and 2007, the growth among OECD[2] member countries of service imports was highest in Ireland and was also well above average in Greece, Luxembourg, and Poland. Imports of services grew relatively slowly in Japan. In the same period, the growth rate of service exports for Ireland was again well above average and a relatively high growth was also recorded for Luxembourg and Denmark. A rather low relative growth occurred in Turkey, Mexico, and France.

---

[1]Services cover government activities, communications, transportation, finance, and all other private economic activities that do not produce material goods.

[2]Organization for Economic Cooperation and Development.

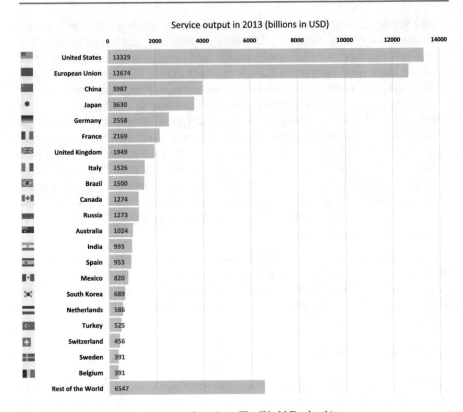

Fig. 1.3 The worldwide importance of services (The World Factbook)

Averaged over the last 3 years, the trade in services was relatively balanced for most countries, but large surpluses were recorded for US and UK, and substantial deficits occurred in Germany and Japan. The fastest growing services in OECD exports are now insurance, and computer and information services, and for imports, insurance and government services. The slowest growing export category has been construction services.

> In the UK, since 16 years new businesses ranging from restaurants to law firms expanded at the sharpest rate. In 2013, the UK service sector growth reached a six-year high.
>
> The Independent, 04.09.2013

In most countries, one of the largest and most important providers of services is the government which operates in sectors such as water management, public safety, and basic healthcare.

Cost reduction and flexibility are often two main arguments for studying services from a scientific perspective. For example, in Denmark the use of various channels to deliver a service has the following costs per transaction [6]: electronic services and self-services € 4.2; telephone calls € 7.8; emails received € 11; letters (paper) € 11.7; personal services (face-to-face) € 14.

The economic value and importance of services raise one question, "how can science and research provide a solution to create services with a higher quality?" Since the internet and the web are now an integral ingredient of the fabric of worldwide societies, economies, and commerce, it can intuitively provide a fundamental infrastructure to enable the realization of the Internet of Services (see Chap. 2).

1.1.3 Service Industries

One approach to promote the understanding of real world, digital, and everyday services across service industries is to provide examples. The service sector is amazingly varied. A brief reading of the listings in the Yellow Pages shows an overwhelming number of services directed at individual consumers as well as to corporate purchasers. Most consumers use services almost every day. Traveling by bus, visiting the dentist, mailing a letter, getting a haircut, refueling a car or sending clothes to the cleaners are all examples of service consumption. This section provides a small set of examples of services categorized by industry. The focus is on presenting examples of everyday services for which a simple grouping mechanism was developed based on intrinsic characteristics. The services are categorized into six industries (Fig. 1.4[3]): logistics, infrastructure, government, financial, entertainment, and business.

Logistics For the logistic domain, two classes of services are provided as examples: transportation and distribution services. *Transportation services* represent an essential element of economic spaces since developments are based on an increase in freight and passenger transportations. This class of services covers transportation such as sea, air, and land services and involves the carriage of passengers and the movement of goods. *Distribution services* enable providers to choose a wide variety of methods to distribute products. Direct distribution methods include, for example, direct mail, retail, catalogs, and the internet.

Infrastructure The infrastructure domain includes a vast number of services. Two classes of services were selected as examples: utilities and city planning services. *Utility services* include telecommunications, postal services, electrical power, natural gas, and also water and wastewater treatment services. Each type of service can be decomposed further. For example, telecommunication services include the transmission of sound, images, and other digital information by devices such as telephone, cable, broadcasting, and satellite. *City planning*

---

[3]Photos used under the public domain dedication license (http://all-free-download.com/).

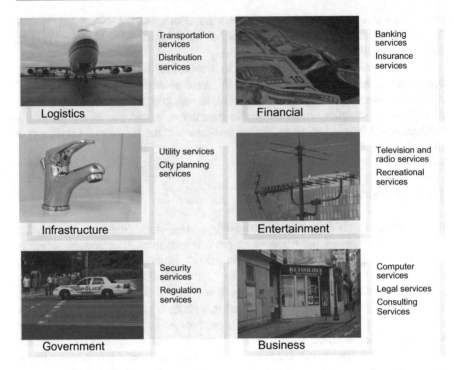

Fig. 1.4 Examples of service industries

services include engineering and technical services related to architectural design and planning of urban projects and supervision of large infrastructures such as dams, bridges, airports, and hospitals.

Government The government domain covers classes of services such as security and regulation. *Security services* provide many different types of support to citizens and are arguably the most important type of services during crisis situations. For example, the Department of Homeland Security, in the US, provides an integrated approach to security allowing a more efficient exchange of information, using IT, among government agencies. *Regulation services* refer to the mechanisms by which governments consign requirements (i.e., legislation, regulations, and administrative policies) on enterprises, citizens, and the government itself.

Finance The financial domain includes services such as banking and insurance services. *Banking services* cover services such as credit, leasing, foreign exchange transactions, asset management, and financial market operations. In recent years, banking markets became integrated at the national level and have increasingly become global. IT has contributed to an increased productivity, lower costs and prices, improvements in quality, variety, and flexibility. *Insurance services* cover the provision of various types of insurance such as freight and car insurance, life and health insurance, and real-estate insurance.

Entertainment   Entertainment covers several service classes, including television and radio, and recreational classes. *Television and radio services* include audio-visual services related to the production of motion pictures, radio and television programs, and musical recordings. It also includes receipts and payments for distribution rights. *Recreational services* comprise services such as those associated with museums, libraries, concerts, and other cultural activities.

Business   The business domain most likely covers the largest spectrum of service classes. Popular examples of classes include: computer, legal, and consulting services. *Computer services* include hardware and software consultancy, and analysis, design, documentation, and programming of systems. *Legal services* cover legal advisory and representation services in any law, judicial, and statutory procedures. Other popular services include drafting of legal documentation, certification consultancy, auctioning, escrow, and settlement services. Finally, *consulting services* help firms adapt to changes in their markets, environment, and their own structure. They involve business process design, marketing advice, change management, training, and re-skilling.

1.2   Basic Principles of Services

A prerequisite for services is the *division of work*, a practice that is known since early history. The division of work—dividing a job into smaller tasks—goes along with the *division of labor*—the specialization of individuals who develop special skills, tools, and experience to perform these tasks. There is a hypothesis that the Neanderthals were not able to survive because of their lack of labor division—other than the Homo sapiens who was familiar with this practice. Durckheim [7] considers the division of labor as "the supreme law of human societies and the condition of their progress". In modern society, division of work does not only occurs between individuals, but also between larger economic units like firms or even nations. What an individual or firm cannot do by itself, it is requesting as a service from others.

In the French feudal society of the eighteenth century, the aristocrats enjoyed fine dining prepared in their own grand kitchens by their personal chefs. During the 1789 revolution many aristocrats fled to the countryside and could not afford this luxury anymore. The chefs were laid off and had to seek new opportunities of income. With their staff and equipment they opened restaurants in Paris and attracted the upper-class bourgeoisie to their establishments. This is how Paris became the birthplace of the modern-day restaurant.

In our times, firms are often in situations comparable to the eighteenth century French households: they consider if they should afford to have their own kitchens and chefs, their own security staff, their own IT equipment—or outsourcing these functions. Catering, security, and IT are provided back to the firms as a service. Catering service providers, security service providers, and IT service providers emerge. This explains the rapid growth of the service industry in today's economy.

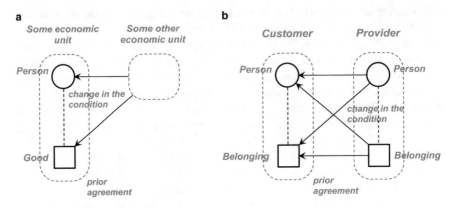

Fig. 1.5 An illustration of Hill's service definition (**a**) and an extension (**b**)

1.2.1 Definition of a Service

Services have many facets. The word service can have different meanings in colloquial language as it will be pointed out later. The academic community has looked at services for many years. Yet, different academic disciplines came up with different views on services. As a consequence, it cannot be expected that there exists a single comprehensive and commonly accepted definition of a service.

One definition worth looking at is the definition of Hill [8]:

▶ **Definition (Service)** A service is a change in the condition of a person, or a good belonging to some economic unit, which is brought about as the result of the activity of some other economic unit, with the prior agreement of the former person or economic unit.

Figure 1.5a illustrates this situation. The essence of this definition is that a service is an *activity* (other terms are *acts*, *deeds*, *performances*, *efforts*) between two economic units (typically denoted as *customer* and *provider*) which changes the condition ("creates value for") of the first economic unit, the customer.

Hill does not get very specific on the economical units. His definition implies that the receiver of the service is a single person or the belongings of a single person. This certainly reflects simple situations like a hairdressing service or a car repair service. But it does not expresses more complicated situations like consulting services in a business-to-business environment. In the latter case, the receiving economic unit is a company (an organization) incorporating different people and "belongings" (assets belonging to a company). Putting the words "person" and "good" into the plural form, Hill's definition becomes general enough to cover all kinds of service situations. It is implicit in this definition that the receiving economic unit (the unit requesting and eventually paying for the service) and the realities being acted upon (persons, goods) can, but must not be different entities. In the simple example of hairdressing, requestor and receiver of the service are typically identical, but in the case of a business consulting service, the requestor and the targeted reality can be quite different.

Also, Hill does not get very specific on the "prior agreement". This agreement can be implicit (tacit consent) or explicit (written contract), it can be the result of a simple request ("please cut my hair") or the result of a complex negotiation. The service delivery, in response to the request, can be a single activity or a complex combination of activities, its duration can be short (telephone directory inquiry) or long-lasting (insurance policy).

It should be noted that the activity *per se* does not distinguishes a service. One and the same activity can be at one time a service and at another time not a service. If somebody has the tires of his car changed by a mechanic, this is a service. If somebody changes the tires of his car by himself, there is no service involved.

Hill and other authors who later built on Hill's definition of a service (e.g., Gadrey [9]) are more explicit on the customer's side (who is receiving the service, which realities are acted upon) than on the provider's side (who is performing the service).

As persons and their belongings can *receive* a service, persons and their belongings can be needed to *provide* the service. For example, the hairdresser uses facilities (shop, chairs, mirrors), tools (scissors, combs, brushes), and materials (shampoo, conditioner, colorant) to deliver his or her service. This is illustrated in Fig. 1.5b. The two symbols for "person" and "belonging" are meant to represent the general situation in which a service provider has *people* (i.e, persons with skills, competencies, and knowledge) and *belongings* (like facilities, tools, and materials) to deliver a service.

1.2.2 Service System

The term *service system* has been widely used in the service literature. While the term appeared already in the 1960s in the context of queuing systems [10], most authors since believed that everybody knows what a service system is and left it largely undefined. Most of the characteristics of a service system, however, can easily be derived from the general and well-defined concept of a system.

A *system* is a set of interacting units or elements that form an integrated whole [11]. A system has a boundary delineating the elements which are inside the system and which are outside—part of the system's surroundings or environment. A system has a *structure* defining its elements and their *relationships*. It might be possible to describe the *behavior* of a system that is intended to fulfill a *function* or *purpose* [12]. The system behavior is often described as a *process* or *mechanism*. There might be a *set of rules* that govern behavior and structure. An open system usually interacts with some elements in its environment. A closed system is isolated from its environment.

The traditional perception of a service system is that of a *service delivery system*. The service system consists of elements (resources like people with skills, competencies, and knowledge, but also things like facilities, tools, materials, computer programs) that have a structure (organization and configuration), a behavior (described as a process or mechanism), and a purpose (to deliver a service). The smallest service system could be an individual person with or without his or her belongings (e.g., a carpenter with his tools), but also a single computer program (e.g., a web service). Larger service systems are service businesses (e.g., a rental car company) or complex networks of businesses and organizations (e.g., the national healthcare system).

▶ **Definition (Service System)** A service system consists of elements (e.g., people, facilities, tools, and computer programs) that have a structure (i.e., an organization), a behavior (possibly described as a process), and a purpose.

The modern perception of a service system is based on the principle of value co-creation and, accordingly, includes the customer within its boundaries: "Service systems comprise service providers and service clients working together to coproduce value in complex value chains or networks" [13]. The smallest service system in this case is represented by the dyadic relationship between just two entities, the customer and the provider [14]. Larger service systems are services businesses or complex service networks including their customers (e.g., the healthcare system with its patients). It should be noted that even if a complex service system might have only one end customer (the patient), it might consist of a multitude of dyadic customer-provider relationships that have been established to deliver the service. And according to the co-creation paradigm, even the end customer assumes the role of a provider, e.g., by sharing information with other actors in the service system.

Complex service systems have been studied under different perspectives, and different terms have been used such as service networks [15, 16], service ecosystems [17], value networks [18, 19], service value networks [20], and service supply chains [21]. Chapter 10 will further discuss service networks.

1.2.3 Interaction Between Customers and Providers

The general scheme in Fig. 1.5b can be used to explain different service scenarios according to the varying involvement of persons and their belongings. Figure 1.6a shows the situation where a person (the provider) delivers a service to another person (the customer). No belongings (things) are involved on either side.

▶ **Definition (Customer and Consumer)** The terms consumer and customer are often used interchangeably, but a consumer and customer are not always the same entity. A customer (also known as a client, buyer, or purchaser) is someone who buys services or goods from someone else, while a consumer is someone that receives a certain service or consumes a product. Clearly, a customer may or may not also be a consumer. It happens often that both terms are use interchangeably. When no ambiguity arises, this textbook can use one or the other term as they are better suited to the context.

Figure 1.6b displays the situation where a person equipped with belongings (provider) acts on another person (customer). The simple hairdressing example is representative for a large variety of services encompassing beauty services, medical services, education services, etc., all targeted towards human beings. Figure 1.6c depicts a service that is targeted towards the belonging of a person, exemplified by car repair. Again, the person on the provider's side (mechanic) is equipped with belongings (tools). The customer is not involved in the actual repair process. This situation is representative for cleaning, maintenance and repair services, and for any kind of transportation or storage of things (mail, cargo, parts).

Example (Customer Involvement)

Today, several food chains, like Subway, have a menu with a strong emphasis on customer involvement. Customers decide the ingredients they want in their sandwich. This entails more than 50 % of involvement of customers.

Two other service scenarios will be more extensively discussed in the next chapter of this book. The first case is *self-service*, a service provided without or with little human involvement on the provider's side. The provider typically sets up facilities or equipment that the customer can use to perform a certain task. Examples are self-service gas stations, ticket vending machines, rental cars, and electronic services. This is shown in Fig. 1.6c. The last case becomes more and more prevalent with recent advances in technology: belongings (things) provide services to belongings (things). For example, computer programs can request services from and deliver services to other computer programs. This situation is illustrated in Fig. 1.6d.

For some of the service scenarios described in Fig. 1.6, a terminology has been used that comes from communications technology. In this field, people describe different *types of communication* such as person-to-person or *human-to-human (H2H), human-to-machine (H2M)*, and *machine-to-machine (M2M)*. Since communication is considered bi-directional, M2H is typically not distinguished from H2M, and therefore rarely used. This terminology has been used to indicate the type of service interaction in different service scenarios. Also service interaction, like communication, is considered bi-directional (request and response). Accordingly, the service scenarios described in Fig. 1.6a, b are characterized by their person-to-person or human-to-human (H2H) interaction (belongings in Fig. 1.6b are not considered to interact with the customer). Self-service in Fig. 1.6d is a typical example for human-to-machine (H2M) interaction (a person requests a service from a machine, and the machine delivers a service to a person), and the situation in Fig. 1.6e is representing machine-to-machine (M2M) interaction. The situation in Fig. 1.6c has not received one of these tags. The belongings on the customer's

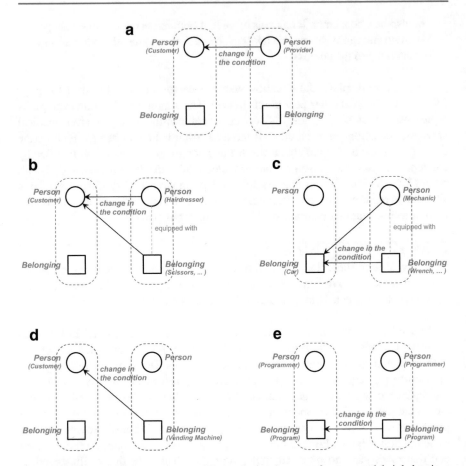

Fig. 1.6 Different service scenarios according to the involvement of persons and their belongings. (**a**) Person acting on person. (**b**) Person with belonging acting on person (Example: Haircut). (**c**) Person with belonging acting on belonging (Example: Car Repair). (**d**) Belonging acting on person (Example: Self Service). (**e**) Belonging acting on belonging (Example: Web Service)

side are not considered to interact with the service provider. In the case where the "machines" are software applications, the terms *human-to-application (H2A)* and *application-to-application (A2A)* have been used.

1.2.4   Operations Management View on Services

In the related disciplines of *operations management (OM)* and *operations research (OR)*, services have been the objects of research long before service science emerged as an autonomous discipline. In German-speaking countries, a sub-discipline of OR, queueing theory, used to be called "Bedienungstheorie" that translates into "service theory" [22]. Most books on queueing theory and discrete event simulation exemplify service scenarios, e.g., Hall's "Queueing Methods for Services and Manufacturing" [23]. The application of OR methods to services will be discussed in Chap. 7 on Service Optimization. In this section, it will be shown that OM provides an appropriate model and terminology to describe services in a structured way. It will be shown that the definition of services presented by Hill [8] can easily be translated into OM terms.

Transformation Process

One of the basic concepts of OM is the *transformation process* [24, 25]. A transformation process is any activity or group of activities that takes one or more inputs, transforms and adds value to them, and provides outputs for customers or clients. This so-called *input-transformation-output model* is shown in Fig. 1.7a. When the inputs are raw materials, it is relatively easy to identify the transformation involved, as when milk is transformed into cheese and butter or when thousands of parts are assembled to build an automobile. When the inputs are information or people, the nature of the transformation might be less obvious. For example, a hospital transforms ill patients (the input) into healthier patients (the output), a teacher transforms less educated students (the input) into well-educated students (the output).

Resources

In operations management, the inputs to the transformation process are called *resources*. Resources can be persons or things (compare with Fig. 1.6 and Hill [8]). Things are typically distinguished into assets and materials. Resources can be *transforming* and *being transformed* [25]. In a typical manufacturing process, the transforming resources are workers together with assets (facilities, machines and tools) that transform materials (the transformed resources) into finished goods (Fig. 1.7b).

Service as a Transformation Process

A service is also a transformation process that can be described with the input-transformation-output model. The difference compared to manufacturing is that both provider and customer give input to and participate in the transformation process (compare with Sampson's service I/O model [26]).

Fig. 1.7 The input-transformation-output model from operations management and the I-T-O model of a manufacturing process (**a**) Process. (**b**) Manufacturing process

Table 1.1 Examples of service processes with input resources and transformations

	Provider's resources	Customer's resources	Transformation
Hairdressing service	Facilities (shop, chair, mirror) Tools (scissors, combs, brushes) Materials (shampoo, conditioner, colorant) Hairdresser	Customer him- or herself	Change in hairstyle
Car service/repair	Facilities (garage, lifting ramp) Tools (wrench, hammer, screw driver) Materials (spare parts, oil) Repair person	Customer's car	Change in condition of car
Medical service	Facilities (hospital, operating rooms) Instruments (stethoscope, syringe) Materials (medicaments, plasters, dressings, disinfectants) Doctors, nurses, paramedics, admin	Customer (patient) him- or herself	Change in health condition
Electronic service (e.g., stock report)	Computing infrastructure with internet connectivity (web server) Software application (web application) (No human resources)	Customer him- or herself Internet access device (personal computer, smartphone)	Change in level of information

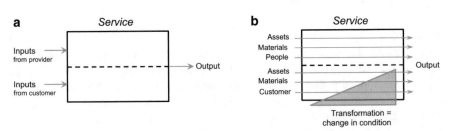

Fig. 1.8 The input-transformation-output model from operations management and its translation to services (**a**) I-O-T model for operations management. (**b**) I-O-T for services

As already illustrated in Fig. 1.5b, the input resources can be persons or belongings (goods, things) on both sides (provider and customer). The "change of condition" (Hill) or "transformation" (OM) can be of very different nature: e.g., changes in the physical characteristics of resources (repair services, cleaning services, beauty services), changes in the location of resources (transportation services), or changes in the physiological or mental state of people (healthcare services, well-being services, education services, entertainment services). Table 1.1 presents a few examples of service processes with their respective input resources and transformations.

To accentuate the special nature of the service process in Fig. 1.8a, b, a horizontal dotted line is drawn to divide the transformation box into a supplier's and a customer's side. Resources "don't change sides" during the service process—this means, there is no change in ownership involved. Both sides participate in the transformation process. Even if the main target of the condition change is on the customer's side (symbolized by the triangle representing increase of value), this does not mean that the resources on the supplier's side don't experience a change during the service process. The service person might get tired from the service delivery, but also more experienced and more knowledgeable. Assets might become worn, materials be consumed. For this close interplay between provider and customer in the service process, the term "co-creation of value" was coined. co-creation of value is one of the most important principles of modern service science (see Chap. 8).

A frequent misconception is that services are the outputs of service processes as goods are the outputs of manufacturing processes. Even OM textbooks are often not precise in this respect. From the preceding discussion it should have become clear that a service is not the *output* of a transformation process, a service *is* a transformation process.

1.2.5 Resource Intensity of Services

Resources are a fundamental element of services. An important characterization of services is based on the *proportion*, or *intensity*, with which different types of resources or capabilities are used in the service process. The following main types of services have been distinguished according to their resource intensity (they are naturally not mutually exclusive):

- Labor- and capital-intensive services.
- Knowledge-intensive service.
- Information-intensive service.
- Technology-intensive service.

Labor- and Capital-Intensive Services

A *labor-intensive service* is a service in which the labor costs outweigh the costs for equipment and materials. A *capital-intensive service* (also *equipment-intensive service*) is a service in which the capital costs (for facilities, equipment, tools) prevail. A hospital, even if it employs many doctors, nurses, administrative staff, and technicians, is a capital-intensive service due to its expensive facilities and equipment (operating rooms, X-ray, tomography, dialysis). Schmenner [27] provides an overview of the capital-labor-ratio for different service industries.

Knowledge-Intensive Services

Knowledge-intensive services, mostly used in the form of *knowledge-intensive business services*, are services that heavily rely on *professional knowledge*. Similarly, *skills-intensive services* [28] rely on *professional skills*. Both knowledge-intensive services and skills-intensive services are forms of labor-intensive services. Cedefop [28] further distinguishes between elementary manual resources (workers), skilled manual resources (agricultural, craft and trade workers, machine operators), skilled non-manual resources (clerks and service/sales workers), and high-skilled non-manual resources (legislators, managers, professionals and technicians). The latter are certainly coincident with knowledge-intensive resources. Physicians are generally distinguished by their professional knowledge, but surgeons or dentists additionally need special manual skills to perform their work.

Information-Intensive Services

Information-intensive services are services in which the activities involve substantial information processing [29]. This might include collecting, manipulating, interpreting, and transmitting data to create value [30]. Information can be collected and processed by people. Examples are opinion surveys (over telephone or face-to-face) or criminal investigations.

More and more information is nowadays available in electronic form, so that the collection and processing can be automated using *information and communication technology (ICT)*. Examples of ICT-based information-intensive services are news ticker services, financial information services, traffic information services, remote diagnostic services, or internet search engines. With the continuing dissemination of instrumentation technology in everyday life (sensors, GPS, vehicle telematics, surveillance cameras) the amount of data available gets bigger and bigger ("big data"), and the task of extracting valuable information becomes more and more sophisticated ("big data analytics").

Technology-Intensive Services

Technology-intensive services are services in which the proportion of labor is very low or zero. The service is delivered by resources that are purely technological—machines or computer programs. These technology-based services can be used by customers in a self-service mode (cf. Fig. 1.6d) or in turn by technological resources (typically computer programs) on the customer's side (cf. Fig. 1.6e). Technology used in services today is predominantly ICT. The dissemination of ICT, and especially the internet, has revolutionized the world of services and has led to concepts like *Electronic Services*, *Web Services*, *Cloud Services*, the *Internet of Things*, and the *Internet of Services*. These concepts will be discussed in the next chapter.

1.3   Services and Goods

Why should one compare services with goods? Services and goods are quite different realities. Operations Management has come up with a clear picture: Goods are "things" that are typically the output of a manufacturing process, and services are transformation processes by themselves.

The attempt to compare services with goods, and, moreover, to define services in contrast to goods, arose in the discipline of Service Marketing. For marketing people, services and goods have one thing in common: both are economic commodities that are promoted and sold by companies. Very often not only goods, but also services, are called the *products* of a company. Since the marketing discipline traditionally focused on goods, the orientation towards services was mainly governed by the question: What are the differences between marketing goods and marketing services? This legitimate question resulted in a considerable but questionable effort to answer a different question: What differentiates services from goods?

The most popular outcome of this discourse are the so-called *IHIP criteria*: *intangibility, heterogeneity, inseparability*, and *perishability*. IHIP criteria have been embraced by many scholars in lectures and textbooks, because they are easy to understand and easy to memorize. Unfortunately, they have led to misconceptions like "services are intangible goods" or "the more intangible, the more something is a service". It is long known that IHIP criteria "do not distinguish services from goods" [13] and "should not be used as generic service characteristics" [31]—no wonder, because "services and goods belong to quite different logical categories" [8]. But IHIP criteria are not useless. They indeed can help to understand the differences in marketing and management of services versus marketing and management of goods.

1.3.1 Differences in Marketing and Management

In the following, two cases will be discussed in which the difference between services and goods is particularly crucial.

Inseparability and Demand Management
The first case addresses the consequences of separability/inseparability on *demand management* and *pricing* of services and goods. Figure 1.9 shows two situations: (a) the fluctuating demand curve for automobile tires, with peaks in fall for winter tires and in spring for summer tires, and (b) the fluctuating demand for a call center with peaks of incoming calls daily around noon. (a) describes a situation that a manufacturer has to handle, (b) a problem for a service provider.

The tire manufacturer has one advantage: due to the separability of production and consumption, he can produce the tires ahead of time and can thus prepare for the peaks occurring in fall and spring. This requires good forecasting methods to predict the upturn and peak point of the demand curve for the coming season. If this is done intelligently, the manufacturer can fulfill all demands and yet smooth out the tire production so that the manufacturing resources are almost constantly utilized throughout the year.

The service provider does not have this advantage: calls need to be answered by the call center agents at exactly the time when they are coming in. There is no "pre-production" of responses (due to inseparability). If the demand shall be completely fulfilled, the call center has to employ as many agents as calls come in at the peak time period. The agents are only fully utilized at this peak time period—in other periods, a number of agents are idle. This is a phenomenon common to many

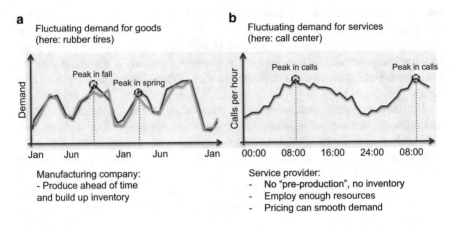

Fig. 1.9 Fluctuating demand of goods and services (**a**) Fluctuating demand for goods. (**b**) Fluctuating demand for services

different service situations: the demand for electricity is heavily fluctuating during the day, the demand for flights and hotel rooms is fluctuating during the year, etc.

Example (Fluctuating Demand of a Call Center)

To avoid customer waiting-times, call centers employ enough agents to cover peak demands. As a consequence, call center agents are often idle during off-peak periods. This is costly for the employer and tedious for the agents. A German call center decided to provide an additional workload when they are not busy answering calls. Agents were assigned the transcoding medical diagnoses written with free text into machine-readable ICD-10 codes (the International Classification of Diseases coding system). Results showed that agents were more satisfied with the new steady workload than they were before.

To cope with this challenging situation, service providers have taken advantage of different management practices. One practice is *demand aggregation*: the provider tries to acquire loads with different demand patterns to take advantage of the statistical effects that reduce variability in the aggregate demand. An example is a call center that serves different time zones: the peaks of one time zone might fall into the quiet periods of the other time zone, and thus the overall demand smooths out.

Another practice is *demand conditioning*: the provider offers incentives to customers to use the service in off-peak periods. These incentives are typically lower prices in off-peak periods and higher prices in peak periods. This is common practice in the travel industry (hotels, airlines, railways). Prices can vary over the year (depending on the attractiveness of the traveling location in a particular season), over the week (working days, weekends) and sometimes even over the day (early morning, late night).

Electricity service providers also experience high demand variability. They have seasonal, weekly and daily fluctuations which are caused by climate/temperatures, length of daylight and dark, working hours in offices and factories, and behavioral characteristics of private households (lighting, heating, cooling, cooking, washing). With the availability of smart meters, energy providers can offer flexible electricity prices on an hourly basis to their customers. If customers change their consumption patterns in reaction to lower prices, the energy providers will be able to avoid costly demand peaks, smooth out demand, and increase the efficiency of their operation.

Intangibility and Advertising

The second case addresses the consequences of "intangibility" on advertising of services. Advertising relies on the *presentation* of products (goods and services) in marketing channels. Only in shops and showrooms, products can be physically presented and are "tangible" for the customer (can be touched). In all other channels, such as newspapers, advertising walls, TV, or internet, products can only be virtually presented or *pictured* for advertising. Tangibility is no longer an issue, one should rather talk about the *picturability* of a product.

It is clear that "tangible goods" are easiest to be displayed in showrooms and pictured in ads. The situation for services—but similarly for intangible goods like music and videos—is more difficult. The advertisement of services has been a major concern of marketing people for many years [32, 33]. Services are activities or transformation processes. An activity or transformation process is not picturable like a tangible good (call this intangibility if you will). But substitutes can be found that make services picturable. A popular substitute is to picture physical delivery resources of a service (a friendly and caring courier) or happy customers while receiving or after having received a service (Fig. 1.10). The condition of a customer can be pictured before and after the service (hair transplant, cosmetic surgery).

Other possibilities are citing past performance characteristics, or presenting customer testimonials [33]. Substitutes are also used in advertising intangible goods.

Fig. 1.10 Advertising services (images courtesy of DHL and ClubMed)

An ad for a newly released CD cannot picture the musical content, but can picture substitutes like the CD cover, a portrait of the musician, or the musician in action interpreting the music in a concert room.

Example (IBM Stand on CeBIT with Mercedes-Benz Actros)

An eye-catcher on the computer fair CeBIT 2012 was a big Mercedes Actros truck on the IBM stand. It attracted people who were curious to understand what a truck has to do with IBM's offerings. They learned that the Actros symbolized an intelligent logistics solution that IBM had developed for the Mercedes-Benz truck manufacturing plant within a service project. IT services are hard to present on a fair. As a substitute, the truck was a perfect tangible object that helped to promote IBM's service capabilities.

1.3.2   The Dual Nature of Services

The word "service", as it was used in this book so far, refers to an *activity* or *transformation process* as defined earlier. But in colloquial language, the word "service" sometimes has a slightly different meaning. It might refer to the *resources* that are provided to deliver the service. Consider the following two sentences:

- A turbulence hit the airplane during the meal service.
- My neighbor owns a dry cleaning service.

In the first sentence, clearly an activity or transformation process is meant, in the second sentence, a set of resources. This colloquial ambiguity is another reason why the IHIP criteria are so difficult to digest. In the first case, intangibility and perishability are clearly given (the meal service is an activity—and as such intangible, other than a thing—and it has a beginning and an end). In the second case absolutely not (the dry cleaning service consists of tangible resources that continue to exist).

The Process and Resource Nature
One could speak of two natures or dimensions of a service. This subtle difference has hardly been noticed and conceptualized in the academic literature. Donabedian [34] distinguished between the structural dimension and process dimension of a service. Shostack [35] mentioned that "services exist in two states of being": in a potential state (where they may be "stored") and in a kinetic state corresponding to the actual rendering. Both authors express the same thing in different words. In the terminology that has been used in this book so far, one could distinguish between the "resource nature" or "resource dimension" and the "process nature" or "process dimension" of a service.

In most cases, when people speak about services they have the process dimension in mind. Sometimes, the resource nature is shining through. Would everybody accept—as a theoretician would—that a massage is an intangible service? No—because people think of the hands of a masseur operating on the body of a client. A sensible, tangible experience! Colloquial language does not clearly distinguishes between the two natures of a service.

Services in Computer Science

In the academic discourse, it should be precisely ascertained which service dimension (nature) prevails in a particular context. In computer science, "services" and "web services" are terms that describe fundamental programming paradigms. Services are "software components of distinct functional meaning" [36], or "software programs with distinct design characteristics" [37]. Web services are "self-describing, self-contained software modules" [38], or "software applications with a published programming interface" [33], and web services "can be sold, too" [39]. It should have become clear from these definitions, that computer scientists use the term services consistently in its resource dimension and their service has more the characteristics of a good (can be sold, can be stored) than of an activity or transformation process. However, also the process dimension is sometimes "shining through".

The novelty of this textbook is that it combines the concepts of services as they are used in economics and as they are used in computer science. Both disciplines have an unambiguous understanding of term service. Treated in isolation, there is no problem. But when the concepts of the two disciplines are brought together, the small but subtle difference poses some challenges.

1.3.3 Non-ownership

Recall the example from the beginning: the chef with his staff and equipment moved out of the aristocrat's house, opened a restaurant and could then offered his capabilities to his former employer or to other customers *as a service*. Nothing has changed in the activities of the kitchen and in the utilization of resources except that the resources no longer belong to the aristocrat.

The non-ownership characteristic of services has early been recognized by researchers [40, 41]. "Yet subsequent theorizing has largely ignored this striking characteristic" [42, p. 34]. Lovelock and Gummesson [42] propose a "fresh perspective" on services considering non-ownership or rental/access—and not intangibility—as the main differentiator of services and goods. In the meantime, the treatment of non-ownership has found its way into service management and marketing textbooks [43, 44].

Outsourcing

A modern way of describing this approach of giving up resources and demanding them back as a service without ownership is called *outsourcing*. Companies have begun many years ago to outsource their cafeteria, their security personnel, their facilities management, and even parts of their administration to service providers. The reason is always the same: companies want to turn fixed costs into variable costs and pay for the service only *on demand*. Non-ownership gives more flexibility and avoids risks if the company's business goes up or down. On the other side, the service provider can mitigate risks and handle varying demand better through economies of scale.

Another example is *IT outsourcing*, where all the IT resources of a company (computers, applications, and IT people) are taken over by a third party and provided back to the first company as a service. IT outsourcing can take many different forms ranging from infrastructure outsourcing over application management services (AMS) to business process outsourcing (BPO).

In the last few years, IT outsourcing has seen a renaissance with tremendous momentum in form of *cloud services*. Cloud services are IT services made available over the internet. The easy accessibility has made them attractive not only for companies, but also for private customers. It is again about non-ownership: a user who previously had a license for a software product and had installed it on his or her personal computer is now buying the software "as a service" from a cloud provider (SaaS = Software as a Service). The user has no problem with installation, maintenance and upgrades—all is done within the cloud.

The Culture of Non-ownership

Even if non-ownership is an old phenomenon, the trend towards it is still on the rise. Not only have the firms discovered the benefits of non-ownership, but their intentions to use non-ownership services has increased [45]. The whole society, and especially the youth, is shifting towards a culture of non-ownership [46]. The desire for ownership decreases and owning is replaced by sharing [47, 48]. This can be observed for books, music, videos, fashion, art, software, cars, and many other products. The internet is the predominant platform to facilitate this development. The internet provides services for people to borrow or exchange physical goods. The tremendous growth in bandwidth has created the opportunity to transmit goods that are available in digital format (music, video) directly over the internet. This has resulted in new kinds of services that are known as *on-demand services* (video-on-demand) or *streaming services* (music streaming).

Example (Consumers Want to Rent Their Music, Not to Own It)

When Apple introduced their iPod and iTunes products in 2001, Steve Jobs still argued that consumers want to own their music, not rent it. Over a decade later it turned out that Steve Jobs was wrong. Musical subscription services like Spotify or Deezer are becoming more and more dominant. According to Nielsen SoundScan, CD sales in the first half of 2014 have dropped down 14.9 % from the first half of 2013, and digital downloads 11.6 %. At the same time, audio and video streaming services had a strong growth of 42 %.

What streaming services are for music and video, are cloud services for software (software-as-a-service). They have similar economic models (on-demand, pay-per-use) and are based on the non-ownership paradigm. Both cloud services and streaming services are forms of *electronic services* which will be discussed in the next chapter.

1.3.4 Bundling of Goods and Services

Many companies combine products with services into new offerings with a superior value for their customers. Examples of well-know offerings include Apple's iPod product which was combined with the iTunes service.

Hybrid Offering

Such a combination is called a hybrid offering [49, 50]. If a company offers an extended warranty contract in addition to an electronic product, this is a hybrid offering. If a beauty salon sells expensive cosmetics in addition to their regular beauty services, this is a hybrid offering. Other examples are airlines which sell duty-free merchandise on board, cable TV providers which sell digital TV receivers or recorders, or leasing companies which sell their used cars after the leasing period.

A hybrid offering should not be confused with a pure service that includes tangible elements. A rental car service is such an example. It includes the car as a tangible element, but the car does not go into the ownership of the customer. As the examples illustrate, the trend towards hybrid offerings can take different directions: providers of goods extend their offerings by adding services and providers of services extend their offerings by adding goods (Table 1.2).

Table 1.2 Bundling of goods and services

Pure goods	Core goods & services	Core services & goods	Pure services
Books	Automobiles with maintenance	Beauty salons selling cosmetics	Teaching (high school, university)
Chemicals	Automobiles with financing	Airlines selling duty-free merchandise	Financial services (banking, insurance, taxes)
Food products	Heavy equipment with full service contracts and training	Leasing companies selling used cars	Communication services (telephone, Internet, cable TV)
	Software with maintenance and support		Transportation services (taxi, rental car, bus, train, airplane)

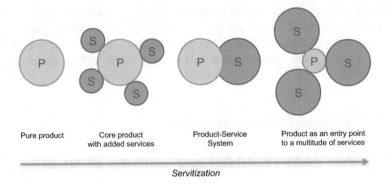

Fig. 1.11 Servitization: adding services to core products (based on Steunebrink [51])

Example (Goods-Services Bundle)

Mobile network operators offer their mobile phone and internet access services often in bundles with smartphones or other access devices. For example, British Vodafone customers (as of December 2014) can sign a 24 month contract with unlimited calling time at monthly payments of £53.50 and get an Apple iPhone 6 for free. At a monthly rate of £43.50, the iPhone is offered at £99. Both offerings are bundled with an additional entertainment service such as Netflix or Spotify.

Servitization

Many manufacturing companies have added services to their core offerings and services have become a dominant portion of their revenues and profits. This process is called servitization [52]. Figure 1.11 illustrates the servitization process. A hybrid offering in which products and services are integrated and have reached a similar level of importance is called a product-service system [53] or a solution [54].

As many recent examples show, the role of the product may become more of an entry point to a multitude of services (smart phones, tablet computers). Even a traditional product like the automobile will be surrounded by an increasing number of services in the future. Examples of services accessible through entry points like smart phones, tablet computers, or cars are news services, e-mail services, navigation services, weather reports, real-time traffic information, and entertainments services.

1.4 Conclusions

Globalization, the steady growth of electronic commerce, the removal of regulatory barriers to economic activities, and the technological advances in computing and telecommunications has enabled the creation of wider service markets.

The term service is used to refer to a range of activities that is difficult to encapsulate within a simple definition. The literature often associates the term service with an act or a performance, or with a change in the condition of a person or of a good belonging to some economic unit under a prior agreement.

A definition becomes even more complex to find since services are also often difficult to separate from the goods with which they may be associated in varying degrees. Nonetheless, it is recognized that services when contracting a service, its ownership is not transferred to the end customer: buying an airline ticket does not entail to own part of the airline. This fact can be contrasted to the action of buying a car, which transfers ownership of the car to the customer.

The differences between goods and services are based on many different factors (e.g., absence of inventories, production and consumption is at the same time, intangibility), which are becoming more and more acute as the services sector expands. These differences are also being explored by using bundling, a marketing tactic that involves offering two or more goods or services as a package deal for a discounted price. Examples of bundling are as widespread as selling iPhone 6, with insurance, a service contract with 6 GB of internet data, 1500 SMS/MMS, and 700 min of local calls.

But one of the major enablers of service markets expansion is IT, which bridges the physical distance between providers and consumers to enable a remote customer involvement during service provisioning. The next chapter will look into this class of services termed *electronic services*.

Review Section

Review Questions

1. Beside the recent developments identified in this chapter, which enabled the dissemination of services in modern society, enumerate other developments which were relevant.
2. Describe the types of digital services the UK government is providing to its citizens.
3. Execute a web search to identify which service industries have a higher market share. Contrast the values found for US, EU, and Asia.
4. Explain how the division of work and labor, and the ownership of resources, are prerequisites for the edification of a service-based society.
5. Compile a list of five distinct definitions for the term service and highlight possible limitations when compared to the definition from Hill [8] adopted in Sect. 1.2.1.
6. Provide four examples of services for each of the interaction types shown in Fig. 1.6.
7. Can the model of interaction types shown in Fig. 1.6 be extended with additional scenarios? Give examples of services for the new scenarios you have identified.
8. Due to the inseparability of production and consumption, services cannot be "stored". What techniques, methods, or tools can be used to manage the supply and demand of services more effectively?

9. How can *crowdsourcing* be used to match service supply and demand more efficiently? Describe two or three services, which could benefit from this sourcing model.
10. Identify and discuss how five well-known companies from various service industries could provide new services using servitization as a differentiating model?

Project

Service systems can consist of hundreds or even thousands of components which are the combination of technology, processes, people skills, and material resources. To ease the comprehension of what constitutes a service, their decomposition and the identification of their main parts is important. Decomposition refers to the process by which a complex system is broken down into parts that are easier to understand, systematize, use, and maintain.

The goal of this project is to select three familiar services (e.g., library loan, internal IT consulting, e-banking, or cloud services) and to use the capstone model [55] presented in Table 1.3 to identify their main components. The final report should constitute a precise service manual that can be used by managers for service operation, management, and improvement.

The capstone model (also known as CAIOPHYKE) was proposed by Kaner and Karni to conceptualize service systems using a five-level hierarchy of components: *major classes*, *main classes*, *attribute description*, *requirement/specification*, and *possible values*. The model enables one to define a service system at several levels. Each level provides another layer of details. The major classes, which are nine, are the most relevant to understand the main components of a service system and are:

1. Customers. The people that benefit or are affected by the service. Customers can be seen as initiators and receivers of a service.
2. Aims. The goals, purposes, and meaning of the system.
3. Inputs. The inputs to the system. They include physical, human, and informational entities to be handled through the service system.
4. Outputs. The outputs from and effects of the system. They can also include physical, human, and informational entities after being handled in the system.
5. Processes. Processes that are performed by the system. They are the transformations for obtaining outputs from inputs.
6. Human enablers. Human enablers are the human resources that own and/or operate the system.
7. Physical enablers. Physical enablers are physical and technological resources which aid or support the operation of the system.
8. Information enablers. Information enablers are information and knowledge resources that support the system.

Table 1.3 The capstone model [55] proposed by Kaner and Karni to conceptualize service systems

	Capstone model			
Customers	Customer organization	Customer features	Customer association	Customer attitudes
Aims	Strategic goals (general)	Strategic goals (service)	Service goals	Customer goals
Inputs	Physical factors	Human factors	Demand factors	Utilization factors
Outputs	Physical factors	Human factors	Informatics	Financial factors
Processes	Service configuration	Service variability	Service initiation	Service provision
Human enablers	Owner organization (enterprise)	Service providers	Support providers	Employee management
Physical enablers	Service center (physical)	Facilities (primary services)	Amenities (supplementary services)	Equipment
Informatic enablers	Product/service information	Promotion	Official documentation	Product configuration
Environment	Market factors	Geographic factors	Economic factors	Technological factors

9. Environment. The system's environment which include all the factors that can influence the system. For example, physical, technological, social, and legal factors.

The term CAIOPHYKE was derived from the letters of the nine major classes of the taxonomy constructed: Customers, Aims, Inputs, Outputs, Processes, Human enablers, Physical enablers, Information enablers (Knowledge), and Environment.

These nine major classes are extended to a second level of 75 main classes. At a third level, they are decomposed into 351 minor classes. The fourth and fifth levels include the actual attributes of a service and their possible values. A complete description of the various levels can be found in [55, p. 264].

Example (CAIOPHYKE)

The major class Customer has the main class Customer Feature, which in turn has the minor class Age, the attribute Age of Customers, and the possible values are: Children, Teenagers, Adults.

The major, main, and minor classes identify aspects of service systems, which can be analyzed to understand how a service is build and structured to, e.g., increase its transparency as well as discover and highlight the aspects that can be improved.

Key Terms

Service-Dominant Logic   A theory which views service as the focus of economic and social exchange.

Service   A service is a change in the condition of a person, or a good belonging to some economic unit, which is brought about as the result of the activity of some other economic unit, with the prior agreement of the former person or economic unit.

I-T-O Model   A basic concept from operations management that represents a service as a transformation (T) process that takes inputs (I), transforms and adds value to them, and provides outputs (O) for customers.

Self-service   A service which is provided without or with little human involvement on the provider's side. The provider often sets up facilities or equipment that the customer can use to perform a certain task.

Knowledge-Intensive Services   Services that heavily rely on professional knowledge.

IHIP   An acronym for four concepts often used to characterize services: intangibility (I), heterogeneity (H), inseparability (I), and perishability (P).

Demand Aggregation   An approach from the field of demand management which aggregates loads with different demand patterns to take advantage of the statistical effects that reduce variability in the aggregate demand.

Demand Conditioning   An approach from the field of demand management which creates artificial incentives for customers to use services in off-peak periods.

Outsourcing   A strategy that many companies follow to turn fixed costs into variable costs by paying for services only on demand to avoids risks if the company's business goes up or down.

Servitization   A strategy that a company may follow which consists in adding services to existing core products. The result is an hybrid offering in which products and services are integrated as one bundle.

Further Reading

James Fitzsimmons and Mona Fitzsimmons. *Service Management: Operations, Strategy, Information Technology*. McGraw-Hill, 2013.
Christopher Lovelock and Jochen Wirtz. *Services Marketing*. Prentice Hall, 2011.
Mairi Macintyre, Glenn Parry, and Jannis Angelis. *Service Design and Delivery*. Springer, 2011.

References

1. Manyika J et al (2010) How to compete and grow: a sector guide to policy. Technical report, McKinsey Global Institute
2. Vargo S, Maglio P, Akaka M (2008) On value and value co-creation: a service systems and service logic perspective. Eur Manag J 26(3):145–152. ISSN:0263-2373
3. Gagliordi N (2015) Enterprise software spend to reach $620 billion in 2015: Forrester. http://www.zdnet.com/article/enterprise-software-spend-to-reach-620-billion-in-2015-forrester/. Accessed 7 Jan 2015
4. EU directive 2006/123/EC of the European parliament and of the council of 12 December 2006 on services in the internal market. Technical report, European Union (2004)
5. Economic Assessment of the Barriers for the Internal Market for Services. Technical report, Copenhagen Economic (2005)
6. Innovation for Better Public Services. Technical report. 48th session of the Public Governance Committee, OECD Conference Centre Paris, France: OECD (2013)
7. Durkheim E (1947) The division of labor in society (trans: Simpson G). The Free Press, New York
8. Hill P (1977) On goods and services. Rev Income Wealth 23(4):315–38
9. Gadrey J (2002) The misuse of productivity concepts in services: lessons from a comparison between France and the United States. In: Productivity, innovation, and knowledge in services: new economic and socio-economic approaches. Edward Elgar, Cheltenham, pp 26–53
10. Riordan J (1962) Stochastic service systems. SIAM series in applied mathematics. Wiley, New York
11. Skyttner L, Rose D (1996) General systems theory: an introduction. Information systems series. Macmillan Press, New York
12. Backlund A (2000) The definition of system. Kybernetes 29(4):444–451
13. Vargo S, Lusch R (2004) The four service marketing myths: remnants of a goods-based, manufacturing model. J Serv Res 6(4):324–335
14. Kieliszewski C, Maglio P, Cefkin M (2012) On modeling value constellations to understand complex service system interactions. Eur Manag J. http://dx.doi.org/10.1016/j.emj.2012.05.003
15. Cardoso J (2013) Modeling service relationships for service networks. In: 4th International conference on exploring service science (IESS 1.3). Lecture notes in business information processing. Springer, Heidelberg, pp 114–128
16. Scott N, Laws E (2010) Advances in service networks research. Serv Ind J 30(10):1581–1592
17. Wieland H et al (2012) Toward a service (Eco)systems perspective on value creation. Int J Serv Sci Manag Eng Technol 3(3):12–25
18. Allee V (2000) Reconfiguring the value network. J Bus Strateg 21(4):36–39
19. Rouse W, Basole R (2010) Understanding complex product and service delivery systems. In: Handbook of service science. Springer, New York, pp 461–480
20. Blau B et al (2009) Service value networks. In: IEEE conference on commerce and enterprise computing, CEC '09, pp 194–201
21. Baltacioglu T et al (2007) A new framework for service supply chains. Serv Ind J 27(2):105–124
22. Gnedenko B, König D (1983) Handbuch der Bedienungstheorie I und II. Akademie-Verlag, Berlin
23. Hall R (1991) Queueing methods: for services and manufacturing. Prentice-Hall international series in industrial and systems engineering. Prentice Hall, Englewood Cliffs
24. Slack N, Chambers S, Johnston R (2010) Operations management. Financial Times/Prentice Hall, Harlow
25. Greasley A (2009) Operations management. Wiley, Chichester
26. Sampson S (2010) The unified service theory. English. In: Maglio P, Kieliszewski C, Spohrer J (eds) Handbook of service science. Service science: research and innovations in the service economy. Springer, New York, pp 107–131

27. Schmenner R (1986) How can service business survive and prosper? Sloan Manage Rev 27(3):21–32. http://www.ncbi.nlm.nih.gov/pubmed/10300742
28. Cedefop (2010) Briefing note—jobs in Europe to become more knowledge—and skills-intensive. http://www.cedefop.europa.eu/EN/Files/9021_en.pdf. Visited on 30 Sept 2010
29. Lahiri A, Seidmann A (2010) The hang-over effect in information-intensive service systems. IEEE Computer Society, Los Alamitos, pp 1–10
30. Lovelock C, Yip G (1996) Developing global strategies for service business. Calif Manag Rev 38(2):64–86
31. Edvardsson B, Gustafsson A, Roos I (2005) Service portraits in service research: a critical review. Int J Serv Ind Manag 16(1):107–121
32. Hill D, Gandhi N (1992) Service advertising: a framework to its effectiveness. J Serv Mark 6(4):63–76
33. Mittal B (1999) The advertising of services: meeting the challenge of intangibility. J Serv Res 2(1):98–116
34. Donabedian A (2005) Evaluating the quality of medical care. Milbank Q 83(4):691–729. ISSN:1468-0009
35. Shostack L (1982) How to design a service. Eur J Mark 16(1):49–63
36. Krafzig D, Banke K, Slama D (2005) Enterprise SOA: service-oriented architecture best practices. The Coad series. Prentice Hall Professional Technical Reference. Prentice Hall, Upper Saddle River
37. Erl T (2005) Service-oriented architecture: concepts, technology, and design. Prentice Hall PTR. Prentice Hall, Upper Saddle River. ISBN:0131858580
38. Papazoglou M (2008) Web services: principles and technology. Pearson Education/Pearson Prentice Hall, Harlow
39. Wilde E, Pautasso C (eds) (2011) REST: from research to practice. Springer, Heidelberg
40. Judd R (1964) The case for redefining services. J Mark 28(1):58–59
41. Rathmell J (1966) What is meant by services? J Mark 30(4):32–36
42. Lovelock C, Gummesson E (2004) Whither services marketing? In search of a new paradigm and fresh perspectives. J Ser Res 7(1):20–41. http://jsr.sagepub.com/content/7/1/20.abstract
43. Fitzsimmons J, Fitzsimmons M (2013) Service management: operations, strategy, and information technology. McGraw-Hill, London
44. Lovelock C, Wirtz J (2011) Services marketing: people, technology, strategy. Pearson Publishing, Harlow
45. Wittkowski K, Moeller S, Wirtz J (2013) Firms intentions to use nonownership services. J Serv Res 16(2):171–185
46. Bruce M (2011) Netflix my life: a culture of non-ownership. http://www.psychologytoday.com/blog/angst/201105/netflix-my-life-culture-non-ownership. Visited on 19 Apr 2014
47. Trendwatching (2006) Transumers: consumers driven by experiences. http://trendwatching.com/trends/transumers.htm. Visited on 19 Apr 2014
48. Botsman R (2010) Sharing is replacing owning. http://edition.cnn.com/2010/OPINION/11/02/botsman.collaborative.consumption/. Visited on 19 Apr 2014
49. Shankar V, Berry L, Dotzel T (2007) Creating and managing hybrid innovations. Presented at the American marketing association winter educators' conference
50. Ulaga W, Reinartz W (2011) Hybrid offerings: how manufacturing firms combine goods and services successfully. J Mark 75(6):5–23
51. Steunebrink G (2012) The servitization of product-oriented companies. http://essay.utwente.nl/62039/
52. Vandermerwe S, Rada J (1988) Servitization of business: adding value by adding services. Eur Manag J 6(4):314–324
53. Baines T et al (2007) State-of-the-art in product-service systems. Proc Inst Mech Eng B J Eng Manuf 221(10):1543–1552
54. Johansson J, Krishnamurthy C, Schlissberg H (2003) Solving the solutions problem. McKinsey Q 3:116–125
55. Kaner M, Karni R (2007) Design of service systems using a knowledge-based approach. Knowl Process Manag 14(4):260–274

Electronic Services

2

Jorge Cardoso and Hansjörg Fromm

Summary

This chapter provides an overview of two streams—the automation of activities and programming paradigms—which drove and supported the evolution of electronic services. These services are service systems implemented using important elements from the fields of automation and programming. It presents several classifications to understand the nature of services according to different views. Since services can take various forms, the chapter explains and contrasts electronic services, web services, cloud services, the internet of services, and service-oriented architectures.

Learning Objectives
1. Describe the evolution of electronic services as a result of the automation of economic activities and self service.
2. Describe the evolution of electronic services as the improvement of programming paradigms.
3. Classify service systems based on the role of information technology, service architectures, strategies, and business models.
4. Compare the various service types and paradigms that exist: electronic services, web services, cloud services, and internet of services.

J. Cardoso (✉)
Department of Informatics Engineering, Universidade de Coimbra, Coimbra, Portugal

Huawei European Research Center (ERC), Munich, Germany
e-mail: jcardoso@dei.uc.pt; jorge.cardoso@huawei.com

H. Fromm
Karlsruhe Institute of Technology (KSRI), Karlsruhe, Germany
e-mail: hansjoerg.fromm@kit.edu

© Springer International Publishing Switzerland 2015
J. Cardoso et al. (eds.), *Fundamentals of Service Systems*, Service Science: Research and Innovations in the Service Economy, DOI 10.1007/978-3-319-23195-2_2

► **Opening Case** Amazon Web Services

AMAZON EMBRACES SOAP AND REST WEB SERVICES

Amazon.com is known by most people as the largest e-commerce web site which sells books and other goods. Less known is the fact that Amazon has close to 1,000,000 servers. Why so many computers? To support millions of customers, Amazon had to build a massive storage and computing infrastructure with high availability and failure resistance to operate its web store. Once the infrastructure was built, it became clear that it could be exploited as a commodity by selling services which would be billed based on their usage. The platform was officially launched in 2006 and named Amazon Web Services (AWS). Nowadays, AWS is responsible for providing services to well-known web companies such as Foursquare, AirB&B, Netflix, Pinterest, Reddit, and Spotify.

What are Web Services?

The technology selected to make the infrastructure remotely available to customers was web services running over web protocols. Web services are a method of communication between computers using the world wide web. They offer functionalities that developers can use in their software applications to invoke and execute remote functions or methods using open and standardized protocols.

AWS offers more than 40 proprietary web services ranging from e-mail services to sophisticated database services. For example, Amazon SimpleDB provides a highly available and flexible non-relational data store. Amazon Glacier is an extremely low-cost storage service that provides secure and durable data archiving and backup. Amazon Simple Email Service is a scalable and cost-effective email-sending service for the cloud and Amazon Flexible Payments Service facilitates the digital transfer of money.

Hundreds of thousands of companies are using AWS to build their businesses. One interesting example is Foursquare.com.

Foursquare Use Case

Foursquare.com is a location-based social app used by 40 million people worldwide to check-in to places (e.g., restaurants and stores), to exchange travel tips, and to share locations with friends. The platform performs business intelligence and analytics over more than 4.5 billion check-ins each day.

The major asset of Foursquare is the large amount of data generated by check-ins. The data needs to be continuously stored and processed with business intelligence applications to create reports and long-term trend analysis. In the past, the use of property databases to process data came with high annual licensing costs and the need for qualified engineers to administer the platform.

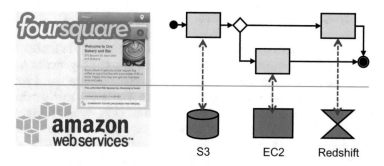

Fig. 2.1 Foursquare relies on Amazon Web Services for storage, processing, and business intelligence

To reduce costs, Foursquare uses Amazon Web Services (Fig. 2.1). For analytics, it adopted Amazon Redshift, a simple, fast, and cost-effective petabyte-scale data warehouse service which offers an efficient solution to analyze data. Simple Storage Service (S3) was also used to store images and Elastic Compute Cloud (EC2) was contracted for a fast and scalable processing.

The Benefits of Using Web Services

For most adopters, the key benefits of using web services include cost reductions, flexibility, and higher productivity.

Costs   The services provided by AWS can free businesses from high initial capital costs. Samsung has achieved reliability and performance objectives at a lower cost by relying on cloud services instead of using on-premise data centers which have high hardware and maintenance expenses.

Elasticity   AWS provides elasticity which enables to increase the computer resources allocated (e.g., the number of CPU or the storage available). This elasticity has enabled SEGA to reduce costs by more than 50 % with new servers when unplanned load spikes occur after the launch of new games.

Investments   Cloud services free organizations from setting up dedicated IT teams and infrastructures. NASA was able to construct a robust, scalable web infrastructure in a few weeks instead of months to support the Mars exploration program (mars.jpl.nasa.gov).

But Amazon AWS is not the only player in the cloud computing arena. Amazon is leading the cloud race, but Windows Azure and Google Cloud are not far behind. Other major players such as IBM, Oracle, and HP are also taking a dominant position in this market.

▶ **Opening Case**

2.1   Perspectives on Services

Already in 1968, Fuchs [1] presented a study that clearly indicated that the future employment growth would be almost entirely absorbed by service industries. Nowadays, the most developed countries have become service-based economies in terms of the distribution of people employed. While the first services were certainly delivered by humans to humans, the advances in computer systems over the past 60 years allowed computers to deliver services to humans. *Information and communication technology* (ICT) has significantly contributed to the evolution of services. Over the years, each wave of innovation has created solutions to automatically execute activities that were once done by human beings.

Services and self services were covered in Chap. 1. It shed some light on the difficulties of finding one single definition for the concept of service. One of the causes of these difficulties is related to the fact that the evolution of services can be observed from two distinct perspectives:

- As the automation of economic activities and self service.
- As the improvement of a programming paradigm.

Figure 2.2 illustrates these two perspectives on service evolution. Their most relevant milestones (represented with a circle) will be discussed in this chapter.

The first perspective looks into how traditional services, such as banking and trading, have benefited from automation and information technologies over the years to enable new forms of service delivery such as e-banking and e-commerce. The second perspective analyzes how the notion of service has emerged in the discipline

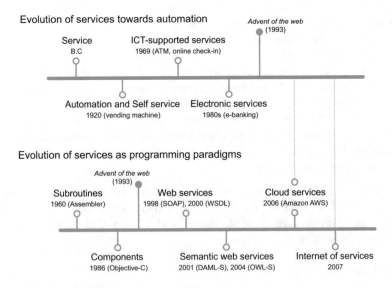

Fig. 2.2 The two perspectives on service evolution

of computer science, more precisely from the fields of software development and distributed systems, to ultimately give rise to software services such as web services.

A third perspective can also be identified as being the intersection of the first two perspectives (shown with dotted lines in the figure). Cloud services and the internet of services label a set of solutions which have a component of business from the first perspective and a component of technology from the second perspective.

2.2 Services as the Automation of Activities

This section presents the evolution of services in the last 100 years that has seen milestones like the advent of automation and self services in the 1920s, the emergence of ICT-supported services in the 1970s, and the dissemination of the internet which started in the 1990s and has led to a wide proliferation of electronic services.

2.2.1 Towards Automation and Self Service

In the old times, most services were delivered by human resources. As the costs of labor increased in industrialized countries, companies were seeking for new ways to deliver services with less human involvement. The answer was automation.

Automation

The manufacturing industry had already introduced automation in their production processes in the early twentieth century. At the same time, the first modern (mechanical) vending machines were introduced for stamps, postcards, tickets, cigarettes, chewing gum, or candy. The vending machines automate the sales process, so that no sales personnel are required anymore. In telephony, modern switching systems were invented to allow the caller to directly dial and automatically get routed to the desired telephone number. This was previously only possible with the assistance of a telephone operator. After automation, hardly any operator assistance was required.

Self Service

All of these service automation examples have in common that the person delivering the service was replaced by a machine and the customer took over the role of the traditional service person. This was the beginning of self-service as a direct consequence of service automation. Even if not all customers accepted self services from the beginning, the advantages of self services were soon being recognized [2]: The machines—other than shops or offices with service personnel—have no opening hours, they are typically available 24 h a day and 7 days a week. When using self service, the customer has the service encounter completely under his or her own control.

The customer does not feel rushed, influenced, or pressured by a service person. The customer can easily change his or her mind and interrupt the service process without annoying the service provider. The emergence of electronics in the second half of the twentieth century, and subsequently, the increasing use of computers and ICT, accelerated the progress of service automation. Self-service gasoline stations appeared in the 1950s, automatic teller machines (ATM) in the 1960s, interactive kiosks in the 1970s, electronic ticket machines (railway, metro, tram) in the 1980s.

In 1969, the first ATM made its public appearance by providing a cash service to customers of Chemical Bank in Rockville Center, New York.

Most of the service providers offering self-service technology give their customer a choice. The customers can use the self service, or still request a service person. At a bank, the customer can go to the teller or use an ATM. At many gas stations, the customer can pump the gas by him or herself, or ask an attendant to do it. At the railway station, the customer can go to the ticket counter or use a ticket vending machine.

2.2.2 The Role of Technology

Froehle and Roth [3] have identified five different classes that describe the role of technology in the service encounter (Fig. 2.3). Each class groups interactions which can be further classified as *face-to-face* or *face-to-screen*.

Technology-Free and -Assisted Services
Technology-free services (Fig. 2.3a) are hardly to be found anymore. Almost every little business like a hairdresser, newspaper store, or beauty salon has nowadays at least an electronic cash register or credit card reader to support their operations.

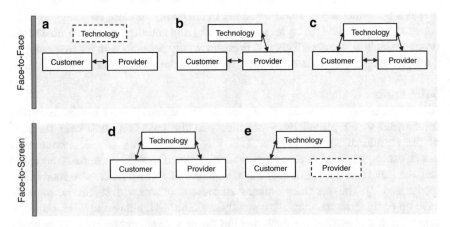

Fig. 2.3 The role of technology on electronic services (adapted from [3]). (**a**) Technology-free service. (**b**) Technology-assisted service. (**c**) Technology-facilitated service. (**d**) Technology-mediated service. (**e**) Technology-generated service

This would qualify as a *technology-assisted service* (Fig. 2.3b), where the service provider uses technology to improve the customer service, but the customer does not have access to this technology. Other examples are bank tellers, airline representatives, rental car clerks who all have access to the customer's data on their computer terminals while they interact with the customer at the counter. In a technology-assisted service situation, the provider is still in physical contact with or in proximity to the customer.

Technology-Facilitated Services

In a *technology-facilitated service* (Fig. 2.3c), both service provider and customer have access to the technology, and are still co-located. An example is an architect who develops a house design interactively with the customer at the computer terminal or a consultant who uses a personal computer attached to a projector to give a presentation to his clients.

Technology-Mediated Services

In the *technology-mediated service* (Fig. 2.3d), customer and service provider are not in face-to-face contact. The service is still delivered by people, who, due to the wide dissemination of communication technology like telephone or internet, can work from almost anywhere in the world. Examples are call-center services (communication typically by phone, but also e-mail), internet crowdsourcing platforms such as Amazon Mechanical Turk, and labor-intensive administrative services (accounting, human resources management) provided to companies typically from low-wage countries over electronic networks (also known as *offshoring*). Remote maintenance is an example of a technology-mediated service where a person on the provider's side (technician) directly acts with the belongings of a customer (machines, computers) over a distance.

Example

The Amazon Mechanical Turk (www.mturk.com), an online service, enables human intelligence tasks to be completed by anonymous people. This is an example of a technology-mediated service, where service providers and customer, not physically co-located, are brought "together".

Technology-Generated Services

In *technology-generated services* (Fig. 2.3e), the task of a human service provider is completely replaced by technology. The customer uses the service in a self-service mode. Technology can be mechanical (vending machine), a mixture of mechanical and electronic devices (ATM, check-in kiosk), or purely electronic (home banking). In the context of services, the terms "electronical" or "electronic" are less related with transistors, diodes, or integrated circuits—they mainly refer to the use of information and communication technology. If ICT is the major technology in support of services, one could speak of ICT-mediated or ICT-generated services according to Froehle and Roth's classification.

Table 2.1 The costs of self
services and assisted services

Technology	Type	Cost
Web	Self service	$0.24
IVR	Self service	$0.45
E-mail	Assisted	$5
Chat	Assisted	$7
Phone	Assisted	$5.5

Technology-generated services are gaining a wide acceptance amount companies and governmental agencies for three main reasons. First, self services are generally cost-reducers. In many cases, a customer self-service interaction is approximately 1/20th of the cost of a telephone call. A Yankee Group research report[1] indicates that, within self-service channels, the web-based self-service costs just $0.24 for an interaction and $0.45 for an interactive voice response (IVR), as opposed to $5.50 for a customer service representative assisted interaction via the telephone (Table 2.1). Second, self service can improve customer experience by providing a broad spectrum of choices. Nowadays, the number of features available to e-banking customers has never been so wide. Customers can trade stocks, download bank statements, and make bill payments. Some features may even only be available using a self-service mode. Third, self service can provide a solution to eliminate inefficient provider-customer interaction bottlenecks, i.e., customers having to wait on the telephone for the availability of staff or to wait in a line to be served by customer support. Customers often prefer to perform routine tasks over the internet without requiring any interaction with a representative of an enterprise.

2.2.3   Electronic Services

Both technology-mediated and technology-generated services are better known as *electronic services* or *e-services*. They are labeled as face-to-screen services. The technology required for electronic services can typically be distinguished into three architectural components:

1. Electronic components on the customer's side.
2. Electronic components on the provider's side.
3. An electronic communication line or network connecting the two.

Figure 2.4 gives four examples of electronic services.

Electronic Components
Figure 2.4a shows an automatic teller machine. In this case, the bank has set up (and typically owns) a user access device (the ATM) and connects it invisibly for the

---

[1]http://www.ccng.com/files/public/Yankee_SelfService.pdf.

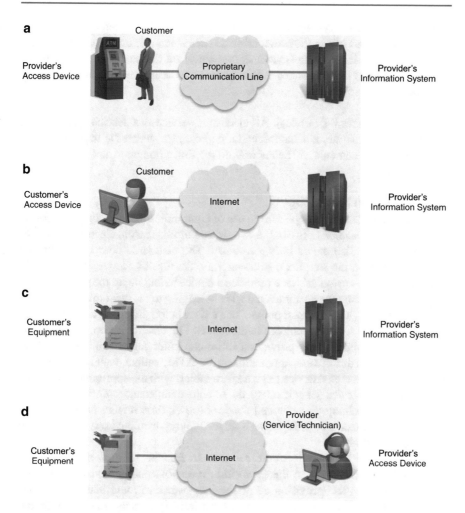

Fig. 2.4 Examples of electronic services. (**a**) Automatic teller machine (ATM). (**b**) Home banking. (**c**) Remote condition monitoring. (**d**) Remote maintenance

customer with a proprietary communication line to its backend information systems. ATM enabled banks to reduce costs by decreasing the need for tellers.

Even with the high cost of IT in the late 70s and early 80s, the cost of automated processing with ATM was less than the cost of hiring and training a teller to carry out the same activity. In this case, a complex and specialized machine, interconnected to the bank mainframe, was developed to replace a human activity.

Figure 2.4b illustrates *home banking*. In this case, the customer has his or her own access device (which could be a personal computer, tablet computer, or a smart phone) and uses the internet to connect to a computer application that the bank has made available for conducting different financial transactions. Figure 2.4c, d show examples of *remote maintenance*. In this case, an automated system (c) or a maintenance expert (d) on the provider's side uses electronic equipment to connect to a remote technical system (machine, computer) on the customer's side via the internet to conduct a maintenance task. A person may or may not be involved on the customer's side.

► **Definition (Electronic Service)** An electronic service is a service system (with elements, a structure, a behavior, and a purpose) for which the implementation of many of its elements and behavior is done using automation and programming techniques.

Communication Technology

Common to all of these examples is the use of communication technology establishing an *online connection* between the two sides. For this reason, electronic services or e-services are also called *online services*. The electronic components on the customer's and on the supplier's side can vary. As Fig. 2.4 shows, the electronic component on the customer's side might be a device belonging to the provider (e.g., an ATM) operated by the customer, a device belonging to the customer and used by the customer (e.g., a PC or smart phone), or a device belonging to the customer acted upon by the provider (e.g., remote maintenance). The electronic component on the provider's side might be the provider's entire computer center running a number of internet-enabled software applications (for ATM, online banking, condition monitoring) or a personal device (e.g., a PC or tablet) with the appropriate programs that allows the service technician to do remote maintenance. The examples of Fig. 2.4a–c are technology-generated services (no or little human involvement in delivery) and the example of Fig. 2.4d is an technology-mediated service according to Froehle and Roth [3].

In most definitions of electronic services so far, the *mediation role* of ICT received more attention than the *generation role*. Rust and Kannan [4] defined electronic services as "provisioning of services over electronic networks", Rowley [5] as "deeds, efforts or performances whose delivery is mediated by information technology". For the EU [6], electronic services are "services delivered over the internet or an electronic network". All these definitions emphasize the communication component of electronic services and leave the question open, how services are created or generated. Hofacker et al. [7] give a clue in remarking that an e-service is created "through a process that is stored as an algorithm and typically implemented by [...] software". They describe the case of an ICT-generated service in which the service is rendered ("generated") by software programs running on the provider's computer systems.

The First Electronic Services

ICT-supported services have been around since the 1960s. The online information service CompuServ started in 1969, electronic funds transfer (SWIFT) in 1977. Online banking began in 1981. This was long before the advent of the internet. In the early times, telephone networks with modems for data communication were used, and a variety of communication standards. With the advent of the internet, "other electronic networks" lost more and more importance. Nowadays, electronic services are predominantly provided over the internet. And accordingly, most people today equate electronic services with internet-based services. This perception has become particularly common for the short form *e-services*, from which specializations like e-banking, e-learning, and e-government have been derived.

▶ **Definition (e-Banking, e-Learning, e-Government)** The Oxford Dictionary defines *e-Banking* as "a method of banking in which the customer conducts transactions electronically via the internet", and e-Learning as "learning conducted via electronic media, typically on the internet". The OECD [8] defines e-Government as "the use of information and communication technologies, and particularly the internet, as a tool to achieve better government", and the IRS defines their e-services as "a suite of web-based tools that allow tax professionals and payers to complete certain transactions online with the IRS".

Since electronic internet-based services are offered through web sites and require user interaction via web pages, one might be inclined to call these services *web services*. However, the term web service is already used by computer scientists with a different, precise technical meaning. It is therefore not recommended to equate the technical term web services with the term electronic services in the sense of economic interactions [9] (web services will be discussed in Sect. 2.3).

2.2.4 The Value of Electronic Services

Many automated self-service technologies like ATMs or ticket vending machines have made services available independent from office hours. The user, however, has to be physically present at the machine in order to request and receive the service. The internet has revolutionized the access to services. Given the widespread availability of the internet, the user needs only a personal device like a desktop, a tablet computer or a smart phone in order to get access to services. Electronic services have inherently several characteristics such as facilitated accessibility and personalization.

Accessibility
With the easy *accessibility* over standard internet devices, the comfort in using electronic services has been brought a big step forward. E-services can be used from home, from public places like libraries or internet cafés, or even while traveling— given a connection of the access device to the internet can be established using local area networks or wireless communication. Electronic mail or e-mail was the first service widely accepted by the internet community. It has largely replaced traditional paper mail like postcards and letters. And it has the advantage that it is almost instantaneously delivered.

Delivery

The *delivery* of electronic services, though, is not unlimited. For example, they cannot replace an ATM for cash withdrawal. However, they have begun to substitute ticket vending machines. Railway companies, theater offices, and concert agencies allow their customers to buy tickets electronically and print them out on their home printer. Airlines offer the possibility to electronically check-in to flights and print out the boarding pass on paper or receive an electronic boarding pass on the smart phone which can be scanned at the airport. Even if cash withdrawal is only possible at the bank counter or at an ATM, electronic banking has received widespread acceptance for personal bank transactions like paying bills, transferring funds, or viewing recent transactions and account balances. Books, music, and videos can be ordered electronically—and even be delivered electronically, if the customer prefers an electronic version of the media.

Standing in line at authorities and filling out paper forms is an annoyance for many people. Moreover, authorities' office hours are typically colliding with most citizens' working hours. Therefore, it was very important for local authorities and government agencies to offer public e-services to their citizens independent of their limited office hours. Such services can be requesting the issuance of a new passport or renewal of the old passport, reporting changes of address or marital status, or renewing a vehicle registration.

All these electronic or online services are known under terms like electronic mail, e-mail, electronic banking, e-banking or online banking, e-government, public e-services, electronic ordering, and e-ordering.

Human Touch

Traditional human-based services are characterized by the personal service encounter involving *human touch* and *service experience*. Very often, the provider and customer know each other well from past service experiences. The provider quickly understands what the customer wants and can deliver a very individual, personalized service. This advantage was lost in automated services: the vending machine treats all customers the same. The machine is typically programmed in a way that all customers have to follow the same path in order to get the desired result. Even if a customer uses a vending machine the 100th time, the machine would not behave differently.

Service experience is influenced by the outcomes of the interactions that occur between service systems and their customers. The outcomes can take the form of functional, behavioral, and emotional effects and directly shape service experience. The interactions occur between people, technology, resources, and customers. They are considered to be a crucial part of a memorable service experience.

Personalization

This disadvantage can be overcome with electronic services. Electronic services—even if delivered by technology—provide possibilities to focus on the customer almost like traditional human-based services do. The keywords are *personalization* and *customization* (yielding individuality), *interaction* (leading to relationship), and *localization* (allowing location-based services). In all cases, a difference can only be made if customers are willing to share their personal information like preferences, transaction details, or whereabouts with the service provider. The customer can benefit considerably from personalization and customization, but will accept the service only if privacy and security are guaranteed. For the service provider, gathering customer data can help to provide focused service offerings, enhance the services, and build a profitable customer relationship [4]. More information on personalization and customization is provided by Vesanen [10], on interaction by Bolton and Saxena-Iyer [11], and on localization by Junglas and Watson [12].

2.2.5   E-Service Strategy

A notable classification has been given by Hofacker et al. [7] to evaluate the strategic position of services. It includes three types:

1. Complements to existing offline services and goods.
2. Substitutes for existing offline services.
3. New core services.

Complementary Services

Many companies are adding value to their existing offline services or goods by providing *complementary e-services*. Examples are parcel service companies such as DHL, FedEx, and UPS that allow their customers to track parcel deliveries online; electronic companies who offer their customers technical support via their website and provide materials like instruction manuals downloadable on the internet; and retailers who offer mobile apps that enable consumers to scan products and obtain information on country of origin, processing dates, quality, and nutritional value.

Substitute Services

Companies who offer *substitutes e-services* to existing offline services are well known. Amazon was the pioneer in offering online book ordering and thus became a painful competitor of brick-and-mortar bookstores. Spotify, a provider of digital music services, and Netflix, a provider of digital video services, are challenging traditional CD and video stores and video rental businesses. Online ordering offers big advantages over the traditional business: while brick-and-mortar stores are pretty limited in the number of products they keep on stock, this is less the case for online companies. Electronic products require little space (only computer storage, a single copy), and physical products sold online can be stored in large remote warehouses. This allows the electronic businesses to serve the long tail [13]: this means a much larger variety including niche products. Google Maps can substitute traditional paper road maps. Online news and online stock reports are competing with financial newspapers. Skype, an internet-based communication service, becomes a challenge for traditional landline or mobile telephony.

New Core Services

New core e-services that arose with the dissemination of the internet are search engines like Google or Yahoo, social networking services like Facebook, LinkedIn, or Twitter, videosharing services like Youtube, Vimeo, or Dailymotion, image and video hosting services like Flickr or Instagram, data storage services like Dropbox, or deal-making services like Groupon.

2.2.6 Electronic Business Models

Section 2.2.3 distinguished three architectural components of an e-service: customers' and providers' electronic components, and the network connecting the two. Electronic business models characterize the role that the provider and the customer take during interactions.

Electronic services have enabled the generalization and rapid dissemination of several business models for electronic commerce: B2B, B2C, and G2C. These terms are short forms for Business-to-Business, Business-to-Consumer, and Government-to-Citizen, respectively. While many more models exist, such as G2G (Government-to-Government), G2E (Government-to-Employee), G2B (Government-to-Business), B2G (Business-to-Government), G2C (Government-to-Citizen), C2G (Citizen-to-Government), this section covers B2B, B2C, and G2C models.

Business-to-Business

Business-to-Business refers to transactions between two parties where the buyer and seller are both businesses. Therefore, products or services are not sold to end users. Buyers purchase goods in large quantities to satisfy the demand of their consumers. Two examples are salesforce.com AppExchange, a provider of business apps, and ariba.com, an e-procurement platform. In B2B environments, the integration of businesses at the application level (known as application-to-application (A2A) integration) was important to improve not only efficiency but also to reduce transaction costs. A2A integration aims to make independently designed software applications work together.

Example

Ariba Inc. uses the internet to enable businesses to facilitate and improve their procurement processes. It was founded in 1996. Until then, typical procurement processes were labor intensive and often costly for large corporations. Ariba supplied the software to create and host vendors' catalogs online as well as the software to enable purchasing staff to remotely buy items. This required to provide electronic services to both provides and customers. In 2012, SAP AG, the largest maker of enterprise applications software, agreed to buy Ariba for $4.3 billion.

Business-to-Consumer

Business-to-Consumer is distinct from B2B since the business (the B) offers products or services to consumers (the C) rather than to other businesses. Amazon.com is a good example of a successful business that has initially started its operations using the B2C model. Customers could simply use a browser to interact with the bookstore. Another example is eBay.com. Although, eBay started as an auction site involving only end users which would take the role of suppliers and consumers, nowadays, it also enables businesses to market their products to end users. B2C environments involve human-to-application (H2A) or application-to-human (A2H) interactions and communications. The machine-like nature of many activities executed by B2C platforms made it possible to develop services that no longer required a human provider in the loop unless there was a problem.

Government-to-Citizen

Governments are important stakeholders which are recognizing the value of using electronic services for improving citizens experience and lowering costs. Therefore, a third model also emerged: *Government-to-Citizen* (G2C). The goal is to provide one-stop, online access to governmental information and services to citizens, quickly, and easily. This model can offer a large spectrum of services such as employment offers, business opportunities, voting information, tax filing, license registration, and payment of fines.

2.2.7   Government-to-Citizen Services

Despite the high availability and adoption of e-government services in Europe, satisfaction can be improved since it is not yet at the levels of e-banking and e-commerce. Europe aims to increase the use of e-government services to 50 % of citizens and 80 % of businesses by 2015. While public services such as income tax declaration have already been modernized there is still room for improvements. Recent budget constraints are pushing governments to drastically increase productivity and reduce costs. Electronic services are a targeted area.

The European Commission is addressing these concerns through its 2020 Strategy and its Digital Agenda flagship. The "Digital by Default or by Detour?" report published in May 2013 surveyed 28,000 internet users across 27 European countries. The study found that 73 % of citizens declare taxes, 57 % change their address, and 56 % apply for a higher education online. Among the many points focused, five important key findings are highlighted:

Innovation   Transformation is needed to drive the development of innovative e-government services. New solutions that use technology in a smarter way, capitalize on social media and collaborative platforms, implement stronger citizen-oriented strategies, and open up data to exploit the value of hidden knowledge are indispensable. Nonetheless, generating innovative services is far from trivial.

Design   Governments have not yet fully embraced a service-oriented thinking. A shift needs to take place to change the ad hoc management of services to their systematic design centered around user needs. There is a variation in the satisfaction of online service users, from 41 to 73 %, which may be a symptom of the use of different approaches for service design.

Efficiency   The increasing number of automated services and self services currently available generate precious data which can benefit from advanced algorithms and analytical tools. Service analytics can extract information to enable public agencies to improve service delivery efficiency and customer experience. The report indicates that 80 % of online public services save citizens time, 76 % provide flexibility, and 62 % reduce costs.

Transparency   Currently, services are presented as black-boxes since citizens are unaware of how processes are internally conducted. In fact, the transparency of service execution rates below 50 %. This indicates that more transparency is still needed. Governments are providing basic data about their agencies, but information on services that empower citizens.

Business models   Opening up data will enable to implement new business models to reach economic gains from various perspectives. The direct impact of Open Data in Europe was estimated at € 32 billion in 2010, with an estimated annual growth rate of 7 %. Nonetheless, few governments are exploiting the full economic benefits of Open Data.

There is no doubt that digital technologies will be a fundamental pillar of future public service delivery taking a different direction from how government operates to date. While Europe is taking a serious strategy to implement digital services[2] at the government level, similar efforts are visible at the global scale.

Three of the most advanced governments in this field include the UK, New Zealand, and US. UK adopted a digital by default approach and offers a guide and resources (gov.uk/service-manual) for delivering digital services in the government. New Zealand has followed the same steps and is mirroring UK progresses (see beta.govt.nz). In the US, The White House issued the directive "Building a 21st Century Digital Government"[3] on May 23, 2012, announcing a strategy to enable a more efficient digital service delivery by requiring agencies to establish specific, measurable goals by using web performance analytics and customer satisfaction measurement tools on all .gov web sites (Fig. 2.5).

2.2.8   Developing Electronic Services

Electronic services are realized by software programs that utilize existing technical infrastructures like the customer's access device, the internet, and the provider's data center and information systems. To develop an electronic service means to develop a software program.

---

[2]The term digital services has the same meaning as electronic services.

[3]The White House, Building a 21st Century Digital Government, May 23, 2012, http://www. whitehouse.gov/sites/default/files/uploads/2012digital_mem_rel.pdf.

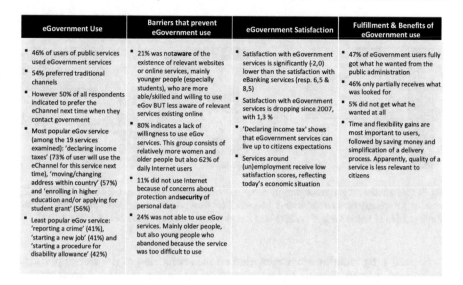

eGovernment Use	Barriers that prevent eGovernment use	eGovernment Satisfaction	Fulfillment & Benefits of eGovernment use
▪ 46% of users of public services used eGovernment services ▪ 54% preferred traditional channels ▪ However 50% of all respondents indicated to prefer the eChannel next time when they contact government ▪ Most popular eGov service (among the 19 services examined): 'declaring income taxes' (73% of user will use the eChannel for this service next time), 'moving/changing address within country' (57%) and 'enrolling in higher education and/or applying for student grant' (56%) ▪ Least popular eGov service: 'reporting a crime' (41%), 'starting a new job' (41%) and 'starting a procedure for disability allowance' (42%)	▪ 21% was not **aware** of the existence of relevant websites or online services, mainly younger people (especially students), who are more able/skilled and willing to use eGov BUT less aware of relevant services existing online ▪ 80% indicates a lack of willingness to use eGov services. This group consists of relatively more women and older people but also 62% of daily Internet users ▪ 11% did not use Internet because of concerns about protection and **security** of personal data ▪ 24% was not able to use eGov services. Mainly older people, but also young people who abandoned because the service was too difficult to use	▪ Satisfaction with eGovernment services is significantly (-2,0) lower than the satisfaction with eBanking services (resp. 6,5 & 8,5) ▪ Satisfaction with eGovernment services is dropping since 2007, with 1,3 % ▪ 'Declaring income tax' shows that eGovernment services can live up to citizens expectations ▪ Services around (un)employment receive low satisfaction scores, reflecting today's economic situation	▪ 47% of eGovernment users fully got what he wanted from the public administration ▪ 46% only partially receives what was looked for ▪ 5% did not get what he wanted at all ▪ Time and flexibility gains are most important to users, followed by saving money and simplification of a delivery process. Apparently, quality of a service is less relevant to citizens

Fig. 2.5   Key findings from the "Digital by Default or by Detour?" report [14]

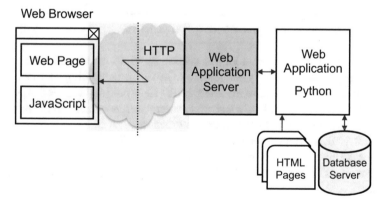

Fig. 2.6   Architecture of a web application

In software engineering, web-accessible programs are called *web applications* (see Fig. 2.6). A web application is a software program residing on the provider's *web application server* which uses the client's web browser as the presentation layer in a client/server fashion. Client and server communicate via standard internet protocols such as HTTP. On request of the client, the web application creates a response in form of *web pages* containing static and dynamic content. Programs may be downloaded and executed on the client's web browser. The *database server* will be responsible for the persistence of data stored for the web application.

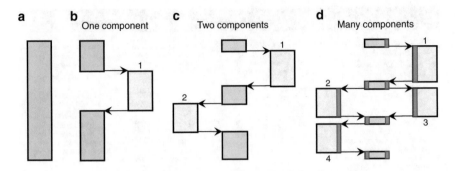

Fig. 2.7 Evolution of programming models. (**a**) "Monolithic" program. (**b**) Programming using reusable, pre-programmed components (services). (**c**) Less programming; more use of components (services). (**d**) Extensive use of components (services); programming has become "modeling"

Popular programming languages used on the server side of the web application are Java, Perl, PHP, Python, Ruby, or .NET. Most web applications use HTML or XHTML to create web pages. They often send JavaScript and/or Flash to make the content dynamic and more interactive.

2.3   Services as Programming Paradigms

In contrast to the previous section, this section describes an evolution in software engineering that has started with service-oriented programming and has seen a similar boost with the advent of the internet like electronic services. It has led to the concepts of *web services*, *cloud services*, *semantic web services*, and the *internet of services*, which are covered in the following sections.

Naturally, these developments are closer to the fields of computer science and information technology rather than to the fields of economics, business, or management as it was the case of Sect. 2.2 on services as the automation of activities.

2.3.1   Subroutines

The origins of service orientation can be traced back to the early days of programming. In the 1950s, programmers realized that certain functions, e.g., date conversion routines, were used over and over again throughout their applications [15]. They isolated the function from the rest of the code and put it into a subroutine (see Fig. 2.7a). This subroutine could then be called from any point in the main program where it was needed. It returned the result back to the main program at the point from where it was called. The programmer kept the subroutine in a library for the case that it could be reused in another application. Subroutines could also be shared with other programmers. A sound use of subroutines often reduced the cost and increased the quality and reliability of developing and maintaining large applications.

2.3.2 Components

Over time, programmers realized that business applications exhibited many of these recurring, separable functions. It became common practice to extensively reuse pre-programmed objects or components as the subroutines were now called (see Fig. 2.7b–d). In the end, programmers did not write many lines of codes anymore—they mainly composed pre-built, reusable components stored in software libraries. The organization of the code in separable functions made code easily reusable due to its inherent modularity, high cohesion, and separation of concerns. This new style of programming was called component-based software development. This style was an indication that components would eventually evolve into distributed services to achieve a higher reuse and decoupling.

Parnas, an early pioneer from the field of software engineering, proposed the concept of *module* [16], which latter evolved into the concept of component. Modules were introduced to enable software developers to implement segments of code independently. They enabled to change one module without affecting other modules, and ease the understanding of the overall system by analyzing one module at a time.

There are some analogies with the French restaurant example introduced in Chap. 1 (page 9): the chef with his staff and kitchen equipment was separated from the aristocrat's household and moved to someplace else, now called a restaurant—much like a particular function was separated from the main application program and moved into a subroutine (component). The restaurant has become a self-contained, autonomous service which (theoretically) could be used by the former owner, but is now available to many other people having a proper physical interface. The subroutine (component) is a self-contained, autonomous program which can be called from the originating main program, but also (potentially) from many other programs.

An important prerequisite for reusability is the separation of the service's implementation from its interface. Application builders should not be concerned with *how* a service works, only with *what* the service accomplishes and *how* it is invoked. For this purpose, the service needs a well-defined interface and its functionality has to be described in a form understandable by the requestor.

2.3.3 Business Process Modeling

Once a reusable set of services is available, the developer can start building a business application based on these building blocks. By intention, the word programming is no longer used for this activity, but rather the words composing or modeling. This different wording indicates a paradigm shift in software engineering. A widely used approach for the composition of services into business applications is *business process modeling* (BPM). BPM provides graphical notations, which are intuitive to business users yet formal enough to represent complex business semantics.

Business process modeling is used by business analysts and consultants to describe business processes in reengineering projects, and it is used by software developers to document business processes as a starting point for application development. The business process model notation (BPMN) has emerged as a widely accepted standard for BPM. Other well-known graphical languages include event-driven process chains (EPC), simple process state diagrams, and even Petri nets (generally used in academic environments).

Once processes are modeled, they can be executed using an orchestration language. For example, the business process execution language (BPEL) defines processes that can be executed on an orchestration engine. During execution, the externally observable interactions between services is called the choreography and describes collaborations between services.

2.3.4   Service-Oriented Architecture (SOA)

Service-Oriented Architecture (SOA) and Service-Oriented Computing (SOC) are programming paradigms that were introduced to overcome the inflexibility of monolithic software. They utilize services as fundamental elements for developing applications [17].

▶ **Definition (Service-Oriented Architecture)** An architectural style and business-centric programming paradigm to develop distributed systems where systems consist of software clients, which act as service consumers, and software providers, which act as service providers.

Composition and Decomposition
Programmers made the observation that smaller functions like "check customer status", "check order status", or "determine product availability" were repeatedly used in larger business applications like order processing, account management, or service scheduling. It appeared meaningful to separate the repetitive tasks from the business applications and to put them as services into a *service repository*. Once a service repository is available, applications could be developed by *composition* of existing services.

Many companies decided to use the SOA paradigm for new application development. They also reengineered existing applications by breaking them down into smaller, manageable services, which were then glued together again in a more flexible way. This process of *decomposition* is not trivial. There are better and worse decompositions. A good decomposition is one which has little interaction between the components and a high functional coherence within the components. In this case,

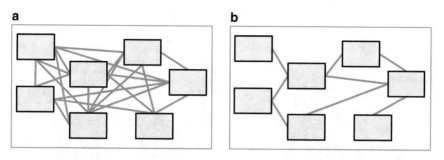

Fig. 2.8 Decomposition of a system into smaller, manageable components. (**a**) A bad decomposition: too many interactions between the components. (**b**) A good decomposition: little interaction between the components; interfaces can be better managed and easily be described

components are more "self-contained" and "loosely coupled"—characteristics that are desired from a service. In his seminal work "The Architecture of Complexity", Simon [18] points out that many natural (e.g., biological) and man-made systems (e.g., technical and organizational) exhibit this kind of "near decomposability".

Figure 2.8a shows a "bad decomposition" with too many interactions (interfaces) between the components and a "good decomposition" with little interaction between the components. In the latter case, the interfaces are better manageable and can be described with less effort (Fig. 2.8b).

Software Paradigm

SOA has increased the speed of development and the ability to quickly adapt existing applications to a changing business environment. Accordingly, many companies readily adopted the paradigm. SOA is not directly related with standards and technologies (even if certain standards become prevalent for SOA). Many companies have started to use SOA within the boundaries of their own organization. They used proprietary standards and technologies to implement a service-oriented architecture.

Enterprise Application Integration

Before the introduction of SOA, *enterprise application integration* (EAI) was the traditional solution to integrate the array of systems and applications of an organization. EAI became a top priority in many enterprises as a result of the emergence of the internet and B2B (Business-to-Business). Both accelerated the need for integration. As shown in Fig. 2.9a, EAI was an approach based on a point-to-point integration of systems which created a high complexity in large organizations. The SOA approach enabled to decompose large applications into standard services which were managed by business processes exposing the business logic of organizations (Fig. 2.9b).

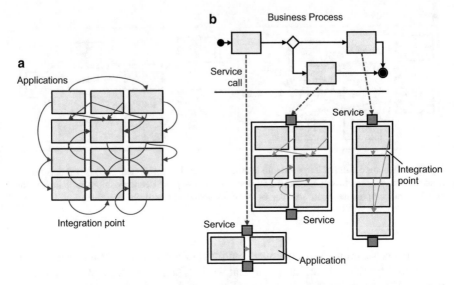

Fig. 2.9 Integration of software systems using EAI and SOA approaches. (**a**) Enterprise application integration. (**b**) Service-oriented architecture

---

Example (EAI Complexity)

The application of an EAI approach requires a systematic and organized management. Otherwise, the number of point-to-point connections can easily reach unmanageable proportions. For example, the grid of applications shown in Fig. 2.9a has 12 systems. Assuming that each application needs to communicate with all the other applications using point-to-point connections, this requires to establish $\frac{n(n-1)}{2}$ connections, with $n = 12$. Therefore, fully connecting the grid requires $\frac{12 \times 11}{2} = 66$ point-to-point connections.

2.3.5 Web Services

The internet established connectivity between a huge number of people, companies, and organizations. In consequence, software exchange and reuse became theoretically possible between very different and distant software providers and consumers. Such software services provided over the internet are called *web services*. Web services can be seen as an extension of the principles of service-orientation and SOA to the internet.

> In contrast to electronic services, web services are designed for machine-to-machine interaction and have only a programmatic interface. Electronic services can be used by virtually everyone, web services can only be used by programmers.

Web Services and Electronic Services

Web services are often not precisely distinguished from web-enabled electronic services (e-services). Both electronic services and web services are services available over the internet (the "web"). But as it was pointed out earlier, an electronic service, such as online banking, has a user interface designed for *human interaction* (web pages displayed in a web browser). Web services are designed for *machine-to-machine interaction* and have only a programmatic interface. Electronic services can be used by virtually everyone, web services can only be used by programmers. An electronic service can, but does necessarily not need to be developed using web service technologies.

▶ **Definition (Web Service)** The World Wide Web Consortium defines a web service as "a software system designed to support interoperable machine-to-machine interaction over a network".

Service Directory

Prerequisites for the development of web services were mechanisms that allowed providers (programmers) to describe and publish their services, and consumers (application builders) to search and find suitable services (Fig. 2.10). For this purpose, a new role has emerged, the *web services broker*, who keeps a *web service directory* listing all web services that service providers have developed, described, and published. The web service directory is often compared with the yellow pages in a telephone directory that allow someone to find a suitable service provider.

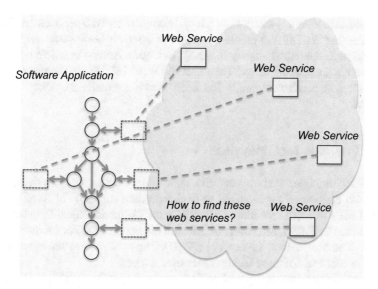

Fig. 2.10 The use of web services for application development (composition)

Two alternatives of identifying a web service are conceivable:

1. The web service directory is human-readable and the application builder (a person) looks it up to find a suitable web service.
2. The web service directory is machine-readable and the application program itself is capable of conducting the service discovery process.

It should be clear that alternative (b) is far more sophisticated than alternative (a). It requires a formalized description of the service and a formalized search algorithm. It requires semantic in addition to syntactical methods to consider meaning and context.

Discovery Protocol

Figure 2.11 shows how the different actors in a web service environment work together [19]. The service provider has created a web service together with its description and publishes it in the web service directory. A service requester (application programmer) searches for a web service via the discovery interface and checks if the description matches his requirements. If an appropriate service is found, the programmer can invoke the service. Finally, the web service answers with a response message.

The fully automated web service engagement, as illustrated in Fig. 2.11b, is still a futuristic scenario. Even if the automated querying of service directory is possible, the understanding and interpretation of the search results and the selection of the appropriate web service matching based on functional and non-functional requirements (price, availability, etc.) still needs human intervention and judgment [20].

The ultimate vision is that web services discover other web services and interact with each other in a fully automated way and without any human intervention. This vision has been described already in a 2001 Scientific American article by Berners-Lee, Hendler, and Lassila titled "The Semantic Web" [21]. Since then, the semantic web services research community has been working steadily to make this vision come true.

2.3.6   Previous Technologies

Previous technologies that covered the same objectives as web services, i.e., to enable two distributed applications to exchange data and call software functions included SUN Remote Procedure Call (RPC), the Common Object Request Broker Architecture (CORBA), Microsoft Distributed Component Object Model (DCOM), and Java Remote Method Invocation (JRMI). Table 2.2 shows the chronological introduction of each of these technologies over the years.

Listing 2.1 shows an example of an RPC protocol specification file that describes the remote version of the PRINTACCOUNT procedure. This specification can be

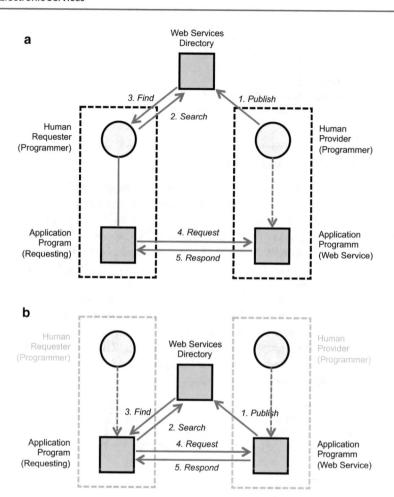

Fig. 2.11 The process of engaging a web service. (**a**) With human involvement. (**b**) Fully automated

Table 2.2 Previous technologies to web services

Technology	Year
Sun RPC	1985
CORBA	1992
Microsoft DCOM	1996
Java RMI	1996

seen as the precursor of WSDL. It contains the information needed for a client to invoke a service or remote procedure.

The differences and similarities between RPC and WSDL can be evaluated by contrasting the examples of interface definition languages given in Listing 2.1 and Fig. 2.13

```
1 /*
2 * msg.x: Remote printing account protocol
3 */
4 program ACCOUNTPROG {
5         version ACCOUNTVERS {
6                 int PRINTACCOUNT(string) = 1;
7         } = 1;
8 } = 0x20000099;
```

Listing 2.1 Example of the RPC interface definition language

These technologies had drawbacks that were considered significant when developing distributed systems, especially in heterogeneous environments. For example, the RPC mechanism had mainly implementations for the UNIX platform and had, therefore, a reduce market share. CORBA and DCOM were fierce competitors which lead to a low acceptance and adoption from the industry. Furthermore, their programming was cumbersome. Finally, Java RMI technology was limited to the Java programming language.

These limitations were a clear indicator that a more open and consensual approach to develop distributed applications was necessary. Web services were the answer to allow software applications to easily communicate, independently of the underlying computing platform and language. The development of web services is substantially less complex than the prior solutions available for creating interoperable distributed systems.

 As a side note, CORBA already used the term service in its specification: "a service is basically a set of CORBA objects with IDL interfaces. The main characteristics of the objects composing a service is that they are not related to any application but are rather basic building blocks, usually provided by CORBA environments (e.g. transactions, naming, events)."

2.4   Web Service Technologies

The goal of web services is to ease the development of distributed systems. Services require to be autonomous and platform-independent, and need to be described, published, discovered, and orchestrated using standard protocols for the purpose of building distributed systems. The emphasis is on the definition of interfaces from a technical and programming perspective. The objective is automation and computerization, since web services provide a technological solution to enable transaction systems, resource planning systems, customer management systems, etc. to be integrated and accessed programmatically through the web (Fig. 2.12).

Nowadays, two types of web services can be identified:

- Operations-based web services.
- Resource-based web services.

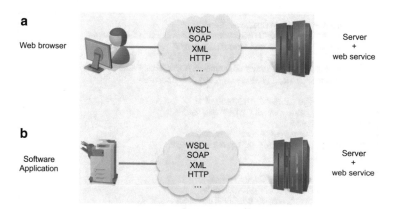

a

Web browser

WSDL
SOAP
XML
HTTP
...

Server
+
web service

b

Software
Application

WSDL
SOAP
XML
HTTP
...

Server
+
web service

Fig. 2.12 Remotely accessing web services. (**a**) A web browser accessing a web service. (**b**) A software application accessing a web service

2.4.1   Operations-Based Web Services

The emergence of the internet forced components to expose their functionality to internal as well as external applications in the form of services. Since the preferred communication medium was the WWW, existing web standards and protocols were adopted and new ones were created, such as HTML, HTTP, XML, WSDL, SOAP, and UDDI, to support web services.

▶ **Definition (XML and HTML)** XML (eXtensible Markup Language) is a specification language used to create schemas to share data on the web using standard ASCII text. HTML (HyperText Mark-up Language) is a language to describe the presentation of a document so that it can be rendered in a web browser in a human readable form.

▶ **Definition (WSDL, SOAP, and UDDI)** Three specifications used to develop distributed systems. The interface of services is described with WSDL, the web services description language; SOAP, originally defined as simple object access protocol, enables providers and clients to exchange messages and call software functions; and UDDI, an acronym for universal description, discovery and integration, is a directory where services are listed using WSDL.

A web service is an autonomous software component that is uniquely identified by a universal resource identifier (URI) which uses the hypertext transfer protocol (i.e., HTTP) to request and transport data as documents, the simple object access protocol SOAP to invoke remote functions, and languages, such as the extensible markup language XML, to structure data.

Figure 2.13 illustrates the skeleton of a WSDL interface definition that a client can use to invoke a remote operation provided by a web service. The service is

```
1.    <definitions name="Customer_Service"
2.      targetNamespace="http://www.store.com/wsdl/CustService.wsdl"
3.      xmlns="http://schemas.xmlsoap.org/wsdl/"
4.      xmlns:soap="http://schemas.xmlsoap.org/wsdl/soap/"
5.      xmlns:tns="http://www.store.com/wsdl/CustService.wsdl"
6.      xmlns:xsd="http://www.w3.org/2001/XMLSchema">
7.
8.      <message name="CustIDRequest">
9.        <part name="CustID" type="xsd:long"/>
10.     </message>
11.     <message name="AddressResponse">
12.       <part name="address" type="xsd:string"/>
13.     </message>
14.
15.     <portType name="Cust_PortType">
16.       <operation name="getAddress">
17.         <input message="tns:CustIDRequest"/>
18.         <output message="tns:AddressResponse"/>
19.       </operation>
20.     </portType>
21.
22.     <binding name="Cust_Binding" type="tns:Cust_PortType">
23.     <soap:binding style="rpc" transport="http://schemas.xmlsoap.org/soap/http"/>
24.     <operation name="getAddress">
25.       <soap:operation soapAction="getAddress"/>
26.       <input>
27.         <soap:body encodingStyle="http://schemas.xmlsoap.org/soap/encoding/"
28.             namespace="urn:store:getaddress" use="encoded"/>
29.       </input>
30.       <output>
31.         <soap:body encodingStyle="http://schemas.xmlsoap.org/soap/encoding/"
32.             namespace="urn:store:getaddress" use="encoded"/>
33.       </output>
34.     </operation>
35.     </binding>
36.
37.     <service name="Cust_Service">
38.       <documentation>WSDL File for CustService</documentation>
39.       <port binding="tns:Cust_Binding" name="Cust_Port">
40.         <soap:address location="http://www.store.com/getAddress/"/>
41.       </port>
42.     </service>
43.   </definitions>
```

Fig. 2.13 Example of a WSDL interface definition

called Customer_Service (line 1) and provides the operation getAddress (line 16–19) which accepts as input the message CustIDRequest (a long) and returns the message AddressResponse (a string) as output (lines 8–13 and 17–18).

SOAP-based web services achieve a loose coupling of distributed systems since a contract is specified between services using WSDL. It describes the operations (methods) a web service makes available to clients; which parameters operations receive and return; and which ports are used for communication. WSDL acts as a specification, very much like the interface definition languages used by RPC and CORBA middleware, to describe the interfaces, operations, and parameters of a web service. Separating the logical and technical layers leaves open the possibility to adopt different programming languages for the implementation of web services.

2.4.2   Resource-Based Web Services

REST web services are resource-based services. The term REST refers to an architecture style for designing distributed applications, which uses the set of well-known HTTP operations GET, PUT, POST, and DELETE to change the state of remote resources. The underlying idea is that, rather than using complex mechanisms such as CORBA, RPC, or SOAP to connect applications, the simple HTTP protocol (and its associated methods) is used to interact directly with exposed resources. Unlike SOAP web services, it is not necessary to use fairly complex specifications such as SOAP itself. The main focus is on interacting with stateful resources, rather than operations (as it is with SOAP and WSDL). The communication is stateless. That is why REST services are often referred to as "stateless".

▶ **Definition (REST Service)** An application-accessible web service that uses REST architectural principles and web specifications as underlying paradigms and technologies, respectively.

Roy Fielding [22] describes REST objectives in the following way: "The name Representational State Transfer (REST) is intended to evoke an image of how a well-designed web application behaves: a network of web pages (a virtual state-machine), where the user progresses through an application by selecting links (state transitions), resulting in the next page (representing the next state of the application) being transferred to the user and rendered for their use."

Figure 2.14 shows an example of a REST request submitted as a URL to update an object (with several attributes) stored at Amazon AWS. The response to this action is an XML message with the return status. In contrast to operations-based web services, there is not formal definition of the remote interface. Nonetheless, and in this case, Amazon makes a web page available so that software developers know the parameters to use with REST requests.

2.5   Cloud Services

Web services provide a technological infrastructure that enables organizations to outsource computing resources as a service to support their business operations, including data storage, hardware, servers, and networking. These services are called *cloud services*. The term "cloud" is used to indicate that the service is remotely accessed using the internet. The cloud service provider owns the computing resources and is responsible for its acquisition, operation, and maintenance. The customer pays only on a per-use basis for the services used.

REST Request as a URL

```
1.   https://sdb.amazonaws.com/?Action=PutAttributes
2.   &DomainName=MyDomain
3.   &ItemName=Item123
4.   &Attribute.1.Name=Color&Attribute.1.Value=Blue
5.   &Attribute.2.Name=Size&Attribute.2.Value=Med
6.   &Attribute.3.Name=Price&Attribute.3.Value=0014.99
7.   &AWSAccessKeyId=your_access_key
8.   &Version=2009-04-15
9.   &Signature=valid_signature
10.  &SignatureVersion=2
11.  &SignatureMethod=HmacSHA256
12.  &Timestamp=2010-01-25T15%3A01%3A28-07%3A00
```

REST Response

```
1.   <PutAttributesResponse>
2.     <ResponseMetadata>
3.       <StatusCode>Success</StatusCode>
4.       <RequestId>f6820318-9658-4a9d-89f8-b067c90904fc</RequestId>
5.       <BoxUsage>0.0000219907</BoxUsage>
6.     </ResponseMetadata>
7.   </PutAttributesResponse>
```

Fig. 2.14 Example of a REST request and a response

According to the US National Institute of Standards and Technology (NIST), cloud services are part of the cloud computing paradigm which is "a model for enabling ubiquitous, convenient, on-demand network access to a shared pool of configurable computing resources (e.g., networks, servers, storage, and applications) that can be rapidly provisioned and released with minimal management effort or service provider interaction."[4]

▶ **Definition (Cloud Computing)** The delivery of computing as a service rather than a product. Resources, software, data, and information are provided to customers, computers, and other devices as a utility (like the electricity grid) over a network (typically the internet).

Cloud computing enables consumers to establish a contract to use an application (a cloud service) hosted by the company that develops and sells the software. Common hosted solutions include enterprise resource planning (ERP) or customer relationship management (CRM) systems. The model does not require consumers to buy software licenses. The hosted cloud services give consumers more flexibility to switch providers and reduce the complexity and cost in maintaining the software.

Figure 2.15 shows the two types of services provided by Amazon Elastic Compute Cloud (EC2). On the left side (a), the screenshot in the background shows how EC2 can be accessed using the web console which is an electronic service

---

[4]http://csrc.nist.gov/publications/nistpubs/800-145/SP800-145.pdf.

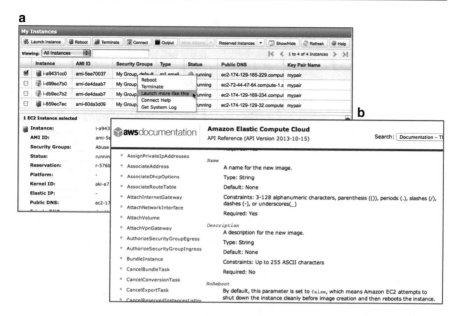

Fig. 2.15 Services provided by Amazon AWS EC2. (**a**) Electronic service interface of EC2. (**b**) Listing and description of web services made available by EC2

accessible via the web. On the right side (b), the screenshot in the foreground shows the SOAP application-accessible web services made available to programmers.

2.5.1 Economies of Scale

As in many areas of the industry, and society in general, new business models often distinguish themselves by bringing cost reductions when compared to existing solutions. Cloud computing also fits nicely into this category. Compared to traditional enterprise data centers, there are large economies of scale that make this model a compelling alternative. Cloud services adopt the utility computing paradigm to provide customers on-demand access to resources in a very similar way to accessing public utilities such as water and energy.

Figure 2.16 shows why cloud computing is an interesting economic solution. The left side of the figure illustrates one of the main drawbacks of the traditional approach that forced companies to invest in computing capacity to respond to occasional, high demand. This can typically be triggered by seasonal demand or to daily peaks of requests. This leads to a waste of capacity when demand is low since only a fraction of the computing infrastructure is utilized. The right side of the figure shows the cloud approach, where the company may request as much or as little computing resources as needed, and pays for these resources per use

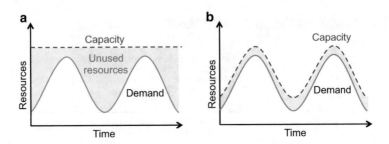

Fig. 2.16 The economical model behind cloud computing. (**a**) Traditional approach. (**b**) Cloud approach

(pay-per-use model). On the provider's side, cost savings are achieved with a more efficient system administration, lower investments in infrastructure, and high levels of equipment sharing.

Administration In a large cloud computing center, one administrator can be responsible for several thousand servers which reduces operation costs. Additional cost savings are also made possible since many applications running in the cloud are accessed using a web browser. Browser-based applications require less administrative overhead on the customer side than traditional software since there is no need to install patches or upgrades. The provider is responsible for carrying out these tasks.

Infrastructure Owning infrastructure, equipment, and servers requires upfront capital costs. Cloud computing shifts high investments to service providers avoiding spending on hardware, software, and licensing fees. Customers can use software with minimal upfront costs using flexible pricing models such as pay-per-use.

Sharing Virtualization technologies allow many virtual servers to run on the same physical machine. Servers, applications, and databases are uncoupled from physical hardware and presented as logical resources. This enables the rapid deployment of resources from a shared pool. Workloads share the infrastructure with other organizations' computing needs which leads to a reduction of costs.

Cloud computing is not without risks. Some issues have been pointed out. Standards are needed to ensure the interoperability of solutions so that cloud services, virtual images, applications, and tools can be moved across cloud environments without high engineering efforts. The transfer of data across cloud providers requires security, encryption, and privacy management. Cloud providers often advertise service levels but no solutions are in place for an effective monitoring and management of the quality of service rendered to customers (Chap. 10 will dive into service level engineering as an approach to make providers accountable when an insufficient quality of services is provided.)

2.5.2 Characteristics

Cloud computing is not a technology[5] but rather refers to a new business model based on a computer platform delivering on-demand services. Therefore, the characteristics of cloud services are not technical but refer to the particular set of features that is offered to consumers. NIST describes five typical characteristics that cloud services should exhibit.

On-demand self service enables customers to decide when to use resources and pay only when using them. A consumer can unilaterally request or release computing resources, such as processing time and data storage services, without requiring human interaction with service providers.

Broad network access allows services to be offered over the internet or private networks. Services are available from any computer, laptop, or mobile device.

Resource pooling enables customers to draw from a pool of computing resources usually located in remote data centers. Customers do not have to know where the resources are maintained. Several consumers can share the same resources which decreases final costs.

Rapid elasticity makes possible to scale services up or down to offer an adjustable number of resources. New resources can be added almost immediately when they are needed.

Measured services enable customers to pay only for the services used. The service provider has to measure, collect, and offer specific information about the services used to bill customers accordingly.

For example, Amazon EC2 is a cloud service that provides elastic compute capacity. It provides a simple web-based self-service interface to obtain and configure capacity with minimal effort (Fig. 2.15a). Users can easily control computing resources such as boot new server instances, scale capacity—both up and down—as their computing requirements change.

2.5.3 Delivery Models

Cloud services can be categorized into three different main types (Table 2.3). Each type describes to which level a customer has control over the software, platform, and/or infrastructure.

The first level, *Software as a Service* (SaaS), enables consumers to use the provider's applications running on a cloud infrastructure. A popular example of SaaS is Google Docs (docs.google.com), an online productivity suite to create, manage, and share documents, spreadsheets, presentations, and surveys. The service

---

[5]Cloud services are usually provided via SOAP or REST web services but any other technology to support and implement distributed systems can be used.

Table 2.3 Cloud delivery models

Delivery model	Examples
SaaS	dropbox.com, docs.google.com, salesforce.com, freshbooks.com.
PaaS	heroku.com, appengine.google.com, force.com.
IaaS	rackspace.com, aws.amazon.com/ec2, windowsazure.com.

provided by Google is accessible directly from a web browser and does not require software installation. Other well-known applications that also belong to this category include dropbox.com,[6] salesforce.com, and freshbooks.com.

The second level, called *Platform as a Service*, or PaaS, provides sophisticated platforms which can be used by customers to develop and run software applications. The provider often makes available programming languages, libraries, and tools so that customers can easily and quickly develop and compile new applications. Examples of PaaS include Google App Engine (appengine.google.com) which enables programmers to build and host web applications on Google's infrastructure; Heroku (heroku.com), a cloud platform to build and host web applications which support several programming languages (it was acquired by Salesforce in 2010); and force.com, the PaaS from Salesforce which enables customers to build new custom business apps to run on Salesforce's servers.

The lowest level, *Infrastructure as a Service* or IaaS provides physical servers, virtualised infrastructures, storage, networks, and other fundamental computing resources such as virtual-machine disk image library, block and file-based storage, firewalls, load balancers, IP addresses, and virtual local area networks. Servers can be fitted with any platform, operating system, and software applications.

Examples include Amazon EC2 (aws.amazon.com/ec2) which provides computing power, Windows Azure (windowsazure.com), Microsoft's cloud platform, and RackSpace (rackspace.com), a company which has built its solution on OpenStack, an open source cloud which does no lock customers into a specific private technology.

2.6   The Internet of Services

The term *Internet of Services* (IoS) appeared in 2007, introduced by SAP and supported by several research projects financed by the European Union. Nowadays, the term web of services is also being used with the same meaning. The IoS addresses the challenge of transforming services into "tradable goods" that are offered, sold, executed, and consumed via the web. The term service is used to

---

[6]Dropbox has a software module which requires its installation in a computer to use the service to synchronize files transparently.

identify services (e.g., human services, e-services, web services, and cloud services) provided through the web which are potentially linked and interconnected, in the same way that the web of pages or documents is connected.

Supporting the IoS requires models, platforms, and tools to make services tradable on the internet and composable into value-added services. Consumers select services from different providers based on their functionalities, best pricing, offered quality of service or rating. After selecting a service, it is delivered by its provider. Finally, the consumer will pay for the service consumption. This procedure is very similar to the operation of cloud services. The difference lies on the type of services provisioned.

Many research challenges around the mapping between services into the IoS are still unresolved. Some of the most critical and urgent questions which still need to be addressed by research and by developing new prototypes include service descriptions, service architectures, service level agreements, monitoring mechanisms, and computer processable legal terms, just to name a few.

2.6.1 Service Descriptions

Service marketplaces need to offer search mechanisms that allow for comprehensive search criteria. At the base for such mechanisms, a framework for describing different aspects of services is needed. A suitable *service description* framework covers not only the functional and technical description of a service but also aspects such as pricing, quality of service, user rating, and legal terms among others. Consumers need to be able to search for service functionality based on functional classifications such as UNSPSC, eClass, eOTD, Rosettanet Technical Dictionary (RNTD), or natural language descriptions. The search results may then be further refined taking into consideration a large variety of non-functional properties.

A good example of achievements in the field of service descriptions is the Unified Service Description Language (USDL). It was developed in 2008 for describing business, software, or real world services using computer-understandable specifications to make them tradable on the internet [23]. Later, in 2011, based on experiment results from the first developments, a W3C Incubator group[7] was created and USDL was extended. In 2012, a new version named Linked USDL[8] based on semantic web technologies was proposed [24].

> Service descriptions are explored in more detail in Chap. 5 which explains how to enrich the description of cloud services with semantic knowledge. The enrichment is applied to a Web API built using the REST architecture style. The chapter also explains how semantics can contribute to develop more effective search algorithms.

---

[7]http://www.w3.org/2005/Incubator/usdl/.
[8]http://linked-usdl.org/.

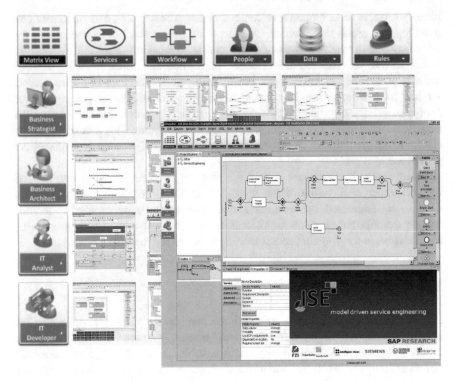

Fig. 2.17 The ISE workbench to engineer services [25]

2.6.2 Service Engineering

Methodologies, methods, reference models, and tools are required to enable a faster development of higher-quality, lower-cost services. *Service engineering* is an approach to the analysis, design, implementation, and testing of service-based ecosystems in which organizations and IT provide value for others in the form of services. Figure 2.17 shows a software workbench called ISE to engineer services. The prototype relied on various models, such as process models, organizational role, business rule, and data models to specify the behavior and technology required to design and implement a service.

Service engineering does not only provide methodologies to handle the increasing complexity of numerous business actors and their value exchanges, but it also provides reference models and tools for constructing and deploying services that merge information technology and business perspectives. Challenges include modeling, validation, and verification of services and their associated business processes, the smooth evolution and execution of business processes and the reliable management of services compositions.

2.6.3   Service Level Agreements

Prior to interacting with a service, the consumer can create a *service level agreement* (SLA) with the service provider stating the terms under which the service needs to be provided. Rights as well as obligations of both parties regarding the service consumption can be described. The aspects specified in a service level agreement (e.g., quality of service and pricing) need to be linked and derived from the service description as it provides the base for negotiation.

To enable trust among the participants, there is a requirement for monitoring SLAs and interactions. Creating monitoring environments for services requires mechanisms to display and analyze information flows between services participating in complex compositions to detect security risks and assess performance. Monitoring also needs to provide mechanisms to ensure trust and confidence in services created by end-users themselves. The goal is to make sure that service providers deliver services under the terms promised to the consumer. The monitoring of functionality may be provided by marketplaces or by trusted third parties. The base for the monitoring is the service level agreement negotiated between the provider and the consumer.

2.6.4   Business and Legal Models

To extract value from services, providers need appropriate business models since they enable to convert new technology into economic value. A special emphasis has to be given to the generation of new business models for all stakeholders (e.g., service providers, aggregators, and consumers) and corresponding incentive mechanisms. It is also an important determinant of the profits to be made from a service innovation and, in some cases, the innovation rests not in the service but in the business model itself [26].

The combination and integration of world-wide regulations and policies is fundamental when provisioning services to end consumers. Legal aspects are subject to extensive government regulations. In European countries, regulation is a combination of central and local controls. Frameworks are needed to facilitate the reasoning about IoS ecosystems across their geographic, economic, social, and legal dimensions. Crafting an appropriate and customized legal framework will help building a service economy that is as robust as existing economies for manufactured goods, commodities, and human-provided services. Technical and legal mechanisms which promote law-abiding attitudes need to be studied.

2.7   Conclusions

This chapter presented two distinct perspectives used to characterize the evolution of services over the past 50 years: (1) the automation of economic activities and self service and (2) the improvement of a programming paradigm.

The first perspective focuses on the creation of electronic services and identifies services from an economic perspective. The aim of this perspective was to reduce the cost of providing services by replacing humans by automated machines. For example, undertaking a trip by train has traditionally required passengers to purchase a ticket from an office and show it for inspection when required by the train operator. As a response to technological development, automatic dispensers and on-line services accessed with web browsers have reduced the cost of service provisioning.

The second perspective looks into services from a computer science view and led to the development of web services and cloud services. These services resulted from the adoption of standards and unified interfaces to enable the interoperability of heterogeneous components to truly support distributed systems. Services, such as web services, use specifications, protocols, and interfaces to enable remote software applications to communicate. Computers located anywhere in the world can request for services to store data, send e-mails, perform complex computations, or encrypt documents.

Review Section

Review Questions

1. ATM machines were one of the first electronic services to be developed in the late 60s. Identify other electronic services introduced in the 70s and 80s.
2. Use Froehle and Roth [3] classification to characterize the following services: expedia.com, booking.com, 99designs.com, redbeacon.com, lulu.com, thread-less.com, odesk.com, and facebook.com. Give additional examples to cover all types of the classification.
3. Identify existing technology-free, -assisted, and -facilitated services which can constitute good candidates for their transformation into technology-mediated and -generated services.
4. Find programming examples of applications implementing the client-server model using RPC, CORBA, DCOM, and JRMI. The client–server model is a distributed application structure that partitions tasks between the service providers (requested service) and service requesters (requesting application). Contrast the benefits and difficulties of each programming techniques.
5. The interface of a SOAP web service is described with the specification language WSDL. Provide an example of a WSDL description of a web service with two operations: `string getAddress(long custID)` and `setAddress(long custID, string regionID)`.

6. Which benefits can cloud services provide to businesses? What type of cost savings can be achieved? How flexible and agile are cloud services? Who typically owns the data and where it is stored?
7. Classify the following cloud services as SaaS, PaaS, or IaaS: lunacloud.com, scalextreme.com, cirrhus9.com, logicworks.net, cohesiveft.com, and app-core.com.
8. Contrast and compare web services, cloud services, and Internet of Services.

Project

This project analyzes the cost differences of deploying an on-premise physical and software infrastructure versus adopting services from a cloud computing provider. You will use the calculator provided at tco.2ndwatch.com to compare the total cost of ownership (TCO) of both approaches and highlight key points when considering cost. The total cost of ownership accounts for the costs to run a software system over its lifetime. It is the best metric to compare the costs of cloud computing and on-premise software deployments. It includes the fees paid to vendors, maintenance and support, and hardware, equipment, and staff costs. The service tco.2ndwatch.com calculates the TCO of using Amazon Web Services versus running applications on on-premise infrastructures.

In a first step, select a company or organization you are familiar with (e.g., a university, library, or research center) and make a comprehensive description of its ICT needs, staff, operations, and infrastructure. Afterwards, estimate the following parameters which are used by tco.2ndwatch.com to calculate the TCO (the web site of the service provides additional information on each parameter):

- Web application servers
- Database servers
- Overall storage
- Data centers
- Growth rate
- Administrative overhead
- Usage pattern

Download the report generated and examine the total expenditures for both strategic approaches. Which one is more cost-effective? What are the main reasons? What characterizes the borderline which can make one of the approaches more attractive over the other?

In a second step, use the service provided at planforcloud.com to determine which cloud provider would supply the most cost-effective solution for the company under study. What are the reasons?

In a last step, write a concise expert report with all the findings recommending to a (possible) manager the best approach to follow (cloud computing or on-premise) and, if a cloud computing approach is recommended, which cloud provider would be best suited to contract.

Key Terms

Electronic Service   An electronic service, or shortly e-service, is a service that allows a remote interaction using information and communication technologies (ICT) such as the internet, software applications, and computing resources.

Web Service   A web service is a technology and approach of communication which enables a software system to support interoperable machine-to-machine interaction over a network.

SOAP Service   A SOAP service is an application-accessible web service that uses the SOAP protocol for exchanging structured information between the two parties involved, i.e., the service provider and the service client.

REST Service   A REST service is an application-accessible web service that uses REST architectural principles and web specifications as underlying paradigms and technologies, respectively.

Cloud Service   Cloud services are designed to provide easy, scalable access to applications and resources. They are managed by cloud service providers. Services are made available on-demand from a cloud computing provider's servers in contrast to being provided from a company's own on-premise servers. Popular cloud services include Google Docs (documents), Dropbox (files), and Flickr (photos).

Cloud Computing   Cloud computing refers to the delivery of hosted services over the internet (i.e., the cloud). Services are predominantly divided into three categories: Infrastructure as a Service (IaaS), Platform as a Service (PaaS), and Software as a Service (SaaS).

Service-Oriented Architecture   An architectural style and business-centric programming paradigm to develop distributed systems where systems consist of software clients, which act as service consumers, and software providers, which act as service providers.

Internet of Services   The internet of services envisions to provide an ecosystem to foster the trading of application and human services over the internet. Beyond downloading music, ordering books, storing files remotely, and booking flights, services can also be traded as commodities.

Service Descriptions   Service descriptions are generally formal representations of functional and non-functional characteristics of services. SOAP web services use WSDL, and electronic services can use Linked USDL for their descriptions.

Further Reading

Olaf Zimmermann, Mark Tomlinson, and Stefan Peuser. *Perspectives on Web Services: Applying SOAP, WSDL and UDDI to Real-World Projects.* Springer, 2013.

Leonard Richardson, Mike Amundsen, and Sam Ruby. *RESTful Web APIs.* O'Reilly Media, 2013.

Thomas Erl, Ricardo Puttini, and Zaigham Mahmood. *Cloud Computing: Concepts, Technology & Architecture.* Prentice Hall, 2013.

Jorge Cardoso and Amit Sheth. *Semantic Web Services, Processes and Applications.* Springer, 2006.

References

1. Fuchs V (1968) The service economy. National Bureau of Economic Research, New York
2. Castro D, Atkinson R, Ezell S (2010) Embracing the self-service economy, Information Technology and Innovation Foundation, p 103
3. Froehle C, Roth A (2004) New measurement scales for evaluating perceptions of the technology-mediated customer service experience. J Oper Manag 22(1):1–21. ISSN:0272-6963
4. Rust R, Kannan P (2003) E-service: a new paradigm for business in the electronic environment. Commun ACM 46(6):36–42
5. Rowley J (2006) An analysis of the e-service literature: towards a research agenda. Internet Res 16(3):339–359
6. EU directive 2006/123/EC of the European parliament and of the council of 12 December 2006 on services in the internal market. Technical report. European Union (2004)
7. Hofacker C et al (2007) E-services: a synthesis and research agenda. J Value Chain Manag 11(2):13–44
8. The e-government imperative: main findings. Technical report. OECD (2003), pp 1–8
9. Baida Z et al (2004) A shared service terminology for online service provisioning. In: Proceedings of the sixth international conference on electronic commerce (ICEC04). ACM Press, New York
10. Vesanen J (2007) What is personalization? a conceptual framework. Eur J Mark 41(5/6): 409–418
11. Bolton R, Saxena-Iyer S (2009) Interactive services: a framework, synthesis and research directions. J Interact Mark 23(1):91–104 [Anniversary Issue]
12. Junglas I, Watson R (2008) Location-based services. Commun ACM 51(3):65–69. ISSN:0001-0782
13. Anderson C (2008) The long tail: why the future of business is selling less of more. Hyperion Books, New York. ISBN:9781401309664
14. Public Services Online: Digital by Default or by Detour? Technical report. European Commission (2013). http://ec.europa.eu/digital-agenda/
15. Wheeler DJ (1952) The use of sub-routines in programmes. In: Proceedings of the 1952 ACM national meeting, p 235
16. Parnas DL (1972) On the criteria to be used in decomposing systems into modules. Commun ACM 15(12):1053–1058. ISSN:0001-0782. doi:10.1145/361598.361623. http://doi.acm.org/10.1145/361598.361623

17. Papazoglou M, Georgakopoulos D (2003) Introduction: service-oriented computing. Commun ACM 46(10):24–28
18. Simon H (1962) The architecture of complexity. Proc. Am. Philos. Soc. 106(6):467–482
19. Booth D, McCabe F, Champion M (2004) Web services architecture—W3C working group note. Technical report
20. Cerami E (2002) In: Laurent SS (ed) Web services essentials, 1st edn. O'Reilly, Sebastopol. ISBN:0596002246
21. Berners-Lee T, Hendler J, Lassila O (2001) The semantic web. Sci Am 284(5):34–43
22. Fielding RT (2000) Architectural styles and the design of network-based software architectures. Ph.D. thesis, University of California
23. Cardoso J et al (2010) Towards a unified service description language for the Internet of services: requirements and first developments. In: IEEE international conference on services computing (SCC), Florida, pp 602–609
24. Pedrinaci C, Cardoso J, Leidig T (2014) Linked USDL: a vocabulary for web-scale service trading. Lecture notes in computer science, vol 8465. Springer, Heidelberg, pp 68–82
25. Cardoso J et al (2011) IoS-based services, platform services, SLA and models for the Internet of services. In: Software and data technologies. Communications in computer and information science, vol 50. Springer, New York, pp 3–17
26. Chesbrough H, Rosenbloom R (2002) The role of the business model in capturing value from innovation: evidence from Xerox corporation's technology spin-off companies. In: Social science research network working paper series, journal Industrial and Corporate Change, 11(3):529–555

Service Innovation

3

Marc Kohler, Björn Schmitz, and Andreas Neus

Summary

This chapter gives an introduction to innovation management in a services context. First, basic definitions and types of innovation are presented. The history of service innovation research and its origins in manufacturing innovation are outlined. The main part of this chapter introduces and applies relevant methods that can support projects for new services development. The last section elaborates on the servitization of manufacturing. It emphasizes the importance of services for the manufacturing industry and presents five types of integrated product service offerings.

Learning Objectives
1. Understand the basic concepts and types of innovation.
2. Identify particular challenges and opportunities of innovation in services.
3. Know how to approach a service innovation project and be able to apply relevant methods to support it.
4. Understand the motivation of companies to servitize and be able to differentiate different types of product service systems.

M. Kohler (✉) • B. Schmitz
Karlsruhe Service Research Institute (KSRI), Karlsruhe Institute of Technology (KIT), Karlsruhe, Germany
e-mail: marc.kohler@kit.edu; bjoern.schmitz@kit.edu

A. Neus
Karlsruhe Service Research Institute (KSRI), Karlsruhe Institute of Technology (KIT), Karlsruhe, Germany

GfK Verein, Nuremberg, Germany
e-mail: andreas.neus@gfk-verein.org

© Springer International Publishing Switzerland 2015
J. Cardoso et al. (eds.), *Fundamentals of Service Systems*, Service Science: Research and Innovations in the Service Economy, DOI 10.1007/978-3-319-23195-2_3

▶ **Opening Case** Massive Open Online Courses (MOOCs)

In late 2011, the internal training services provider of a large German logistics corporation was faced with a challenge. The unit found itself in a currently comfortable, yet fragile position: The department still had an exclusive supply-agreement with the entire company, as it used to be the case for many internal service providers. However, as presented in Chap. 1, the last decades have shown that a large share of services that used to be provided internally are now being outsourced to specialist companies. Examples for this development include IT departments, call centers, helpdesks, and building services.

The CEO of the training services provider envisioned similar possibilities for his unit, meaning that they would have to become competitive in the market place in order to win future training engagements. This implied a number of challenges for the organization. The central question to be addressed was identified as:

How can we use modern IT infrastructure and teaching formats to offer competitive training services?

IT infrastructure was identified as a key challenge for the organization, since competitors had increasingly been using modern IT technology to support their training programs, and were therefore at an advantage. However, in combination with new teaching formats, this could also represent an opportunity for the organization, through which it might be able to differentiate itself from other providers, and offer attractive, competitive training packages.

A promising format that was quickly identified is called Massive Open Online Courses (MOOCs) (Fig. 3.1). MOOCs were first used at universities in the United States, and were introduced with the idea of making education and knowledge available to anyone with an internet connection. Consequently, courses that had previously only been taught live at universities to a comparably small number of anywhere from a few to several hundred students, were made available to anyone signed up with one of the MOOC platforms—a theoretically unlimited number of participants.

Examples for MOOC platforms in the United States include edX (www.edx. org) and Coursera (www.coursera.org). Last year, a consortium consisting of Stanford University, Google, MIT, and other leading universities, enabled an open source adaptation of edX, called OpenEdX, which will allow universities and other organizations to use the existing know-how contained in the platform to offer their own courses, and to integrate them with the courses already available on the edX platform.

But how would the training provider be able to react to and make use of these developments? The identified opportunities quickly led to the question of how they could re-invent their business model and offer new services, based on the MOOC concept. A service innovation project involving experts from different areas of the organization was kicked off. The key challenge in the project was getting the employees and managers to think outside their current organization's processes, routines, and service portfolio.

Fig. 3.1 A MOOC platform offering several online courses for free

The methods used to guide the team in exploring the design space available to them, in finding ideas, evaluating, developing, and selecting promising solutions, are a defining factor of such a service innovation project. This means that the services address actual needs of current or potential customers not being met by competitors' offers. This can be supported by methods analyzing the customer ecosystem, the competitive structure of the industry, and available services in the market. Being feasible on the other hand means that a newly developed service can be integrated with the company's existing resources, capabilities, employee base, and customer channels. This is supported by specific methods, which analyze the components of a service offering, from required resources to the value proposition.

In the case of the training provider, the service innovation methods helped define a new training package that can be used to educate employees in highly specialized areas, such as machine and infrastructure maintenance. However, the application of these methods is not bound to a specific context or domain—it is perfectly appropriate to apply the methods in other sectors, such as entertainment, health care, professional services, as well as banking and insurance services.

▶ **Opening Case**

3.1   Introduction

Due to its importance for companies' competitive advantage, innovation has been a focus of management and business research for many decades. One of the first authors to formally define innovation was Schumpeter [1]. The following seminal definition is based on his works and is still the foundation for many recent definitions of innovation:

▶ **Definition (Innovation)** An innovation is the combination of a novelty and its introduction to a market. The novelty can either be newly discovered, or re-used in the context of this innovation.

The study of innovation has traditionally been rooted in manufacturing and goods-based industry settings. With a growing share of economic value being created in the service sector and through the servitization of many established industry firms (see Sect. 3.3), increasing attention has been directed towards service innovation.

R   As in Chap. 1, the terms *service* and *good* are used to distinguish the two concepts, and
           product is used to refer to them together.

3.1.1   Types of Innovation

Among the many typologies that formalize degrees of innovativeness or novelty of innovations, Henderson and Clark [2] have supplied a frequently used one. The authors analyze innovations along two dimensions, thus introducing a categorization of possible types of innovation (cf. Fig. 3.2). The first dimension describes the degree of change in the employed core concepts, the other dimension describes the degree of change in the linkages between these core concepts. The core concepts represent the building blocks of an innovation and can be existing products, technologies, infrastructure, or resources in general. The linkages between the core concepts characterize the way in which the concepts are connected to form a new offering. This can include technical interfaces, physical integration, and the connection of different service components.

For example, the introduction of video-chat technologies, such as the service Skype, was an innovation that reused existing core concepts in the sense of existing infrastructure and communications protocols, and arranged them in a novel way (changed linkages between core concepts) to produce a service innovation. This is categorized as an architectural innovation according to Henderson and Clark, a category that many service innovations belong to.

The other three categories are named incremental, modular, and radical innovation. An incremental innovation exhibits only minor changes in comparison to an existing product, and does not significantly change the core concepts or the linkages between them. A service example of an incremental innovation would be to add storage space to an existing website hosting service. A modular innovation changes some of the core components of a product, while their linkages remain mostly

Fig. 3.2 Types of innovation according to Henderson and Clark [2]

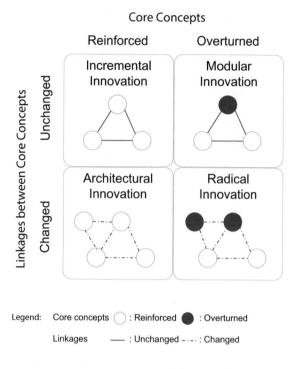

unchanged. An example of a modular service innovation would be to introduce a new fitness and spa program at a hotel, which previously only had a basic wellness offering. The wellness component of the service offered by the hotel is new, but it is linked with the other components in an unchanged way. Lastly, a radical innovation introduces new core concepts, and links them in a new way. A radical innovation was for example constituted by the introduction of the PayPal payment service. This service introduced new concepts, for example an account based on a user's email address, which allows payments by credit card without revealing the user's credit card information. This service also introduced new linkages, for example by integrating itself with existing payment services offered by other financial institutions and by offering interfaces to webshop providers.

As a consequence, PayPal has had a significant impact on the market of payment services. Research applying such a market-oriented perspective has led to a distinct stream of research and definitions. For example, the introduction of micro-payment loans may be considered innovative by a traditional retail bank today, but judging from the market's point of view, this service already exists and does not constitute any mentionable innovation.

Another widely discussed type of innovation is *disruptive innovation* as introduced by Christensen [3]. A disruptive innovation is novel for an entire market or industry, and which changes established industry structures.

As suggested in this short example on banking services, the classification of an innovation depends on the perspective employed. For example, an innovation from an industry-leading company does not need to be radical to be disruptive for a market. As an example, various Google services come to mind that reuse parts of existing Google services, databases and infrastructure, but have completely changed established markets, such as online navigation. On the other hand, a laggard company might develop what they consider a radical innovation, but this does not mean that it is going to be considered novel or disruptive by its customers or other players in the market. Whether to classify an innovation as incremental, radical or disruptive thus depends heavily on the perspective taken.

3.1.2 Service Innovation

The traditional economic and marketing view of value creation and innovation is based on manufacturing and exchanging goods and is therefore called a goods-dominant logic. With the increasing economic importance of services, this view has been challenged. In the marketing literature, Vargo and Lusch [4] have introduced the alternative concept of a service-dominant logic, which has become a foundation for the area of service science.

While important to companies and economies, *service innovation* is a complex phenomenon. Early research on this topic posed the question of whether service firms actually innovate at all [5]. Having established that service firms do innovate, but differently than industrial firms, service innovation has been studied from a variety of perspectives. One difficulty is posed by the large variety of service sectors (see Chap. 1), which makes it important to concentrate on a certain service environment in order to yield relevant insights [6].

Service innovation is an area of research of high relevance for service science [7], however it is still a nascent area. As a consequence, no commonly agreed upon definition has been established. A definition that captures several important dimensions of a service innovation is provided by den Hertog [8].

▶ **Definition (Service Innovation)** The novelty in a service innovation can be constituted by changes in one or several of the following dimensions: Service concept, customer interaction, value system, business partners, revenue model and organizational or technological service delivery system.

Authors have taken different approaches in delineating service innovation from innovation in goods-based industries. Broadly speaking, three approaches can be identified [9]:

- The *assimilation approach* implies that innovation in the manufacturing and in the services domain are, generally speaking, of the same nature and pose comparable challenges to organizations. Consequently, the two phenomena would not have to be studied separately.

- The *demarcation approach* represents the extreme opposite opinion. According to this point of view, innovation in goods innovation in services are entirely distinct and need to be investigated separately, with regard to their challenges, and their supporting methods, processes, etc.
- The *synthesis approach* introduces the thought of mutual enrichment: In tackling the challenges of innovation in service organizations, one can learn from the rich history of research on manufacturing and industry-based innovation. On the other hand, services and service innovation prominently feature some aspects that might become increasingly important for goods-based innovation, and which might inform management decisions in that domain as well.

Due to the emergent nature of service innovation research, there is an ongoing debate on the applicability of the individual approaches. As in many contemporary publications, this contribution builds on the synthesis approach to service innovation.

An important determinant for the management of service innovation in an organisation is what type of innovation the firm aims to introduce. This has important implications for the firm's innovation activities, partner management, and so on.

3.2 Managing Service Innovation

The management of service innovation is impacted by a large number of factors. Besides the design of roles and responsibilities, processes and other organizational characteristics, on an individual innovation project level, the methods employed by the team have a determining role. There is a multitude of methods available to support service innovation projects.

In this chapter, the focus is placed on the early phases of such projects, concentrating on methods that support the development of goals and a scope, as well as ideas that can subsequently be further developed and implemented. The subsequent phases of an innovation process are addressed in the following chapters. Chapter 4 on service design ties in particularly closely with the concepts and methods presented here. To get a wider understanding of the area of service innovation management, please consider the section further reading at the end of this chapter.

The definition of service innovation introduced above highlights the multiple dimensions of the concept. This ties in closely with recent publications on business model innovation. Osterwalder and Pigneur [10] introduce the business model canvas as a way of analyzing the features and newness of a new product. This illustrates that a service innovation does not necessarily have to deliver a new value proposition to a customer to qualify as such. Offering an existing value proposition by means of different channels, or in different organizational configurations, also is an important facet of service innovation. The business model canvas decomposes a business model into complementary units, which can be analyzed and modified

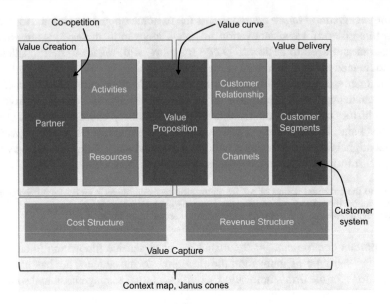

Fig. 3.3 Overview of the business model canvas and connection to the presented service innovation methods (based on Osterwalder and Pigneur [10])

to identify potentials for service innovation, and which can act as a framework for pulling together and complementing the insights collected through the application of the service innovation methods presented in the following. Figure 3.3 shows an overview of the canvas and connects its with the individual methods.

The following methods for service innovation projects represent a selection from a wide range of available methods and tools. This selection cannot be exhaustive, but attempts to cover a reasonable range of the dimensions of a service innovation, while still staying manageable. Further methods and tools can be found in the literature pointed out in Sect. 3.4 and through the URLs given at the end of this section.

Context Map The context map is one of the methods for the first steps in an innovation project and part of the foresight and innovation methodology developed at Stanford University [11]. The context map puts the central topic or opportunity to be addressed by the team in the center, and arranges the relevant dimensions around this topic. By capturing and discussing these dimensions, the problem space defining the team's challenge is properly explored.

Janus Cones Another early-stage method from the foresight and innovation methods collection are the Janus cones. They get their name from the ancient Roman god Janus, who is characterized by looking into the future and the past at the same time, and is typically depicted with two faces looking in opposite direction. Similarly, the Janus cones capture past events relevant to one's innovation project, allowing a projection of potential future events and their timing.

Customer System   Services and hybrid offerings are often characterized and differentiated from pure goods-based offerings by their extent and frequency of customer interaction. However, especially in B2B contexts and more complex service networks, the customer is not necessarily a single entity. Therefore, the customer system differentiates the buyer, the user, and the influencer, and helps analyze their needs in a systematic way. This is a simplified version of the roles in a firm's buying centre as identified in the marketing literature [12].

Co-opetition   The co-opetition framework by Brandenburger and Nalebuff [13] enables a view beyond an individual industry to connect a service provider's offering with those of suppliers, competitors, complementors, and customers across industries. This allows a view on a consumer's choice across the spectrum of offers, as well as the realization of synergies with and differentiation from competition.

Value Curve   The value curve is a frequently used benchmarking and innovation method, introduced by Kim and Mauborgne [14]. Using this visualization, firms are able to compare their value propositions to those of the competition in a structured manner. This comparison is based on the identification of the relevant dimensions or attributes of the value proposition.

While the customer system, co-opetition model, and value curve help analyze particular aspects of the innovation, the context map and Janus cones methods help establish a general overview of the innovation topic and to generate ideas that guide further development in the course of the innovation project. In the following, each of the methods is discussed in turn. In this discussion, the methods are being applied to a case study in the area of health care services. Further application scenarios for the methods can be found in the exercises section at the end of the chapter.

3.2.1 Context Map

Service innovation projects aim to develop new offerings, sometimes even for unknown markets. As a consequence, often no concrete, objective, and measurable goal exists that a project team could work directly towards. First of all, consequently, the problem space and the concrete topic that the team wants to work on have to be elicited in greater detail. A helpful method to employ in this step is the context map [11]. When applying the context map method, the team should follow these steps:

1. Identify central topic.
2. Discuss and identify key dimensions.
3. Record related topics.

First, the central topic of the service innovation project is discussed in the team. This might sound trivial, but only by actually discussing and writing down the topic,

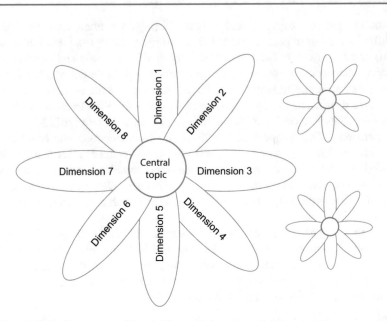

Fig. 3.4 Generic context map with two adjacent context maps for related topics

the team can make sure to obtain a shared understanding. Achieving this shared understanding of the topic to be tackled is essential, and investing time and effort here will pay off over the course of the project. Once a shared understanding of the central topic has been reached, it is written down in a circle in the middle of a sheet of paper, whiteboard, flipchart, or similar. This will form the center of the context map, as illustrated in Fig. 3.4.

Subsequently, the team should bring up, discuss and explore the most important dimensions of the considered topic, following standard brainstorming best practice [15]. In this phase, it is key to preserve all input that is brought up by the team members while discussing the innovation topic. It should be noted that at this point, the aim is not to come up with solutions for the topic discussed. This means that the team should capture all salient dimensions identified in the discussion, whether there is agreement or intense disagreement and argument on one of the dimensions.

Depending on the complexity and scope of the topic one chooses to tackle, several iterations or rounds of discussion might be required to get a good and mutually agreed-upon set of identified dimensions. The dimensions are then added to the central circle of the context map, giving it the appearance of a flower. It is recommended by the authors to draw eight petals [11], since this allows to capture a satisfying number of relevant dimensions, without introducing too much complexity. While this range of dimensions will help the team develop a focused understanding of the topic at hand, the number of relevant dimensions could of course be varied depending on the case at hand. It is important not to lose focus, though. One of the main advantages of the context map method over others, such as mindmapping,

Fig. 3.5 Context map for
topic stroke patient care

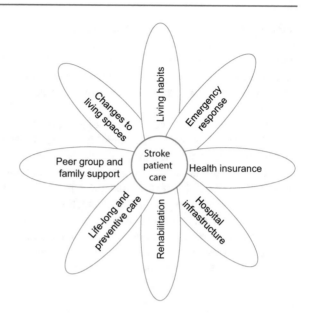

is its deliberate limitation to a small number of dimensions and to only one level
of analysis (no sub-categories). This supports the team in sustaining a joint effort
towards a common goal and makes the context map an important asset that should
be compared to project developments on a regular basis.

Lastly, if dimensions are brought up that seem relevant, but more remote than
the ones making up the original context map, the team can collect them in adjacent
context maps. This can happen in concurrence with the second step and is also
shown in Fig. 3.4. As with any of the methods presented here, the context map
should be used iteratively. This means that at any point it is possible to jump back
to an earlier topic or dimension and investigate it in more detail. The exercise ends
when the team agrees on a (set of) context map(s), which capture the problem space
adequately.

An application of the context map method to our health care services case
study is illustrated in Fig. 3.5. Following the procedure described above, the topic
stroke patient care is put at the heart of the discussion. Subsequently, the relevant
dimensions of the topic are explored. Some dimensions, such as emergency
response, health insurance, and hospital infrastructure directly come to mind
when thinking about the acute and hospitalized phase of a patient's stroke. Other
dimensions, such as rehabilitation, peer group and family support, and changes to
living spaces are challenges that the health care system has to address in the post-
hospital phase of stroke patient treatment.

Two other identified dimensions, life-long and preventive care and living habits
could also be associated with this ongoing care phase. However, these dimensions
highlight another aspect of stroke care: By taking certain actions proactively, and by
changing some living habits, the risk of suffering from a stroke can be significantly

reduced. Two other dimensions were identified in this exemplary discussion. They are, however, not as closely related to the health care system as the other dimensions, and are therefore captured separately. Succession plans and personal finance and investments could be used to create adjacent context maps, or to check the topic's core dimensions for interaction with these personal finance and career planning aspects.

Having compiled this context map of the topic stroke patient care, an innovation team has gained a solid understanding of the relevant problem space, and has highlighted dimensions touching on all phases of the associated life cycle: From proactive care all the way to long-term changes and interventions in the post-phase of a stroke. These dimensions and the entities providing corresponding services represent a basis for exploring and evaluating the innovation topic further. Having gained a satisfactory understanding of the current state of stroke patient care, the next method presented helps explore possible development paths and future events that might change power structures in this system, or the needs of the people the new service concepts are aiming to support.

3.2.2   Janus Cones

Having identified the central topic and its most relevant dimensions, one of the next questions in an innovation project is how they will develop in the time to come. As a newly developed service will address future markets and customer needs, it is vital to explore likely developments and potential future events in addition to the status quo. This step in the innovation project can be supported by the *Janus cones* method, which helps in extrapolating historic events and developments to future ones. When a team employs this method, it should observe the following activities:

1. Decide on time frame to consider.
2. Collect and analyze past events and developments.
3. Try to extrapolate.

First, the team has to choose a time frame for the historic (and future) analysis. It is recommended to go back about twice as many years as one wants to look into the future [11]—the exact number of years will depend on the specific service innovation topic and its context. In the health care domain, for example, many historical events might have an influence on today's market situation, and an analysis should go back a number of decades. In other areas, nanotechnology for example, a focus on more recent developments might be sensible.

Next, past events and significant changes in markets and society, which have influenced the central topic of the innovation project, are captured. Carleton et al. [11] advise to perform some research before performing this group exercise— this can include desk and internet research and interviews with persons knowl- edgeable on the time frame and topic considered. The topics are captured in a dual-cone illustration, as shown in Fig. 3.6 for the health care case study. The left cone represents the past, and the further back an event lies, the further left it is put on

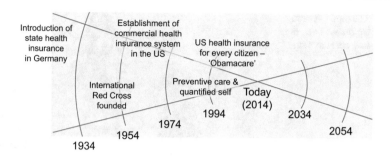

Fig. 3.6 Janus cones analyzing selection of health care history

the visualization. The circular lines indicate time intervals, which make the figure easier to read and support the comparison of individual events. Historical events and major changes are collected until the team judges the figure as informative and complete. As illustrated in the figure, the collected topics can be of very different nature—from major historic events to societal trends and development of technologies. However, they are characterized by their relevance for the investigated topic.

In this example, the consideration begins with the introduction of state health insurance in Germany, which was one of the first insurances in general and built the foundations for many services, such as the one being developed in the course of this chapter. Moving along the time axis, the foundation of the Red Cross is considered an important event, since it represents a major part of the infrastructure needed for the emergency response in the acute phase of stroke care. Health insurance systems in other countries, as exemplified by the US here, also play an important role as benchmarks for the new service development—both the introduction of the first commercial insurance system and the recent introduction of a comprehensive federal insurance system, colloquially often referred to as Obamacare. Lastly, the presented illustration considers recent relevant societal trends, such as the introduction of preventive care practices and the trend of measuring and quantifying oneself through personal logs and sensors. Of course, this is a small selection of possible relevant events and trends, and many more could be identified in the course of an innovation project tackling this topic.

White spots that are left in the collection of events can be filled by additional research, and further interviews with older relatives, etc. Once a rich left cone depicting relevant events and changes has been established, discussing these and their connections allows the team to move towards making statements about future developments and to start filling out the right-hand side of the picture. The most important insights can be gained by putting the past events and developments into relation with each other: When did certain trends and developments start? Have they gone in the same direction, or have there been opposing forces? What is the maturity of certain trends, topics, and technologies—are they still under development, or are they nearing their peak? Are there any constants in the emerging patterns that might be extrapolated into the considered future?

Fig. 3.7 Customer system
highlighting relevant actors in
purchase and consumption of
a service

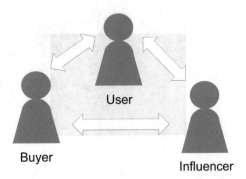

3.2.3 Customer System

When creating a new offering, it is essential to properly consider the customer's
and other parties' perspectives. This is increasingly true in service systems that
are growing more complex and are involving more actors. However, when talking
about these other actors, it is usually difficult to consider a single, well-defined
customer. As illustrated in Fig. 3.7, one does not only have to consider the person
who purchases our service (buyer), but also the people he purchases the service for
(user), as well as other people in his business and social environment, who might
have an opinion on his purchase decision (influencer).

In our health care services case study, these categories would typically be
populated by the relatives (buyer), the patient (user), and other actors, such as friends
or health insurance companies (influencers). In designing a new service offering
for stroke patients, consequently not only the affected person (the patient) has to
be considered, but also the people making the decision between different service
providers, and other parties such as friends, advertisement, etc., who influence their
judgement. Please consider that the categories of the Buyer and the User can be
populated by the same person(s). While this method is called the customer system
here, it should also be used to understand other players involved in the service
system, such as suppliers and partner organizations.

 The next chapter contains additional information that is relevant for enriching the customer
system, in particular the persona method.

3.2.4 Co-opetition

The *co-opetition* framework [13] considers five groups of market participants: The
service provider itself, its suppliers, competitors or substitutors, complementors,
and of course, customers. Drawing out this model for a given service provider
helps understand explicit and implicit connections it has with both the organizations

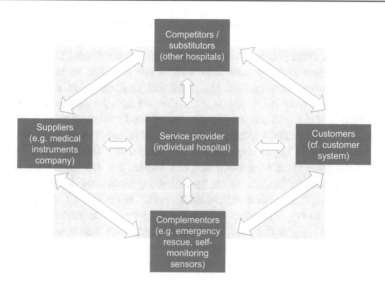

Fig. 3.8 Co-opetition framework for analyzing industries (based on Brandenburger and Nale-buff [13])

increasing (complementors) and decreasing (competitors) the value they deliver to their customer. While this appears relatively straightforward in some instances, particularly for identifying the customers and suppliers, other connections might not be as apparent. Applying this to the health care services case study, the goal is to analyze the connections of hospitals as service providers in the context of stroke patient care, as shown in Fig. 3.8.

The hospitals are depicted in the middle of the figure. If a person suffers from a stroke, they usually receive first treatment and transport to the hospital by emergency rescue services, consequently shown as a complementary service to the hospitals. For a relative, arguably, an alternative to calling emergency rescue would be to call a taxi to transport the patient to the hospital, or to even use one's own car. Thus, this could in turn be captured a substitute to the emergency rescue services.

Further connections suggested in the illustration can fall outside of the traditional medical landscape, and may consequently be less obvious. This is illustrated for example by considering the connection with self-monitoring sensors. Nowadays, many self-monitoring sensors and devices are readily available for consumers' use in stores, and with increasing interest in so-called quantified self communities, a growing number of people are tracking their vital signs and other health data on a regular basis. Having up-to-date information on one's vital signs, such as heartrate, blood pressure, and so forth, of course increases possibilities of proactive care and thus may reduce the number of acute strokes that have to be treated in hospitals. Accordingly, this industry is shown as a complementor to the hospital services. In turn, the use of self-monitoring sensors and devices is supported by a broad availability of smartphones, which help to record and visualize the data gathered by the sensors. The other branches shown in the figure can be interpreted in an analogous manner.

Analyzing a service provider's complementors and substitutors in this way helps gain a broader view of the organization's connections within its industry, as well as across industries. This method highlights the importance of considering the ecosystem of the service being developed. If one neglects the perspective of service complements and complementors, the quality of the developed service might not matter after all, since it will likely not receive a lot of attention in the market. The success of Apple's iOS operating system for example is often attributed largely to the vast number of applications and services available for it—these are however not provided by Apple themselves but by their complementors. A natural next step for dealing with the identified substitutors would be the use of the value curve model discussed after this, to illuminate potential ways of differentiation from this competition. The insights obtained on complementors and their connections can be used for example in the creation and modification of the provider's business model through the business model canvas discussed at the end of this section.

3.2.5 Value Curve

With the insights collected through the application of the methods presented above, the innovation team can formulate a first rough value proposition for the new service they want to develop. In order to do so, it is important to benchmark the service innovation with existing offers. As described by Kim and Mauborgne [16] in their article on implementing a blue ocean strategy—a move into a market space with low competitive pressure and high margins—applying the *value curve* method helps identify strengths and weaknesses in competitors' value propositions. This effectively helps the team avoid undifferentiated imitation strategies, which will limit the success of the newly developed services.

In order to prepare for the development of a new value curve, one first has to identify the most relevant dimensions of a value proposition in the analyzed industry or marketplace. These are captured on the y-axis, as shown in Fig. 3.9. After that, through prior knowledge and additional research, value curves for selected industry incumbents are drawn—these are two of the value curves shown in this figure.

The remaining curve illustrates the value proposition for a hypothetical new stroke patient focused insurance. But how does the innovation team come up with the value curve for their novel service? Kim and Mauborgne [16] advise to investigate four options for change within the identified relevant dimensions:

Create Which factors should be created that the industry has never offered?
Eliminate Which of the factors that the industry takes for granted should be eliminated?
Raise Which factors should be raised well above the industry's standard?
Reduce Which factors should be reduced well below the industry's standard?

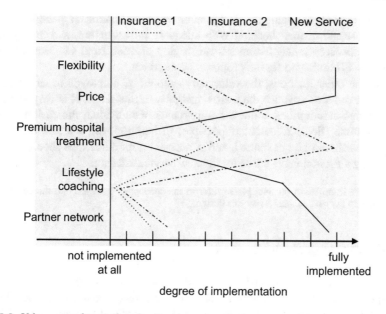

Fig. 3.9 Value curves for novel stroke care insurance

It is important to note the recommended order in thinking about the value proposition's fulfillment of the individual dimensions. Making incremental changes from incumbents' value curves will likely not produce a well differentiated and promising new service offering—it is about really finding a new need or market niche to target. On the other hand, dimensions that potential customers do not value as high as generally assumed in the industry can be treated with less priority without losing to much appeal in the customer's eyes. This also allows to stay competitive on pricing, since one will likely not be able to provide a better service in all relevant dimensions at a price level comparable to existing services.

In our example, the new insurance service focuses on the needs of stroke patients. An important aspect of that is flexibility, since the post-hospital phase of treatment is usually long and, thus, entails very different experiences for individual patients. Consequently, the fulfilment of this dimension is raised well above the competitors' standards.

There are two dimensions, which are not addressed at all in our example, namely lifestyle consulting and providing an extensive partner network between institutions, and with special deals for patients. These are implemented on a high level in the new service, in order to differentiate it from existing competitors. Consequently, the new service is positioned in the premium segment, as indicated by the dimension price.

In addition, previously held assumptions in the industry are challenged. The importance attributed to premium hospital treatment, such as having a room to oneself or being treated by a more senior physician is hypothesized to be comparably low to the considered stroke patients in comparison to the other value dimensions.

One possible reason behind this is that in emergency situations, a patient is always delivered to the nearest hospital with adequate infrastructure, and among these hospitals, processes and treatments are highly standardized. Consequently, this dimension is eliminated for the proposed new service.

Like the other methods, the value curve should be employed in an interactive fashion in order to advance the team's insights. In this sense, it is very important to challenge assumptions about the importance of individual dimensions, and to conduct some (field) research, if possible. In addition, the selected dimensions themselves should be questioned, and if necessary, modifications should be made in creating a desired value curve for the new service offering.

> ⓡ   For more information on this, please refer to the concept of personas and the customer journey in the next chapter on service design.

3.2.6 Business Model Canvas

The *business model canvas* [10] was introduced as one of recent academic attempts at capturing the most important aspects of a company's business model. In our context, it can be used to pull together the insights obtained through the application of the other methods presented. Filling out the categories of the canvas allows the innovation project team to make connections with existing resources, activities, competencies, and the customer base in the case of an established service firm.

In the case of a start-up company, this methods helps the project team identify areas, which will have to be developed and invested in. In both contexts, the business model canvas helps to analyze the interplay of the individual elements of a service and its value proposition. In addition, it provides a first glimpse at a potential business case, in the form of rough revenue and cost considerations.

An exemplary canvas is depicted in Fig. 3.10. In line with the performed analyses and obtained insights above, this case study's aim is to develop a service for stroke care and a corresponding business model. The three broad areas of the canvas, value creation, value delivery, and value capture, are discussed in turn below, with the value proposition connecting value creation and delivery.

Value Creation

Partner   As highlighted in the application of the value curve method above, our new service is positioned as a premium service, and is intended to offer an attractive partner network to customers. Consequently, this includes for example interactions with other health insurance companies, specialized hospitals and doctors, but also specially trained lifestyle and nutrition coaches.

Activities   In terms of activities, the new full service is specialized for stroke patients, and should address their needs from very early stages to sustainable care. This means that our service should offer for example dedicated emergency contact and rescue services to reduce potential response times. Other important

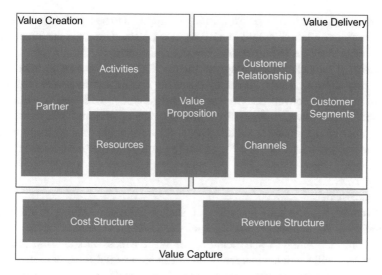

Fig. 3.10 Business model canvas (based on Osterwalder and Pigneur [10])

activities include offering coaching and access to support groups, as also indicated in the partner category above.

Resources   Resources and competencies constitute an important basis for success-fully providing a new service. Key resources required in our case could be trained hotline staff for the contact service described above, as well as personal advisors and corresponding office spaces to assist patients in adapting to changes and transitioning between individual phases of stroke care. It is important to note that a company does not need to provide all necessary resources and competencies on its own. In order to introduce a new service, it can integrate its offers with other providers and use for example outsourcing to create a service system.

Value Proposition

The new service's value proposition has already been identified using the value curve method above. It is positioned as a premium service, which specifically targets stroke patients and offers them a full service package. This clearly differentiates it from the more generic offers of other health insurance companies. In particular the integration with other specialized providers and the broad range of service elements provide a high value to the customer.

Value Delivery

Customer Segments   It is somewhat difficult to define the potential customer segments for the discussed kind of new service. What is feasible, though, is analyzing the customer bases and segments of existing health insurance providers, and collecting this information here.

Customer Relation   As the new offering is supposed to be a premium full service, the customer relation should ideally be very personal, and the customer should always have access to his personal advisor and coach.

Channels   Channels for reaching and interacting with the customer in our example span different media. As discussed above, it is important for the customer to have maximum convenience in reaching our service provider and the associated service providers. Consequently, a combination of personal, telephone, email and other online channels could be used. Personal communication and physical advertisement could be done for example through partner hospitals and private practices.

Value Capture

Cost Structure   The cost structure of such a complex service is difficult to anticipate. At this stage, the relevant cost categories should be captured to guide further research and detailing of the business model. Important cost categories will include emergency services and hospital bills, commissions for associated service providers and partners, hotline staff, infrastructure, marketing and advertisement.

Revenue Structure   Revenues for the discussed kind of service will likely be based on a monthly or yearly payment scheme, since it would be difficult to determine a one-off fee for a service with such high delivery length and volatility. Optional premium services that customers can choose will provide additional revenues, also on a recurring, or on a one-time basis.

Of course, the presented methods can be supported by electronic tools, which facilitate their application in service innovation projects. For many methods, templates for their use are readily available, or can be created with relative ease. An interesting web resource to check out in this context is service design tools (http://www.servicedesigntools.org), an open collection of such tools. In particular for the business model canvas, since this is a commercially supported method, there is a whole ecosystem of tools available, from workshop support to electronic resources.

The importance of innovating in services is not restricted to *pure* service companies, however. In recent years, services have gained momentum in manufacturing and other industries, and are becoming integral parts of many companies' business models. Innovation in services is thus considered to be one of the core drivers for growth and competitive advantage in the future. This increasing investment in services and their development results in the *servitization of manufacturing* [17].

3.3   Servitization of Manufacturing

When asked to name pioneers in service innovation, people list names like Amazon, Facebook or Google. Such companies have a reputation for introducing cutting-edge services which frequently enthuse their customers. The need to innovate in services goes far beyond *pure* service companies, however. (Former) Manufacturing companies such as ABB, IBM, Rolls-Royce, Xerox, and others have (re-)discovered the potential of services as well. Despite their focus on goods and technology, they have heavily expanded their service business; by providing solutions of integrated product and service offerings instead of selling products only.

ABB, a global player in the automation and power industry, offers a wide range of industrial services along the entire life cycle of its products: from installation, to maintenance, to end of life services and replacement. An example for an integrated product and service offering are ABB's *Maintenance Outsourcing Services*, where the company takes over the maintenance management for entire industrial plants in form of a full service solution [18]. Rolls-Royce, known for providing the airline engines for Boeing's 787 Dreamliner and Airbus' A380, offers a rich portfolio of integrated product service offers as well. Within their *Total Care Service* Rolls-Royce takes over the entire engine and maintenance management for civil aerospace clients. Airlines are charged based on the performance they receive, i.e., per flying hour of engine [19].

The strategy to offer integrated product service solutions has been pursued by a number of manufacturing companies worldwide. Many of them—for instance IBM, Rolls-Royce, and Xerox—generate more than 50 % of their total annual revenues with services [20–22].

3.3.1 Servitization

In literature, the trend to offer integrated product and service offerings—so called *product service systems (PSS)*—is summarized by the phrase *servitization of manufacturing*. The concept goes back to Sandra Vandermerwe and Juan Rada, who published an article on the *servitization of business* in the European Management Journal in 1988 [23]. Since then the concept has received increasing attention, both, in industry and from an academic point of view. Baines et al. [17] define servitization in the following way:

▶ **Definition (Servitization)** Servitization is the innovation of an organisations capabilities and processes to better create mutual value through a shift from selling product to selling product service systems.

The definition emphasizes three key aspects. First, servitization is about innovation. Moving into services requires the redesign of business models, the innovation of respective capabilities and processes with a focus on value creation. Second, servitization is about mutual value creation, i.e., it involves the cooperation and coordination among provider and customer to obtain a beneficial outcome for both of them. Third, servitization comes with the shift from selling products to providing integrated solutions of products and services. Baines et al. [24] define this concept in the following way:

▶ **Definition (Product Service Systems)** An integrated product and service offering that delivers value in use.

Reasons for manufacturing companies to servitize are manifold. Yet, most of them go back to two reasons: to the realization of financial benefits and to the establishment of closer relationships with customers.

In times of declining margins, low growth rates in mature markets, and an increasing commoditization of products, manufacturing companies are under pressure. Customers are highly price sensitive and in many cases product characteristics alone are not sufficient to successfully differentiate oneself from competition. In such an environment services offer additional sources for differentiation, thereby enabling providers to customize their offerings and to realize higher profits. Moving into the service business enables the development of entirely new business models allowing to enter into entirely new markets and to compete in existing ones. In contrast to products, services business models usually generate continuous cost and revenue streams. That is, cash flows from services are usually distributed over a period of time which smoothes the effect of economic cycles.

The second line of reasoning assumes that servitization allows manufacturing companies to establish closer relationships with customers. As the development of product service systems is about mutual value creation, servitization requires closer customer integration quasi per definition. Once a closer relationship is established, manufacturing companies can use the additional insights they gain to even further customize their offers which leads to a customer lock-in. One way to achieve this—and this point is frequently made in this context—is to service the installed base. Besides its additional revenue potential (in many industries, the total expenditures invested in the installed base is much greater than the sales of new assets per year), servicing the installed base allows equipment providers to gain a deeper knowledge of their customers' business, processes and needs.

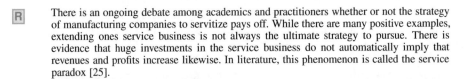

> There is an ongoing debate among academics and practitioners whether or not the strategy of manufacturing companies to servitize pays off. While there are many positive examples, extending ones service business is not always the ultimate strategy to pursue. There is evidence that huge investments in the service business do not automatically imply that revenues and profits increase likewise. In literature, this phenomenon is called the service paradox [25].

> The trend towards extending the service business is not restricted to the manufacturing industry. Examples can be found in all kinds of industries in both, business-to-business and business-to-consumer markets. From an academic point of view, research on servitization shares many ideas with related fields. One example is research evolving around the paradigm of *service dominant logic* (see Chap. 1). It postulates a new dominant logic for marketing stating that services rather than goods are the fundamental basis of economic exchange [26].

3.3.2 Product Service Systems

Once a manufacturing company has decided to servitize the question remains how to move into the service business, i.e., how to integrate products and services. Depending on the industry, customer requirements, maturity of a company's service

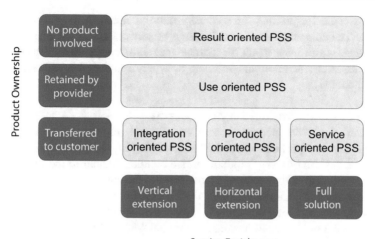

Fig. 3.11 Types of product service systems (based on Neely [28])

business, etc., companies may offer different types of product service systems (e.g., product oriented, use oriented, and result oriented PSS). In literature, various typologies to distinguish different types of product service systems have evolved (see e.g. Tukker, Neely, Meier et al. and van Ostaeyen et al. [27–30]).

For example, Neely [28] distinguishes five types of product service systems which are organized along two dimensions, product ownership and service enrichment (cf. Fig. 3.11). With regard to product ownership, the product might be transferred to the customer, retained by the provider, or there might no product be involved at all. Service enrichment may happen vertically (i.e., companies go down- or upstream), horizontally or in form of full solutions.

Integration Oriented Product Service Systems
Companies that offer integration oriented PSS seek to go downstream, i.e., they aim to move into retail and distribution, transport, financial services, consulting, etc. The physical product builds the core offering and is transferred to the customer. It is enriched with services from the vertical supply- and distribution chain.

Integration oriented product service systems can for instance be found in the automotive industry. Car manufacturers do not only produce cars, they increasingly move into retail services themselves, thereby bypassing independent car dealers.

Product Oriented Product Service Systems
Product oriented PSS are very similar to integration oriented product service systems. Product ownership is still with the customer. However, in contrast to integration oriented product service systems, the service offered is directly related to the product. That is, services relate to the product life cycle and may comprise activities such as design and development, installation, maintenance support, replacement, etc.

An example for product oriented PSS may be found in the service portfolio of ABB. The company offers a wide range of services along the entire life cycle of its assets, from installation, to maintenance and repairs, to advanced services such as asset optimization and software as a service, to end of life services and replacement [31].

Service Oriented Product Service Systems

Service oriented PSS incorporate services directly into the product. In contrast to integration and product oriented PSS (product plus service), services build an integral part of the offering (product service bundle). Similar to the first two types of PSS, ownership of the product is transferred to the customer.

An example for such a service is BMW's Intelligent Emergency Call service [32]. In case of an accident the system automatically sets off an emergency call connecting the passenger to a trained personnel who will take further action (e.g., call emergency services, transmit current position, etc.). In this example, the service (the ability to automatically set off an emergency call) is directly integrated into the product, i.e., the car.

Use Oriented Product Service Systems

Use oriented PSS focus on the provision of the functionality that is contained in a product. Instead of purchasing a product that provides a particular functionality, the utilization of this functionality is sold as a service. Use oriented product service systems can typically be found in the context of leasing or outsourcing, in sharing or pooling. The product used to provide the functionality is owned by the service provider and does not pass on to the service customer.

One company that provides use oriented PSS is Xerox. The company's focus is no longer on selling printers. Instead, Xerox has introduced leasing contracts for their printers and even offers full managed printing services. Thereby, customers can purchase the actual functionality—the printing of documents—only, without having to invest in the actual product, the printer [22].

Result Oriented Product Service Systems

Result oriented product service systems constitute the most service centric product service system. In this case, the product is entirely replaced by a service, i.e., there is no product ownership any longer.[1]

A typical example, as stated by Neely [28], is the replacement of answering machines by voice mail services. In this case, the functionality of the tangible

---

[1]This does not mean that there are no physical resources involved in providing a service. The difference to other PSS types is rather that the customer does not buy a product but a certain result or capability which was prior delivered through a product. The way in which these results or capabilities are achieved is not specified any more. Instead, the provider is free in choosing how the predefined results or capabilities are to be achieved.

product is entirely replaced by the service which leads to the result that there is no need for individuals to own an answering machine and thus a physical product any longer.

To distinguish clearly between the different types of product service systems is not always possible. Instead, a value proposition for a customer may consist of various types of product service systems. Take BMW's Intelligent Emergency Call service as an example: though the service itself may be a service oriented PSS, the car may be leased or be part of BMW's mobility service DriveNow (use oriented). In this case, the overall value proposition for a customer is realized by a combination of various types of product service systems.

3.4 Conclusions

The transition of manufacturing companies towards integrated solution providers is far from trivial and there are various challenges and managerial implications to address. Entering into the service business requires a change of mindset, closer integration of customers and the establishment of long term relationships to name just some requirements [23, 28].

Manufacturing companies need to change their mindsets in order to develop a service culture that focuses on customers and their needs instead of discrete features of products. Providing integrated product service solutions requires providers to understand how value is created for and perceived by their customers. To achieve this, companies need to rethink their traditional, transactional way of doing business and need to move to a relational marketing approach that focuses on the establishment of long-term relationships. If such a strategy coincides with an increasing engagement in long-term contracts, long-term risks and uncertainties have to be modeled, understood and managed.

The establishment of a service culture and the shift towards relational marketing inevitably comes with a closer customer integration. As service is all about co-creation of value, solution providers and their customers need to collaborate in the design, provision and utilization of product service systems. To achieve an effective coordination among involved stakeholders, information, people, technology as well as other internal and external service systems have to be managed accordingly. Manufacturing companies need to cope with the increasing complexity that results from this integration. Only if all involved parties have a mutual understanding of how value is created, can beneficial outcomes for both parties be achieved.

What is still unclear is how readily learnings from pure service organizations can be applied to manufacturing companies that are transforming into servitized organizations. Many issues are yet to be researched further, such as promising capability constellations for supporting service innovation, and managing the trade-off between exploitation in existing business and the exploration of new business opportunities [33]. In service firms, this has often been a challenge affecting every level of corporate hierarchy, rather than being solved centrally through a dedicated research and development department in industrial companies. Understanding the capabilities that these different organizational modes require further, and transferring learnings on service innovation management, could play a key role in the success of companies' servitization initiatives.

Review Section

Review Questions

1. What is the definition of innovation that was used in this chapter?
2. What are the four basic types of innovation according to Henderson and Clark? Name the two dimensions along which they are distinguished, draw the resulting framework and give an example for each category.
3. What are the three approaches to studying innovation in services and how do they relate to existing knowledge in the manufacturing innovation domain?
4. What are the essential elements and steps in applying the Janus Cones method? Please apply the method to a service topic not presented in this book and record your results.
5. Which method presented in this chapter is most suitable for analyzing the current and potential stakeholders of a service system? What value can you derive from applying it to your innovation challenge? Please compare the services offered by a budget airline, such as Ryanair, and those offered by a full-service provider, such as Emirates, using the value curve method.
6. Using the customer system method, please analyze the involved parties in the following situation: A start-up is considering to offer a novel service that allows college students to mentor highschool students in order to give them profound insights into their colleges of interest before they start with their studies.
7. Which types of product service systems are there? Find an example from practice for each type of product service system defined.
8. What are the challenges posed by servitization and how could each of them be addressed?

Project

This chapter has briefly touched on the concept of Massive Open Online Courses (MOOCs) as instruments in online teaching. A comprehensive overview of courses offered, as well as further information can for example be found at https://www.mooc-list.com.

Imagine your university wants to create its own MOOC format and maybe even delivery platform. The key question, of course, is how to make the new service stand out from the large number of already established MOOCs in the market. This entails the consideration of the customers', as well as the teachers' perspective at your university.

The following questions should be answered in your report:

- What characterizes the existing MOOC landscape and offerings? What unique advantages and shortcomings do they have? You may use for example the value curve and the business model canvas method to perform this analysis.
- In designing a novel MOOC service, what are the key dimensions your university has to address? A suitable method to tackle this question is the context map.
- Who are the stakeholders you have to address in the creation and delivery of the service? What are their individual requirements and motivations? You can use the customer system method to answer this point.
- How can you ensure that the newly created service is not only more attractive to students than existing MOOCs, but potentially more attractive than traditional classroom teaching? How is your university going to implement the service? You can build on your previous value curve and business model canvas analysis to answer this question.

In writing your report, please provide the visual application of the introduced methods, as well as corresponding explanatory text. Furthermore, your report should of course follow standard academic practices and present references for material and information that you have retrieved and used in your work.

Key Terms

Innovation   Innovation is the introduction of a novelty to a market.

Service Innovation   The creation of a new market offering in the form of a service.

Types of Innovation   Different types of innovation can be differentiated. One popular categorization was developed by Henderson and Clark, based on the dimensions change in key concepts and change in linkages between these concepts.

Service Innovation Methods   There are a number of specific methods that can be employed in service innovation projects. The methods presented here focus on the early phases of such projects.

Innovation Process   Innovation processes are simplified models for describing the individual phases that an innovation project usually goes through. They can also be used in a prescriptive way, when a company designs their own innovation process and has projects follow it.

Business Model Canvas   The Business Model Canvas is a relatively recent and comprehensive tool for describing a business model for an existing company, for a new offering, or for a start-up.

Product Service System   An integrated product and service offering that delivers a certain value in use to the customers.

Servitization   The transformation of industrial companies from selling products to selling product service systems.

Further Reading

Renu Agarwal, Willem Selen, Göran Roos, and Roy Green. *Handbook of Service Innovation.* Springer, 2015.

Lance Bettencourt. *Service Innovation: How to go from customer needs to breakthrough services.* McGraw-Hill, 2010.

Henry Chesbrough. *Open Services Innovation: Rethinking your business to grow and compete in a new era.* John Wiley & Sons, 2010.

Rod Coombs and Ian Miles. *Innovation, Measurement and Services: The New Problematique.* In Economics of Science, Technology and Innovation, 18, pp. 85–103, 2000.

Faïz Gallouj, and Faridah Djellal. *The Handbook of Innovation and Services: A Multi-disciplinary Perspective.* Edward Elgar Publishing, 2010.

Jan Leimeister. *Dienstleistungsengineering und-management.* Springer, 2012.

References

1. Schumpeter J (2013) Theorie der wirtschaftlichen Entwicklung: Eine Untersuchung über Unternehmergewinn, Kapital, Kredit, Zins und den Konjunkturzyklus (1926), 9th edn. Duncker Humblot, Berlin
2. Henderson RM, Clark KB (1990) Architectural innovation: the reconfiguration of existing product technologies and the failure of established firms. Adm Sci Q 35(1):9–30
3. Christensen CM (1997) The innovator's dilemma. The management of innovation and change series. Harvard Business School Press, p 225
4. Vargo S, Lusch R (2004) The four service marketing myths: remnants of a goods-based, manufacturing model. J Serv Res 6(4):324–335
5. Sundbo J (1997) Management of innovation in services. Serv Ind J 17(3):432–455
6. Tidd J, Hull FM (2006) Managing service innovation: the need for selectivity rather than 'best practice'. N Technol Work Employ 21(2):139–161
7. Ostrom AL et al (2010) Moving forward and making a difference: research priorities for the science of service. J Serv Res 13(1):4–36
8. den Hertog P, van der Aa W, de Jong MW (2010) Capabilities for managing service innovation: towards a conceptual framework. J Serv Manage 21(4):490–514
9. Coombs R, Miles I (2000) Innovation, measurement and services: the new problematique. In: Metcalfe JS, Miles I (eds) Innovation systems in the service economy - measurement and case study analysis, 2nd edn. Springer, Berlin, pp 85–103
10. Osterwalder A, Pigneur Y (2010) Business model generation. Wiley, New York, 281 pp
11. Carleton T, Cockayne W, Tahvanainen A-J (2013) Playbook for strategic foresight and innovation, Tekes, 264 pp
12. Webster FE, Wind Y (1972) A general model for understanding organizational buying behavior. J Mark 36(2):12–19
13. Brandenburger AM, Nalebuff BJ (1996) Co-opetition: a revolution mindset that combines competition and cooperation: the game theory strategy that's changing the game of business, p 304

14. Kim WC, Mauborgne R (1999) Creating new market space. Harv Bus Rev 77:83–93
15. Stanford University d.school (2014) https://dschool.stanford.edu/blog/2009/10/12/rules-for-brainstorming/. Last accessed 25 March 2014
16. Kim WC, Mauborgne R (2005) Blue ocean strategy: from theory to practice. Calif Manag Rev 47:105–121
17. Baines TS et al (2009) The servitization of manufacturing: a review of literature and reflection on future challenges. J Manuf Technol Manag 20(5):547–567
18. ABB (2013) http://www.abb.com/service/. Last accessed 25 Nov 2013
19. Rolls-Royce Holdings plc (2013) http://www.rolls-royce.com/civil/services/totalcare/. Last accessed 23 Oct 2013
20. IBM (2013) http://www.ibm.com/annualreport/. Last accessed 23 Oct 2013
21. Rolls-Royce Holdings plc (2013) http://www.rolls-royce.com/Images/rolls_royce_annual_report_2012_tcm92-44211.pdf. Last accessed 23 Oct 2013
22. Xerox (2013) http://www.xerox.com/assets/pdf/partners/studiocom/annual/2012_Xerox_Annual_Report.pdf. Last accessed 23 Oct 2013
23. Vandermerwe S, Rada J (1988) Servitization of business: adding value by adding services. Eur Manag J 6(4):314–324
24. Baines TS et al (2007) State-of-the-art in product service-systems. Proc Inst Mech Eng B J Eng Manuf 221(10):1543–1552
25. Gebauer H, Fleisch E, Friedli T (2005) Overcoming the service paradox in manufacturing companies. Eur Manag J 23(1):14–26
26. Vargo SL, Lusch RF (2004) Evolving to a new dominant logic for marketing. J Mark 68(1):1–17
27. Tukker A (2004) Eight types of product-service system: eight ways to sustainability? Experiences from SusProNet. Bus Strateg Environ 13(4):246–260
28. Neely A (2008) Exploring the financial consequences of the servitization of manufacturing. Oper Manag Res 1(2):103–118
29. Meier H, Roy R (2010) Seliger G Industrial product-service systems — IPS2. CIRP Ann Manuf Technol 59(2):607–627
30. Van Ostaeyen J et al (2013) A refined typology of product-service systems based on functional hierarchy modeling. J Clean Prod 51:261–276
31. ABB (2013) http://new.abb.com/service Last accessed 25 Nov 2013
32. BMW (2013) http://www.bmw.com/com/en/insights/technology/connecteddrive/2013/services_apps/intelligent_emergency_calling.html Last accessed 25 Nov 2013
33. O'Reilly CA, Tushman ML (2004) The ambidextrous organization. Harv Bus Rev 82(4):74–83

Service Design

4

Niels Feldmann and Jorge Cardoso

Summary

This chapter provides an overview of service design as a human-centric approach for creating, describing, and operationalizing new or improved services. It outlines how service design relates to topics such as service innovation and new service development, as well as the key characteristics associated with the concept today. The service design process includinga selection of specific methods is introduced and illustrated.

Learning Objectives
1. Explain how service design relates to service innovation and new service development.
2. Examine the meaning of service design over the past three decades.
3. Understand the key characteristics of service design and the specific perspective designers contributed to the creation and improvement of services.

(continued)

N. Feldmann (✉)
Karlsruhe Service Research Institute (KSRI), Karlsruhe Institute of Technology (KIT), Karlsruhe, Germany
e-mail: niels.feldmann@kit.edu

J. Cardoso
Department of Informatics Engineering, Universidade de Coimbra, Coimbra, Portugal

Huawei European Research Center (ERC), Munich, Germany
e-mail: jcardoso@dei.uc.pt; jorge.cardoso@huawei.com

© Springer International Publishing Switzerland 2015
J. Cardoso et al. (eds.), *Fundamentals of Service Systems*, Service Science: Research and Innovations in the Service Economy, DOI 10.1007/978-3-319-23195-2_4

4. Explain what a typical service design process looks like and what specific
   methods are used by service designers.
5. Apply core methods such as stakeholder maps, personas, customer journey
   maps, and blueprints in practice.

▶ **Opening Case** Accommodation Services

Sleepless in Iceland : Why parties are not everybody's piece of cake

"I love Iceland! I adore it for its geological uniqueness, for the beauty of its
nature, its literature and music scene and, in general, its people. Upon arrival of
my last trip to the country, my spouse and I checked into a pleasant four-star hotel
in Reykjavik's city center to be close to the domestic airport for an early morning
departure to northern Iceland the next day. The friendly receptionist gave us a nice
room on one of the upper floors. So, all was good and we went out for dinner in
town.

Around 10 pm, back in our hotel room, we realized loud music coming from
somewhere nearby. "Just some young people out on the street enjoying Reykjavik
at night and playing music in their car; they will be gone soon", we thought. But not
so. Over time the noise level rose and by 11 pm we could feel the vibrations of the
music's constant beat in our room. I decided to explore where the music came from.
So, I left our room and walked along the hallway. The closer I got to the staircases,
the louder it got. Level by level, I went down the stairs until I stood right in front
of the backdoors of the hotel's conference venue. Obviously, this evening our hotel
was the place to be for Reykjavik's nightlife scene.

Down in the lobby, a group of sleepless hotel guests had already gathered and
the receptionist confirmed everybody that she would take care of the situation. The
music would be turned down soon. Hoping for the best, I headed back to our room,
only, to return back to the reception 30 min later due to unchanged loudness and
vibrations. This time the receptionist told everybody, there was nothing she can do
about the noise. The event department of the hotel had rented out the venue to a
large party until later that night. But we could feel free to complain to the hotel's
management the next morning.

Most people left upset, yet, I did not want to yield and asked whether they were
fully booked. The lady denied. So, I asked whether there are still some rooms
available in the building's wing that was most distant from the venue and if she
would be entitled to change us into another room if we are not satisfied with the one
we've got. She confirmed all of these points. Lucky me! And, off I went with a new
room key, ready for a good night of sleep. However, most of the other disappointed
guests probably stayed sleepless for another couple of hours (Fig. 4.1).

Fig. 4.1 Rustic Icelandic hotel

Stories like this are common. Nevertheless, it is worth having a closer look at what happened in the opening case. Services lead to experiences on the customer side [1] and service providers aim to optimize this experience. The traveler is looking forward to a great vacation experience starting with a quiet night in a pleasant hotel. The other customers, the participants of the party, are looking for a great experience as well, namely a great, loud party until late at night. However, the night ended with both customer groups being unhappy, i.e. the hotel guests being sleepless and the party guests probably having to finish their party sooner than expected. How could this happen? The hotel serves as two service providers, a lodging provider and an event provider, and potentially runs two corresponding business units which operate rather independently. While both units are experienced in providing good services within their own domain, the trouble began when the event department contracted for a service that interfered with the service of the other unit. In other words:

- The business units operated in silos.
- They designed their services from their perspective instead from the customers.
- They did not put a proper mechanism in place to handle exceptions.

As an old consultants' wisdom says "perception is reality", i.e., the customer's perception of a service determines the level of experience gained from a service rather than the imagination of the service provider. Correspondingly, in this chapter we will discuss methods to deeply understand customers' needs and design services from their perspective aiming for an optimized service experience.

▶ **Opening Case**

4.1   Introduction

Based on the opening case and its analysis it can be conjectured that *service design* is about making (new) services work as properly and smoothly as possible, i.e. to operationalize them by laying out processes, defining roles, responsibilities, permissions, and prerequisites for the provision of a service. And in fact, as discussed later, this is an essential part of service design [2]. However, the concept of service design as it is used and researched today goes far beyond the operational aspect. So far, the story has emphasized aspects such as meeting customers' expectations, handling exceptions, and avoiding disappointments. But, designing a service to provide positive experiences includes the opportunity to delight customers, e.g. to offer more than they expected, or conduct a service in a more convenient way. Nowadays, the term service design is often used with a broader meaning. But, if service design is about improving or even creating new services in order to positively surprise customers, the terms *service design, new service development*, and *service innovation* start to conceptually overlap.

Hence, this section will shed some light on the definitions and key characteristics of service design and discuss its relation to the other two concepts. The following sections of this chapter will then introduce methods used for service design and tools that help applying these methods in projects.

4.1.1   Service Design

Service design consists of the two rather broadly defined terms *service* and *design*. Chapter 1 of this book already reflected on the various types of services and what people have in mind when talking about services. This leaves the second term, design, for discussion. Design is used in a broad variety of contexts such as the design of products, communication design, web design, software or IT-system design, and even (design) methods themselves. Furthermore, design is a verb describing a creative process as well as a noun describing the result of this process. Surprisingly or perhaps not surprisingly, given the variety of contexts, scholars struggle to agree on a shared definition for the term [3]. Hence, due to the context-bound nature of the term, subsequent focus lays on how the service community defines and uses the term service design.

Early publications on the topic of service design focus on the modeling and *description of services*, e.g., blueprinting of services [2]. Correspondingly, and similar to our discussion in the opening case, their definitions of the term service design emphasize the description of a service concept primarily through visualizations. Further definitions are broader and refer to the process of creating a concept for a (new) service including the early creative steps to come up with an idea for a new service [4]. Some authors from the late 1990s and early 2000s specify what a *service concept* should look like (e.g., [5,6]). According to them the service concept ranges from customers' needs to operationalized action on how to address them.

▶ **Definition (Service Concept)** The service concept describes in detail the needs of the targeted customers, what actions to take to meet these needs, and how to operationally implement these actions.

Since the first service design researchers originated from various design backgrounds, service design was influenced by a wide range of design disciplines. Therefore, the concept of service design became broader and recent publications define service design as the process of "systematically applying design methods and principles to the design of services" [7].

In an overview on service design as a field of research, Blomkvist et al. [8] point out that academics initially focused on putting service design in relation to their home disciplines and establishing service design as an own field of research. Meanwhile, research became much wider and deeper and now deals with service design itself, e.g., reflecting on underlying theories, exploring new design techniques, analyzing case studies, or moving towards product-service systems.

Given the diversity of the research field of service design, synonyms and variations to the term service design have emerged and are worth highlighting. Building on the close relation of service design and *design thinking* [9, 10]—a similar approach originating from product innovation—some authors have framed the term *service design thinking* [11]. Moreover, other researchers emphasize that investigating the needs of customers as well as provider-customer interactions may lead to more than just a good service process. It may also lead to insights about the physical environment, the service employees, the service delivery process, fellow customers, and back office support [12]. Thus, these authors framed the term design for services rather than service design [13]. However, this chapter uses the term service design.

▶ **Definition (Service Design)** The systematic application of design methods and principles to the creation of service concepts for new or improved services (following [7]).

4.1.2 New Service Development and Service Innovation

As the definition and current understanding of research imply, service design is about creating new or improving existing services. This raises the question how service design differs from the concepts of service innovation as well as *new service development* (NSD)—another term found in scientific literature addressing the creation of new services. Johnson [14, p. 5] defines new service development as the "overall process of developing new service offerings". To delimit the term NSD, the author refers to service design as specifying "the detailed structure, infrastructure, and integration content of a service operations strategy".

▶ **Definition (New Service Development)** Addresses the "overall process of developing new service offerings" [14, p. 5].

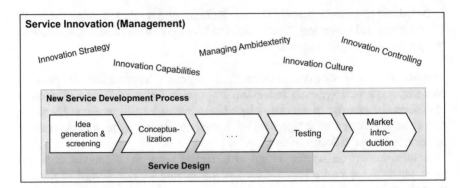

Fig. 4.2 Schematic overview of service innovation, new service development, and service design

Looking more closely at the NSD process shows that it covers all the steps of a classical innovation process, from idea generation to market introduction [15]. Service design on the contrary aims for a service concept and therefore overlaps only partly with the NSD process. What is more, service design primarily "contributes to service development in areas such as user orientation, contextualization, and design as a strategic instrument" [7, p. 342]. While service innovation was initially seen as a process of service development [16], and therefore was highly overlapping with NSD, today service innovation has become more of a management discipline. As seen in Chap. 3, recent service innovation literature covers a wide range of topics such as service specific challenges of innovation management, capabilities to sustainably innovate services or processes, and methods and tools for developing new services.

Service innovation is the overall discipline dealing with the service specifics of innovation management. It includes new service development as the process of creating and establishing new services. Service design covers part of this new service development process and adds the specific perspective of designers to it (Fig. 4.2).

4.1.3   Service Design Characteristics

The previous section introduced the three terms: service innovation, new service development and service design. One key differentiator between the new service development process and service design was the application of design methods and principles to the creation of services. This raises the question why the perspective of a (service) designer is so valuable for the development of new services.

Service designers aim to understand and improve service experiences by focusing on customers and their interactions with a service provider. In more detail, professionals agree on the following cornerstones [11, 13, 17, 18]:

- Human-centric
- Interactive
- Holistic

- Iterative
- Prototype-based

Some experts emphasize further characteristics of service design which support and complement these five cornerstones. For instance, they point out the importance of working in interdisciplinary teams to accommodate a multi-perspective understanding of a service and its environment as well as receive a broader range of ideas for possible solutions. Furthermore, a visual description of the interactions between parties involved in a service, for instance, to ensure the right speed of service provision is considered to be a key element of service design.

Human-Centric

In companies R&D traditionally approaches innovation projects from a technology point of view and innovation departments apply a management perspective focusing on market niches, key resources of an organization, revenue models or whole business models. In terms of customers, it is common practice to define customer segments which are then used in the innovation process. Service design takes a slightly different but complementary approach: It looks at customers on an individual level rather than on a segment level. This means, service designers put themselves into the shoes of a customer or other stakeholders when creating new or improving existing services. Hence, if there is a "true north" of service design it is this paradigm of *human centricity*. Everything else feeds into this notion.

Interactive

To put themselves into the shoes of other humans, service designers have a strong motivation for going out and working as *interactively* as possible with customers. As the subsequent sections will show, service designers leverage several techniques and tools to interact with and learn from people. The aim of this strong interaction is to understand how individuals perceive a service as comprehensively as possible. Asking and observing customers and engaging in their actions lead to valuable insights.

Holistic

Furthermore, service designers want to understand customers or other stakeholders *holistically*. This takes place on two levels: first, the designers strive to go far beyond the typical demographics used for customer or stakeholder segments and see their representatives as individuals. Actors try to get an almost tangible picture of the role they shall slip in. Designers want to reach a similarly deep understanding of the customers or stakeholders they look at, including their personality, their social environment and many more. Secondly, service designers try to understand the system a service takes place in as comprehensively as possible. Hence, they try to get a grip on all relevant settings, e.g., environment, service employees, or service delivery. With regards to the stakeholders, as discussed above, they are again seen from an individual point of view with their goals and driving forces.

Iterative

Understanding humans on an individual level as well as systems a service takes place in can be complex. To address this complexity, service designers consider their work to be highly *iterative*, i.e., as an ever-learning cycle. The steps of understanding people and systems, ideating over new solutions, prototyping solutions, testing them with different stakeholders to gain feedback and learn from it, and again better understand people and systems are all applied from the very beginning of a project. Steps can be short and cycles can be extremely fast at the beginning, slowing down with the increasing maturity of the project.

Prototype-Based

Service designers use *prototypes* throughout the service design process. In fact, research shows [19] that they perceive prototyping as a core activity and use it for a range of purposes such as visualizing services, communicating about them, collaborating with users to explore important needs and the wider context of services, as well as evaluating ideas. Thus, service designers use prototypes for problem understanding at the beginning of the project to almost final prototypes for new services at the end. Throughout the process, the number and granularity of prototypes vary. At the beginning, many simple prototypes are applied to gain more concrete input from stakeholders. Towards the end, less prototypes are used but with far more details to demonstrate a potential final service.

Prototypes are mostly thought of as physical drafts of ideas. Typical prototypes in service design often appear in the form of scripted stories, comic-like visualizations, or role plays. For many service designers, these kinds of prototypes pose many challenges. Among others, they report on difficulties with intangibility when prototyping social interactions, inconsistency between instances of role play, or unauthentic behavior of participants [19]. Researchers addressed to these challenges by building conceptual frameworks to gain a deeper understanding of the exact shortcomings of service prototyping and contribute to their enhancement [20].

4.1.4 Designers' Skills

Human-centricity and understanding customers (stakeholders) in a holistic way are two cornerstones of service design. The application of design principles and methods enables service designers to follow these cornerstones. This raises the question why design principles and methods help us to take human-centric and holistic perspectives. Recently, an increasing number of companies started to open design centers, even if they are not in a typical design business. What do they try to achieve? (Fig. 4.3).

Having a closer look at the *curriculum* of a design study unveils that up-and-coming designers get trained in various disciplines to acquire *skills* that help them to better understand humans as individuals. As expected, the curriculum includes subjects like holistic thinking, interdisciplinary thinking, and various artistic methods. What is more, aspects of human sciences, social sciences, and psychology and related methods are taught. For instance, Meroni and Sangiorgi [13],

News room > News releases >
IBM Unveils New Design Studio to Transform the Way Clients Interact with Software and Emerging Technologies
50,000 square foot Austin Design Studio leads effort to redesign the face of enterprise software

Fig. 4.3 IBM announces new design studio in Austin, TX

amongst others, stress the importance of education in empathic design, experience design, and methods derived from ethnology, a branch of anthropology that studies people and the relationships between them. Related methods include the observation of people, the documentation of their behavior, and their social structures. Based on these disciplines and their methods, designers develop capabilities to have a closer look at humans, to document their observations and retrieve interesting findings from them. While not all of those various disciplines and their methods can be covered in detail in this chapter, a selection of popular approaches will be introduced in the following section.

4.2   Design Process

The literature provides several *service design processes* which differ in terms of number of steps as well as wording. However, on a higher level the processes show many similarities. This book builds on the four high-level steps of the service design process by Mager and Gais [18]. With regards to the detailed activities taking place in each of these phases, input from several authors is considered to ensure a more comprehensive picture. Thus, as shown in Fig. 4.4, the service design process consists of the four iterative and highly interconnected phases *exploration*, *creation*, *reflection*, and *implementation*. Each of these phases, their key steps as well as the interaction between them is described in detail below. Additionally, Table 4.1 provides a schematic summary of the service design process including an overview of typical activities for all phases and steps as well as common methods.

Exploration Phase

Service design projects typically start with an extensive *exploration phase*, during which the designers focus on: (a) better understanding and (re-)framing the challenge they have been given; (b) investigating the perspectives of the involved humans in detail; (c) deciding which of the gained information needs to be considered in the subsequent phases; and (d) optimizing their team and methods to solve the challenge. While the last two are fairly straightforward, there is a strong emphasis on the first and second step, i.e., identifying the real challenge and better understanding the humans with their emotions and needs. For the first, design teams

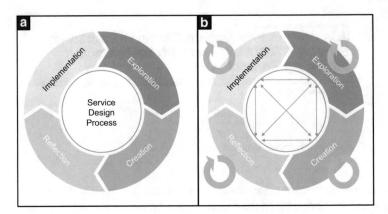

Fig. 4.4 The (**a**) general service design process (adapted from Mager and Gais [18]) and (**b**) its highly iterative nature within each phase as well as across the various phases

often create a so-called design space map as well as a stakeholder map. The design space map is a visual representation of the challenge depicting everything related that might be relevant throughout the project. The stakeholder map as well as some of the methods applied to address the second step will be explained in detail in this section. In fact, these initial steps are one of the key differentiators of the service design approach from classical new service development (NSD) processes, such as the one of Scheuing and Johnson [21]. While their NSD process starts with the formulation of objectives, reflecting on a given strategy, and then generating ideas for solutions, the designers question the actual challenge and put a lot of effort into understanding it more deeply before starting with the creation of ideas [11].

Creation Phase

After the exploration of the challenge and the humans involved, the *creation phase* for solving the identified challenge starts. This means to (a) ideate on solutions for the challenge, to (b) conceptualize those ideas, as well as to (c) assess and select ideas to pursue on. With regards to ideating, designers apply a mix of classical brainstorming methods, foresight methods—to go beyond the obvious and design for the future—for examples see Chap. 3 on Service Innovation), and role-play like approaches to maintain the human centric perspective during their creative phase. Conceptualizing the ideas is almost inseparably bound to the first step. Since service design aims to make concepts as tangible as possible, the creation of prototypes during as well as after the ideating step becomes critically important. Typical kinds of prototypes generated during the ideation and conceptualizing steps include mock-ups (often made of paper), comic-like story boards, or role plays. In fact, and as a side note, service designers often already employ simple prototypes in the exploration phase to engage in more concrete discussions with stakeholders and

Table 4.1 Characteristics of the phases of a service design process

Phase	Step	Objective	Typical activities	Methods (examples)
Exploration	Understand challenge	Understand and (re-)frame the challenge	Frame the actual challenge or problem Identify impact factors and stakeholders	Design space map Stakeholder map Janus Cones, Context Map Customer System
	Investigate humans	Understand the customers, further stakeholders and the service environment	Identify customers' needs, requirements, and demands Identify touchpoints between provider and customer Assess the overall experiences made by customers as well as their development over time Assess the service from the perspective of the provider and other stakeholders Analyse the environment Identify initial options for improvement	Persona A day in a life Shadowing Observe, interview, engage with customer Empathy map Customer journey maps
	Set focus	Synthesize the findings from the discovery phase in order to facilitate the subsequent creation phase	Aggregate and abstract the data points found Identify core findings and room of further action	
	Setup Project	Setup the project for success	Form the right teams Create or tailor methods/tools	
Creation	Ideate	Enable radical and outside the box thinking & ideas	Conduct divergent activities oriented towards the far future Open approaches: Involve employees and customer	Creativity methods Value curve methods Co-opetition model Service theater (enacting)
	Conceptualize	Detail out a service concept from an experience perspective	Create low-resolution prototypes (often made of paper) to discuss functionality with customers / stakeholders rather than graphics	Mock-ups Prototypes Storyboards
Reflection	Assess & Select	Reduce the amount of ideas to follow up with	Compile alternative service episodes based on ideas and test them with customers and stakeholders	Story-telling Request customer feedback
		Explore feasibility and fit of the service	Compare to existing portfolios and strategies	SWOT analyses Business cases Customer acceptance tests
Implementation		Detail out a service concept from an operational perspective	Organization-, process-, and (IT-)technology-specific competences	Service Blueprint High-resolution prototype Graphical design Business Model Canvas

to gain richer insights. Assessing and selecting ideas involves the identification of complementary ideas and their aggregation into bundles. The film industry may serve as an analogy for this: ideas for characters, actions, stage scenery, etc. get compiled to film sequences which then get integrated into an overall storyline. Similarly, service designers form alternative service episodes out of the many ideas they have created and conceptualized earlier on. Using intensive feedback from customers and other stakeholders, these alternatives then get evaluated and prioritized. The most convincing sequences are pursued.

Reflection Phase

So far, all steps have been undertaken from a customer experience and perception point of view without considering the feasibility of ideas generated. Hence, in the *reflection phase* the feasibility and fit lenses are applied. This involves an assessment of the technical, legal, and financial feasibility as well as the fit to the service provider's strategy and potential other service offerings. For this, classical instruments such as business cases or a SWOT analysis are typically applied. Therefore, the reflection phase has a filter function. However, amongst service designers it is a common practice to take some of the ideas considered to be "totally unrealistic yet very persuasive if implementable" and elaborate more deeply on them. Sometimes these types of ideas are referred to as dark-horse prototypes due to their mystic and unpredictable character.

Implementation Phase

While the previous phases have primarily dealt with generating ideas for services from a customer perspective and evaluating their general feasibility, the service is yet to be implemented in detail—in particular from an operational perspective. This is done within the *implementation phase*. This means, the service provider has to conceptualize the service including all aspects from the targeted service experience on the customer side to the organizational and technical processes inside the organization that ensure the service experience. One of the most frequently used methods for this is service blueprinting.

Process Execution

Although the outlined process looks linear, professionals from academia and practice emphasize its highly iterative character—if not to say sometimes chaotic. Within each phase the steps are conducted iteratively. Likewise, the phases are implemented iteratively and, what is more, jumps between steps of the various phases are common practice (Fig. 4.4b). For instance, the findings derived from identifying customers' needs in detail may change the formulation of the challenge, or the discussion of the prototypes with customers during the creation phase may uncover needs that require to go back to the exploration phase.

R Service design processes are highly iterative—within each of its phases as well as across the various phases.

In service design projects the initial exploration phase receives a strong focus and takes a significant amount of time. Also, this is where the service design approach differs the most from more classical service innovation or new service development processes which often start with idea generation.

4.3   Design Methods

This chapter introduces key *design methods* primarily used in the exploration phase of the service design process, namely, the *stakeholder map*, the *persona* concept, and the *customer journey map*. These methods will demonstrate how to better observe and interpret humans' needs, visualize, and choreograph what others cannot see, and observe services from the perspective of experiences. In addition, *service blueprinting*, one of the founding methods of service design from the early 1980s, is explained to address the objective of operationalizing the service provision. Notably, according to Hollins and Hollins [22], who call service design a *practical craft*, the methods can be tailored to the specific project situation, i.e., they are themselves subject to prototyping.

4.3.1   The Stakeholder Map

At the beginning of a project, service designers aim to get a grip on the issue to solve. For this, they visualize all information and questions they perceive as relevant in a map. As a team, the designers strive for a common understanding of the overall challenge, its related sub-challenges, main impact factors, etc. Gray et al. [23] call this type of visualization a *context map* and give instructions on how to create it in a workshop-like setup. Amongst practitioners this map is sometimes also called a *design space map*. Notably, this map is maintained throughout the whole design project, i.e., the team regularly uses it to reflect on a given challenge, to question it, and potentially redefine it. One key aspect of the context map is the identification of critical stakeholders that need to be taken into consideration.

▶ **Definition (Stakeholder)** "A stakeholder [...] is [...] any group or individual who can affect or is affected by the achievement of the firm's objectives" [24].

Freeman [24, p. 46 and 54] refers to a stakeholder map as a (visual) representation of groups or individuals who either affect or are affected by an organization's objectives.

▶ **Definition (Stakeholder Map)** A stakeholder map for a service design project is a visual representation of groups or individuals who either affect or are affected by an organization's objectives naming the stakeholders and showing essential relations between them (based on Freeman [24]).

Hence, to create a stakeholder map, service designers need to undertake two essential steps:

Identify Stakeholders Initially, relevant stakeholders need to be identified, if necessary grouped, and positioned onto the map. Naming stakeholders is a rather challenging task. Stakeholders can be classified into primary stakeholder, i.e., those groups without whose participation an organization cannot survive, and secondary stakeholders, i.e., those groups who have mutual influence with the organization but are neither critical for the survival of the organization nor do they engage in transactions with it [25]. At a high level, many stakeholder groups, in particular the primary stakeholder groups, might be named quite easily, e.g., customer, suppliers, and investors. However, for the service design process a more detailed level of granularity is needed. Hence, service designer spend significant effort on uncovering important yet not obvious stakeholders. For instance, they think of experts, skeptics, extreme users, misusers, early adopters, and many more. In Chap. 3 (Service Innovation), the customer system tool introduced can help service designers to think of different customer roles, i.e., buyer, user, and influencer.

Draw Relations To complete the stakeholder map, relations—or *mutual stakes*—between the various parties (stakeholders) need to be visualized as well. There are many perspectives on what a stake is and how to categorize stakes, e.g., owning equity, economic impact, and political influence. In practice, for the sake of simplicity and overview, service designers tend to represent all types of stakes between stakeholders as arrows in the map and simply label arrows in natural language rather than category names.

Similar to a context map, the stakeholder map is created at the beginning of a service design project and is maintained throughout its whole lifecycle (Fig. 4.5).

4.3.2 The Persona

The stakeholder map provides an overview of the most critical groups to consider during a service design project. Nonetheless, the names of the groups and their most essential relations to other domain players do not yet allow designers to step into the "shoes" of individuals of these groups and view the world as they would do it, i.e., to act human-centric.

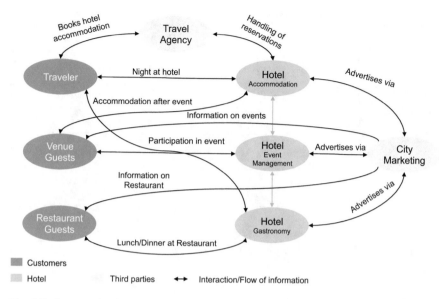

Fig. 4.5 An example of a stakeholder map for the opening case

The *persona concept* stems from Human-Computer Interaction (HCI) research [26–28] and helps to bridge the gap between more abstract customer segments and the aim to design from the perspective of an individual. For each stakeholder group of the stakeholder map, one or more archetypical representations are created. Rather than simply aggregating the typical requirements and characteristics of a stakeholder group, a persona is an almost real, typical yet individual description created to represent a group.

▶ **Definition (Persona)** A persona is a "fictitious, specific, concrete representations of target users" that puts "a face on the user—a memorable, engaging, and actionable image that serves as a design target." [27, p.11].

One can think of a persona as a role in a theatre play. Similar to an actor, service designers can slip into this role or can engage in dialog with it. In terms of creating a persona, Cooper [26, p. 123] emphasizes that they are rather discovered by thorough investigation than being made-up. To make the persona more "relatable", it gets a fictional name, personal information, and a picture, though. Regarding the information retrieved from investigation, demographic information, e.g., age, gender, marital status, children, relationships, level of (available) income, and level of education provide a factual basis.

Furthermore, context-oriented information related to the service design challenge needs to be added to the persona. This, for instance, includes requirements, needs or wishes the persona typically expresses. To gain an even more personal and holistic picture, softer information is added such as a description of the persona's personality

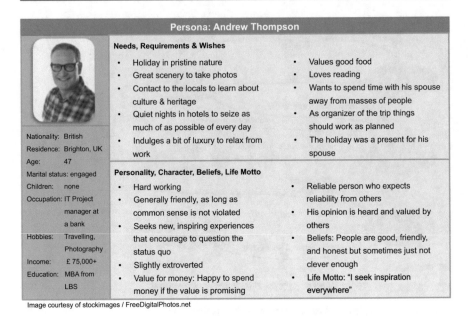

Image courtesy of stockimages / FreeDigitalPhotos.net

Fig. 4.6 An example of a persona from the opening case

including character, believes, life mottos as well as feelings and mood (Fig. 4.6). This type of information may help to uncover less obvious needs or underlying motivations of the persona. Creating an empathy map [23] helps to generate some of this information. This approach suggests reflecting on how a person perceives a certain situation, i.e., what the person thinks, sees, says, does, feels, and hears [28].

> The objective of using a persona in a service design project is to: (1) understand behavior, needs, and preferences of typical representatives of stakeholder groups; (2) make the underlying motivations clearer; and (3) enable service designers to put themselves into the personas' shoes when analyzing situations and creating solutions.

Notably, templates for personas vary dramatically based on the project they are applied to and the preferences and experiences of the designers. Three critical success factors for the implementation of the persona concept emerge:

- The customization of the template to use in a service design project is crucial. Depending on how a project develops, additional or different information which was not expected at the beginning, is required.
- Over the course of a project a persona will mature in terms of its description. The information gained over time needs to be reflected and incorporated into the persona. This will make it more real and complete. Hence, creating a persona is an iterative, evolving process.

- Practitioners report about the importance of treating a persona like a project team member. The physical representations of the persona, such as posters in the project room, role plays or even dolls at the meeting table, support the designers endeavor to put themselves into the shoes of the personas.

4.3.3 The Customer Journey Map

The methods outlined so far enabled service designers to step into a persona's shoes. Now, an approach is needed to help the service designer to walk in those shoes and capture what they see with the persona's eyes. For this, the idea of a *customer journey map*—a visual representation of a service customer's experience—is used.

▶ **Definition (Customer Journey Map)** "A customer journey map provides a vivid but structured visualization of a service user's experience" [11].

According to Zomerdijk and Voss [29, p. 74], it "involves all activities and events related to the delivery of a service from the customer's perspective", and—as nicely phrased by one of their interviewees—it is used to understand the behavior, feelings, motivations, and attitudes of customers throughout the journey.

Structurally, customer journey maps are closely linked to the key concepts service episodes and service encounters (see also the Chap. 8—Service Co-creation). Services comprise several episodes with a defined start and end points, and consist of several encounters, i.e., interactions between a service provider and a service customer [30]. In our hotel opening case, "booking a hotel room" or "staying at the hotel" are examples of episodes of the service "hotel visit". Check-in, ordering a drink at the bar, or check-out are typical encounters of the episode "staying at the hotel". A customer journey visualizes a service with its episodes (also referred to as *phases*) and encounters (often called *touchpoints*).

There are no standards in terms of what a customer journey looks like and thus, as Fig. 4.7 shows, many different templates are used. Nonetheless, based on the analysis of several case studies, Voss and Zomerdijk [12] identify the following commonalities of the various customer journey maps:

Perspective The customer and customer's experience play the central role in a customer journey. The focus is on the customer perspective. Operational aspects of the service provider beyond the direct interaction with the customer are not displayed in the map.

Touchpoints The elements and actions depicted in the customer journey map are touchpoints between the customer and the provider, i.e., every situation where a customer gets in touch with the provider. Touchpoints range from hearing the provider's name (e.g., by word of mouth) to interactions during the actual service provision.

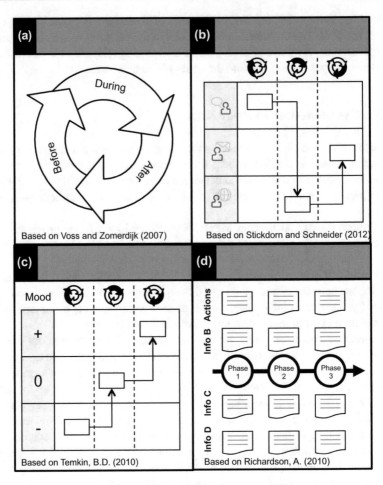

Fig. 4.7 Schematic representations of customer journey maps. (**a**) Wheel style. (**b**) Process map. (**c**) Perception map. (**d**) Descriptive map

Timeframe   As the variety of touchpoints suggests, customer journeys start long before the service takes place and end after it is provided. Thus, the timespan to consider for service design is questioned and, most likely, extended compared to the limited perspective on direct interactions between customers and service providers.

However, until today, the customer journey map is subject to experimentation and further development by many professionals from academia, consulting, and industry. The development and usage of a customer journey map involves: *identify persona, frame the timespan, envision journey,* and *evaluate journey map.*

Identify Persona

A customer journey map is the visual representation of a specific service customer's experience. Thus, determining one of the previously defined personas as the customer whose perspective to take is the initial step to create a map.

Frame the Timespan

Voss and Zomerdijk [12] pointed out that the timeframe covered by a journey exceeds the duration from sales to provision of a service. Hence, when is a journey supposed to start and when is it supposed to end? As the journey incorporates all touchpoints between the customer and provider, one might start the journey with the customer recognizing the provider or its name for the first time. However, this would still be a provider-centric mindset to a certain extent. In fact, following this idea, important steps might be missed. The guiding question should rather be "when does the customer recognize a requirement for the first time that may result in demand for a service?" This may be long before a provider's name even crosses the customer's mind.

To give an example, people who consider buying a house or an apartment typically get motivated by events such as moving to a new location or seeing friends buying a house. They probably start asking themselves whether buying a property is a good idea. Walking around looking at other people's houses more reflectively might be the next step before they start screening the Internet for real estate prices in their region and comparing them to their personal financial situation. From the perspective of a real-estate agent or a bank most of the steps may have taken place long before the customer comes across their names or offers. However, supporting people in early phases and providing guidance might be an opportunity for extending their business. These opportunities can be seen as potential touchpoints for a provider. To summarize, the intention of a customer, when it starts and ends, is what should determine the timeframe of a customer journey rather than existing touchpoints with a provider. Once the timeframe is determined, it is recommended to split it into phases to further develop the journey.

Envision Journey

With a persona, a timeframe, and phases at hand, the service designer can conduct the mapping of the customer journey, i.e., walking in the persona's shoes and visualizing its experiences. In line with the service design cornerstones, this process is of iterative nature. Designers alter between:

1. Anticipating the persona's steps, behavior, and emotions.
2. Observing, interviewing or engaging with real customers who are similar to their persona to gain additional information.
3. Abstracting from the gathered real-world data.

For the second step in particular, learning from real customers, service designers draw from a broad set of tools. *Shadowing* customers in terms of immersing into their world, documenting their behavior on video, photo, recordings, notes, etc.

to learn from them is one of those tools. Another popular tool is called *a day in a life*. It is quite similar to the shadowing tool and works with the same recording devices. However, the focus is a typical day in the life of a person rather than how a person experiences and behaves with a particular service. Thus, this tool is strong in enabling designers to understand everyday life of a person as an environment for the service. For instance, if service designers want to find out when a given service is least disturbing for a customer, knowing the typical patterns in his daily life can be crucial.

All gathered data is then mapped onto a canvas, the customer journey map. Since all services with humans as customers entail an experience on their side, keeping track of the emotions that contribute to the overall service experience of the customer are worth recording. Thus, the perception map (see Fig. 4.7c) showing the mood level associated with each touchpoint is a strong visualization. Connecting the touchpoints sequentially supports the impression of a journey. Additional text on aspects such as *obstacles to continuation* or *motivation to proceed* may complement the map (Fig. 4.8).

Evaluate the Journey

By building a persona, the service designer learned a lot about its personality and needs. Generating a journey map as outlined in Fig. 4.8, uncovered the persona's emotions and overall experience based on its needs. From analyzing the emotions and further information provided by the journey map, the persona's needs, motivations, etc. can be better understood and prioritized. For this, a framework like Kano's model of customer satisfaction (Fig. 4.9) comes in handy [31–33]. Concrete representations of needs are requirements. While needs are relatively stable, requirements, i.e., how and to what extend a need should be satisfied, may vary.

Kano et al. suggest there are requirements which customers express explicitly—subsequently called type 1 requirements. With regards to the tourist from the opening case, this would be "a hotel room for x nights including breakfast". However, there are also requirements that typically are not expressed explicitly but considered to be obvious: requirements of type 2 in Fig. 4.9. For the traveler, this would have been—for instance—a clean and quiet room. A customer cannot be positively excited by fulfilling these requirements since they constitute what was taken for granted. However, as seen in the opening case, if any of these requirements are not met, satisfaction drops dramatically.

Finally, there are requirements of type 3, which a customer does not expect to be fulfilled. However, they provide an opportunity to delight a customer. In hotels, complementary upgrades, free pralines in the room, an invitation to a get-together, etc. belong to this category. Notably, no matter how well a provider serves type 3 requirements, if he misses out on type 1 or—in particular—type 2, the overall experience will suffer dramatically. As a side note, type 1, 2, and 3 have received several names in literature such as one-dimensional, or key (type 1), must-be or hygiene requirements (type 2), and delighters, motivators, or attractive requirements (type 3). This chapter stays with the neutral terms type 1 to 3.

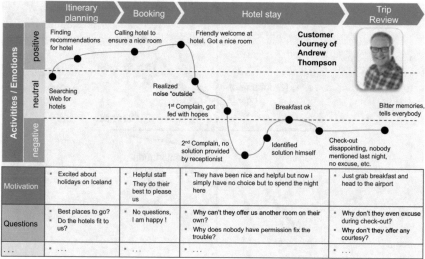

		Itinerary planning	Booking	Hotel stay	Trip Review

Finding recommendations for hotel
Calling hotel to ensure a nice room
Friendly welcome at hotel. Got a nice room
Customer Journey of Andrew Thompson

Searching Web for hotels
Realized noise "outside"
1st Complain, got fed with hopes
Breakfast ok
Bitter memories, tells everybody

2nd Complain, no solution provided by receptionist
Identified solution himself
Check-out disappointing, nobody mentioned last night, no excuse, etc.

Motivation		▪ Excited about holidays on Iceland	▪ Helpful staff ▪ They do their best to please us	▪ They have been nice and helpful but now I simply have no choice but to spend the night here	▪ Just grab breakfast and head to the airport
Questions		▪ Best places to go? ▪ Do the hotels fit to us?	▪ No questions, I am happy !	▪ Why can't they offer us another room on their own? ▪ Why does nobody have permission fix the trouble?	▪ Why don't they even excuse during check-out? ▪ Why don't they offer any courtesy?
. . .		▪ ...	▪ ...	▪ ...	▪ ...

Activitites / Emotions — positive / neutral / negative

Image courtesy of stockimages / FreeDigitalPhotos.net

Fig. 4.8 An example of a customer journey map for the opening case

With regards to evaluating the customer journey map, service designers reflect on the shape of the journey, i.e., what it looks like overall, how many touchpoints are positioned in the negative emotions zone, what types of requirements were violated that made the persona perceive a given touchpoint negatively. In addition, designers question what it would take to change the shape of the curve, to move up the experience made at specific touchpoints from a neutral to a positive level. In a nutshell, each touchpoint as well as the journey's shape provide opportunities for innovation [12].

Remarkably, the customer journey approach can be applied to a given situation as well as—hypothetically—to an idea for a new or changed service. In the latter case, it can facilitate a comparison of the original state of the service with the expected impact of a design change.

As seen, the customer journey map enables to visualize the customer experience when interacting with a service. Taking the inspiration from the journey, possibly reframing the project's challenges based on the findings from the journey, and then ideating on how to improve or overturn the service are the next logical steps. However, the steps outlined primarily cover the customer perspective. No matter how compelling ideas for a new service experience might be, feasibility needs to be ensured, i.e., the service needs to be operationalized on the provider side. For this, service blueprinting comes into play.

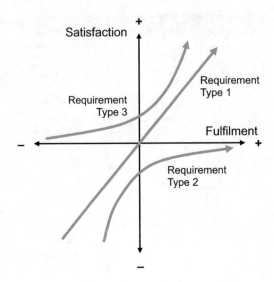

Fig. 4.9 A model of customer satisfaction (based on Kano et al. [31])

4.3.4   Service Blueprinting

Service blueprinting is a simple method to identify and describe the processes that
support services. While the Karni and Kaner approach presented in Chap. 1 looked
into a service as a system composed of many components (e.g., inputs, outputs,
environment, and resources), blueprinting looks mainly at service processes and
their activities.

▶ **Definition (Service Blueprinting)** A technique to help organizations understanding their service offerings and delivery processes by enabling to examine service
processes from a customers point of view.

The output of service blueprinting consists of a graphical representation of a
service process as shown in Fig. 4.10. This example corresponds to the service
blueprint of a typical hotel stay. It identifies process activities, the interaction points
between the customer and the service provider, and the roles of customers and
employees. In more details, the process describes the management of the life cycle
of an overnight stay, which includes activities such as check in, registration, food
delivery, and check out.

Service blueprinting was introduced by Shostack in 1984 [34] and has its origin in service
quality, customer experience, and customer satisfaction research.

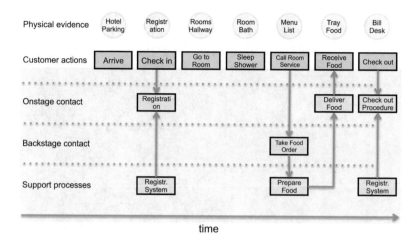

Fig. 4.10 An example of a service blueprint modeling a typical overnight stay at a hotel. *Rectangles* represents activities which together, with edges, form a service process

Benefits

The benefits of service blueprinting are wide-ranging. Organizations are able to make explicit how services are provisioned to customers. Benefits range from fostering innovation, quality management, training support, to efficiency improvements, and to service standardization:

Innovation Service blueprinting is a planning and analysis tool which can be used to develop new innovative services as well as for improving existing ones. The processes and activities identified can provide the grounds to discover areas for innovation and suggest ways to customize services to address niche markets with specific needs.

Quality The graphical representation of processes enables to quickly identify possible failure points. This provides managers the facts and the possibility to redesign procedures leading to an increased customer satisfaction. Over time, it becomes possible to develop operating procedures with a proven high quality.

Training Detailed descriptions of service designs provide an important documentation which can be used during the training of new employees. Staff can grasp and understand *who* executes *which* activities, and *when*.

Efficiency The visual representation of processes provides the opportunity to parallelize the execution of activities to reduce the time to complete services. It also enables to highlight which activities are fundamental, optional, and which should be adapted to better satisfy customer requirements.

Standardization The codification of the knowledge associated with the operation of services enables to identify best practices which can lead to the creation of organizational standards. Once identified, golden service blueprints can be distributed and implemented at several locations, ensuring a consistent service quality.

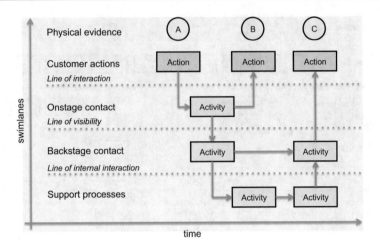

Fig. 4.11 The structure and components of service blueprints

In practice, service blueprinting is used by process managers and service designers to conceive how a service will work. Service managers, and employees in general, can use service blueprints as a guide to operate services on a daily basis. While service blueprinting has many benefits, one disadvantage is that it typically looks at processes from a managerial perspective and process orientation rather than a customer perspective.

Structure and Components

A blueprint consists of a *structure* and several *components* as illustrated in Fig. 4.11. The structure can be viewed as a two-dimensional structure: the vertical axis provides several *swimlanes* which identify various areas of action and the horizontal axis identifies the timeline of activities conducted by the customer and service provider.

A blueprint has five main vertical components: four swimlanes separated by what is called a line, and a special area capturing any physical evidence of the occurrence of customer actions:

Physical evidence   are identifiable and visible outcomes that result from executing activities. It is a way to recognize that a service exists and that also attests the progress of a service delivery process. For example, the registration desk, a central point of contact between service providers and customers where requests can be made, is a physical evidence of the service.

Customer actions   are the steps that customers are required to take as part of the process of service delivery. They are drawn sequentially from left to right and are located above the *line of interaction* which separates the interactions between customers and providers. For instance, to request for a specific service, customers know that they must make a phone call, send an email, or go to the service/registration desk.

Onstage contact   are activities taken by employees that are visible to customers as part of the service process. Therefore, they are located above the line of visibility. Every time the customer and provider interact, the line of interaction is crossed and a *moment of truth* occurs. For example, when a clerk receives a request from a customer, the first step is to register the request with the management systems. Then, the request is categorized and prioritized for a better utilization of the resources and the support staff time.

Backstage contact   are activities taken by employees that are not visible to customers. They happen behind the scenes to support onstage activities. The line of internal interaction separates the onstage contact employee activities from support processes and activities. For example, the staff that takes a food order by phone may not be visible to customers. In such a case, they are classified under the label backstage contact.

Support processes   are activities carried out that are not directly related to a particular customer but that need to exist for a service to be delivered. Thus, they are located below the line of internal interaction. For instance, the activity registration calls for a support process managed by an information system which will determine if the record of a customer already exists, what are his preferences concerning the view of the room, and what rooms are available.

While the four lanes that decompose a service delivery process are kept physically separate, they are connected by channels of communications.

How to Develop a Blueprint

The process of building a service blueprint can be decomposed into six distinct steps [35]:

1. Identify the service to be blueprinted.
2. Identify the customer or customer segment target for the service.
3. Map the service process from the customer's point of view.
4. Map contact employee and/or technology activities.
5. Link contact activities to the required support functions.
6. Add physical evidence of service delivery at each customer action.

The first step to develop a service blueprint consists in identifying the service to be blueprinted. Services may need to be prioritized to select the most important services to model or to start by modeling the most simple ones to gain experience with the technique. Identifying the segment which represents the target customer(s) of the service, is the second step. There is often no "one-size-fits-all" solution when developing services which bring a high level of satisfaction to customers. When too many distinct customers are considered, it becomes difficult to take design decisions.

Once services and customers are identified, the actual service blueprinting starts. Two activities are executed: map the customer's process and map the service providers' own processes. Reconstructing or finding how providers' processes operate is not always an easy task, especially when complex information systems, such as enterprise resource management systems, are involved. Afterwards, the fifth steps links contact activities to support activities.

Finally, the physical evidence and tangible aspects of a service are added to customers' contact activities. In this step, as well as in step two, blueprinting requires designers to consider the manner customers experience service delivery since designers are most likely not part of the customer segment under study. In other words, designers should replace their perceptions of the service delivery by what is important for customers.

Other Modeling Approaches

Modeling is a common activity in organizational settings. Business models, process models, and enterprise architecture models are frequently used to create abstract representations of important organizational artifacts. Service blueprinting is also a modeling approach but compared to other initiatives—which place emphasis on a formal control-flow (e.g., business process modeling) or provide a wide view on organizations (e.g., Zachman framework)—service blueprinting focuses on the customer processes which are identified first. All the other tasks are then defined so that they support the value proposition offered to customers.

4.3.5   Design Tools

Figure 4.12 and Table 4.2 provide examples and an overview of resources on the internet to learn more about service design, engage with the service design community, and support the creation and maintenance of some of the maps outlined in the chapter.

Portals providing service design tools are subject to constant change. Hence, the links provided are only an excerpt of what is available on the Internet.

4.4   Conclusions

Service design is the process of systematically applying methods and principles to the design of services. The focus is on the *process*. Design experts and professionals agree that a process must be human-centric, interactive, holistic, iterative, and makes use of prototypes. A typical design process starts with an exploration phase, which identifies the challenges and the humans involved. The second phase, the creation phase, generates ideas for solving the challenges. Afterwards, the reflection phase will make an assessment of the technical, legal, and financial feasibility of the ideas. Finally, the last phase, implementation, will build a service from an operational perspective.

During each phase, the design process relies on the use of methods that assist service designers to capture information using various lenses. Well-known methods

Fig. 4.12 Popular web sites with information about design tools

Table 4.2 Overview of web sites to service design tools on the internet

Resource	Description
service-design-network.org	Professional society of service designers; editor of the service design journal "Touchpoint".
servicedesigntools.org	An open collection of communication tools used in design processes, build, and maintained by the Politecnico di Milano.
usability.gov	Web resource on best practices and guidelines for user experience including overviews of related disciplines. Provided by the U.S. Department of Health and Human Services.
innovationgames.com	Innovation games provides some service design tools such as the empathy map as online facilitation tools.
thisisservicedesignthinking.com	Website to the book "This is Service Design Thinking". The website provides free templates is several languages.

include stakeholder maps to represent groups or individuals who either affect or are affected by an organization's objectives; personas which enable to understand customers' goals and behavior patterns; customer journey maps, which illustrate the steps customers go through when participating in service delivery; and service blueprinting, which describes graphically the processes, activities, and physical evident of services' interactions that occur during service provisioning.

Review Section

Review Questions

1. Remember a disappointing service situation you experienced yourself and reflect on why you were disappointed. What was worse, the fact that something went wrong or the way the service provider reacted to your complaint?
2. What could the service provider have done to fix the issue in a satisfactory way? Do you see a possibility how a service provider could turn the unlucky accident into a positive experience for the customer?
3. What types of education that business students as well as technical students typically do not receive do bring designers to the table when it comes to designing a service?
4. As discussed in the chapter there is no standard template for a persona. What pieces of information would you include in your template and why?
5. Where exactly do you see a difference between the typical description of a customer segment and a persona? What do you reckon is the ratio between a customer segment and the number of personas needed to represent the segment? Is it 1:1?
6. What are the pros and cons of the various customer journey maps as shown in Fig. 4.8?
7. Can you think of any downside of deriving ideas for innovations from the customer journey?
8. Thinking about the Kano model, do you expect the association of a requirement to type 1, 2, or 3 to be stable over time?
9. Explain how service blueprinting achieves the following goals: map the value exchanges and identify touchpoints; explain the interactions between customers and provider's staff; and expose how interactions are supported by backstage activities.
10. Self-service technologies are technological interfaces that enable customers to co-produce services without a direct employee involvement (e.g., ATM, gas pump terminals, and hotel check out kiosks). Can blueprinting also be used to model the services provided by self-service technologies? If the modeling is feasible, explain any adaptation that needs to be made to the method. Otherwise, justify why blueprinting is not adequate to use with self-service technologies.

Project

As a challenge, imagine you were asked by your local public transport company to overturn ticket sales. Try to improve the existing ticket sales process or develop a new one by applying service design methods. Start by building a team of three to five students, conduct a short workshop, and brainstorm on ideas for an improved ticket sales process.

Next, put those results aside and start applying the service design methods: sketch a stakeholder map for your challenge. On the customer side there may be the young Generation-Y student, the pensioner, the business person, or a parent with kids. Can you think of other typical customers? What are further stakeholders do you see, who are not customers? After drawing the stakeholder map, pick two types of customers and try to create a persona for them. Try to make them as real as possible without exaggerating or even turning them into ridicule. Start building the personas in a brainstorming session at your desk. Then go out, observe, and interview people who are similar to your personas and incorporate your observations into the persona maps. How did the picture of the personas change during this exercise? Did they get richer? Did some of your clichés of a persona turned out to be wrong?

For both of your personas start creating a customer journey map for the existing ticket sales process as outlined in the chapter. Take a camera or your smartphone, go out, observe, and interview people alike to your persona. Pay attention to the timeframe you cover in your journey map. After completion and review of the journey maps start generating ideas for improvement of the ticket sales process again by conducting a brainstorming workshop.

Finally, take out the idea map you generated at the very beginning and compare it to the result of your second brainstorming session. How do they differ?

Key Terms

Service Concept   The service concept describes in detail the needs of the targeted customers, what actions to take to meet these needs, and how to operationally implement these actions.

New Service Development   Describes the process of developing a new service from the early development stages to its market introduction.

Service Design   The systematic application of design methods and principles to the creation of service concepts for new or improved services.

Stakeholder Map   A visual tool that allows to represent groups or individuals who either affect or are affected by an organization's objectives, their level of commitment with the organization, and their relevance to the organization.

Persona   A fictitious representation of an individual that puts a face on an archetypical member of a group of people—mostly users. It serves as a memorable design target and, therefore, helps to guide design decisions.

Customer Journey Map   A diagram that illustrates the steps customers go through when participating in service delivery. This map provides a structured visualization of a service customers' experience.

Service Blueprinting   An operational tool that describes graphically the processes, activities, and roles of services' interactions in a level of detail which enables implementation, verification, and maintenance. The output of the tool is a service blueprint which contains a process model-like structure.

Further Reading

Andy Polaine, Lavrans Løvlie and Ben Reason. *Service Design.* Rosenfeld Media, 2013.

Anna Meroni and Daniela Sangiorgi. *Design for Services (Design for Social Responsibility).* Gower Publishing Ltd, Farnham, 2011.

Marc Stickdorn and Jakob Schneider. *This is Service Design Thinking: Basics, Tools, Cases.* Wiley, 2012.

The bootcamp bootleg. http://dschool.stanford.edu/use-our-methods/the-bootcamp-bootleg/. Stanford D. School, 2014

The virtual crash course in service design. http://dschool.stanford.edu/dgift/. Stanford D. School, 2014

References

1. Johnston R, Kong X (2011) The customer experience : a road-map for improvement. Manag Serv Qual 21(1):5–24
2. Shostack L (1982) How to design a service. Eur J Mark 16(1):49–63
3. Ralph P, Wand Y (2009) A proposal for a formal definition of the design concept. In: Lyytinen K. et al (eds) Design requirements engineering: a ten-year perspective. Lecture notes in business information processing, vol 14. Springer, Berlin, pp 103–136
4. Zeithaml V, Parasuraman A, Berry L (1990) Delivering quality service: balancing customer perceptions and expectations. Free Press, New York
5. Edvardsson B, Olsson J (1996) Key concepts for new service development. Serv Ind J 16(2):140–164
6. Goldstein SM, Johnston R, Duffy J, Rao, J (2002) The service concept: the missing link in service design research? J Oper Manag 20(2):121–134
7. Holmlid S, Evenson S (2008) Bringing service design to service sciences, management and engineering. In: Hefley B, Murphy W (eds), Service science, management and engineering education for the 21st century. Service science: research and innovations in the service economy. Springer, Norwell, pp 341–345
8. Blomkvist J, Holmlid S, Segelström F (2010) This is service design research: yesterday, today and tomorrow. In: Stickdorn M, Schneider J (eds), This is service design thinking: basics, tools, cases. Wiley, New York
9. Dym CL, Agogino AM, Eris O, Frey DD, Leifer LJ (2005) Engineering design thinking, teaching, and learning. J Eng Educ 94(1):103–120
10. Brown T (2008) Design thinking. Harv Bus Rev 86(6):84–95
11. Stickdorn M, Schneider J (2012) This is service design thinking: basics, tools, cases. Wiley, New York
12. Voss C, Zomerdijk L (2007) Management of innovation in services. Innov Serv 44(9):97–134
13. Meroni A, Sangiorgi D (2011) Design for Services (Design for Social Responsibility). Gower Publishing, Ltd, Farnham
14. Johnson SP, Menor LJ, Roth AV, Chase RB (2000) A critical evaluation of the new service development process: integrating service innovation and service design. In: Fitzsimmons MJ, Fitzsimmons JA (eds) New service development: creating memorable experiences. SAGE Publications Inc, Thousand Oaks, pp 1–33

15. Fitzsimmons JA, Fitzsimmons MJ (2013) Service management: operations, strategy, information technology. McGraw-Hill Higher Education, New York
16. Sundbo J (1997) Management of innovation in services. Serv Ind J 17(3):432–455
17. Erlhoff M, Mager B, Manzini E (1997) Dienstleistung braucht design. Design for social responsibility. Luchterhand
18. Mager B, Gais M (2009) Service design. Wilhelm Fink GmbH und Co, Verlags-KG, Stuttgart
19. Blomkvist J, Holmlid S (2010) Service prototyping according to service design practitioners. Linköping University Electronic Press, Linköping
20. Blomkvist J, Holmlid S (2011) Existing prototyping perspectives : considerations for service design. In: Proceedings of the Nordes'11: the 4th Nordic design research conference, making design matter, 29–31 May, Helsinki, pp 31–40
21. Scheuing E, Johnson E (1989) A proposed model for new service development. J Serv Mark 3(2):25–34
22. Hollins G, Hollins B (1991) Total design - managing the design process in the service sector. Pitman, London
23. Gray D, Brown S, Macanufo J (2010) Gamestorming: a playbook for innovators, rulebreakers, and changemakers. O'Reilly Media Inc, Sebastopol
24. Freeman E (2010) Strategic management: a stakeholder approach. Cambridge University Press, Cambridge
25. Clarkson M (1995) A stakeholder Framework for analyzing and evaluating corporate social performance. Acad Manag Rev 20(1):92–117
26. Cooper A (1999) The inmates are running the asylum. Sams, Indianapolis.
27. Pruitt J, Adlin T (2010) The persona lifecycle: keeping people in mind throughout product design. Elsevier, Amsterdam
28. Nielsen L (2012) Personas - user focused design. Springer, London
29. Zomerdijk L, Voss C (2010) Service design for experience-centric services. J Serv Res 13(1):67–82
30. Liljander V, Strandvik T (1995) The nature of customer relationships in services. Adv Serv Mark Manag 4(141):67
31. Kano N, Seraku N, Takahashi F, Tsuji S (1984) Attractive quality and must-be quality. J Jpn Soc Qual Control 14(2):147–156
32. Matzler K, Hinterhuber HH, Bailom F, Sauerwein E (1996) How to delight your customers. J Prod Brand Manag 5(2):6–18
33. Matzler K, Hinterhuber H (1998) How to make product development projects more successful by integrating Kano's model of customer satisfaction into quality function deployment. Technovation 18(1):25–38
34. Shostack L (1984) Designing services that deliver. Harvard Business School Reprint, Harvard
35. Zeithaml V, Bitner M, Gremler D (2012) Services marketing. McGraw-Hill Higher Education, New York

Service Semantics

5

Steffen Stadtmüller, Jorge Cardoso, and Martin Junghans

Summary

The chapter looks at how to enrich the description of cloud services with semantic knowledge. This enrichment is conducted using Linked USDL (Unified Service Description Language), a service description language built with semantic web technologies. Linked USDL provides a business and technical envelope to describe services' general information and their Web API. This improves the search and contracting of services over the web. Using the LastFM cloud service as a starting point, the chapterdelves into semantic description and explains the development of a Web API build using the REST paradigm to access cloud services pragmatically.

Learning Objectives
1. Understand the limitations of describing cloud services in natural language.
2. Understand how cloud services are programmatically accessed using a Web API.
3. Use Linked USDL and semantics technologies to describe cloud services.

(continued)

S. Stadtmüller (✉) • M. Junghans
Karlsruhe Service Research Institute (KSRI), Karlsruhe Institute of Technology (KIT), Karlsruhe, Germany
e-mail: steffen.stadtmueller@kit.edu

J. Cardoso
Department of Informatics Engineering, Universidade de Coimbra, Coimbra, Portugal

Huawei European Research Center (ERC), Munich, Germany
e-mail: jcardoso@dei.uc.pt; jorge.cardoso@huawei.com

© Springer International Publishing Switzerland 2015
J. Cardoso et al. (eds.), *Fundamentals of Service Systems*, Service Science: Research and Innovations in the Service Economy, DOI 10.1007/978-3-319-23195-2_5

Facebook	developers.facebook.com	Facebook data can be connected with countless business apps for endless possibilities.	
Twitter	dev.twitter.com	Enables applications to send and read tweets.	
YouTube	developers.google.com/youtube/	YouTube Data and Player API allow programmers to access functionality and content.	
Dropbox	dropbox.com/developers/	Grants access to data from external applications for easy revisions, file sharing, and search.	
Instagram	instagram.com/developer/	Enables applications to access user, relationship, media, comments, etc. of pictures and videos uploaded.	
LinkedIn	developer.linkedin.com	Companies can search for new employees and advertise job offerings.	
Wordpress	codex.wordpress.org/WordPress.org_API/	Enables companies to apply new functionality and features to WordPress.	
Lastfm	last.fm/api/	Clients can access information about albums, events, users, and artists.	
Google	developers.google.com/products/	Google API allowing access to their products' data such as maps, social networking, and email.	

Fig. 5.1 The most well-known companies contributing to the API economy

4. Use graph patterns to describe REST services.
5. Develop search algorithms which leverage semantic service descriptions.

▶ **Opening Case** Cloud Services foster the API economy

ACCESS TO CLOUD SERVICES VIA WEB API TECHNOLOGIES IS PROVIDING A NEW FORM OF INNOVATION

The API economy is an economy where companies providing cloud services expose their data assets to third parties using Web-accessible Application Programming Interfaces (Web API). Many well-known companies are already taking advantage of this new movement by exposing their businesses through a Web API, including: Facebook, Twitter, YouTube, Dropbox, and Instagram (Fig. 5.1).

The emergence of Web API technologies goes back to the year 2000. The first mover was salesforce.com who offered application interfaces to its clients. The largest impact was made by ebay.com who offered a Web API to the general public.

In the past, a technique called web scraping was the way developers programmatically retrieved data from web pages. It consisted of developing and customizing a web client to parse the HTML pages of a targeted website to extract formatted data.

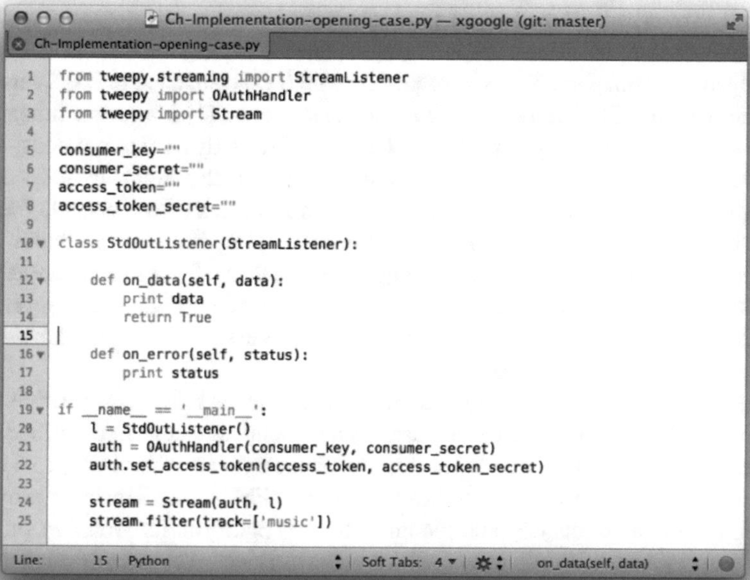

```
○ ○ ○              Ch-Implementation-opening-case.py — xgoogle (git: master)
○ Ch-Implementation-opening-case.py
1   from tweepy.streaming import StreamListener
2   from tweepy import OAuthHandler
3   from tweepy import Stream
4
5   consumer_key=""
6   consumer_secret=""
7   access_token=""
8   access_token_secret=""
9
10  class StdOutListener(StreamListener):
11
12      def on_data(self, data):
13          print data
14          return True
15
16      def on_error(self, status):
17          print status
18
19  if __name__ == '__main__':
20      l = StdOutListener()
21      auth = OAuthHandler(consumer_key, consumer_secret)
22      auth.set_access_token(access_token, access_token_secret)
23
24      stream = Stream(auth, l)
25      stream.filter(track=['music'])

Line:      15 | Python                    ▲ | Soft Tabs: 4 ▼ | ✿ ▼ |  on_data(self, data)    ▲ | ●
```

Fig. 5.2 Access to the Twitter Web API to retrieve tweets with the term "music"

This process was complex, laborious, expensive, and required the reprogramming of client applications each time the provider made a change to the structure of web pages. With the emergence of Web API technologies, access to remote data became extremely simple as shown in Fig. 5.2 using, e.g., Python.

Two trends deserve to be mentioned: internal Web API and API Mashups.

Internal Web API   While many interfaces are made publicly visible, a trend is for companies to also start using Web API technologies internally to capitalize on important collections of data assets.

Web API Mashups   The use of Web API technologies enables third parties to mash data and functionality from various providers to create and deliver new products and services in response to emerging demand.

► **Opening Case**

5.1   Semantics in Cloud Services

As already explained in Chap. 2, cloud computing and cloud services are computing solutions based on the Internet. In the past, companies would run applications on computers physically located in their building, cloud computing allows users to access the same types of applications over the Internet. Google Docs and Dropbox are well known examples of cloud services.

The landscape of cloud computing is expanding rapidly in size, diversity, and heterogeneity. Amazon AWS Marketplace,[1] which was launched in 2012, has up to now more than 1250 cloud services available. Noor et al. [1] found that almost 6000 cloud services are already available on the web. The study carried out consisted of searching the web using a customized cloud service crawler engine to find websites that offered cloud services. More than half a million links were parsed. Websites were individually analyzed using a text mining classifier because these cloud services were described in natural language. Additionally, ProgrammableWeb,[2] a popular registry for web-based services lists over 10,000 interfaces to different services. There is an exponential growth of the service ecosystem on the web that can be seen over the last years.

The increasing size of the cloud computing landscape brings several challenges. One of the difficulties is related to search since cloud services are described using web pages in natural language at providers' websites. As an example, Fig. 5.3 shows LastFM (last.fm) and its Web API (last.fm/api). LastFM is a SaaS instance providing a large online music catalog and recommendation platform. Its Web API provides programmers access to all data stored by the service. Web search engines like Google, Yahoo, or Bing work relatively well for finding popular articles on a specific subject using keywords. However, when search engines based on keyword matching are applied to the search of a specific type of cloud service, they fail to provide adequate results. In fact, all currently available search tools suffer either from poor precision (i.e., too many irrelevant documents) or from poor recall (i.e., too few relevant documents are found). For example, using the Google search engine to find a cloud redundant storage service with a cost per TB lower than $25 per month, will return roughly 125,000 matching documents, but unfortunately it is not possible to immediately see any that matches the query. The results are littered with many other types of cloud services (e.g., "Amazon EC2 computing"), news articles on cloud services (e.g., "Top tips for doing a cloud storage cost analysis"), and reports (e.g., "How AWS pricing works").

This chapter describes how semantics can be used to address problems like the service search by enriching the description of cloud services using formal languages that enable computers to automatically interpret the description of the cloud services. Section 5.2 introduces semantic technologies that can be applied to create effective machine-readable service descriptions, as well as foundational design principles of Web APIs. Section 5.3 illustrates how Linked USDL [2], a semantic description language for services, can be used to enrich the description of a cloud service. Finally, Sect. 5.4 explains how formal descriptions can be explored by algorithms to support tasks such as search, matching, and ranking.

Throughout this chapter S-LastFM is used as an example for a cloud service with a Web API that leverages semantic technologies. S-LastFM is derived from LastFM, but offers slightly different functionalities and employs a formal language

---

[1] Amazon AWS Marketplace http://www.aws.amazon.com/marketplace.

[2] ProgrammableWeb http://www.programmableweb.com.

a Web API methods

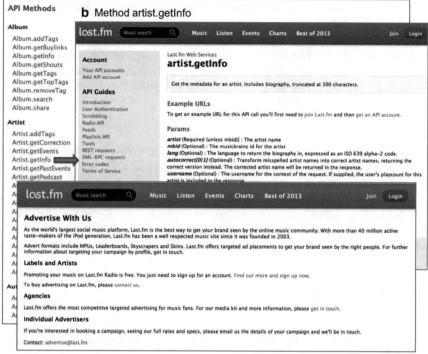

c Business characteristics

Fig. 5.3 The natural language description of technical (**a** and **b**) and business characteristics (**c**) of LastFM

to describe these functionalities: For the purpose of this chapter S-LastFM supports via its API the lookup of information of music artists, as well as the order of tickets for upcoming concerts. Further S-LastFM supports two interfaces that allow to search for such concerts.

5.1.1 Comprehensive Descriptions

Cloud services are complex entities that are not exhaustively characterized with descriptions for technical access via a Web API. In fact, pricing models, legal aspects, and service levels are elements that often need to be described explicitly when dealing with cloud services. While in the past the description of web services was mainly done at the technical level. Service description languages like WSDL [3] define the syntactical structure of service functionality descriptions. So-called semantic service description languages and frameworks like semantic annotations for WSDL (SA-WSDL) [4] and the semantic markup for web services OWL-S [5] allow functionality descriptions that can be interpreted by machines. However, cloud services are more complex entities that also require the description of business and operational information.

▶ **Definition (WSDL)** The Web Service Description Language (WSDL) is an XML format for describing network services as a set of endpoints operating on messages containing either document-oriented or procedure-oriented information (http://www.w3.org/TR/wsdl).

Business Perspective

A business-sensitive perspective represents a paradigm shift from the IT view on cloud services to a commercial view. For example, LastFM includes a natural language description of legal terms and policies, a pricing model, contact information, and a network of partners. This information is expressed in the form of natural language published as web pages, which makes it difficult for a computer to interpret it. Table 5.1 provides a set of examples extracted from the LastFM website. Section 5.3 explains how Linked USDL is used to include this information in structured descriptions.

Operational Perspective

The operational perspective is concerned with the elementary operations that a service provides. For example, LastFM provides more than 140 operations classified in 14 categories. Figure 5.3 shows the web page that displays all the operations, which are part of the LastFM Web API. These operations can be orchestrated to develop more advanced and complex cloud services, which can in turn be sold to consumers. Formally capturing this information using Linked USDL is also described in Sect. 5.3.

Technical Perspective

Cloud services are programmatically accessed using a Web API, an application-to-application communication technique. A Web API enables businesses to integrate

Table 5.1 The business perspective of LastFM

Charact.	Description	Web page (last.fm)
Terms of use	Terms that customers agree to follow to use the website. It also includes the definition of what it is considered to be "Acceptable Use"	/legal/terms
Privacy policy	A legal document that discloses some or all of the ways LastFM gathers, uses, discloses, and manages customers' data	/legal/privacy
Subscription terms	The terms that subscribers agree to when they purchase and use their LastFM subscription	/legal/subscription

third party cloud services, such as a customer relationship management system (e.g., SugarCRM[3]), with a minimal effort into their own local software systems. The technical perspective indicates, which web standards can be used to interact with cloud services. For example, the Web API provided by LastFM is supported by REST services. Although the approach to describe a Web API in natural language (see Fig. 5.3a, b) is the one most often used, it is far from adequate for the goal of increasing the degree of automation of tools managing cloud services. Section 5.2 looks into the technological approaches to construct a Web API and Sect. 5.3.3 explores how they can be enriched and described using semantic knowledge in the form of graph patterns.

5.1.2 Cloud Service Tasks

Enriching cloud service descriptions usually does not only provide more comprehensive technical access to, and understanding of, the offered functionality, but also enables a higher degree of automation in performing high level tasks. Examples include search, composition, comparison, and clustering of cloud services [6]. Section 5.4 explains how algorithms that make use of semantic service descriptions can be developed to execute high level tasks, specifically, the task of service search, which consists of:

- Matching a service request with cloud service descriptions.
- Ranking available services according to their degree of match with a request.

Search is particularly interesting as it often serves as the foundation of tasks related to cloud services, e.g., the development of mashups, which are characterised as applications that combine content from several sources on the web. Mashups are often focused on an ad-hoc integration of involved cloud services. In order to build mashups, an identification of suitable cloud services is necessary, which demands service search capabilities that go beyond simple keyword search. Additionally, semantic cloud service descriptions mitigate the challenge of the actual combination of cloud services [7–9], e.g., by providing a clear understanding of involved input and output data. Semantic descriptions mitigate the problem of integrating data from various cloud services within the mashups [10] as data integration based on Semantic Web Technologies is more robust than the development of individual data schema mappings between pairs of cloud services.

---

[3]http://www.sugarcrm.com.

5.2 Foundational Technologies

This chapter looks into the use of semantic technologies as a solution to describe cloud services from a business and technical perspectives. Therefore, this section provides a brief introduction to the technologies that are used, namely, web semantics and Linked Data. It also introduces a Web API architecture, which is broadly used to implement cloud services. The presented material is a prerequisite to understand the description of cloud services using Linked USDL and graph patterns in the following sections.

5.2.1 The Semantic Web

The World Wide Web Consortium (W3C) started to work on the concept of a Semantic Web with the objective of developing solutions for data integration and interoperability. The goal was to develop ways to allow computers to interpret (sometimes termed understand) information on the web. The Semantic Web identifies a set of technologies and standards that form the basic building blocks of an infrastructure that supports the vision of a meaningful web.

▶ **Definition (Semantic Web)** The Semantic Web, as defined by the W3C (http://www.w3.org/standards/semanticweb/), is an extension of the classical *web of documents* and describes a set technologies and standards with regard to common data formats and exchange protocols to support a *web of data*.

Linked USDL is a fixed service description schema that was formalized using two technologies from the Semantic Web: the Resource Description Framework (RDF) [11] and RDF Schema (RDFS). RDFS was used to define a schema and vocabulary to describe services. This schema is applied to create RDF graphs that describe individual services. Both, RDF and RDFS, are used by applications that need to interpret and to reason over the meaning of information instead of just parsing data for display purposes.

▶ **Definition (RDF)** The Resource Description Framework (RDF) is a standard model for data interchange on the web (http://www.w3.org/RDF/).

RDF

The Resource Description Framework was developed by the W3C to provide a common data model enabling the description of information that can be read and interpreted by computer applications. RDF provides a graph model for describing resources on the web. A resource is an element (document, web page, printer, user, etc.) on the web that is uniquely identifiable by a universal resource identifier (URI).

A URI serves as a means for identifying abstract or physical resources. For example, http://wikipedia.org/wiki/Metallica identifies the location of a web page about the band Metallica, and the following encoding `urn:isbn:1-420-09050-X` identifies a book using its ISBN. The RDF model is based upon the idea of making statements about resources in the form of a subject-predicate-object expression, a triple in RDF terminology. Each element has the following meaning:

Subject   is the resource; the "thing" that is being described.

Predicate   is an aspect about a resource that expresses the relationship between the subject and the object.

Object   is the value that is assigned to the predicate.

RDF is based on a directed graph data model: A set of nodes are connected by (directed) edges. Nodes and edges are labeled with identifiers (i.e., URIs) that make them distinguishable from each other and allow for the reconstruction of the original graph from the set of triples. RDF offers a limited set of syntactic constructs—only triples are allowed.

Every RDF document is equivalent to an unordered set of triples, which describe a graph. For example, the RDF triple that describes the statement: "Metallica is the artist of Garage Inc." is shown in Listing 5.1.

```
1  http://s-last.fm/album/garageInc , http://s-last.fm/artist ,
     http://s-last.fm/artist/metallica
```

Listing 5.1 Example of an RDF triple

The subject, `http://s-last.fm/album/garageInc`, is a resource representing a particular album. This resource has the property `http://s-last.fm/artist` with the value `http://s-last.fm/artist/metallica`. The statement can also be graphically represented as depicted in Fig. 5.4.

RDF blank nodes are used to express statements about individuals with certain properties without denominating the individual. The anonymity of blank nodes ensures that nothing besides the existence of the node can be inferred. Blank nodes, as the name suggests, may only occur in the subject or object position of a triple.

RDF literals describe data values that may only occur as property values. They are represented as strings and a shared interpretation is assumed to be given. Therefore, literals can be typed with a data type, e.g., using the existing types from the XML Schema specification [12]. Untyped literals are interpreted as strings.

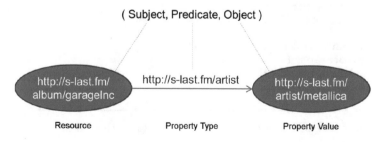

Fig. 5.4 An example of an RDF graph

Turtle Syntax

While RDF is a data model, there are several serialization formats that can represent RDF graphs. Originally, XML was proposed and has been widely adopted by RDF data processing and management tools. Note that the data model is not affected by the choice of any of the serialization formats; the graph structures remain unchanged. Turtle, the Terse RDF Triple Language, is one of the serializations. It is a compact syntax for RDF that allows for the representation of graphs in natural text form [13]. It will be used in the remainder of this chapter.

In Turtle, every triple is completed by a full stop. A URI is represented in angle brackets and literals are enclosed in quotation marks. White spaces outside identifiers and literals are ignored. One way to represent the RDF statement from Fig. 5.4 using Turtle is shown in Listing 5.2.

Turtle permits abbreviations to further increase readability. For example, multiple triples with the same subject or triples with same subject and predicate can be pooled as shown in Listing 5.3 for an extended example.

The first lines introduce prefix abbreviations of the namespaces used. `rdf:type` is a property to state that the resource `sfmalbum:garageInc` is an instance of the class `sfm:Album`.[4] The property `rdf:type` is often abbreviated to a. Capital first letters are used to indicate class names in contrast to individual and property names. The description of the location of the concert `sfmconcert:663239` makes use of a blank node representing the location resource. The location resource is not named but specified by its geographic coordinates embraced by square brackets.

```
1 <http://s-last.fm/album/garageInc> <http://s-last.fm/artist>
      <http://s-last.fm/artist/metallica> .
```

Listing 5.2 Turtle syntax representation of the RDF graph in Fig. 5.4

```
1 @prefix rdf: <http://www.w3.org/1999/02/22-rdf-syntax-ns#> .
2 @prefix sfm: <http://s-last.fm/> .
3 @prefix sfmalbum: <http://s-last.fm/album/> .
4 @prefix sfmartist: <http://s-last.fm/artist/> .
5 @prefix sfmconcert: <http://s-last.fm/concert/> .
6 @prefix geo: <http://www.w3.org/2003/01/geo/wgs84_pos#> .
7
8 sfmalbum:garageInc sfm:artist sfmartist:metallica ;
9    rdf:type sfm:Album .
10 sfmartist:metallica rdf:type sfm:Artist .
11
12 sfmconcert:663239 a sfm:Concert ;
13   sfm:location [
14     geo:lat "48.7932" ;
15     geo:long "9.2258"
16   ] .
```

Listing 5.3 Turtle syntax representation of an RDF graph using abbreviations

---

[4]Compare to the collection resources of a REST architecture introduced in Sect. 5.2.2.

```
1  <?xml version="1.0"?>
2  <rdf:RDF xmlns:sfm="http://s-last.fm/"
       xmlns:rdf="http://www.w3.org/1999/02/22-rdf-syntax-ns#">
3    <sfm:Album rdf:about="http://s-last.fm/album/garageInc">
4      <sfm:artist>
5        <sfm:Artist
             rdf:about="http://s-last.fm/artist/metallica"/>
6      </sfm:artist>
7    </sfm:Album>
8  </rdf:RDF>
```

Listing 5.4 RDF/XML serialization of the RDF graph from Listing 5.3

Many tools have been recently developed to support users in modeling structured data. Knowledge can be described with the support of ontology modeling tools like Protégé.[5] A traditional text editor can also be used to create service descriptions, but dedicated applications, such as TextMate for Mac, provide syntax highlighting for Turtle, auto-completion, syntax validation, and format conversions. All helpful features that facilitate the modeling task. RDF graphs can be validated against a schema and converted to different serialization formats (including RDF/XML, Turtle, and others) with web-based tools like validators[6,7] and translators [14]. Listing 5.4 shows the RDF graph of Listing 5.3 using the RDF/XML serialization.

RDF Schema

RDF Schema is a vocabulary language for RDF and allows the modeling of simple ontologies [15]. RDFS describes the logic dependencies among classes, properties, and values. While RDF provides universal means to encode facts about resources and their relationships, RDFS is used to express generic statements about sets of individuals (i.e., classes). RDFS associates the resources with classes (as shown in Listing 5.3), states the relations between classes, declares properties, and specifies the domain and range of properties.

▶ **Definition (RDFS)** RDF Schema (RDFS) provides a data-modelling vocabulary for RDF data. RDF Schema is an extension of the basic RDF vocabulary (http://www.w3.org/TR/rdf-schema/).

Classes in RDFS are much like classes in object oriented programming languages. They allow resources to be defined as instances of classes (by using the property rdf:type) and subclasses of classes. Subclass hierarchies can be specified by the RDFS property rdfs:subClassOf. The intuitive set theoretic semantics of class instances and subclasses (defined as member-of- and subset-of-relationships, respectively) ensures the reflexivity and transitivity of rdfs:subClassOf. The semantics of RDFS are specified in a W3C Recommendation [16].

---

[5]Protégé ontology editor and knowledge-base framework http://www.protege.stanford.edu.
[6]http://www.rdfabout.com/demo/validator/.
[7]http://www.w3.org/RDF/Validator/.

```
 1 @prefix rdfs: <http://www.w3.org/2000/01/rdf-schema#> .
 2 @prefix xsd: <http://www.w3.org/2001/XMLSchema#> .
 3
 4 sfm:artist rdf:type rdfs:Property ;
 5   rdfs:subPropertyOf sfc:contributor ;
 6   rdfs:label "Album artist"@en ;
 7   rdfs:domain sfm:album ;
 8   rdfs:range sfm:artist .
 9
10 sfmalbum:garageInc sfm:artist sfmartist:metallica ;
11   sfm:released "1998-11-23"^^xsd:date .
```

Listing 5.5 Specification of domain and range of properties in RDFS

Properties can be seen as attributes that are used to describe the resources by assigning values to them. RDF is used to assert property-related statements about objects, and RDFS can extend this capability by defining the class domain and the class range of such properties.

As the example shown in Listing 5.5 indicates, property hierarchies can be specified with the RDFS property rdfs:subPropertyOf. A complete overview over the language concepts is provided in [12]. Literals, as shown in line 6 of Listing 5.5, describe data values for properties. A language tag, such as @en for English, is used to specify the language of the literal. Data type information can also be appended to literals following the double caret (cf. line 11). Each data type is also identified by its URI, which in turn allows applications to interpret their meaning.

The adoption of semantic technologies in the context of services implies an increased modeling and development effort. The development of appropriate domain ontologies, if required, can be time consuming. In order to mitigate this burden, different ontology learning approaches can automatically compute an ontological representation of the domain, e.g., from given text documents describing the domain [17, 18].

Given the logical statement nature of the knowledge represented with ontologies, traditional relational databases are not the ideal storage and query platform for RDFS. Knowledge is represented as sets of subject-predicate-object-triples and these are most efficiently stored and accessed in dedicated triple stores, such as Jena TDB[8] and AllegroGraph.[9] Likewise, querying triple stores is done via specific query languages: the current standard language for querying RDF(S) is SPARQL [19].

---

[8]Jena TDB http://www.jena.apache.org/documentation/tdb/index.html.

[9]AllegroGraph http://www.franz.com/agraph/allegrograph/.

SPARQL

The RDF information encoded is readable and interpretable by machines, e.g., software programs that utilize the knowledge in applications like a concert ticket selling application. SPARQL is an SQL-like query language that allows the retrieval of data from RDF graphs. Answers are computed by matching patterns specified in a query against the given RDF graph.

▶ **Definition (SPARQL)** The Simple Protocol and RDF Query Language Protocol (SPARQL) is a query language for RDF (http://www.w3.org/TR/rdf-sparql-query/).

Basic graph patterns are used in SPARQL queries when a set of triple patterns is matched. Listing 5.6 shows the SPARQL graph pattern query syntax. In SPARQL, Turtle is used to describe the graph patterns. In this example of a query, the set of artists, i.e., the individuals of the class sfm:Artist, are retrieved and returned.

The answer of SELECT queries are bindings for the variables (denoted with a question mark) listed directly after the keyword SELECT. In the example, the query results in variable bindings for ?artist, which comprises, as shown in Table 5.2, a list of three artists represented by their URI as used in the RDF graph. Other query forms, e.g., ASK, DESCRIBE, and CONSTRUCT, allow queries for other kinds of information. ASK returns a boolean answer about the existence of a solution for a specified graph pattern. A DESCRIBE query returns an RDF graph describing specified resources.

SPARQL is also able to build RDF graphs and return them as results. The example from Listing 5.7 shows how the CONSTRUCT query form can be used to list places in which bands have played. Therefore, this query specifies a template used to build a graph-based on the matching results of the query.

```
1 PREFIX rdf: <http://www.w3.org/1999/02/22-rdf-syntax-ns#>
2 PREFIX sfm: <http://s-last.fm/>
3
4 SELECT ?artist
5 WHERE
6 {
7   ?artist rdf:type sfm:Artist .
8 }
```

Listing 5.6 SPARQL query to retrieve instances of the class Artist

Table 5.2 Results of the SPARQL query shown in Listing 5.6

Artist
<http://s-last.fm/artist/metallica>
<http://s-last.fm/artist/rihanna>
<http://s-last.fm/artist/eminem>

```
1 CONSTRUCT { ?artist sfm:playedIn ?place }
2 WHERE
3 {
4   ?artist rdf:type sfm:Artist .
5   ?artist sfm:event ?event .
6   ?event geo:located ?place .
7 }
```

Listing 5.7 SPARQL query asking for artists and the places they have performed at

Linked Data

Linked Data is a subset of the Semantic Web that adheres to the principles of the Semantic Web architecture: commitment to the use of RDF(S) and URIs to denote things. In particular, Linked Data adheres to the following four design principles [20]:

- Use URIs to name "things".
- Use HTTP URIs so that people can lookup the names.
- Lookups on those URIs provide further information describing the "things" in RDF.
- Include links to other URIs in the descriptions to allow people to discover further "things".

The use of an HTTP URI allows machines and humans to lookup the name and get useful information about resources adhering to the RDF and SPARQL standards. The HyperText Transfer Protocol (HTTP) is prevalently used to exchange data on the web.[10] The use of an HTTP URI further guarantees the uniqueness of the identifier.

The resolvable resource description should contain links to other resource identifiers so that users can discover more things.[11] Linkage comprises external and internal links (for any predicate) and the reuse of external vocabularies, which can be interlinked. The special property `owl:sameAs` specifies the equivalence of different identifiers that refer to the same thing. For example, the band Metallica is described in different vocabularies or websites. Overlapping data of different sources can be aligned by equivalence statements as illustrated in Listing 5.8.

Adhering to the Linked Data principles has many advantages that apply in the context of structured representation of data on the web but also in the context of the formal description of services. For example, for service search, selection, composition, and analysis.

---

[10]See IETF RFC7230 at http://tools.ietf.org/html/rfc7230 et seq. for details.

[11]Linked Data—Design Issues http://www.w3.org/DesignIssues/LinkedData.

```
1 @prefix owl: <http://www.w3.org/2002/07/owl#> .
2
3 <http://dbpedia.org/resource/Metallica> owl:sameAs
     <http://s-last.fm/artist/metallica> .
```

Listing 5.8 Establishing the equivalence of resources using the property `owl:sameAs`

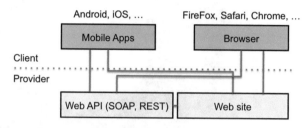

Fig. 5.5 Architecture of services provided over a web API and described using web pages

5.2.2 Web API Design Principles

Application Programming Interfaces (API) are used to provide general access to the functionality of a services. Client applications like mobile applications (apps) or web pages containing interactive web forms can make use of an API to offer these functionalities to end users. The resulting layered architecture depicted in Fig. 5.5 provides the advantage that applications using the Web API can be developed by the service provider as well as third party developers, thus increasing the potential reach of the service.

For example, the provider of S-LastFM offers the service functionality with an API described at s-last.fm/api. The S-LastFM homepage makes use of this API to offer the services to the consumers. Additionally, third party developers can develop mobile or web applications to provide the services of S-LastFM on mobile devices. According to a W3C note,[12] when constructing a Web API two general alternatives for the implementation exist:

- An API that exposes an arbitrary set of operations.
- A resource-oriented API with a uniform set of stateless operations.

Both types correspond to the types of cloud services described in Chap. 2. This section only gives a brief overview of operations oriented approach and focuses on the architecture of resource-oriented interfaces, since the latter are predominantly used on the web (see Fig. 5.6): A detailed comparison of both API paradigms is available from [21, 22].

---

[12]http://www.w3.org/TR/ws-arch/#relwwwrest.

Fig. 5.6 Protocol usage of
public web interfaces
according to
ProgrammableWeb

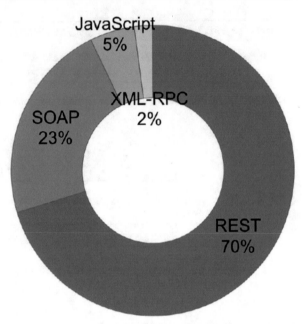

ProgrammableWeb.com 12.09.2013

Operation-Oriented API

An API with arbitrary operations is often designed by adhering to the variety of specifications and languages commonly referred to as the WS-* stack. However, other variants exist, e.g., remote procedure calls. The main characteristic of this style of API is that the operations that make out the service are directly defined and offered. When implemented for cloud services such an API uses the web as a transport layer for the data and entails a high degree of freedom. For example, the S-LastFM API can offer the following operations. Client applications can invoke these operations to invoke the desired functionalities.

- `findArtistInfo` using the name of an artist as input.
- `findConcerts` using an identifier of concerts as input.
- `orderConcertTicket` using an identifier of the concert as input.

Resource-Oriented API

A resource-oriented API complies to the constraints of a Representational State Transfer (REST) architecture [23]. According to the Richardson maturity model [24], REST is identified as the interaction between a client (i.e., an application) and a server based on three principles:

1. The use of URI-identified resources.
2. The use of a constrained set of operations, i.e., the HTTP methods, to access and manipulate resource states.

3. The application of hypermedia controls, i.e., the data representing a resource contains links to other resources. Links allow a client to navigate from one resource to another during interaction.

According to statistics from ProgrammableWeb, the majority of publicly accessible interfaces are designed according to REST principles (cf. Fig. 5.6). Therefore, this chapter will elaborate in the following on the concepts of REST in more detail.

Resources

A REST API offers the service functionality under the primacy of resources rather than operations. A resource can be a real world object or a data object on the web. Resources are uniquely identified with a URI. The representation of a resource details its current state, i.e., relevant information associated with the resource. Resources can be grouped into collections. These collections in turn are also URI-identified resources themselves (so called *collection resources*). The resulting tree-like structure of the resources is similar to the well known directory structure of file systems. In the case of the S-LastFM API, collection resources representing artists, concerts, etc. correspond to the folders of a file system, while the concrete instances of artists and concerts correspond to files put into the corresponding folders. In order to illustrate this concept, Table 5.3 lists examples of instances and collection resources of the S-LastFM Web API.

Constrained Operations Set

The interaction of client applications with cloud services via a REST API is not based on the call of API-specific operations but rather on the direct manipulation of exposed resource representations or the creation of new resource representations. A manipulation of the state representation implies that the represented resource is manipulated accordingly. For such manipulations, REST offers only a constrained set of operations that can be applied to a resource. These operations are shared by all interfaces following REST principles, which increases interoperability and understandability of the interfaces. Nevertheless, not all resources must necessarily allow the application of all possible methods.

Some of the methods can carry input data as a payload, which describes the intended new state of the addressed resource.[13] On the web, the allowed operations are the HTTP methods (cf. Table 5.4) and the identifier of a resource is an HTTP URI, which makes the web the underlying platform for the API. For example, S-LastFM uses the following methods:

- GET. Almost all resources of S-LastFM allow for the application of GET to retrieve information. A GET on one of the collection resources gives an overview of the known instances of concerts and artists. The retrieval of the information

---

[13]The HTTP POST method is a noteworthy exception as it permits the submission of data to process, which is similar to an RPC call and therefore should be used carefully.

Table 5.3 Resources of the S-LastFM web API

URI/description
http://s-last.fm/artist
A collection resource of music artists with a representation that contains links to all artists
http://s-last.fm/artist/metallica
http://s-last.fm/artist/rihanna
http://s-last.fm/artist/eminem
Resources representing individual music artists. The representation contains information about the artist (e.g., name and genre) and links to upcoming concerts
http://s-last.fm/concert
A collection resource of concerts with links to all concerts
http://s-last.fm/concert/1234
http://s-last.fm/concert/1235
http://s-last.fm/concert/1236
Resources representing individual concerts with information about the concert (e.g., location, date, and price per ticket) and links to the performing artist and to the `ticketorder` resource
http://s-last.fm/ticketorder
Collection resource of ticket orderings with a representation containing links to all ticket orderings
http://s-last.fm/ticketorder/567
http://s-last.fm/ticketorder/568
http://s-last.fm/ticketorder/569
Resources representing individual ticket orderings with information about the ordering (e.g., delivery and address) and link to corresponding concert

Table 5.4 Overview of HTTP methods (excerpt)

Method	Safe	Idempotent	Description
GET	✓	✓	Retrieve the current state of a resource
OPTIONS	✓	✓	Retrieve a description of possible interactions
DELETE		✓	Delete a resource
PUT		✓	Create or overwrite a resource with the submitted input
POST			Send input as subordinate to a resource or submit input to a data-handling process

of a specific ticket order however is only allowed with the correct credentials. Only a user who created the ordering can look it up again. The retrieval of the collection resource for all orderings is generally not permitted.

- POST. The collection resource for ticket orderings allows POST to enable users to add a new ticket order for a specific concert.
- PUT. S-LastFM allows PUT only to overwrite existing ticket orders, to enable users to update an order.
- DELETE. Ticket orders can also be canceled with DELETE up to a predefined time before the concert takes place.

Two types of methods exist: safe and unsafe. Safe methods guarantee not to affect the current states of resources, while unsafe methods change the state of the resources. Furthermore, most of the methods are idempotent. The repeated application of an idempotent method on a resource does not change the state of the resource beyond the first application of the method. For example, if a client application deletes a resource, deleting it again has no effect.

Hypermedia Controls

A REST API fosters loose coupling between clients and services on the premise that client applications do not need to know about all resources in advance. The retrievable representations of some known resources contain links to other resources that the client can discover during runtime. Applications can use such discovered resources to perform further interaction steps. Collection resources specifically contain links to all the resources in the collection. This architectural design allows client applications to be robust toward changes in the API, because the application has to react to whatever it finds when it interacts with the API [24, 25].

For example, at the behest of an end user a client application can interact with the resources of S-LastFM in the following way:

1. Retrieve the information (i.e., representation) of a specific artist, which contains links to upcoming concerts (method GET).
2. Retrieve the information of one of the concerts, which contains a link to the collection of ticket orderings (method GET).
3. Create in this collection a new resource representing a new ticket order (method PUT).

Note that only the identifier of the resource representing the artist needs to be known in advance (i.e., before the interaction can start). This could be further refined by providing a search interface over the available artists as contained in the artist collection resource.

In a REST architecture, no constraints are given on how the status of a resource has to be represented. There is no defined standard regarding data model or serialization format of the data that detail the current state of a resource or the input and output data of a method. Client application and API are, however, supposed to agree on the format of the exchanged data and implicitly on how the data is supposed to be interpreted. The process of establishing this agreement is called *content negotiation*. For different application scenarios such an agreement requires vendor specific content types (i.e., content types defined by the service provider) for the individual services to convey the meaning of the communicated data. The idea behind vendor specific content types is that service providers can reuse content types and application developers can make use of specific content type processors in their applications to work with the data. In practice, however, most Web API providers simply make use of standard non-specific content types, e.g., text/xml or application/json [26]. Developers therefore have to write applications that are individually adapted for the API they make use of. Section 5.3.3 details another solution to this problem based on Linked Data resource representations.

5.3   Linked USDL

The need for descriptions at the business and operational levels redirected efforts to the development of new languages to capture these perspectives beside the technical one. USDL [27], the Unified Service Description Language, is probably the most comprehensive attempt. It provides a shared semantic vocabulary[14] to describe services.

▶ **Definition (USDL and Linked USDL)** The Universal Service Description Language (USDL) is a platform-neutral language for describing services. Linked USDL is a remodeled version of USDL build upon the Linked Data principles.

The initial USDL development started in 2008 to describe business, software, and real world services using a computer-understandable specification to make them available on the web. The Internet of Services (see Chap. 2) requires services to be traded and, thus, places emphasis on the description of business characteristics such as pricing, legal aspects, and service level agreements. This was the main motivation to create USDL. In 2012, a new version named Linked USDL [28] was developed based on Linked Data principles and represented with RDFS. This is the version which will be explored in this chapter.

5.3.1   Linked USDL Family

Linked USDL is segmented into modules. The objective of this division is to reduce the overall complexity of service descriptions by enabling providers to only use the modules needed. Currently, five modules exist:

usdl-core   The core module covers concepts central to a service description. It includes operational aspects such as interaction points between the provider and consumer that occur during provisioning and the description of the business entities involved.

usdl-price   The pricing module provides a range of concepts which are needed to adequately describe price structures in the service industry.

usdl-agreement   The service level agreement module gathers functional and non-functional information on the quality of the service provided, e.g., availability, reliability, and response time.

usdl-sec   This module aims to describe the main security properties of a service. Service providers can use this specification to describe the security goals, profiles, and mechanisms.

---

[14]A vocabulary is also known called a "schema", a "data dictionary", or an"ontology".

usdl-ipr   This module captures the usage rights of a service. Rights are often
associated with the concept of copyright which implicitly exists with the creation
of an artifact (i.e., a service) and does not need to be registered with an office in
order to be granted.

For example, customers and providers can use usdl-agreement [29] to
create service level agreements to monitor whether the actual service delivery
complies with the agreed service level. In case of violations, penalties or com-
pensations can be directly derived. The module usdl-ipr is fundamental for
business environments to define rights and obligations when consuming a service.
The official Linked USDL website is available at linked-usdl.org and the current
Linked USDL modules, use cases, and documentation are available at GitHub –
http://www.github.com/linked-usdl/.

5.3.2   The Core Module

The Linked USDL Core can be regarded as the center of the Linked USDL family
since it ties together all aspects of service description distributed across the USDL
modules. Figure 5.7 shows the conceptual diagram on the core module. Classes
are represented with an oval, while properties with an edge. Linked USDL Core
has 12 classes (e.g., Service, ServiceOffering, InteractionPoint,
and Role) and 13 properties (e.g., receives, hasInteractionPoint,
withBusinessRole, and hasInteractionType).

To explain how a service can be described with Linked USDL, S-LastFM will be
used as an example. Most of the information used for the modeling was retrieved
from the LastFM web site and shown in Fig. 5.3. The description was written using
the Turtle language.

Before starting with the formal representation of the S-LastFM service, a set
of prefixes needs to be defined to ease the modeling with Turtle. Listing 5.9
shows the prefixes that refer to the Linked USDL modules which will be used in
this running example (lines 1–5). Other prefixes required, but not shown, refer to
vocabularies such as Dublin Core[15] (shown in the example with :dcterms) and
GoodRelations[16] (:gr). The extract also shows the standard heading statements
required to create a service instance (lines 7–13).

```
1 @prefix usdl: <http://linked-usdl.org/ns/usdl-core#> .
2 @prefix usdl-br:
       <http://linked-usdl.org/ns/usdl-business-roles#> .
3 @prefix usdl-it:
       <http://linked-usdl.org/ns/usdl-interaction-types#> .
```

---

[15]The Dublin Core Schema is a vocabulary that can be used to describe web resources (video,
images, web pages, etc.), as well as physical resources such as books.

[16]GoodRelations is a vocabulary for product, price, store, and company data that can be embedded
into web pages to be automatically processed by intelligent applications.

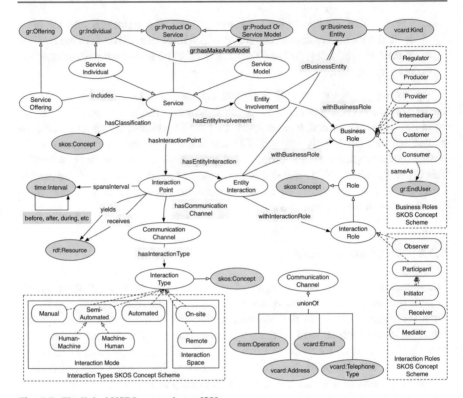

Fig. 5.7 The linked USDL core schema [28]

```
4 @prefix usdl-ir:
      <http://linked-usdl.org/ns/usdl-interaction-roles#> .
5 @prefix usdl-pr: <http://linked-usdl.org/ns/usdl-pricing#> .
6 ...
7 <> a owl:Ontology ;
8   rdfs:label "S-LastFM service description" ;
9   dcterms:title "S-LastFM service description" ;
10  dcterms:description "Enhanced description of last.fm, a
        popular music recommendation service." ;
11  dcterms:created "2014-01-17"^^xsd:date ;
12  dcterms:modified "2014-01-18"^^xsd:date ;
13  owl:versionInfo "001" .
```

Listing 5.9 Prefixes and standard statements for the S-LastFM service description

The Service

The next step is to specify the actual service to be described. The class
usdl:Service provides the entry point for the description. As shown in
Listing 5.10, the new service was named service_SLastFM. The specification
also includes:

```
1  :service_SLastFM a usdl:Service ;
2    gr:description "A semantic recommendation service for
       music." ;
3
4    usdl:hasServiceModel :model_SLastFM ;
5    usdl:hasEntityInvolvement [
6      a usdl:EntityInvolvement ;
7      usdl:ofBusinessEntity :be_SLastFM_Ltd ;
8      usdl:withBusinessRole usdl-br:provider
9    ] ;
10   usdl:hasInteractionPoint :ip_Advertise ;
11   usdl:hasInteractionPoint :ip_TicketOrder .
```

Listing 5.10 The S-LastFM service class

- Associating a service model with the service.
- Specifying the business entities participating during service provisioning.
- Enumerating the interaction points provided by the service.

The class usdl:ServiceModel is used to create groupings of services that share a number of characteristics. For example, a service model for S-LastFM can group services characterized by supplying online music. In the same line of thought, the service "Vodafone unlimited internet service" may belong to the grouping "Internet provisioning service". The example from Listing 5.10 associates the service service_SLastFM with the service model model_SLastFM[17] using the property usdl:hasServiceModel (line 4).

The class usdl:EntityInvolvement captures the gr:BusinessEntity involved in the service delivery and the usdl:Role they play (lines 5–9). Entity involvement is a fundamental construct introduced in Linked USDL to enable capturing service networks [30]. This enables specifying, for instance, that a given music service is provided by a certain company or that a third party is involved in the service delivery chain. The properties usdl:ofBusinessEntity and usdl:withBusinessRole enable to specify the business entities involved during the provisioning of a service and also the role that each one takes. In Listing 5.10, the business entity is defined with the class be_SLastFM_Ltd and its role is defined as usdl-br:provider. Linked USDL provides a default taxonomy of basic business roles that cover the most typical ones encountered during service modeling such as regulator, intermediary, producer, and consumer. The prefix usdl-br identifies the taxonomy usdl-business-roles[18] which defines the default roles available.

---

[17]The definition of the service model model_SLastFM is not provided in this running example.
[18]http://www.linked-usdl.org/ns/usdl-business-roles.

```
1  :be_SLastFM_Ltd a gr:BusinessEntity ;
2    foaf:homepage <http://slast.fm/> ;
3    foaf:logo
         <http://cdn.last.fm/flatness/badges/lastfm_red.gif> ;
4
5    gr:hasISICv4 "5920"^^xsd:string ;
6    gr:hasNAICS "512220"^^xsd:string ;
7    gr:legalName "SLast.fm Ltd."^^xsd:string ;
8    gr:taxID "830 2738 46"^^xsd:string ;
9
10   vcard:hasAddress
11     [ a vcard:Work ;
12       vcard:country-name "UK"@en ] .
```

Listing 5.11 Description of the business entity providing the S-LastFM service

Listing 5.11 illustrates the description of the company providing the S-LastFM service with the class be_SLastFM_Ltd. The description includes the ISIC (International Standard Industrial Classification of All Economic Activities) code for S-LastFM: 5920 – sound recording and music publishing activities. It also specifies the NAICS (North American Industry Classification System) code, legal name, tax ID number, and country where the company is located (lines 5–8).

 The North American Industrial Classification System (NAICS) and the International Standard of Industrial Classification (ISIC) codes are six digit numbers used to describe the primary economic activity of businesses. They classification codes can be used for looking up reports on specific industries or to find companies within a certain industry.

Interaction Points

The extract from Listing 5.10 also defines two interaction points, ip_Advertise and ip_TicketOrder, for the service service_SLastFM. An interaction point (usdl:InteractionPoint) represents an actual step in performing the operations made available by a service. On a personal level, an interaction point can model that consumer and provider need to meet in person to exchange service parameters or resources during service delivery (e.g., documents that are processed by the provider). On a technical level, this can translate into calling a web service operation (most cloud services are accessed and invoked via web services). An interaction point can be initiated by the consumer or the provider. Since interaction points may be long running and have an ordering with respect to other interaction points, they are subclasses of TimeSpanningEntity. It is, therefore, possible to express temporal relationships between interaction points such as "before" or "after". For richer expressions, the time ontology constructs can be used.

Listing 5.12 shows the interaction point ip_Advertise which enables customers to book advertising campaigns and inquire about rates and specs. Interaction points define four main pieces of information:

```
1   :ip_Advertise a usdl:InteractionPoint ;
2   dcterms:title "S-LastFM Advertisement"@en ;
3   dcterms:description "If you are interested in booking a
        campaign, seeing our full rates and specs, please send
        us the details of your campaign and we will get in
        touch."@en ;
4
5   usdl:hasCommunicationChannel [
6     a usdl:CommunicationChannel ;
7       vcard:country-name "UK";
8       vcard:locality "London";
9       vcard:postal-code "SE1 0NZ";
10      vcard:street-address "Last.fm Ltd., 5-11 Lavington
            Street" ;
11      usdl:hasInteractionType usdl-it:manual ;
12      usdl:hasInteractionType usdl-it:remote
13  ] ;
14
15  usdl:hasCommunicationChannel [
16    a usdl:CommunicationChannel ;
17      vcard:hasEmail <mailto:advertise@slast.fm> ;
18      usdl:hasInteractionType usdl-it:manual ;
19      usdl:hasInteractionType usdl-it:remote
20  ] ;
21
22  usdl:hasEntityInteraction [
23    a usdl:EntityInteraction ;
24    usdl:withBusinessRole usdl-br:provider ;
25    usdl:withInteractionRole usdl-ir:participant
26  ] ;
27
28  usdl:hasEntityInteraction [
29    a usdl:EntityInteraction ;
30    usdl:withBusinessRole usdl-br:customer ;
31    usdl:withInteractionRole usdl-ir:participant
32  ] ;
33
34  usdl:receives dbpedia:Advertising ;
35  usdl:yields dbpedia:Contract .
```

Listing 5.12 An interaction point involving human interaction

- The communication channels that customers or applications can use to interact with a service.
- The entities that are involved during the realization of the interaction point.
- The resources that are needed for an interaction point to execute properly.
- The resources that are generated from the execution of an interaction point.

The example identifies two types of communication channels (lines 5–20):

- `vcard:Address`
- `vcard:Email`

These classes are not shown in the example since they are all grouped by the class `usdl:CommunicationChannel`.

Communication Channels

Communication channels are additionally characterized by their interaction type. Linked USDL provides two default taxonomies covering the main modes (i.e., automated, semi-automated, or manual) and the interaction space (i.e., on-site or remote). The example describes how customers can ask for information to advertise a campaign with S-LastFM. This can be done by using "snail" mail or email. All the communication channels of the example require a manual (`usdl-it:manual`) and remote (`usdl-it:remote`) interaction. This means that humans, not software applications, will be involved in the interaction with S-LastFM.

The example also indicates the role of the two entities that will interact (lines 22–32): both the provider and customer are participants. This information is represented using the class `usdl:EntityInteraction` which links interaction points to business entity types (e.g., provider, intermediary, and customer) using the property `usdl:withBusinessRole` and the role they play within the interaction (e.g., initiator, mediator, and receiver) using the property `usdl:withInteractionRole`.

Receives and Yields

Listing 5.12 shows that the interaction point receives (`usdl:receives`) and yields (`usdl:yields`) resources (lines 41–42). Receives is the input required and yields corresponds to the outcome produced by an interaction point. The example shows that the interaction point `ip_Advertise` receives a resource identified by the concept `dbpedia:Advertising` and yields a resource identified by the concept `dbpedia:Contract`. Since dbpedia is the computer-understandable formal mirror of wikipedia, the use of these two properties reach twofold objectives:

- Provide a natural language description via wikipedia.com which is suitable to be interpreted by humans.
- Provide a formal description via dbpedia.org which is suitable to be processed by software applications.

Naturally, other computer-processable data sources such as freebase.com can also be used.

Automated Communication Channels

While the previous example of an interaction point involved only human participants, the example from Listing 5.13 illustrates a fully automated interaction which

```
1  :ip_TicketOrder a usdl:InteractionPoint ;
2    dcterms:title "Ticket Orders"@en ;
3    dcterms:description "Collection of all ticket orders;
         allows to submit new ticket orders"@en ;
4
5    usdl:hasCommunicationChannel [
6      a sfm:TicketOrder ;
7        usdl:hasInteractionType usdl-it:automated ;
8        usdl:hasInteractionType usdl-it:remote ;
9    ] ;
10
11   usdl:hasEntityInteraction [
12     a usdl:EntityInteraction ;
13     usdl:withBusinessRole usdl-br:provider ;
14     usdl:withInteractionRole usdl-ir:participant ;
15   ] ;
16
17   usdl:hasEntityInteraction [
18     a usdl:EntityInteraction ;
19     usdl:withBusinessRole usdl-br:consumer ;
20     usdl:withInteractionRole usdl-ir:initiator ;
21     usdl:withInteractionRole usdl-ir:receiver ;
22   ] ;
23
24   usdl:receives sfm:Concert ;
25   usdl:yields sfm:TicketOrder .
```

Listing 5.13 An interaction point for an application-driven interaction

does not require human intervention (lines 5–9). This means that on both sides of the communication channel, applications will be involved during service provisioning by exchanging data. This requires a well-defined API which must be understood by applications.

The most well-known approaches to describe services semantically are OWL-S, WSMO, SAWSDL, and WSMO-Lite when it comes to SOAP Web services, and MicroWSMO and SA-REST for REST Web services [28]. In order to cater for interoperability, Linked USDL Core uses what can essentially be considered the maximum common denominator between these formalisms: the minimal service model.[19] The MSM is a simple RDFS vocabulary to capture the semantics of SOAP and REST Web services in a common model.

The resources exposed in a REST architecture can be seen as communication channels of the service. However, the hypermedia constrains (cf. Sect. 5.2.2) of REST imply that clients are supposed to discover many of the resources by following links. Therefore, not all the exposed resources need to be described and covered by a Linked USDL description: only the resources a client is expected to start its interactions with need to be included as interaction points in a Linked USDL

---

[19]http://www.iserve.kmi.open.ac.uk/ns/msm/.

description. Additional resources will be discovered. In the case of S-LastFM, the resource sfm:TicketOrder can be considered an entry point for an interaction. In contrast, the individual resources representing the artists or concerts are not necessary to include in the Linked USDL description, since clients do not start their interactions with these resources directly.[20]

Listing 5.14 shows how the operation sfm:TicketOrder can be semantically described. In this example, the class msm:Operation is extended with the property gdp:graphPattern to provide a link to graph pattern-based descriptions (explained in Sect. 5.3.3) that detail the exchanged data when ordering a concert ticket by interacting via the communication channel. This new property is attached to the only given part of the message content of input and output respectively.

Service Offering

A usdl:ServiceOffering is an offer made by a gr:BusinessEntity of one or more instances of usdl:Service to customers. An offering usually associates a price, legal terms of use, and service level agreement with a service. In other words, it makes a service a tradable entity. Listing 5.15 illustrates an offering named offering_SLastFM for the service service_SLastFM (lines 1 and 11). Such a service offering may have limited validity over geographical regions or time, the offering adds various pieces of information such as temporal validity, eligible regions, and accepted payment methods (lines 2–10).

Finally, the last part of the example indicates that the classes legal_SLastFM and price_SLastFM describe the legal aspects and the price of the S-LastFM service, respectively (lines 12–13).[21]

```
1  sfm:TicketOrder a msm:Operation ;
2    msm:hasInput _:input ;
3    msm:hasOutput _:output ;
4    hrest:hasMethod "POST"^^xsd:string .
5
6  _:input a msm:MessageContent ;
7    msm:hasPart _:in1 .
8  _:in1 gpd:graphPattern <http://s-last.fm/ticketorder/input> .
9
10 _:output a msm:MessageContent ;
11   msm:hasPart _:out1 .
12 _:out gpd:graphPattern <http://s-last.fm/ticketorder/output> .
```

Listing 5.14 Example of a communication channel of type msm:Operation from Listing 5.13

---

[20]Since clients might require descriptions for all resources to interact with them, not included resources have to provide similar information directly, which can be retrieved at runtime for example via the HTTP OPTIONS method.

[21]The description of the legal and price modules are not covered in this chapter.

```
1  :offering_SLastFM a usdl:ServiceOffering ;
2     gr:validFrom "2014-01-24T00:00:00+01:00"^^xsd:dateTime ;
3     gr:validThrough "2015-12-24T00:00:00+01:00"^^xsd:dateTime ;
4     gr:eligibleRegions "DE"^^xsd:string, "US-CA"^^xsd:string ;
5     gr:acceptedPaymentMethods gr:VISA,
          gr:ByBankTransferInAdvance ;
6     gr:eligibleDuration [
7        a gr:QuantitativeValue ;
8        gr:hasValueInteger "1"^^xsd:int ;
9        gr:hasUnitOfMeasurement "MON"^^xsd:string
10    ] ;
11    usdl:includes :service_SLastFM ;
12
13    usdl:legal :legal_SLastFM ;
14    usdl:price :price_SLastFM .
```

Listing 5.15 A concrete offering of a service

5.3.3 Technical API Descriptions

A Linked USDL description of an application web service with a remote and automated communication channel also entails a description on the technical level, besides the business and operation levels. Such technical information can be used by clients for the invocation of the service or the automation of high level tasks (see Sect. 5.4). This section explains how technical information can be provided for REST architectures, where resources are represented with Linked Data.

Service Resource States

For resource-driven or REST-based services, the technical description of the API does not have to be focused on the operations. Since REST architectures only use a constrained and shared set of operations, the intuition or meaning of the operations is always inherently clear and well defined. For example, in the case of a REST API based on HTTP, the semantics of the available operations[22] (cf., Table 5.4) are defined in an RFC specification[23] and therefore do not need to be explicitly described further in the service description.

A REST architecture offers the functionality of a service by allowing the states of resources to be changed. It is these possibilities to manipulate a resource that need to be described. The manipulation of a resource state is the result of an application of an unsafe method at a resource, where the payload (i.e., input data) details the desired state change. The output data that is returned after the application of a method details the new state of the affected resource [31]. Therefore, to describe the manipulation possibilities of a resource, it is sufficient to detail the possible inputs

---

[22]The operations of an HTTP-based REST API are also referred to with the term *HTTP methods*.
[23]See IETF RFC7230 at http://tools.ietf.org/html/rfc7230 et seq. for details

and the resulting outputs for the available operations of the resource. Furthermore, the relation between the input and output (i.e., how the input influences the resulting state) needs to be made explicit.

In a REST architecture, client application and server are supposed to form a contract with content negotiation, not only on the data format but implicitly also on the semantics of the communicated data, i.e., an agreement on how the data has to be interpreted [25]. Since the agreement on the semantics is only implicit, programmers developing client applications have to manually gain a deep understanding of the provided data and the manipulation possibilities, often based on natural text descriptions. However, the reliance on natural language descriptions for the interfaces lead to mashup designs in which programmers are forced to write glue code with little or no automation and to manually consolidate and integrate the exchanged data.

Linked Data (see Sect. 5.2.1 "Linked Data") unifies a standardized interaction model with the possibility to align vocabularies using RDF, RDFS, and OWL. However, the interactions are currently constrained to simple data retrieval. Following the motivation to look beyond the exposure of fixed data sets, the extension of Linked Data with REST technologies has been explored and many approaches recognize the value of combining REST services and Linked Data [32–35]. These approaches propose to use Linked Data to represent the state of a resource, and as a format for input and output data.[24] The use of unique identifiers as central elements of Linked Data mitigates the problem of the only implicitly negotiated semantics of the communicated data (see Sect. 5.2.2). Furthermore, Linked Data is already focused on the interlinkage of resources, which makes the design of a hypermedia control-driven API architecture straight forward.

Graph Pattern Descriptions

Since Linked Data uses a graph-based data model, many existing approaches [33–35] propose graph patterns as a means to describe the input and output data of possible resource manipulations. The use of graph patterns enable to automatically recognize the vocabularies that are understood by an API and detail how the data representing the resource states is structured. In the scenario of ordering a concert ticket via S-LastFM a user has to (mediated by an application) create a new order resource. An example of the state of an order resource (e.g., identified by http://s-last.fm/ticketorder/567) expressed with Linked Data is shown in Listing 5.16.

The state representation of the resource details the price of the tickets, the amount, and the estimated time until the tickets are delivered (lines 11–13). Additionally, the resource contains links to the user who ordered the tickets and to the concert (lines 8 and 10). Following the link to the resource representing the user can, e.g., bring results regarding the delivery address or credit card details for payment. Some of the elements in the state representation are different for every individual order resource. These variable elements are either provided by the user that submits the order via the client application or they are set by S-LastFM directly:

---

[24]If another format like JSON or XML is used, a description needs to make the implicit semantics of the data explicit.

```
1  @prefix rdf: <http://www.w3.org/1999/02/22-rdf-syntax-ns#> .
2  @prefix sfm: <http://s-last.fm/> .
3  @prefix sfmorder: <http://s-last.fm/ticketorder> .
4  @prefix sfmuser: <http://s-last.fm/user> .
5  @prefix sfmconcert: <http://s-last.fm/concert> .
6
7  sfmorder:567 rdf:type sfm:Ticketorder .
8  sfmorder:567 sfm:user sfm:JohnDoe .
9  sfm:JohnDoe rdf:type sfm:User .
10 sfmorder:567 sfm:event sfmconcert:1234 .
11 sfmorder:567 sfm:price "120 USD"@en .
12 sfmorder:567 sfm:amount "2" .
13 sfmorder:567 sfm:eta "10 days"@en .
14 sfmconcert:1234 rdf:type sfm:Concert .
```

Listing 5.16 An example of a state representation of an order resource

```
1  Method: POST
2  Input:
3
4  _:order rdf:type sfm:Ticketorder .
5  _:order sfm:user ?u .
6  ?u rdf:type sfm:User .
7  _:order sfm:amount ?a .
8  _:order sfm:event ?c .
9  ?c rdf:type sfm:Concert .
```

Listing 5.17 Input data in the form of a graph pattern

- **Provided by the user.** For example, the user name sfm:JohnDoe and the amount of the ordered tickets "2".
- **Provided by S-LastFM.** For example, the URI of the newly created order resource sfmorder:567 and the price of the tickets "120 USD".

Input Graph Pattern

To create a new ticket order, a client application has to POST data (see Listing 5.17) detailing the desired new resource to the collection resource of the ticket orders. A graph pattern-based description for the input data of a POST to the ticket order collection resource (http://s-last.fm/ticketorder) uses variables for the elements that are different for every individual order resource. The client has to use a blank node _:order for the input data, since it is not possible to know in advance what identifier the API will assign to the new resource.

Output Graph Pattern

The returned data after the application of POST characterizes the state of the created resource (see Listing 5.18). Therefore, the description of the output data is similar to the input description, but contains, additionally, variables for the information added by the API (e.g., the price of the ordered tickets).

```
 1 Method: POST
 2 Output:
 3
 4 ?order rdf:type sfm:Ticketorder  .
 5 ?order sfm:user ?u  .
 6 ?u rdf:type sfm:User  .
 7 ?order sfm:amount ?a  .
 8 ?order sfm:event ?c  .
 9 ?c rdf:type sfm:Concert  .
10 ?order sfm:price ?p  .
11 ?order sfm:eta ?t  .
```

Listing 5.18 Output data in the form of a graph pattern

Input and output descriptions share common variables (e.g., ?u, the user that ordered the tickets). The use of the same variable implies that it will be bound by the same value. This establishes a connection between input and output descriptions and allows to describe the relation between both.

Finally, it is important that input as well as output descriptions of resources can be treated as URI-identified resources as well:

- `http://s-last.fm/ticketorder/input` as URI for the input description
- `http://s-last.fm/ticketorder/output` as URI for the output description

Since the descriptions are URI-identified resources themselves, it is possible provide links to the descriptions. Such links can be used as a response when the `HTTP OPTIONS` method is applied to the collection resource of the ticket orders, which allows a client to look up the descriptions. The links are also used to refer to the graph pattern descriptions in the USDL document detailing a communication channel of the service (cf. Sect. 5.3.2).

5.4   Service Search Algorithm

Descriptions for services can be utilized to increase the degree of automation of higher level tasks, such as service search, composition and discovery. This section details how graph pattern-based descriptions, which can be provided as part of a Linked USDL description, can be leveraged for *service search* [36]. Given a specific functionality that is required to be fulfilled by a service (e.g., the order of tickets for concerts), the process of searching for a service refers to the problems of

- Matching, i.e., identifying the subset of services that are suitable to provide the functionality out of a potentially large set of services
- Ranking, i.e., comparing the identified services in terms of their capability to satisfy the given requirements.

However, service descriptions can be leveraged to improve the automation of other tasks such as the invocation of a service or the composition of several services to create a complex service.

5.4.1 Matching

In a scenario where services are described with Linked USDL, which provides links to graph pattern-based input and output descriptions, service search requests can be formulated as *service templates*. These templates follow the same syntax as the graph pattern descriptions. Therefore a service template consists of two graph patterns that represent a template of:

- all possible *input* RDF graphs a client can provide for the invocation of a service,
- the *output* RDF graphs such an agent expects to be delivered by the service.

Similar to the graph pattern descriptions a service template details a clients possibilities to provide input for a service operation. Further the template describes the requirements of the client on the output of a service operation, as well as the expected relation between the input and output.

Therefore, the question of whether a given service description matches a service template correlates to the problem of graph pattern containment. The input graph pattern of a service description must be contained in the service template's pattern. This containment relation implies that every graph that satisfies the template input graph pattern must also satisfy the service description's input graph pattern. Intuitively, the input a client is able to provide fulfils the requirements of the service to be invoked. Note that this also allows for a client to provide additional data, which it can provide for service invocation even though a matching service does not require them.

A client can for example express in an input template that it can provide information about a location and a music genre. If a service details in an input description that it requires just the information about the location, template and description are matching, since the description is contained in the template. However, if a description details that information about location and an artist is required, template and description are not matching.

Matching the output graph patterns works in an analogous way. The output graph pattern of a service description contains the output graph pattern of a template, which implies that every graph that satisfies the service description output graph pattern also satisfies the template output graph pattern. So the required containment relation of the output patterns is dual to that of the input graph patterns. Intuitively again this means a service output has to provide enough to satisfy the request, but can provide more.

A client can for example express in an output template that it is looking for information from a service about a concert. If a service details in an output description that it provides information about concerts and genre, template and description are matching, since the template is contained in the description. However, if template of the client details it requires information about concerts and ticket prices, template and description are not matching.

Formulas 5.1 and 5.2 summarize the relations between the patterns in a service description and a service template in a search process.

$$Service\ Description\ Input\ Pattern \subseteq Template\ Input\ Pattern \tag{5.1}$$

$$Template\ Output\ Pattern \subseteq Service\ Description\ Output\ Pattern \tag{5.2}$$

5.4.2 Ranking

The matching based on graph pattern containment consists of two binary decisions (one for the input and one for the output), of whether a service description completely matches a service template. However, it is sensible to assume that often services only partly satisfy the requirements of an agent, or that an agent has not all the necessary data for the invocation. Therefore, services should be ordered according to the degree they match to a given request. To allow for such a flexible search approach a ranking of service descriptions against service templates has to be enabled with continuously-valued matching metrics, e.g.:

- The *predicate subset ratio* (*psr*) measures to what degree the set of predicates used in one pattern are subsumed within the set used in another.
- The *resource subset ratio* (*rsr*) measures to what degree the set of named resources, in subject or object position, used in one pattern are subsumed with those of another pattern.
- The *containment ratio* (*cr*) measures to what degree triple patterns in one graph pattern are contained in the other pattern.

The metrics *psr* and *rsr* indicate to what degree a service description and a service template are using the same vocabulary. These vocabulary-based metrics allow to test whether a service description and a template use some of the same resources and predicates (and to what degree). Therefore, they provide a mechanism to discover services, which are close to a given template, but are not necessarily completely matching.

Similarly to the pattern containment, metrics for input and output have to be distinguished. A template input graph pattern can offer more data than actually needed by a service without endangering their compatibility. Therefore, the subset ratios for the input patterns have to measure to what degree the resources (respectively predicates) in the service descriptions are used in the service template. For the subset ratios of the output patterns this works the other way around, because a service can offer more output than required by the template. In this case the subset ratios have to measure to what degree the resources (respectively predicates) in the template are used in the service description. The Eqs. (5.3) to (5.6) show how the metrics are calculated.

$$psr_{input} = \frac{|P_{templ} \cap P_{decsr}|}{|P_{descr}|} \tag{5.3}$$

$$psr_{output} = \frac{|P_{templ} \cap P_{decsr}|}{|P_{templ}|} \tag{5.4}$$

$$rsr_{input} = \frac{|R_{templ} \cap R_{decsr}|}{|R_{descr}|} \tag{5.5}$$

$$rsr_{output} = \frac{|R_{templ} \cap R_{decsr}|}{|R_{templ}|} \tag{5.6}$$

where,

P_{templ} the set of all predicates in the template.
P_{descr} the set of all predicates in the service description.
R_{templ} the set of all resources in the template.
R_{descr} the set of all resources in the service description.

Let the input description pattern use the predicates rdf:type, sfm:performer and sfm:location. The input template uses rdf:type, sfm:performer and sfm:artist. Then $p_{input} = 2/3$, because only two out of three predicates in the description are used in the template.

The metric cr measures to what degree a graph pattern P_{sub} is contained in another pattern P_{super}. To realize this, the measurement cr is based on the power set $\mathscr{P}(P_{sub})$ of triple patterns derived from the graph pattern P_{sub}. The largest set of triple patterns $T_{max} \in \mathscr{P}(P_{sub})$ (i.e., the set with the most triple patterns) in the power set is identified, that is contained in P_{super}:

$$T_{max} \subseteq P_{super} \tag{5.7}$$

Note that T_{max} is not necessarily unique in $\mathscr{P}(P_{sub})$. However, just one of the largest triple pattern sets that are contained in P_{super} needs to be identified for the calculation of cr. Equation (5.8) shows how the metric cr is calculated. The metric describes the ratio between the number of triple patterns in the identified set T_{max} and the overall number of triple patterns in the original pattern P_{sub}, from which the power set is derived.

$$cr = \frac{|T_{max}|}{|P_{sub}|} \tag{5.8}$$

cr measures precisely to what degree a graph pattern is subsumed by another, thus expressing the containment degree of one pattern in relation to another.[25] Note, that if a graph pattern is completely contained in another one (i.e., $cr = 1.0$), the subset ratios must necessarily result in a metric of 1.0.

The vocabulary-based metrics do not regard the structure of the graph patterns to match service descriptions and templates. The metrics *rsr* and *psr* are therefore less precise search metrics compared to *cr*, i.e., even if all vocabulary-based subset ratios result in a value of 1.0, it is not guaranteed that a service description and a template match in terms of pattern containment. On the other hand, if $cr = 1.0$ for the input and output patterns, a complete match is guaranteed. However, the vocabulary-based metrics are computationally less expensive to calculate. To achieve a scalable service search system *rsr* and *psr* can be used to filter service descriptions for a given template: if either *psr* or *rsr* result in a value of 0.0, it can be inferred without additional calculation that the value of *cr* has to be 0.0. Furthermore, other low values for *rsr* and *psr* can be used as thresholds. If one of the vocabulary-based metrics falls below the defined threshold, the calculation of *cr* can be omitted. The setting of this threshold depends on the required reaction time of the service search system, as well as the desired values for precision and recall.

Figure 5.8 and Table 5.5 illustrate an example of a search process in the S-LastFM scenario. In the example a client is searching for a functionality where the client can interact with a resource to acquire information about upcoming concerts. In the input of the interaction with the resource the client can include information

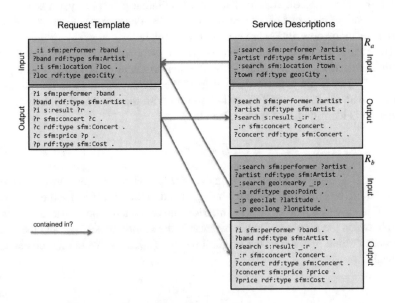

Fig. 5.8 An example of the ranking process

---

[25] For a detailed description of how to calculate the described metrics see [36].

Table 5.5 An example of the ranking process (cont.)

	Service description R_a		Service description R_b	
	Input	Output	Input	Output
Pattern containment	Yes	No	No	Yes
cr	1.0	0.71	0.33	1.0
psr	1.0	0.8	0.4	1.0
rsr	1.0	0.66	0.5	1.0

about the artist and the city in which the client is looking for concerts. As output of the interaction the client expects to find a concert and information about the price for tickets. The example assumes two descriptions are available for:

- Resource R_a to which requests can be submitted with artist and city. R_a provides output information about concerts (but no ticket price information).
- Resource R_b to which requests can be submitted including artist and a geographical point with latitude and longitude. R_b provides output information about concerts including ticket price information.

In this example the client has enough information to invoke the interaction with R_a, but this will not provide all the desired information, since no information about the price of concert tickets are delivered by R_a. Interacting with R_b would provide all the desired information, but the client does not have enough data to invoke it (the latitude/longitude coordinates of the city are missing). This is also reflected in the containment metrics as detailed in Table 5.5. It can be seen how the *psr* and *rsr* metrics can serve as an estimation for the more precise *cr* metric.

Therefore in the given example no perfect match for the template can be found. The client has to resolve this problem and decide:

- Resolution 1: Choose R_a and forgo some of the desired results.
- Resolution 2: Choose R_b and try to acquire missing information (e.g., with the help of another API).

In terms of ranking R_a would be preferred over R_b with regard to the input, but R_b would be preferred over R_a with regard to the output. If a definite order of the resources is required, a weighted average can be calculated from the input and output metrics. The weights reflect which of the resolution strategies is preferred by the client.

5.5 Conclusions

This chapter looked into how rich and comprehensive service descriptions can be constructed to facilitate the search of cloud services. Naturally, rich descriptions improve, not only search, but also other computational tasks such as service selection, discovery, classification, and composition.

The approach followed started by taking a cloud service Web API and used semantic web technologies to enrich and formally describe the Web API structure from a technological perspective as well as from a business perspective. The cloud service selected was LastFM since it is a popular service on the web. The formal description was done by relying on Linked USDL to add semantic knowledge. Linked USDL provides a business and technical envelope to describe services' general information and their Web API. To exemplify the benefits of using semantic service descriptions, an algorithm for service search was developed to demonstrate how semantics can improve precision and recall.

Review Section

Review Questions

1. What are the differences between interfaces and services? What is a Web API?
2. Why is a keyword-based search insufficient for the search for a services or an API?
3. What is the purpose of the operational perspective on services. Compare it to the technical perspective, which also includes a formal description of the operations.
4. Draw the RDF graph of the RDF document shown in Listing 5.13 on page 163.
5. Create a SPARQL query to retrieve the business and corresponding interaction roles of all the entities involved in an interaction from the RDF document given in Listing 5.13. The correctness of the query and the obtained results can be evaluated with existing tools such as Jena TDB or AllegroGraph.
6. Explain the concept of a collection resource?
7. Why does REST restrict the set of available interaction methods? Is this constraint too restrictive?
8. Which aspects of a service can be modeled in the business perspective of Linked USDL?
9. Name use cases in which structured information about the service provider can be useful.
10. What is the relationship between an interaction point and an operation in Linked USDL?
11. What is the main benefit of the use of hypermedia controls?
12. How is the state of a resource described? What kind of information is included?
13. Graph-patterns have been used to describe input and output data of an API. Is it possible to use RDF(S) descriptions instead?
14. In which cases can other relationships (than the ones introduced in Formulas 5.1–5.2 on page 170) between the patterns in service and service template descriptions be useful?

Project

The implementation of services is an extensive task. Besides traditional design, implementation, and testing of the software that already provides the service functionality, a number of further task have to be considered in order to effectively provide a functionality as a service. As this chapter conveyed, the interfaces provide access to resources and methods of the underlying software systems. Further, a formal, i.e., machine-readable and machine-interpretable, description of the provided service is a prerequisite for managing large services automatically.

The use of formal service descriptions increases the degree of automation that is necessary when a large set of service are managed. Different task of management may require that information about different perspectives on services. Due to the importance of expressive and formal service descriptions, the goal of this project is to practice, apply, and gain a more detailed understanding on service descriptions. Within this project, we will continue to use Linked USDL as a service description model in combination with the Semantic Web technologies.

1. Find a service that is publicly available in the Internet. The service should expose at least a few number of different resources and methods, which are provided by a public Web API. This API is described in semi-structured web pages that describe resources and methods in natural language.
2. Make yourself familiar with the involved resources and methods. Identify two non-trivial methods of the API that will be formally described in the subsequent steps.
3. At this stage, a vocabulary of the domain of intercourse is needed. Create an RDFS vocabulary describing the resources of chosen methods. The vocabulary can be sketched in form of an RDF graph drawn on paper. Alternatively, existing modeling tools like Protégé or a simple text editors can be used alike.
4. Furthermore, the Linked USDL service description model is used to create a description for this service and its chosen methods. A complete overview on Linked USDL can be obtained from http://www.linked-usdl.org.
5. Create a Linked USDL description of the technical perspective of the service. This description should cover the methods and all the involved resources, like input and output parameters. Since Linked USDL service descriptions can be serialized to regular RDF documents, a plain text editor or any RDF modeling tool can be used. A dedicated Linked USDL editor is currently under development.
6. Extend this service description, such that the business and operative perspectives are added. The provider of the service describes legal terms, service quality, and other information related to these perspectives within web pages, which may contain large text blocks. The relevant information needs to be identified and expressed formally. The RDFS domain vocabulary can be extended accordingly, if required.

Within this project, it should become obvious how tedious it can be to deal with and to interpret natural language text descriptions of services. It is easy to imagine how difficult it can be to analyze, search, or invoke services from a large service repository. The need and the benefits of formal descriptions as well as the broad spectrum of perspectives gained by the use of Linked USDL were conveyed.

Key Terms

Web API The acronym API stands for application programming interface and enables applications to exchange data. A Web API is the web version of this interface. It is leveraging web technologies (e.g., URI, HTTP, HTML, JSON, and XML) to enable companies to make their data assets available to external developers.

Service Description A service description defines and characterizes the services offered to customers. It includes functional and non-functional characteristics (properties). Typically, services are described in natural language, but more modern approaches use semantic web technologies.

USDL The Unified Service Description Language (USDL) was the first comprehensive language to describe services using computer-understandable formats. It described aspects such as legal constraints, pricing models, service level, and interactions between customers and providers [27, 37].

Linked USDL Linked USDL is a simpler version of USDL which was designed using Linked Data principles. It is more adequate to work on web environments since it uses solely web protocols and specifications, and it describes services semantically [28].

Semantic Web The Semantic Web is a technology stack originally developed by the W3C which enables people to share knowledge beyond the boundaries of websites. The specifications which are part of the stack, and include URI, RDF(S), OWL, and SPARQL, strive to turn unstructured data into computer-readable formats.

Linked Data Linked Data is a paradigm which applies the principles and technologies of the web to share and link data. It can be viewed as a pragmatic way of applying the technology stack provided by the Semantic Web to build worldwide networks of linked knowledge.

Turtle Turtle (Terse RDF Triple Language) is a serialization for capturing knowledge expressed using the Resource Description Framework (RDF). It is relatively simple to read/write when compared to other serializations, e.g., XML.

Further Reading

Jorge Cardoso and Amit Sheth. *Semantic Web Services, Processes and Applications*. Springer, 2006.

Rudi Studer, Stephan Grimm, and Andreas Abecker. *Semantic Web Services: Concepts, Technologies, and Applications.* Springer, 2010.

Leonard Richardson, Mike Amundsen, and Sam Ruby. *RESTful Web APIs Paperback.* O'Reilly Media, 2013.

References

1. Noor T et al (2013) CSCE: a crawler engine for cloud services discovery on the world wide web. In: IEEE 20th international conference on web services (ICWS). IEEE, Washington, DC, USA, pp 443–450
2. Cardoso J, Pedrinaci C (2015) Evolution and overview of linked USDL. In: 6th International conference exploring services science (IESS 2015). Lecture notes in computer science. Springer, Berlin
3. Christensen E et al (2013) Web services description language (WSDL) 1.1. W3C note. W3C, Mar 2001. http://www.w3.org/TR/wsdl. Accessed 10 Sep 2015
4. Kopecky J et al (2007) SAWSDL: semantic annotations for WSDL and XML schema. IEEE Internet Comput 11(6):60–67
5. Martin D et al (2004) OWL-S: semantic markup for web services. W3C member submission
6. Cardoso J, Sheth A (2003) Semantic e-workflow composition. J Intell Inf Syst 21(3):191–225
7. Endres-Niggemeyer B (eds) (2013) Semantic mashups. Intelligent reuse of web resources. Springer, Berlin/Heidelberg
8. Le Phuoc D et al (2009) Rapid prototyping of semantic mash-ups through semantic web pipes. In: Quemada J et al (eds) Proceedings of the 18th international conference on world wide web, WWW 2009, Madrid, 20–24 April 2009. ACM, New York, NY, USA pp 581–590
9. Lathem J, Gomadam K, Sheth AP (2007) SA-REST and (s)mashups: adding semantics to RESTful services. In: Proceedings of the first IEEE international conference on semantic computing (ICSC 2007), Irvine, CA, 17–19 Sept 2007. IEEE, Washington, DC, USA, pp 469–476
10. Di Lorenzo G et al (2009) Data integration in mashups. SIGMOD Rec 38(1):59–66
11. Manola F, Miller E (2013) RDF primer. W3C recommendation. W3C, Feb 2004. http://www.w3.org/TR/rdf-primer/. Accessed 10 Sep 2015
12. Brickley D, Guha RV (2013) RDF vocabulary description language 1.0: RDF schema. W3C recommendation. W3C, Feb 2004. http://www.w3.org/TR/rdf-schema/. Accessed 15 Aug 2013
13. Beckett D, Berners-Lee T (2013) Turtle - terse RDF triple language. W3C team submission. W3C, Mar 2011. http://www.w3.org/TeamSubmission/turtle/. Accessed 10 Sep 2015
14. Stolz A, Rodriguez-Castro B, Hepp M (2013) RDF translator: a RESTful multi-format data converter for the semantic web. Technical report TR-2013-1, Universität der Bundeswehr München, July 2013
15. Staab S, Studer R (eds) (2009) Handbook on ontologies, 2nd edn. International handbooks on information systems. Springer, Berlin.
16. Hayes PJ (2013) RDF semantics. W3C recommendation. W3C, Feb 2004. http://www.w3.org/TR/rdf-mt/. Accessed 10 Sep 2015
17. Maedche A, Staab S (2001) Ontology learning for the semantic web. IEEE Intell Syst 16(2):72–79
18. Lehmann J, Voelker J (2014) An introduction to ontology learning. In: Lehmann J, Voelker J (eds) Perspectives on ontology learning. AKA/IOS Press, Heidelberg, pp 9–16
19. W3C SPARQL Working Group (2013) SPARQL 1.1 overview. W3C recommendation. W3C, Mar 2013. http://www.w3.org/TR/sparql11-overview/. Accessed 10 Sep 2015
20. Bizer C, Heath T, Berners-Lee T (2009) Linked data - the story so far. Int J Semantic Web Inf Syst 4(2):1–22

21. Pautasso C, Wilde E (2009) Why is the web loosely coupled?: a multi-faceted metric for service design. In: Quemada J et al (eds) International conference on world wide web. ACM, New York, NY, USA
22. Stadtmüller S et al (2013) Comparing major web service paradigms. In: Workshop on services and applications over linked APIs and data, vol 1056. CEUR-WS, 2013
23. Fielding R (2000) Architectural styles and the design of network-based software architectures. Ph.D. thesis, University of California, Irvine
24. Richardson L, Ruby S (2007) RESTful web services. O'Reilly Media. Sebastopol, CA, USA
25. Webber J (2010) REST in practice: hypermedia and systems architecture. O'Reilly Media, Farnham, UK
26. Maleshkova M, Pedrinaci C, Domingue J (2010) Investigating web APIs on the world wide web. In: IEEE 8th European Conference on Web Services (ECOWS), IEEE, Ayia Napa
27. Cardoso J et al (2010) Towards a unified service description language for the internet of services: requirements and first developments. In: IEEE international conference on services computing (SCC), FL, pp 602–609
28. Pedrinaci C, Cardoso J, Leidig T (2014) Linked USDL: a vocabulary for web-scale service trading. Lecture notes in computer science, vol 8465. Springer, Berlin, pp 68–82
29. García JM et al (2015) Linked USDL agreement: effectively sharing semantic service level agreements on the web. In: The IEEE international conference on web services (ICWS), New York, 2015
30. Cardoso J et al (2012) Open semantic service networks. In: International symposium on services science (ISSS), Leipzig, 2012
31. Stadtmüller S et al (2013) Data-Fu: a language and an interpreter for interaction with read/write linked data. In: International conference on world wide web. International world wide web conferences steering committee, Geneva, Switzerland, pp 1225–1236
32. Wilde E (2009) REST and RDF granularity. Accessed 10 Sep 2015
33. Krummenacher R, Norton B, Marte A Towards linked open services and processes. In: Future internet symposium. Springer, Berlin, pp 68–77
34. Speiser S, Harth A (2011) Integrating linked data and services with linked data services. In: Proceedings of the 8th extended semantic web conference (ESWC'11) part I, Lecture notes in computer science, vol 6643. Springer, Heraklion
35. Verborgh R et al (2011) Efficient runtime service discovery and consumption with hyperlinked RESTdesc. In: International conference on next generation web services practices, Salamanca, 2011
36. Stadtmüller S, Norton B (2013) Scalable discovery of linked APIs. J Metadata Semant Ontol 8(2):95–105
37. Cardoso J, Winkler M, Voigt K (2009) A service description language for the internet of services. In: International symposium on services science (ISSS), Leipzig, 2009

Service Analytics

6

Jorge Cardoso, Julia Hoxha, and Hansjörg Fromm

Summary

Service analytics describes the process of capturing, processing, and analyzing the data generated from the execution of a service system to improve, extend, and personalize a service to create value for both providers and customers. This chapter explains how services, especially electronic services, generate a wealth of data which can be used for their analysis. The main tasks and methods, from areas such as data mining and machine learning, which can be used for analysis are identified. To illustrate their application, the data generated from the execution of an IT service is analyzed to extract business insights.

Learning Objectives
1. Understand the concept of service analytics and its importance for service systems.
2. Describe the various tasks and methods associated with analytics and how they can be applied to services.

(continued)

J. Cardoso (✉)
Department of Informatics Engineering, Universidade de Coimbra, Coimbra, Portugal

Huawei European Research Center (ERC), Munich, Germany
e-mail: jcardoso@dei.uc.pt; jorge.cardoso@huawei.com

J. Hoxha • H. Fromm
Karlsruhe Service Research Institute (KSRI), Karlsruhe Institute of Technology (KIT), Karlsruhe, Germany
e-mail: hansjoerg.fromm@kit.edu

© Springer International Publishing Switzerland 2015
J. Cardoso et al. (eds.), *Fundamentals of Service Systems*, Service Science: Research and Innovations in the Service Economy, DOI 10.1007/978-3-319-23195-2_6

3. Explain how classification, prediction, and association rules, from the traditional data mining field, can be applied to service systems.
4. Understand how analytics can be used to analyze real-world datasets generated from the execution of IT services.

▶ **Opening Case** Analytics for service improvement

ANALYZING CUSTOMERS' BEHAVIOR WHILE INTERACTING WITH SERVICE SYSTEMS

A couple is traveling with their new car on the expressway. It is cold outside, the heating is on, but they are not pleased with the heat distribution: the upper part of the cabin interior is warm, but the foot space is cold. They try to regulate the temperature using the climate menu of the car's control display—without success.

The co-driver takes the owner's manual out of the glove compartment and finds a section on climate control on page 109. But page 109 does not give the necessary information to solve their problem. From page 109, a reference is made to page 80, where all controls of the center console are described. After browsing backwards and forwards between pages 109 and 80 a number of times, they still have not found the required information.

This simple example is illustrative of many situations that are found in service environments. Consider the car owner's manual as an *information service* that the auto manufacturer provides to customers. After having printed and placed the manual in the glove compartment of every car, the manufacturer knows practically nothing about the usage of this service (the manual).

Possibly hundreds of drivers have been reading page 109 of the car owner's manual. If the car manufacturer would have access to this information, it could reach the conclusion that something is wrong with the temperature control of the car—or at least with the usability of the control display. If the manufacturer would know that many people browse back and forth between pages 109 and 80, it would know that something was wrong with the editorial structure and the content of the manual. Knowledge on the usage could provide important feedback to the engineering department as well as to the department responsible for the owner's manual.

However, if instructions are only printed on paper (Fig. 6.1), there is a "disconnection" between the provider and the user of the service. This disconnection prevents information from flowing from the service consumer to the service provider.

Fig. 6.1 Owner's manuals are typically disconnected from their providers

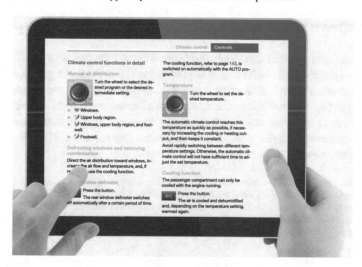

Fig. 6.2 The use of mobile devices enables manufacturers to monitor and analyze customers behavior

If the manual would be electronically accessible in the car and connected to the provider using the internet (Fig. 6.2), the manufacturer could analyze customers' usage patterns. Counting the number of visits to particular pages could easily reveal which dashboard controls the customers have the most difficulties with. Measuring the time intervals between page visits could be an indicator for how well the text is readable and how quickly the customer finds a solution to his problem. The behavior described previously—a user jumping back and forth between two pages—could easily be detected and corrected in the next version of the manual.

▶ **Opening Case**

6.1 Introduction

Automotive manufacturers deliver an increasing number of services with their cars, such as traffic and weather information systems, and communication, driver assistance, navigation, and entertainment services. But they often do not know much about the usage of these services by their customers.

Electricity service providers typically ask their customers to read their meters once per quarter or once per year. Based on the consumption they bill customers. However, electricity providers miss information about weekly or daily consumption patterns, which would allow them to give a useful feedback to customers or offer specially-priced contracts.

In healthcare, service providers, such as family doctors or hospital staff, typically have enough information about the patient while under their custody. But as soon as the patient leaves their facilities, they lose track of their condition, health status, and behavior.

All these examples are characterized by an information gap between the service provider and the customer. This gap is preventing the provider to get more insight into the customer's service usage. But this disconnection is being overcome with the emergence of new information technologies. An increasing volume of data is being collected either by users (e.g., through smartphones) or by technologies like smart metering in energy services, telematics in automotive services, RFID in logistics, condition sensors in engineering, and healthcare.

R   Traditional human-based services are characterized by the personal service encounter. Very often, the provider and the customer know each other well from past service interactions. The provider understands what the customer wants and can deliver an individual, personalized service. This advantage was initially overlooked in technology-enabled services, where the face-to-face contact between customer and provider did not occur anymore.

From the many use case domains available (e.g., automotive, energy, and healthcare), this chapter presents a real-world example from IT service management. Section 6.3 explains how service provisioning can be analyzed with the objective of improving operational performance and increasing productivity. The section analyzes an IT service, more precisely, the incident management service from the Information Technology Infrastructure Library (ITIL) [1]. The objective of this service is to restore normal service operation as quickly as possible and ensure that the best possible levels of service quality and availability are maintained.

The next chapter, Chap. 7, provides a complementary view on service systems by explaining how optimization theories and techniques can be used to improve the efficiency and effectiveness of services.

6.1.1 Sharing Data

If customers are willing to share data with service providers, providers will have the opportunity to study customers' behaviors and preferences to gain insights on the customer almost like it was possible in traditional face-to-face services. But studying service usage does not only provide more focus towards the customer, it can also help to identify weaknesses in the provisioning of the service which in turn gives rise to service improvements. This new focus on studying service usage can be achieved with service analytics.

In the energy scenario above, a move from quarterly or yearly meter readings to almost real-time consumption recordings with smart meters can result in a win-win situation for both customers and providers. With detailed knowledge about the fluctuating energy consumption over the day, energy providers can improve management by more accurately anticipating expensive peak consumption periods. At the same time, the provider can influence demand, e.g., by lowering electricity prices and, thus, incentive consumption in off-peak periods. The provider can give feedback on usage statistics that help the customer to identify power guzzlers in the household to handle energy consumption with greater care. In summary, there are advantages for all parties: lower energy prices for consumers, operational improvements for providers, and environmental benefits for everyone.

6.1.2 Big Data

Reading a smart meter every 15 minutes instead of only once a year generates about 35,000 times more data. Reading it every 15 s generates over 2,000,000 times more data. This is the dilemma of service analytics: when providers and customers were disconnected, there was no data about the service usage available. Now that new technologies like sensors, smart meters, and telematics have been introduced, there are large volumes of data available—often more than desired. This has been recently described with the term *big data* [2].

▶ **Definition (Big Data)** Big data describes large volumes of both structured and unstructured data that are difficult to process using traditional databases and software techniques. The difficulties are associated with the nature of the data: volume (e.g., terabytes and petabytes), velocity (e.g., streaming and near-real time), and variety (e.g., formats).

In the case of service systems, the volumes of captured data have grown extremely fast. Big data processing now often allows to work with the raw data in situations that were not possible before, both in terms of the statistics (enough samples available) and in terms of technology (enough processing power available).

6.1.3 Knowledge Discovery

The process of creating useful knowledge from large data sets and documents is often described as knowledge extraction or knowledge discovery. It describes the overall process of discovering useful knowledge from data, while analytics and data mining refer to one particular step in this process.

▶ **Definition (Knowledge Discovery (KD))** The non-trivial process of identifying valid, novel, potentially useful, and ultimately understandable patterns in data [3].

The KD process starts with data preparation, data selection, data cleaning, and the incorporation of appropriate prior knowledge, before analytics/data mining techniques can be applied. After application of these techniques, the proper interpretation of the results is essential to ensure that useful knowledge is derived from the data.

 The blind application of data mining methods can be a dangerous activity, which can easily lead to the discovery of meaningless and invalid patterns.

6.1.4 Analytics for Service Systems

The application of analytics to service systems is progressing in many domains. Some areas like web analytics are more advanced, while other areas like healthcare analytics are making the first steps [4, 5]. Interesting examples include digital content providers (e.g., iTunes, Spotify, and Amazon Kindle) which use analytics to recommend and personalize content; online gaming services that use analytics to improve their games; telco providers that analyze communications behavior to optimize provisioning of network resources; and price comparison websites and intermediaries (e.g., tour operators) that use demand patterns to optimize pricing.

The goal is to apply basic and advanced analytics to an entire service system to generate the highest benefits for all stakeholders according to the value co-creation principle. The challenge is to draw information and insights out of big volumes of data to study customer behavior and characterize service usage. This requires sophisticated methods for capturing, processing, and analyzing data. These methods are subsumed under the term service analytics [6].

▶ **Definition (Service Analytics)** Describes the methods for capturing, processing, and analyzing data taken from a service system—in order to improve, extend, and personalize the service provided. It also describes how new value is created for both the provider and the customer.

When data is available, the potential is clearly visible—as with electronic services (services fully rendered over the internet) since by design these services require connectivity between providers and customers. For example, customers visit the provider's web pages in order to obtain the service. Thus, the provider is able to analyze customers usage characteristics at several levels of detail. This analysis is known under the terms web analytics or web usage mining [7,8]. Typical data of interest are the overall number of page visits, the number of page visits per customer, the time intervals between page visits, the path that customers take through the web site, etc. With this data, the provider can analyze the behavior and preferences of individual customers, make recommendations, assess the general acceptance and attractiveness of web offerings, and discover usability problems related to navigating and finding information on web pages.

The methods and techniques from web analytics can readily be transferred to analyze service systems. It is mainly due to the difficulties in obtaining usage data and in reducing the vast amount of data to a manageable size that these techniques have not been used extensively in the past.

6.2 General Notion of Analytics

There is no single agreed-upon definition of the term *analytics*. Some authors like Kohavi et al. [9] use the terms analytics and *data mining* interchangeably. Others like Davenport and Harris [10] use analytics as a synonym for *business intelligence*, a term which refers to the applications and best practices to analyze information to improve and optimize business decisions and performance.

▶ **Definition (Data Mining)** Generally, data mining (sometimes called data or knowledge discovery) is the process of extracting useful, often previously unknown information, from large databases or data sets.

Opposing opinions are grounded to the doubt if analytics should include or exclude data management and reporting technologies. Davenport and Harris [11] distinguish between access and reporting, and analytics, both are seen as subsets of business intelligence. Data management and reporting are often considered as basic analytics, which are a prerequisite for advanced analytics (see [12]) built on methods from statistics and operations research. Basic analytics include reporting solutions based on data warehouse and data marts like standard and ad hoc reporting, online analytical processing (OLAP), queries, drilldowns, and alerts [13].

6.2.1 Data Preprocessing

This section identifies the most common tasks, which are part of the process executed in the context of a data analytics project. Such a process usually involves data pre-processing, cleaning, integration, transformation, reduction, and discretization.

Data pre-processing is an important first step in the analytics process. Since data gathering is usually performed with loosely controlled methods, they can generate datasets with several missing and out-of-range values, redundant entries, invalid data combinations, etc. It is often the case that datasets exhibit the following three main problems:

1. Data may be incomplete, for example they lack attribute values or attributes of interest.
2. Data may be noisy, containing errors, anomalies, or outliers.
3. Data may also be inconsistent, for example they contain discrepancies in codes or names.

Performing analytics on data that have not been previously checked against these problems may cause misleading results. The data pre-processing activity screens the gathered data for quality problems. Data pre-processing typically includes the following tasks: *cleaning, integration, transformation, reduction,* and *discretization*.

Data Cleaning
Data cleaning consists in the following activities: fill in missing values, smooth noisy data, identify or remove outliers, and resolve inconsistencies. Missing data is handled in different ways, for example, by manually filling values; using global constants; applying the mean of the attribute values to fill the missing value of a particular attribute; finding the most probable value by applying, e.g., Bayesian rules or decision trees; or simply ignoring the instance whose value is missing. Noisy data are handled by sorting and partitioning the data to detect and remove outliers. This is done by applying automatic binning, clustering methods, or through human inspection.

Data Integration and Transformation
Data integration combines datasets from multiple sources, such as files, databases, or data cubes, into a coherent data store. Integration tasks confront the problem of resolving value conflicts, as well as handling redundant data. Data transformation helps with normalization, i.e., scaling of values to fall within a range, as well as with aggregation techniques.

Data Reduction
Data reduction is a very important step when, as it is usually the case, organizations are dealing with very high volumes of data and need to perform analytics tasks, which are computationally expensive if performed on complete datasets. As such,

the data reduction task consists in finding a reduced representation of the dataset that is smaller than the complete set, yet it enables to yield almost the same analytical results. Among the strategies used in data reduction are data aggregation, dimensionality reduction, numerical reduction, and concept hierarchy generation.

Data Discretization
Data discretization, often considered as part of data reduction, consists in reducing the number of values of a particular continuous attribute by dividing the range of the attribute into intervals. Afterwards, the data values of the attribute are replaced by discrete labels.

6.2.2 Data Analysis

Methods subsumed under the title analytics originate from mathematics (statistics, linear algebra, and operations research) and computer science (database systems, data mining, machine learning, artificial intelligence, and computational linguistics).

Table 6.1 gives an overview of the different analytics methods and how they can be applied to service systems. In Section 6.3, a selection of these methods—data preprocessing, classification and prediction, and association rules—will be presented in more detail. Section 6.4 briefly presents cluster analysis, regression analysis, and text mining. For more information on these and other methods, the reader is referred to textbooks on data mining [7, 14], and business forecasting [15, 16].

Classification of Approaches
Analytics comprise various methods from statistics and operations research, which can follow descriptive, predictive, or prescriptive approaches [17].

Descriptive analytics is the simplest form of analytics. It condenses and summarizes big data into smaller, more useful and manageable pieces of information. For example, creating summarized information about the number of customers or about the page views of an electronic service.

Predictive analytics uses several methods to study historical data to forecast future trends or events. A model is created using past data to predict future data.

Prescriptive analytics extends descriptive and predictive analytics by recommending to decision-makers the possible courses of action that can be taken as well as the likely outcome of each decision.

Several existing methods can be used to support service analytics. Examples include text and image mining, clustering, anomaly detection, forecasting algorithms, and visual analysis:

- Data mining and machine learning algorithms like clustering and association can be used to identify similarities between customers (e.g., segmentation).

Table 6.1 Overview of analytics tasks, methods, and applications

Tasks	Methods	Applications
Preprocessing	Preprocessing Techniques (Data Cleaning, Data Transformation) Dimensionality Reduction (Principal Component Analysis (PCA), Support Vector Machines (SVM), Factor Analysis (FA), Eigen decomposition, Latent Variable Analysis)	Reduction of large volumes of data to manageable size (dimensionality reduction) Removal of incorrect, irrelevant and redundant information
Classification	Decision Tree (C4.5), K-Nearest Neighbor (KNN), Support Vector Machines (SVM), Artificial Neural Networks (ANN), logistic regression	Prediction of user behavior; prediction of customer churn/attrition, loyalty, profitability; prediction of failures (resulting in predictive maintenance)
Association	With candidate generation (k-Means, k-Medoids) Without candidate generation (RELIM, FP-GROWTH)	Co-purchase information (Market Basket Analysis)
Cluster Analysis	Partitioning Approaches (k-Means, k-Medoids) Hierarchical Approaches (AGNES, DIANA) Density-Based Approaches (DBSCAN, OPTICS, CLIQUE) Outlier Detection (ABOF)	Customer segmentation; similarity of interest; combinations of problems/complaints; recommendations; identifying customers requiring similar types of assistance; identifying service objects with similar problems (e.g., auto repair)
Regression	Basic Statistical Techniques (nonlinear, multi-variate, logistic regression) Time Series Forecasting (Moving Average, Exponential Smoothing, Autoregressive Moving Average (ARMA), Autoregressive Integrated Moving Average (ARIMA))	Demand forecasting (electricity consumption, service calls, emergency calls, service parts, etc.); usage trend analysis; next action by customer; customer lifecycle management
Sequence Mining	Apriori-Based Algorithms (AprioriAll, GSP, SPADE) Pattern-Growth Algorithms (FreeSpan, PrefixSpan) Early Pruning Algorithms (SPAM)	Service usage analytics (flow of patients through hospital, user browsing patterns); mobility pattern analysis (mobile phone usage, traffic, sports); repeat visit analysis (repair, hospital); temporal recommendations; service personalization
Text Mining	Preprocessing Techniques (document standardization, tokenization, filtering, lemmatization, stemming) Sentiment Analysis Text Summarization	Customer/patient complaint analysis (from calls or social networks); customer experience analysis; customer emotion and sentiment analysis; analysis of service documentation (e.g., maintenance records and reports, medical records and reports)

- Text mining algorithms are the basis for customer experience, sentiment, and complaint analysis using unstructured data sources like blogs on the internet.
- Temporal data mining algorithms are able to discover sequential usage patterns, e.g., in the browsing behavior of customers on a provider's web pages.
- Visual analytics and visual data mining provide a clearer view and understanding of relationships within a complex service system.
- Time series forecasting and regression analysis methods can be used for prediction and trend analysis (e.g., service demand).

The boundaries between descriptive, predictive, and prescriptive methods are blurred. Association, clustering, sequential pattern analysis, and text mining (also visual data mining which is not mentioned in Table 6.1) are generally classified as descriptive methods, whereas classification, regression, and time series forecasting are clearly predictive methods. Prescriptive methods are in the realm of mathematical optimization and are covered in the Chap. 7 on Service Optimization.

Characterization of Methods
Data mining experts use the following terms to characterize algorithms:

- Supervised learning
- Unsupervised learning

In *supervised learning*, the data records contain attributes (input variables) and a target variable (output variable or label). The objective of learning is to construct a function which relates a given set of attributes with the desired output. If this function has been determined from an existing training data set, it can be used to predict the output for any new combination of attributes. Thus supervised learning methods are clearly predictive.

Unsupervised learning methods do not use labeled data (no target variable)—the goal is rather to find patterns and structures in the data, which were previously unknown [7]. Unsupervised learning methods are therefore descriptive.

6.3   Analyzing IT Services

ITIL is commonly used in the industry for IT service management. It provides a set of best practices, which take often the form of reference models and accepted processes, which are sound and efficient. The adoption of reference models is motivated by the following drivers [18]:

Design.   They significantly speed up the design of services by providing reusable and high quality content.

Optimization.   They optimize the design as they have been developed over a long period and usually capture the business insight of experts.

Compliance.   They ease the compliance with industry regulations and requirements and, thus, mitigate risk.

Alignment.   They are an essential mean to align business needs and IT service
implementations.

Worldwide, many well-known companies are adopting ITIL for IT service
management. Examples include large software providers such as Microsoft, HP, and
IBM; financial services societies such as Bank of America, Deutsche Bank, and
Barclays Bank; manufacturers such as Boeing, Caterpillar, Toyota, and Bombardier;
and departments of defence such as the US Army, US Navy, and US Air Force.

Example

As a concrete example of cost reduction, Proctor and Gamble reduced IT
spending in 10 % of their annual IT budget ($125M) by adopting ITIL. The
efficiency and optimization of service provisioning were the main reasons behind
the savings.

The ITIL Lifecycle

ITIL consists of five main books, which correspond to the five phases of the ITIL
lifecycle: service strategy, service design, service transition, service operation, and
continual service improvement. An introductory book to ITIL service management
is also available. Each of the five main volumes textually describes the best practices
that can be followed by a company to manage IT services. Thus, ITIL should not be
viewed as a piece of code, system, or software application.

This section will look into the service operation phase, and, more precisely, it
will analyze the incident management service.

The Incident Management Service

The primary objective of the incident management (IM) service is to resolve
incidents (e.g., application bugs, disks-usage thresholds exceeded, or printers not
working) in the quickest and most effective possible way. The incident management
service can be characterized as reactive, and a formal working process is put into
place to respond as efficiently and effectively as possible in resolving reported
incidents.

If a user cannot print, he contacts the service desk for help, which creates a record
describing the incident. If the issue cannot be resolved immediately, the service
desk manager opens an incident record, which is assigned to a technician. When the
technician finds the cause of the incident, he fixes the problem. The service desk
manager informs the user to retry to print. If the user can print, the service desk
manager closes the incident record. Otherwise, the record remains open and another
attempt to resolve the incident is made. Figure 6.3 provides a simple representation
of the business process model behind the IM service.

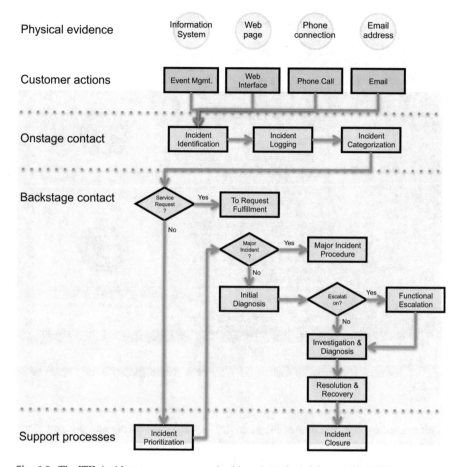

Fig. 6.3 The ITIL incident management service blueprint (adapted from p. 48, [19])

6.3.1   ITIL Software Systems

Nowadays, software solutions to support and manage ITIL services already exist (e.g., ServiceNow, Zendesk, Kayako, UserVoice, and Freshdesk). Depending on the requirements, companies can acquire solutions containing a broad list of features ranging from SLA and escalation management, to the integration with social media platforms, to automated ticket routing, and to graphical forms design.

During service provisioning, incidents are handled using the activity record system. Activities are assigned to appropriate team members, who will deal with the task as appropriate. These systems generate events, which are recorded in a log to provide an audit trail that can be used to understand how services were provisioned. For example, each time an activity of the service illustrated in Fig. 6.3 is executed, an event is generated and stored in a log. Event records typically contain information

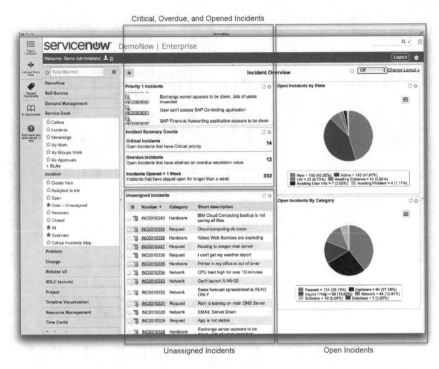

Fig. 6.4 Software application to support the ITIL incident management service illustrated in Fig. 6.3

such as a timestamp, the name of the activity executed, the owner and priority of the incident case, the status of the service, and a description of the incident. Once an incident has been properly dealt with, it is closed.

Figure 6.4 provides an example of an interface that team members use to handle incidents.

These log files need to be integrated into one consistent dataset for analysis. This process includes the detection of errors and inconsistencies to improve the quality of data, the integration of schema, and the consolidation of instances. Afterwards, service analytics are applied to the dataset to extract valuable insights and knowledge about service provisioning patterns.

6.3.2 Dataset Description

A dataset from the automotive industry is used to explain how service analytics can be operationalized. It is a real-life dataset, which contains event records from operational business processes. The dataset was generated by an incident management system called VINST and has the following characteristics.

Table 6.2 The attributes of the dataset (attributes are written using the `typewriter` font)

Attribute	Count	Description
`SR number`	7.554	A unique ticket number for each incident reported.
`Change date+time`	many	The timestamp indicating when the status of an incident case changed.
`Status`	4	The status of the incident management service: queued, accepted, completed, closed.
`Substatus`	13	The substatus of an incident case: assigned, awaiting assignment, cancelled, closed, in progress, wait, unmatched.
`Involved ST function div`	24	The IT organization that provides the service. It is divided into functions (mostly technology wise).
`Involved organization`	25	The business area of the user reporting the incident to the service desk.
`Involved ST`	649	The team responsible for resolving the incident.
`SR latest impact`	4	The impact of an incident for the customer: major, high, medium, low.
`Product`	704	The identification of the product which originated the incident.
`Country`	23	The country of the support team that takes ownership of the incident record.
`Owner country`	32	The country of the owner.
`Owner first name`	1.440	The person of the support team that is the owner of the reported incident.

- It is available from the Business Process Intelligence (BPI) Challenge 2013 web site.[1]
- It contains event records from a three-week period from the 1st of May 2012 up to and including the 23rd of May 2012.
- It contains 65.533 events pertaining to 7.554 incident records.
- It was not preprocessed or filtered, other than anonymized.

Table 6.2 provides the description of the attributes that are part of the log schema and Table 6.3 shows an extract of the dataset.

6.3.3   Preprocessing and Cleaning

It was necessary to preprocess the dataset before conducting the analysis. The basic tool for data munging used for our analyses was Microsoft Excel. Its feature to import CSV files has allowed the original dataset to be imported to a tabular format. The filtering and sorting capabilities of Excel have eased the identification of missing data and have allowed for raw estimations of attributes' count (Table 6.2 shows the count for each attribute).

---

[1] www.win.tue.nl/bpi/2013/challenge.

Table 6.3 Examples of instances of the dataset

Instances
1-364285768;2010-03-31T15:59:42+01:00;Accepted;In Progress;A2_4;Org line A2;V30;Medium;PROD582;fr;France;Frederic
1-364285768;2010-03-31T16:00:56+01:00;Accepted;In Progress;A2_4;Org line A2;V30;Medium;PROD582;fr;France;Frederic
1-364285768;2010-03-31T16:45:48+01:00;Queued;Awaiting Assignment;A2_5;Org line A2;V5 3rd;Medium;PROD582;fr;France; Frederic
1-364285768;2010-04-06T15:44:07+01:00;Accepted;In Progress;A2_5;Org line A2;V5 3rd;Medium;PROD582;fr;France;Anne Claire
1-364285768;2010-04-06T15:44:38+01:00;Queued;Awaiting Assignment;A2_4;Org line A2;V30;Medium;PROD582;fr;France;Anne Claire
1-364285768;2010-04-06T15:44:47+01:00;Accepted;In Progress;A2_5;Org line A2;V13 2nd 3rd;Medium;PROD582;fr;France;Anne Claire
1-364285768;2010-04-06T15:44:51+01:00;Completed;Resolved;A2_5; Org line A2;V13 2nd 3rd;Medium;PROD582;fr;France;Anne Claire

The Python language was used during the loosely process of manually converting the dataset from its original format into another format that allowed for a more convenient analysis. The objective of the conversion was to obtain a better understanding of support tiers, owner names, and to handle missing values.

Support Tiers

The incident management service aims to restore normal service operations after the occurrence of a specific incident. Incident reports are first handled by the 1st line (the service desk) and escalated to the 2nd and 3rd line teams when 1st line engineers are not able to resolve the incident.

To explore the behavior of service provisioning, it was required to know which support tier (1st, 2nd, or 3rd line) handled an incident. Unfortunately, the attribute Involved ST combined, into one field, the support team name and the support tier. For example, S2 2nd combined the name of the support team S2 and the support tier 2nd indicating the 2nd support tier. A 1st line involvement was assumed for activities for which no explicit line number was present in the Involved ST attribute. For example, S2 indicated implicitly a 1st level support tier. Therefore, a new attribute was created to solely indicate the support tier. The Involved ST was divided into two attributes: Involved ST and Support line. The values for Support line were 1st, 2nd, 3rd, and 2nd-3rd.

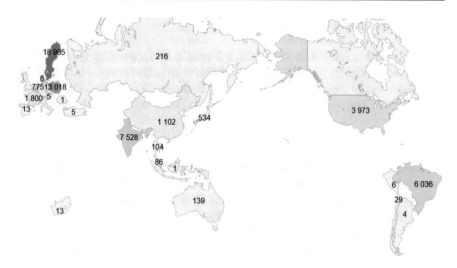

Fig. 6.5 Worldwide distribution of the volume of activities associated with the incident management process [20]

Basemap, a library for plotting 2D data on maps in Python, was used to visualize the results of converting the original dataset. The map in Fig. 6.5 shows that 2.911 (4.44 %) activities are performed in the 3rd line mainly in Sweden, Poland, France, and India. Incidents that require the intervention of the 2nd-3rd support line were handled in France (39 (0.06 %) activities). More than 46.000 (70.26 %) activities are performed by the 1st tier mainly in Sweden, Poland, Brazil, and India. The most active countries that involve the 2nd line to solve incidents are Sweden, India, Poland, and Brazil with 16.541 (25.24 %) activities handled.

Owner Names
The attribute Owner first name has 1.440 unique values (e.g., Frederic and Anne Claire). These names do not map uniquely to the Owner country attribute. The most probable explanation is that several people using the system and located in different countries have the same name. To solve this problem, the Owner country was concatenated with Owner first name to create a new attribute. This generated 1.688 distinct new entities for the incident dataset.

Missing Values
Several values of the attributes Status and Substatus were not specified in the dataset. For example, wait-customer, in-call, unmatched, and resolved. For some activities, no organization or function division were indicated. Instances without these values were removed from the dataset. The format of timestamps was modified to enable their processing by various tools.

6.3.4   Predicting Incident Closure

The goal of this section is to construct a predictive model that will enable to understand the factors that influence an incident to be closed or not. More precisely, the objective is to understand the influence that the number of functional divisions, support teams, and organizations involved in the resolution of an incident has on the closing of incidents.

Classification and Prediction

Classification and prediction are forms of data analysis used to build models that capture important data patterns or predict future data trends. The question that will be answered is: *how to predict whether an IT service incident report submitted will be resolved or not*. The prediction is based on the attributes that describe an incident, e.g., support teams involved, country owning the incident, and functional departments involved. Organizations can make use of classification techniques to answer this question.

Classification is a two-step process (Fig. 6.6). In the first step, a model is built to describe a predetermined set of data classes. A collection of data records is used, such that each record contains a set of attributes. One of the attributes is the target

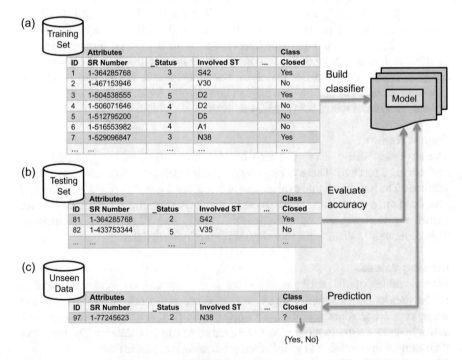

Fig. 6.6 The classification process: (**a**) the training dataset is used to build a classification model, (**b**) the test data is used to evaluate the accuracy of the model, and (**c**) unseen incident reports are classified using the model

class, often referred to as the class label attribute. The goal is to build a model for the class label attribute as a function of the values of other attributes.

The second step is the classification (prediction). The inferred model is used to classify previously unseen records by assigning a class to each of them as accurately as possible. Data records are also referred to as instances, tuples, samples, examples, or observations. The data records analyzed to build the model collectively form the training data set. A test set is used to determine the accuracy of the model. Usually, a given dataset is divided into training and test sets. The training set is used to build the model and the test set is used to validate the model.

Decision Trees

A *decision tree* is a structure resembling a graph, which looks like an upside down tree. It is composed of internal nodes, which contain attribute test conditions, branches to child nodes that correspond to the possible values of the respective attribute, as well as leaf (terminal) nodes representing classes. The starting node in a decision tree is the root node.

Figure 6.7 illustrates a typical decision tree build to classify incident records. This tree can be used to predict whether or not an incident record will be closed. Internal nodes are represented by rectangles, whereas circles represent leaf nodes. To classify an unknown incident instance, the attribute values of the instance are tested along the decision tree, tracing a path from the root node to the leaf node that predicts its class.

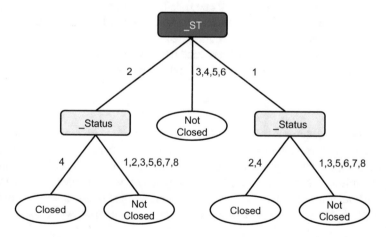

Fig. 6.7 A decision tree for IT service provisioning analysis, which can be used when an IT provider needs to quickly decide whether or not an incident report is likely to be resolved (it should be noted that this tree generated by Weka can be optimized). The underscore (_) in front of ST and Status indicates that the attribute captures the number of times the value of the attribute has changed in the log file

The process of constructing a decision tree out of known samples (observations/-training data) is known as decision tree induction. The basic algorithm uses a greedy strategy, which builds a decision tree in a top-down, recursive, divide-and-conquer way. The basic approach is the following:

1. Create the root node representing all instance records.
2. Choose the best attribute to split the remaining instances and make that attribute a decision node.
3. Repeat this process recursively for each child.
4. Stop when:
   (a) All the instances have the same class attribute label.
   (b) There are no more attributes.
   (c) There are no more instances.

The basic procedure to build a decision tree is the same for most decision tree-based algorithms and only differs on the method used to select the best attribute (node) to split the instances. The best attribute provides most information based on an *attribute selection measure*. It is the best one to split the samples into individual classes. A popular algorithm is the ID3 that uses the measure of *information gain* to select the best attribute for splitting.

Training and Test Set
To build a more accurate predictive model, new attributes were added to the original dataset that was shown in Tables 6.2 and 6.3. This involved changes at the schema level and instance level. The original dataset was parsed and for each incident record, a new instance was created with new attributes.

A Python application was created to read the original dataset (see Table 6.2) and transform its content to contain five additional attributes[2] (see Table 6.4):

$$\_Status, \_FuncDiv, \_Org, \_ST, \_Closed$$

The transformation involved reading the attributes _Status, _FuncDiv, _Org, and _ST from the original dataset, and adding a new attribute indicating how many times the original attribute values changed for each incident reported. For example, _ST = 5 indicated that an incident was handled by 5 support teams. Another new attribute was created to represent the target class: the attribute _Closed. It was set to true to indicate that an incident report was closed.

Attribute Selection
Since many of the attributes present in the original dataset were possibly not relevant for the objective of this study, and, thus, did not contributed to creating a good predictive model, the less significant attributes were removed. The correlation-based

---

[2]New attribute names start with an underscore _.

Table 6.4 The new attributes added to the original dataset (the column *count* identifies how many different values exist for each attribute)

Attribute	Count	Description
_Status	8	The number of distinct states associated with an incident report.
_FuncDiv	4	The number of distinct functional divisions involved in resolving an incident.
_Org	13	The number of organizational divisions involved in resolving an incident.
_ST	24	The number of support teams involved in resolving an incident.
_Closed	2	A Boolean variable indicating if a incident was closed or not.

feature subset selection algorithm [21] was used to evaluate the worth of a subset of attributes by considering the individual predictive ability of each attribute along with the degree of redundancy between them. Subsets of attributes that are highly correlated with the class while having low inter-correlation were preferred. The application of the selection algorithm identified _Status, _FuncDiv, _Org, _ST, and _Closed as the most relevant attributes.

Classifier Construction

The J48 method from Weka (see Sect. 6.5) was used to build a decision tree. Figure 6.8 shows the Weka application and the decision tree constructed. Figure 6.7 shows a simplified view of the decision tree constructed to enable a better interpretation of the results. The most important attribute (the root node) was _ST and represents the number of supporting teams involved in resolving an incident. When _ST is 3, 4, 5, or 6, incidents are typically not closed. On the other hand, when _ST has values 1 or 2, the attribute _Status is used to predict if an incident will be closed or not. In both cases, if the number is equal to 4, incidents are likely closed. Furthermore, for _ST = 1 and _Status = 2, incidents are also closed.

Accuracy Evaluation

Table 6.5 shows a summary of the evaluation of the classification tree created. A high number of instances (incidents) were correctly classified: 92.5 %. Precision and the F-measure were higher for incidents that were not closed; precision was almost 100 %. For incidents that were closed, the precision was of approximately 80 %.

R

The F-measure (or F-score) is calculated based on the precision and recall. The calculation is as follows:

$$Precision = t_p/(t_p + f_p)$$
$$Recall = t_p/(t_p + f_n)$$
$$F - score = 2 * Precision * Recall/(Precision + Recall)$$

Where t_p is the number of true positives, f_p the number of false positives, and f_n the number of false negatives. Precision is defined as the fraction of elements correctly classified as

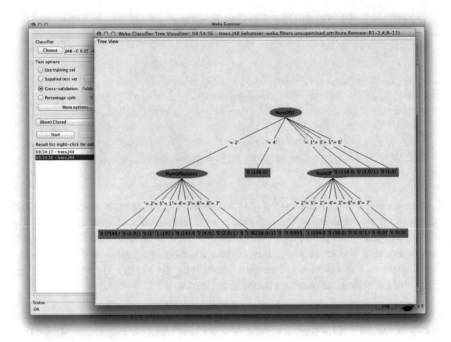

Fig. 6.8 Visualization of the decision tree in Weka

Table 6.5 Summary of the evaluation of the decision tree

Stratified cross-validation (summary)

```
Correctly Classified Instances        19119              92.5904 %
Incorrectly Classified Instances       1530               7.4096 %
Kappa statistic                        0.8207
Mean absolute error                    0.1205
Root mean squared error                0.2462
Relative absolute error               30.9035 %
Root relative squared error           55.7619 %
Total Number of Instances             20649

=== Detailed Accuracy By Class ===

              TP Rate  FP Rate  Precision  Recall  F-Measure  ROC Area  Class
              0.916    0.046    0.982      0.916   0.948      0.944     0
              0.954    0.084    0.804      0.954   0.872      0.944     1
Weighted Avg. 0.926    0.056    0.935      0.926   0.928      0.944

=== Confusion Matrix ===

     a     b   <-- classified as
 13891  1276  |    a = 0
   254  5228  |    b = 1
```

positive out of all the elements the algorithm classified as positive, whereas recall is the fraction of elements correctly classified as positive out of all the positive elements.

Interpretation of the Model

An interesting operational insight from the constructed model, shown in Fig. 6.7, is that the most relevant factor predicting that an incident will be closed is the number of support teams (_ST) involved in its resolution. In other words, a lower number of support teams involved in solving an incident increases its likeliness to be closed. This insight is supported by analyzing the _Status. From the 10.699 instances analyzed, more than 6200 incidents were closed when only one support team was involved. Two hypotheses can be raised:

- Complex incidents require several support teams to be resolved and, thus, are more likely to remain open.
- Incidents that require several support teams introduce communication noise and overhead, which make their resolution less likely.

In both situations, the IT service provider can be recommended to foster the communication and coordination across teams. A notification mechanism can be developed to alert the service desk when an incident is involving more than two teams to resolve an incident as it is likely that the incident will remain unsolved. Management actions such as training and active monitoring can be taken to improve incident closure rate.

6.3.5   Identifying Behavioral Patterns

The next study conducted explored three behavioral patterns that are typically associated with incident management service provisioning: wait-user, push-to-front, and ping-pong.

- Exaggerated use of the status *wait-user*. Incidents must be resolved as soon as possible. Support teams are evaluated based on their timely response. However, when it is necessary to contact and wait for an answer from a customer, the waiting period (labeled as Status = wait-user) is not accounted to evaluate the efficiency of a team. As a result, teams can abuse this phenomenon to increase their evaluation.
- Low occurrence of *push-to-front*. Three lines of support exist for resolving incidents. Each has a higher degree of specialization from the 1st to the 3rd. Thus, 1st line teams can easily be tempted to transfer incidents to 2nd or 3rd line teams to reduce their workload, even though they could be handled at the 1st level. This phenomenon lowers the overall efficiency of the IM service.
- Occurrence of the *ping-pong* effect. Sometimes, because of the difficulties associated with handling certain incidents, the teams responsible for their resolution can transfer incidents to other units or levels, and these, in turn, can return incident in a vicious cycle that does not allow for progress in their resolution.

This phenomenon should be identified and avoided to increase the efficiency of the IM service.

All these phenomena have an impact on service provisioning. Association rules can be used to analyze the incident management dataset to determine if these behaviors occur.

Since good literature on data mining exists, the reader is refereed to the work from Witten et al. [14] and Han et al. [7] to acquire the necessary knowledge on basic concepts underlying association rules—such as the definition of a rule, its support and confidence, and how patterns are mined—to understand this section.

Association Rules

Association rule mining is an approach that finds frequent co-occurring associations among a collection of elements. The goal is to find associations of elements that occur together more often when compared to randomly sampling of all possibilities. An example of this is: when an incident report involves product PROD34, the support team G45 is most often involved in its resolution.

Suppose that the dataset includes the following information:

- There are 60,000 incident records in total.
- 750 records contain PROD34 (1.25 %).
- 6000 records contain G45 (10 %).
- 600 records contain both PROD34 and G45 (1 %).

If there was no association between PROD34 and G45 (i.e., they are statistically independent), then it is expect that only 10 % of PROD34 incidents to be handled by G45 (since 10 % of all records have G45). However, 80 % (600/750) of PROD34 incidents are handled by G45. This is a factor of 8 increase over what was expected—that is called *lift*, which is the ratio of the observed frequency of co-occurrence to the expected frequency. This is determined by counting the records in the dataset. So, in this case, the association rule would state that incidents involving PROD34 also involve G45 with a *lift* factor of 8.

In statistics, *lift* is estimated by the ratio of the joint probability of two items x and y (i.e., $P(x, y)$), divided by the product of their individual probabilities (i.e., $P(x)$ and $P(y)$):

$$lift = \frac{P(x, y)}{[P(x)P(y)]}$$

If the two items are statistically independent, then $P(x, y) = P(x)P(y)$, corresponding to *lift* $= 1$. Note that anti-correlation yields *lift* < 1, which is also an interesting discovery—corresponding to mutually exclusive items that rarely co-occur together. For the incident management service, the objective is to find instance records with a *lift* > 1.

Table 6.6 The new attributes added to the original dataset

Attribute	Description
_Substatus	The number of different substates an incident was.
_InvolvedST	The number of support teams involved in resolving an incident.
_OrgLines	The number of fields of the organization involved in resolving an incident.
_OrgLineA2	Binary attribute indicating if the organizational line A2 was involved in resolving the incident.
_OrgLineC	Binary attribute indicating if the organizational line C was involved in resolving the incident.
_Wait-User	Binary attribute indicating if the incident was placed in the wait-user state.
_Push-to-Front	Binary attribute indicating if the incident was pushed to front.
_Ping-Pong	Binary attribute indicating if teams resolving the incident report exhibited a ping-pong behavior.

Training and Test Set

To extract more meaningful business rules, new attributes were added to the original dataset. A Matlab application was created to read the original dataset and transform its content to contain eight additional attributes (see Table 6.6):

```
_Substatus,_ST,_OrgLines,_OrgLineC,_OrgLineA2,
_Wait-User,_PushFront,_PingPong
```

To account for the valuable information associated with support teams, organizational lines, and substatus of each record, these original attributes were replaced by quantitatively evaluating their value, instead of qualitatively as they were in the original dataset (this approach was already followed in the study carried out in the previous section).

Furthermore, several attributes present in the original dataset were removed. Status was removed since the Substatus attribute includes the needed knowledge of the incidents' states. Owner country was also removed since it provides the same information as the information conveyed by the Country attribute. Finally, attribute Owner first name refers only to the owners of the incidents which was too specific for our analysis.

The main organizational lines, A2 and C, were captured by creating two new attributes, _OrgLineC and _OrgLineA2, respectively, to indicate if an incident was handled by these organizational lines.

All records were analyzed individually to determine if the attribute `Substatus` had the value `wait-user`. When this condition was verified, the new attribute `_Wait-User` was set to true, otherwise it was set to false.

The records of the dataset were also scanned to determine if an incident was handled by the 2nd or 3rd line by analyzing the attribute `Involved ST` of the original dataset. When this condition was verified, the new attribute `_Push-to-Front` was set to true, otherwise it was set to false.

Finally, the ping-pong phenomenon was identified by setting the value of the new attribute `_Push-to-Front` to `true`. This occurred when an incident was initially handled by a particular support team, then sent to another support group, which would send it again to the initial support group. The ping-pong behavior was only identified when the incident report transferred in such a cycle retained its value for the attribute `Substatus`. If this attribute value changed in a cycle, it meant that productive work was performed.

Model Construction

To find association rules in the incident dataset, the *apriori* algorithm [14] was used. It is an influential algorithm for mining frequent itemsets to construct Boolean association rules. The algorithm uses a bottom up approach, where frequent subsets are extended one item at a time. It was designed to operate on datasets containing records, instances, or transactions.

The apriori algorithm implemented in Weka was used with a minimum support of 55 % and a minimum confidence of 90 %. The results generated various rules shown in Table 6.7.

Interpretation of the Model

The results show that a strong relationship exists between the phenomenon push-to-front (handling as many incidents in the 1st line as possible) and ping-pong (sending incidents back and forth between support teams before they are resolved). The following rule expresses this relationship:

$$\_Push - to - Front = 0(4545) \implies \_Ping - Pong = 1(4393)$$

It identifies that the occurrence of push-to-front generally implies a ping-pong phenomenon with a confidence of 97 %. This confidence is the ratio between the number of incidents in which the rule is correct (4.393) and the number of incidents in which the rules is applicable (4.545).

One recommendation can be made based of the association rules found. If the IT service provider concentrates its efforts in alleviating push-to-front, it will also be able to alleviate the ping-pong. This will optimize IT service operations.

Table 6.7 Examples of instances of the dataset

Associator model (full training set)

```
Apriori
=======

Minimum support: 0.55 (4154 instances)
Minimum metric <confidence>: 0.9
Number of cycles performed: 9

Generated sets of large itemsets:
Size of set of large itemsets L(1): 6
Size of set of large itemsets L(2): 10
Size of set of large itemsets L(3): 5
Size of set of large itemsets L(4): 1

Best rules found:

 1. _OrgLines=1 _OrgLineC=1 4416 ==> _OrgLineA2=0 4416               conf:(1)
 2. _OrgLines=1 _OrgLineC=1 _Ping-Pong=0 4246 ==> _OrgLineA2=0 4246 conf:(1)
 3. _OrgLineA2=0 _Push-to-Front=0 4270 ==> _Ping-Pong=0 4175         conf:(0.98)
 4. _Push-to-Front=0 4545 ==> _Ping-Pong=1 4393                      conf:(0.97)
 5. _OrgLines=1 _OrgLineA2=0 4966 ==> _Ping-Pong=0 4779              conf:(0.96)
 6. _OrgLines=1 _OrgLineC=1 4416 ==> _Ping-Pong=0 4246               conf:(0.96)
 7. _OrgLines=1 _OrgLineA2=0 _OrgLineC=1 4416 ==> _Ping-Pong=0 4246
                                                                     conf:(0.96)
 8. _OrgLines=1 _OrgLineC=1 4416 ==> _OrgLineA2=0 _Ping-Pong=0 4246
                                                                     conf:(0.96)
 9. _OrgLines=1 5519 ==> _Ping-Pong=0 5284                           conf:(0.96)
10. _Push-to-Front=0 _Ping-Pong=0 4393 ==> _OrgLineA2=0 4175         conf:(0.95)
```

6.4   Clustering, Regression, and Text Mining

This section reviews three additional methods that can be used to study and improve service delivery. Namely, cluster analysis, regression analysis, and text mining.

6.4.1   Cluster Analysis

Cluster analysis is the process of finding groups of objects such that the objects in a group are similar (or related) to one another and different from (or unrelated to) the objects in other groups. The goal is to have high homogeneity within clusters and high heterogeneity between clusters. For example, cluster analysis is useful to group similar customers when preparing advertisement campaigns. This is often called market segmentation.

▶ **Definition (Clustering)** An important task in data analysis that has the objective to group a set of objects so that objects in the same group are more similar to each other than to those in other groups.

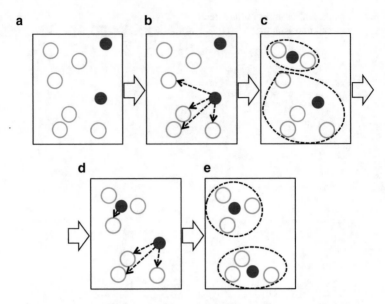

Fig. 6.9 Clustering a set of objects using k-means (**a**) Choose objects as the initial cluster centers. (**b, d**) (Re)assign each object to the closest cluster. (**c**) Update the centroids of the clusters. (**e**) Repeat the procedure until the cluster centroids do not change

Clustering methods are generally classified into the following categories: partitioning methods, hierarchical methods, density-based methods, grid-based methods, and model-based methods. In this chapter, the focus is on the most popular methods: partitioning and hierarchical methods.

The k-means Clustering

The *k-means* method is a partitioning approach, where each cluster is associated with a centroid (center point); each point is assigned to the cluster with the closest centroid, and the number of clusters k is pre-defined. Given a set of objects and a number of clusters k, the algorithm is very simple (Fig. 6.9):

- Step 1. Choose arbitrarily k objects as the initial cluster centers (a).
- Step 2. (Re)assign each object to the closest cluster based on the mean value of the objects in the cluster (b, d).
- Step 3. Update the centroids of the clusters (c).
- Repeat Steps 2 and 3 until the cluster centroids do not change (e).

The initial centroids are often chosen randomly. The clusters are prone to vary from one run to another. The centroid is (typically) the mean of the points in the cluster. The *closeness* is computed by Euclidean distance, cosine similarity, or other related measures. K-means converges for common similarity measures, where most of the convergence usually happens in the first few iterations. It is often the case that the stopping condition is replaced by "until relatively few points do not change clusters".

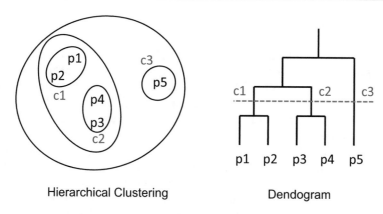

Hierarchical Clustering   Dendogram

Fig. 6.10 Clustering of objects based on hierarchical methods

Hierarchical Clustering

Hierarchical clustering methods work by grouping data objects into a set of nested clusters organized as a hierarchical tree. The clusters can be visualized as a dendogram: a tree like diagram that records the sequences of merges or splits. Hierarchical clustering operates top-down (divisive) or bottom-up (agglomerative). In a top-down fashion, one starts with a large cluster, which is divided until each element is assigned to a cluster. In a bottom-up fashion, one starts with one element per cluster and aggregates clusters together until a global cluster is constructed. Figure 6.10 shows representations of these clustering methods.

Agglomerative clustering algorithms are one of the most popular hierarchical clustering techniques. The basic procedure is the following:

• Compute the distance matrix between the input data points.
• Let each data point be a cluster.
• Repeat
  – Merge the two closest clusters.
  – Update the distance matrix.
• Until only a single cluster remains.

The key operation of this method is the computation of the distance between two clusters. Different distances can be used: maximum distance between elements of each cluster (*complete-linkage* clustering); minimum distance between elements of each cluster (*single-linkage* clustering); and mean distance between elements of each cluster (*average-linkage* clustering).

The final result is a grouping of all the objects in a single cluster, and, of course, the constructed tree hierarchy (dendogram). To generate partitioning clusters, the tree is cut at a given level.

6.4.2 Regression Analysis

The prediction of continuous values can be performed with models that are based on statistical *regression*. Consider the following goal: Determining how fast (time) incident are handled successfully is very important to assess the efficiency of IT service providers. The variables in this case are time and incidents. The goal is to predict the duration of repairs for a given number of incidents (see [22] for a detailed discussion of this type of IT service).

The statistical task is to predict a value of a given continuous-valued variable based on the values of other variables, assuming a linear or nonlinear model of dependency. Regression can be used. It is the model explaining the variation in a dependent variable (Y) using the variation in independent variables (X). If the independent variable(s) sufficiently explain the variation in the dependent variable, the model can be used for prediction. The output of a regression is a function that predicts the dependent variable based upon values of the independent variables.

▶ **Definition (Regression)** Regression is a data analysis task that can be used to predict a number. It creates a linear model from existing data (e.g., from sales, house values, or temperature), and uses the model to predicted unknown occurrences.

A linear regression model defines a line that denotes the relationship between X and Y. The variables may have different levels of correlation, thereby X and Y might be related to each other in many ways: linear or curved. As such, there are distinct methods for linear regression and nonlinear regression, accordingly.

Linear regression fits a straight line to the data. A linear regression model related to the example is depicted in Fig. 6.11. It shows the relation between the dependent variable *time* (in minutes) and the number of incidents, which is the independent variable. Even though the points of the graph do not fall on a straight line, the pattern suggests a linear correlation between the variables.

Other examples of real-world applications of regression include predicting sales of new products based on advertising expenditure, predicting the number of patients with high risk of heart stroke expected to come in the hospital over the weekend to schedule staff, or predicting number of IT incidents expected during the weekend to plan for support technicians.

6.4.3 Text Mining

Text mining is the analysis of data represented in natural language text. Text analytics consists in mining data contained in unstructured, natural language text in order to discover new knowledge and, accordingly, make decisions to solve problems.

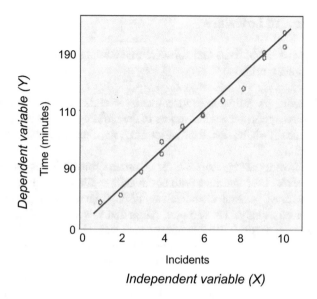

Fig. 6.11 The scatter plot of data suggests a linear relationship between time and the number of incidents

Through an iterative approach, organizations can successfully use text analytics to gain insight into content-specific values such as sentiment, emotion, relevance, and intensity.

▶ **Definition (Text Mining)** A process by which software applications extract specific high-quality information from a large amount of text, usually by recognizing specific terms.

Text mining methods are typically grouped into two main categories: text analysis and document retrieval. Retrieval methods consist in finding from a large corpus of text documents those that are more relevant to a specified query, i.e. user demand. Most prominent examples are web search and retrieval in library catalogs. For example, by analyzing the incident reports submitted to an IT service provider as a corpus of textual documents, text retrieval becomes useful when a technician is searching with a particular query, e.g., incidents related to printers, and the most relevant reports to that query are to be given back as results.

Software that provide text analytics typically transpose words and phrases of the unstructured data representation into numerical values, which can then be analyzed with traditional mining techniques. Important tasks usually performed are document topic detection, text categorization, document clustering, sentiment analysis, and text summarization.

6.5   Tools and Software

The following is a list of tools and software that contain a variety of analytics and machine learning algorithms:

- R and RStudio. A software environment for statistical computing and data mining. It has support for a wide variety of data mining and statistical algorithms, which includes classification, time series analysis, clustering, and linear and non-linear modeling.
- SPSS. A software package suitable for beginners since it is easy to use. It has a "point and click" user interface with commands available via drop-down menus. It performs most general statistical analyses (regression, logistic regression, survival analysis, analysis of variance, factor analysis, and multivariate analysis).
- SAS. In contrast to SPSS, SAS targets power users which can use the application programmability. Users typically write SAS programs that manipulate data and perform data analyses. As with SPSS, it also provides general statistical analyses.
- Mahout. a scalable machine learning and data mining library suitable for Big Data processing. It supports different algorithms such as classification, regression, and recommendation.
- MALLET. A Java based machine learning package for document classification, topic modeling, information extraction, and sequence labeling applications.
- Weka. An open source machine learning software library in Java which includes pre-processing, regression, classification, clustering, and association rules. Figure 6.8 illustrates the visualization of a decision tree generated in Weka.
- Graphlab. A scalable and distributed machine learning library that supports graph-based machine learning algorithms.
- Encog. An advanced machine learning framework that supports a variety of advanced algorithms, as well as methods to normalize and process data. It is available in Java, C++, and .NET.
- Rapid Miner. An open source machine learning in Java, which supports a wide range of machine learning algorithms.
- d3js. Chord diagrams for visualization based on the D3.js javascript library.
- Gephi. An open-source software for visualizing and analyzing network graphs.
- Tableau. A commercial software used for data visualization. The software is suitable for improving the process of finding patterns in data.

Other, more common, tools which can be used include Microsoft Excel for processing of the raw datasets and to explore processed data. Excel is especially helpful for implementing basic and intermediate mathematical functions.

6.6   Conclusions

The large volumes of data available today, generated from service operations, hold implicit information that can be translated into useful knowledge for making intelligent business decisions. In fact, IT service provisioning is often managed by sophisticated information systems, which monitor and log all the activities needed to deliver services with agreed service levels.

Service analytics provides enterprises with powerful mechanisms to convert these logs into in consistent datasets to be analyzed. Extracted insights are important to understand all aspects of service operations to take actions to improve organizational performance and increase customer satisfaction. Service provisioning can be studied to identify human behavior in service intensive organizations at the individual, work group, and organizational levels. Delivery can identify how staff, information systems, and customers arrange themselves to co-create services. Finally, consumption looks into the role of time and place in service delivery.

Existing algorithms from the field of data mining, e.g., classification, association rules, regression, and clustering, can be used with little adaptation and effort. Naturally, in many situations new algorithms must be developed when specific insights need to be extracted.

Review Section

Review Questions

1. Briefly describe the main characteristics that distinguish service analytics from the general data analytics paradigm.
2. This chapter defines three levels under which service analytics methods fall based on the action performed with the discovered knowledge. Briefly describe these levels and give example of analytics methods that fall under each of them.
3. What are the differences between classification and prediction methods?
4. What is cluster analysis? What is a cluster? List the main differences between partitioning methods and hierarchical methods for cluster analysis. Give examples in each method. Describe a scenario in which application of clustering to service systems.
5. Describe the characteristics of the regression method. Define a scenario in which regression can be applied to service systems. How is regression different from cluster analysis?
6. Describe the main types of text mining methods relevant for services. Give one example for each of the following cases: (a) an application that uses document categorization techniques on the data generated by the consumption of a particular service and (b) an application that uses sentiment analysis methods on the data generated by the consumption of a particular service.

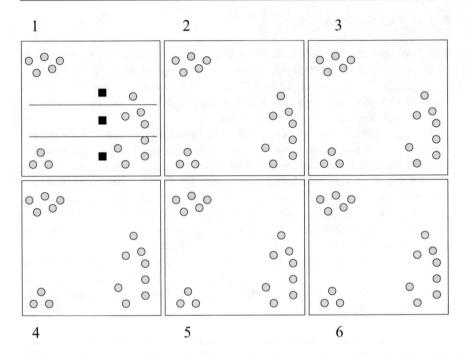

Fig. 6.12 Step-by-step simulation of the k-means clustering algorithm

Project

Clustering

Consider the dataset from Fig. 6.12 as a graphical representation of IT service incident (i.e., each point represents an incident). The company needs to cluster incidents by applying the k-means method in this dataset for the first six iterations. The circles are data points. The initial centroids are given as black rectangles. The separating lines show the clusters boundaries in the first iteration.

1. How do the centroids and boundaries look like in the following iterations? Does the method terminate?
   Hint: this is a quality sketch to demonstrate the main principle of clustering.
2. Show graphically an example that applies k-means algorithm, which for different initializations gives different results.

Decision Tree

Figure 6.13 describes the results of a marketing campaign for a real-estate service. It contains information for each potential client regarding the residential area where he or she lives, the type of household, his earnings, and whether he was a former

Residential Area	House Type	Earnings	Former Client	Result
Suburb	Single-family House	High	No	No Reply
Suburb	Single-family House	High	No	No Reply
Suburb	Townhouse	High	No	No Reply
Suburb	Semi-detached House	Low	No	Replied
Suburb	Townhouse	Low	Yes	Replied
Suburb	Townhouse	High	Yes	No Reply
City	Semi-detached House	Low	Yes	No Reply
City	Townhouse	High	Yes	No Reply
City	Semi-detached House	High	No	Replied
City	Semi-detached House	Low	No	Replied
City	Townhouse	Low	No	Replied
City	Semi-detached House	High	Yes	No Reply
Village	Semi-detached House	Low	Yes	Replied
Village	Townhouse	High	Yes	Replied
Village	Single-family House	Low	No	Replied
Village	Single-family House	High	No	Replied
Village	Townhouse	Low	No	Replied

Fig. 6.13 Dataset with the results of a marketing campaign

client of the company. Use this data to predict whether a person is going to react positively (i.e., send a reply) to an advertisement of the service. Build a decision tree in order to make this prediction.

Key Terms

Analytics   Data management and reporting methods which are a prerequisite for advanced analytics built on methods from statistics and operations research.

Service Analytics   Analytics applied to service systems with the goal to generate the highest benefits for all stakeholders according to the value co-creation principle.

Cluster Analysis   The process of finding groups of objects such that the objects in a group are similar (or related) and different from (or unrelated to) objects in other groups.

Classification and Prediction   Forms of data analysis that can be applied to build models that describe important data patterns or predict future data trends.

Decision Trees   Supervised learning method used for classification. A decision tree is an upside down tree structure, which is used to classify an unknown instance by testing its attribute values along the path from the root node to leaf nodes.

Regression Analysis   A statistical technique used to predict a continuous dependent variable from a number of independent variables.

Text Mining   The analysis of unstructured natural language text to obtain insights.

Further Reading

Gareth James, Daniela Witten, Trevor Hastie, and Robert Tibshirani. *An Introduction to Statistical Learning*. Springer, 2013.

Ian Witten, Eibe Frank, and Mark Hall. *Data Mining: Practical Machine Learning Tools and Techniques*. Morgan Kaufmann, 2011.

Foster Provost and Tom Fawcett. *Data Science for Business: What you need to know about data mining and data-analytic thinking*. O'Reilly, 2013.

References

1. Van Bon J, de Jong A, Kolthof A (2007) Foundations of IT Service Management based on ITIL. Van Haren Publishing, Zaltbommel. ISBN 9789087530570
2. Fromm H, Bloehdorn S (2014) Big data - technologies and potential. In: Enterprise integration, Chap 9. Springer, Berlin, pp 107–124
3. Fayyad U, Piatetsky-Shapiro G, Smyth P (1996) From data mining to knowledge discovery in databases. AI Mag 17(3):37
4. Terry K (2013) Analytics: the nervous system of IT-enabled healthcare. Institute for Health Technology Transformation. Report http://ihealthtran.com/analyticsreport.html
5. Groves P et al (2013) The Big Data revolution in healthcare. McKinsey & Company
6. Fromm H, Habryn F, Satzger G (2012) Service analytics: leveraging data across enterprise boundaries for competitive advantage. In: Globalization of professional services. Springer, Berlin, pp 139–149
7. Han J, Kamber M, Pei J (2011) Data mining: concepts and techniques. The Morgan Kaufmann series in data management systems. Morgan Kaufmann, Los Altos, CA
8. Srivastava J et al (2000) Web usage mining: discovery and applications of usage patterns from web data. ACM SIGKDD Explor Newsl 1(2):12–23
9. Kohavi R, Rothleder N, Simoudis E (2002) Emerging trends in business analytics. Comm ACM 45(8):45–48
10. Davenport T (2006) Competing on analytics. Harv Bus Rev 84(1):98
11. Davenport T, Harris J (2007) Competing on analytics: the new science of winning. Harvard Business Press, Watertown, MA
12. Kobielus J (2010) The Forrester wave predictive analytics and data mining solutions, Q1 2010. Forrester Research, Cambridge, MA
13. Chaudhuri S, Dayal U (1997) An overview of data warehousing and OLAP technology. ACM SIGMOD Rec 26(1):65–74
14. Witten I, Frank E, Hall M (2011) Data mining: practical machine learning tools and techniques. Morgan Kaufmann, Los Altos, CA
15. Wilson H, Keating B (2008) Business forecasting with business ForecastX, 6th edn. McGraw-Hill/Irwin, New York, 513 pp
16. Hanke JE, Wichern D (2008) Business forecasting, 9th edn. Prentice Hall, Englewood Cliffs, 576 pp
17. Analytics (2015) INFORMS online. http://www.informs.org/Community/Analytics. Accessed: 2015-10-17

18. Gerke K, Cardoso J, Claus A (2009) Measuring the compliance of processes with reference models. In: 17th international conference on cooperative information systems (CoopIS 2009). Springer, Algarve
19. OGC (2007) ITIL service operation. ITIL Series. Stationery Office ISBN: 978-0113310463
20. Paszkiewicz Z, Picard W (2013) Analysis of the Volvo IT incident and problem handling processes using process mining and social network analysis. In: van Dongen B et al (eds) CEUR online proceedings, 2013. Proceedings of the 3rd business process intelligence challenge co-located with 9th international business process intelligence workshop (BPI 2013)
21. Hall M (1998) Correlation-based feature subset selection for machine learning. Ph.D. thesis. University of Waikato, Hamilton
22. Cardoso J, Lopes R, Poels G (2014) Service systems: concepts, modeling, and programming. Springer, Berlin

Service Optimization

7

Melanie Reuter-Oppermann and Anne Zander

Summary

This chapter provides an overview of Operations Research and its mathematical models for planning problems arising in the area of services. For a better understanding, a basic introduction into the field of Operations Research is given. Different examples from service areas are presented. Several methods for solving the mathematical problems are discussed. In addition, the optimization software called IBM ILOG CPLEX Optimization Studio is presented that can be used to determine an optimal solution for a mathematical problem. The use of simulation in the area of Operations Research is also discussed and the software AnyLogic is used to provide examples.

Learning Objectives
1. Understand the concept of Operations Research and how it can be used to tackle planning problems.
2. Remember the presented planning problems, be able to reproduce the formulations and to explain them.
3. Implement OPL models and solve them using IBM ILOG CPLEX.
4. Recognize, model, and solve similar planning problems for different service domains.

M. Reuter-Oppermann (✉) • A. Zander
Karlsruhe Service Research Institute (KSRI), Karlsruhe Institute
of Technology (KIT), Karlsruhe, Germany
e-mail: melanie reuter@kit edu; anne zander@kit edu

© Springer International Publishing Switzerland 2015   217
J. Cardoso et al. (eds.), *Fundamentals of Service Systems*, Service Science: Research
and Innovations in the Service Economy, DOI 10.1007/978-3-319-23195-2_7

▶ **Opening Case** Operations Research for Airline Services

Planning problems arising for Airlines or Airports are interesting from both the Operations Research and the Service Research perspective. In this opening case two different examples are presented. One case considers an airline whereas the other presents a planning problem at an airport. Both cases show that by applying Operations Research resources can be used more efficiently in order to save costs, and increase staff and customer satisfaction.

Crew Scheduling at Air New Zealand

For airlines crew scheduling is one of the most important and challenging planning problems. Several years ago, Air New Zealand Limited, an international and domestic airline group that offers both air passenger and cargo transport services, discovered their need to improve the way they scheduled tours of duty and rosters. Both, tours of duty planning and crew rostering are complex planning problems involving scheduling and routing that need to be solved with Operations Research methods. A tour of duty means a sequence of flights with alternating duty periods and rest periods. A duty period can contain one or several flights depending of the flight lengths. For example, a tour could be Auckland–Sydney–Fiji–Auckland. In this tour, a crew member works on the flights Auckland–Sydney and Fiji–Auckland. The flight Sydney–Fiji is a passengering flight that brings the crew member as a passenger to an airport for the subsequent flight as the next duty period. For the tours of duty planning problem at Air New Zealand minimum cost tours of duty were determined in order to cover all scheduled flights. Costs occur for example for passengering flights (as the seat cannot be sold to a customer) or for overnight stays in hotels if necessary. Solving the rostering problem then assigned tours of duty to individual crew members. Air New Zealand developed eight optimization-based software tools together with the University of Auckland that solved all aspects of the two planning problems for national and international flights. It is stated that as of 2000, Air New Zealand saved $13,500,000 per year due to these systems which in addition could better fulfill crew members' preferences [1].

Optimizing Copenhagen Airport

Obviously, it is not only possible to optimize planning problems for airlines, but it is also interesting to look at problems which arise at airports. There, a lot of different allocation, scheduling and location problems arise. For example, check-in counter allocation is important such that passengers can check-in as quickly as possible while maintaining a reasonable cost level for counters and staff. Another problem is the allocation of aircrafts to gates as expressed in Fig. 7.1. This does not seem to be of importance for passengers directly, but of course when an aircraft has to wait before it can finally dock on a gate, passengers might miss connecting flights

Fig. 7.1 Aircraft parking problem

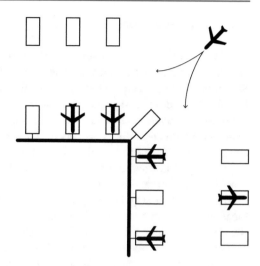

or future flights might be delayed. Therefore, solving both problems is crucial for a good service performance of an airport which was for example recognized by the airport in Copenhagen.

Copenhagen Airport is the wold's first private airport (1925) serving over 150 airlines and 23 million passengers a year. For these 150 airlines only 100 check-in counters are available such that deciding which counter to use for each outbound flight is complex as well as critical to the functioning of the airport. As the airport management did not want to invest in additional check-in counters, they had to find a way to efficiently utilize their existing counters. Therefore, the Operations Research group built an optimization model for the allocation problem that was solved by an optimization software. They were able to improve the utilization of the counters so that they could postpone over $16M in investments for additional check-in facilities.

In 2010 the Operations Research group at Copenhagen Airports also had to face a "parking problem" of the aircrafts. The "parking lot" was often crowded and usually full, not every space (aircraft stand) was able to accommodate every aircraft and the demand was predicted to increase significantly in the future. As building one new stand had a cost of $5M–$10M, they got the task to build a system that could maximize the utilization of each stand as well as minimize costs for an expected future increase of capacity. It took them 2 months to build a mathematical model that included all the requirements and restrictions as constraints. There were hard constraints that had to be fulfilled like for example certain aircraft types could only park at certain stands as well as softer preferences that for example some airlines wanted to be located closer together as they had a high number of passengers transferring between aircrafts. Again, they used the same software as for the counter allocation problem. The results lead to a more efficient plan that served as a basis for new investments in stands and gates with a total cost over $70M [2, 3].

▶ **Opening Case**

7.1   Introduction

In 2003 the President Tom Cook of INFORMS (Institute for Operations Research
and the Management Sciences) initiated a campaign in order to promote Operations
Research and to develop a new way of explaining what Operations Research (OR)
is and what it does. The participants of the campaign came up with the following
definition. "Operations Research is the discipline of applying advanced analytical
methods to help make better decisions." Further they agreed on a new slogan which
captures the essence of Operations Research: "The Science of Better" [4, 5].

Not only airline and airports need "better decisions", but for example in production planning Operations Research can be used to locate facilities, to determine the
production schedule (when to produce how many pieces of which kind at which
location) or to schedule tasks on machines. Another important area Operations
Research is widely used in is Supply Chain Management. But of course also
services can be involved in a Supply Chain, for example if the transport of goods
was outsourced to a hauler. Basically, the same ideas for optimizing production
planning can also be used to improve services. For example, the routes of technical
sales employees serving customers on a B2B level or the management of incident
tickets could be improved. Improving services here not only means to increase the
efficiency, to maximize the profit or minimize costs but also to increase or balance
the utilization of resources (which could be physical resources as well as personnel,
for example). In addition, as often the focus is on the customers when planning
and improving services, minimizing their waiting time, maximizing the availability
or in general maximizing their satisfaction are possible aims. All these goals can
be used as a so-called objective function for the mathematical model that is built
in accordance to the planning problem that needs to be solved. In practice it often
happens that there is not just one goal, but two or more. Then the problem is called
multi-criteria. This is because different aspects and interests need to be balanced
which is especially important in the service industry [6]. In that case often a tradeoff
between different interests and goals needs to be made.

As different types of service industries exist, Operations Research models and
methods for these types can also differ, of course. For consistency reasons services
arising in the area of healthcare are chosen for examples throughout this chapter as
this is an important service area in research as well as in practice. In addition, it will
also be pointed out to which other services the models and methods can be applied.

There already exists a variety of publications on Operations Research (OR) for
services. For example, in 2012 the journal Computers and Operations Research
published a special issue on OR for service science. Especially in the area of
healthcare the use of OR is widespread—at least in literature and depending on
the country also already in practice. For example, the European working group
"ORAHS" (Operations Research Applied to Healthcare Services) organizes a
conference each year only dedicated to OR in healthcare. Every second year, there is
an INFORMS healthcare conference, usually held in the United States of America.

In 2010, Daskin published a whole book on Operations Research for Service Science [6]. Typical planning problems that arise for (public or private) service providers include:

- Location planning: How many hospitals are needed and where should they be located to serve all patients?
- Resource allocation: How should scarce resources (such as operating rooms) be allocated to demands (i.e., surgeries)?
- Short-term workforce planning: How many nurses need to be scheduled for each shift and when should each shift begin?
- Vehicle routing problems: How many routes/vehicles are needed to serve a set of customers (e.g., patients of a home healthcare provider) and how should the routes look like?

The issue of finding the right balance between the demand for services and the supply of those seems especially important when planning and optimizing services and their underlying processes. Obviously, this can be reformulated as finding the balance between the achieved service level for the customer and the cost for providing that level [6].

7.2 Operations Research

Operations Research is characterized by the use of quantitative models and methods to support decisions. Thereby, the quantitative models depict the essential decisions to take considering influencing parameters of a real world problem. The methods of Operations Research are used to determine the best decision possible to solve the problem and to analyze the properties of a given decision. In this section, the basic concepts of Operations Research are described. First, we explain the process of developing a quantitative model based on a real world problem. Then, a basic Operations Research optimization model is described and different planning dimensions as types of input data or planning levels are discussed. At last, different areas within Operations Research that use specific modelling techniques, analyzing methods and solution methods are presented.

▶ **Definition (Operations Research)** The discipline of applying advanced analytical methods, i.e., optimization methods, to help make better decisions.

7.2.1 Idealized Planning Process

The process of an OR based planning, i.e., preparing for problem solving, is displayed in Fig. 7.2. First of all it is important to realize that there exists a "necessity and potential for improvement" and that the corresponding "problem" in the real world can be modeled and solved using OR. This is often realized

Fig. 7.2 OR planning
process

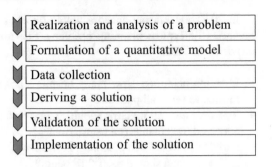

because something went wrong or goes wrong repeatedly. Another possibility is that an analysis of existing data showed the need or the potential for improvement. After the recognition of the problem it needs to be analyzed, and its most important elements such as goals, restrictions and the effect of decisions on the goals have to be abstracted to build a quantitative model. Here, a model is a simplified version of reality where the important real relationships are preserved. A generic quantitative OR model, i.e., an optimization model, will be presented in the next section. Then, data needs to be collected to quantify the model elements. Next, the model has to be solved, i.e., among the possible decisions that fulfill the restrictions the best one with respect to the objective is taken. In the following sections different solution methods are presented. The decision taken is the solution of the problem. It needs to be validated, i.e., it has to be checked if the implementation of the solution in the real world problem really solves it. If this is the case, it can be put into practice. If this is not the case the model formulation needs to be checked again as well as the data used to determine the parameters of the model.

7.2.2 Operations Research Models

In Operations Research different kinds of models exist that play an important role in science as well as in business in general. First of all, there are quantitative or mathematical models (often also called formulations). As described in the previous section, in general these models are idealized representations of reality and represent the consequences of decisions with respect to given goals and restrictions. They are built of mathematical symbols, expressions and systems of equations. In a basic optimization model decisions must be taken which is represented by the decision variables $x = (x_1, x_2, \ldots, x_n)$, with n being a natural number. The goal to be achieved is represented by the objective function f which is a function of the decision variables. Depending on the goal the objective function is to be minimized or maximized $\min_{x \in X}(\max_{x \in X})f(x)$. Given the restrictions of the problem there is only a certain degree of freedom in the decision which is given by a decision space X, i.e., a decision x has to satisfy $x \in X$. Often X is defined by a number of conditions such as equations and inequalities that are called constraints. Now, taking a decision means to choose values for the decision variable x. A decision x with $x \in X$ is called feasible solution, whereas every decision x with $x \notin X$ is called infeasible solution. If there is $x^* \in X$ such that $f(x^*) = \min_{x \in X}(\max_{x \in X})f(x)$, then x^* is called an optimal solution and $f(x^*)$ optimal (objective) value. Finding an optimal solution or at least a near optimal solution is the core of optimization. All constant values appearing in the constraints and in the objective function are called parameters of the model. They are generated from the real world data the problem is based on.

To better understand the previous definition of a basic optimization model we look at a specific example. Imagine a farmer who can cultivate two different grains, e.g., wheat and rye, and has to decide how many acres to assign to which grain. Hereby, he wants to maximize his revenue. Suppose the farmer has 10 acres and selling the wheat from one acre of land yields 10,000 €, whereas for rye it is 12,000 €. Legal guidelines prescribe to cultivate at least three acres of wheat. Let us transform this simple problem into a mathematical model. The farmer has to take two decisions $x = (x_1, x_2)$ where x_1 represents the acres used to grow wheat and x_2 represents the number of acres used to grow rye. The revenue is then given by $10,000\,x_1 + 12,000\,x_2$ which the farmer wants to maximize. Further, he knows that he cannot use more acres than he owns. This leads to $x_1 + x_2 \leq 10$. Similarly, the constraint $x_1 \geq 3$ is obtained. To be sure that the model only accepts decisions that are valid in the real world the constraints $x_1, x_2 \geq 0$ are added. In summary, the farmer ends up with the following model:

$$\max 10{,}000\,x_1 + 12{,}000\,x_2$$

$$\text{subject to}\, x_1 + x_2 \leq 10$$

$$x_1 \geq 3$$

$$x_1, x_2 \geq 0$$

In this case, finding an optimal solution is fairly simple. As both, wheat and rye, are profitable to sell the farmer will till every acre. Given that rye is more profitable than wheat he would cultivate as much wheat as necessary -3 acres $-$ and sow rye on the rest of his land -7 acres. Hence, the optimal solution is given by $x_1 = 3$ and $x_2 = 7$. Unfortunately, not all problems can be solved that easily. Modeling real world problems often leads to having a lot of variables and many constraints that are more complicated than in this example. Then, sophisticated solution methods adapted to the specific problem in order to find an optimal or at least near optimal solution are needed. Therefore, a first simple taxonomy of OR models is presented in the following. Knowing the category of a model in the taxonomy helps to decide for the appropriate solution methods.

Considering real world problems often leads to the definition of more than one goal, e.g., if there are several stakeholder involved in the decision process. Then multiple objective functions must be taken into account. There exist different theories of how to balance various objective functions. So first, single and multi objective models can be distinguished. The example model of the farmer can be categorised as a single objective model. His single aim is to maximize his revenue. But this example model has yet another interesting property. It is linear. This means all constraint terms and the objective function are linear functions, hence they are of the form $a_1x_1 + a_2x_2 + \cdots + a_nx_n$, where the x_i are the decision variables and the a_i are constants/parameters, $i = 1, \ldots, n$. Every model that is not linear is called non-linear. The domain of an optimization model can either be general, which essentially means that the decision variables take real values, or they can be integer, which means the decision variables can only take integer values. If a model is linear with real valued decision variables, we call it a Linear Program (LP). If it is linear and integer, we call it an Integer Linear Program (ILP). Sometimes a linear model has some decision variables that can take real values and others that can only take integer values. Such models are called Mixed Integer Linear Programs (MILP). This chapter will mainly focus on linear models with one objective.

7.2.3 Planning Dimensions

Operations research planning problems can be categorized further with respect to their type and usage of data, to their planning horizon and to their complexity. Considering the data, we can differentiate between the following cases:

- Input data can be either static (fixed) or dynamic (changes throughout the planning horizon).
- Input data can be deterministic (known in advance) or stochastic (often either probability distributions or scenarios are known).
- Input data can be offline (completely known in advance) or online (becomes known along the planning horizon).

There are mainly three levels for the planning horizon:

- Strategic (long term planning, e.g., several years).
- Tactical (mid term planning, e.g., 1 year).
- Operational (short term planning, e.g., daily).

Last but not least, there are two main complexity classes: efficiently solvable, i.e., in polynomial time, and non-efficiently solvable, so called NP-hard problems. Efficiently solvable problems are mostly easy to handle, and using the right methods optimal solutions can be found quickly up to big input sizes. In contrast, non-efficiently solvable problems can take way too long to solve even for small input sizes. In these cases, often near optimal solutions are searched instead, using heuristics which will be explained later on.

7.2.4 Areas of Operations Research

Operations Research can be divided into a number of different areas. Its definition actually varies a bit for different countries due to several possible interpretations of OR. This is supported by the fact that OR is taught and studied by mathematicians, computer scientists and economists. However, there are several basic areas of OR that should be mentioned at this point.

Linear Programming

Linear Programming deals with solving Linear Programs where the decision variables take real values and are bound by linear functions. These programs are generally easy to solve to optimality using the Simplex method [7, 8]. We will learn more about this method in the section Solution Methods.

(Linear) Integer and Combinatorial Optimization

Integer Programming is concerned with optimization problems where some or all the decision variables must be restricted to integer values [9, p. 533]. In the case of integer decision variables one often has a finite set of possible decisions. Hence, one can enumerate and calculate the objective function for all of them in order to solve the problem. Unfortunately, if the set of possible decisions is too large this would take too much time. Therefore, more sophisticated methods have been developed to find optimal or near optimal solutions without testing every single feasible decision. As an example, the Branch-and-Bound method is shortly presented in the Solution Methods' section [8].

Nonlinear Programming

Nonlinear programming is concerned with solving optimization problems, where the object function and constraint functions may be nonlinear [9, p. 547]. General nonlinear problems are often very difficult to solve. But there are some methods that can be applied to specific non-linear problems. For example, there are methods to solve quadratic optimization problems with a quadratic objective function and linear constraints. A quadratic linear function has the following general form: $f(x) = \sum_{i,j=1}^{n} a_{ij}x_i x_j$ where the x_i are the decision variables and the a_i are parameters. There are also specific methods to solve convex minimization problems. A convex optimization problem is characterized by a convex objective function and a decision space X that is also convex. One important property of convex minimization is that local optima are global optima. This means that any decision x which is best in an environment of x is already best considering the whole decision space X.

Stochastic Optimization

Stochastic optimization deals with multiple decision stages where decisions have to be taken before certain parameters become known. These parameters are often characterized by a distribution. The goal is often to take the decision such that the expected value of the objective function over all decision stages is maximized or minimized [10].

Robust Optimization

Another approach to tackle problems with uncertain data is robust optimization. Often the parameters of an optimization model are only known up to a certain degree of accuracy. Depending on the definition a solution to a robust optimization problem is called robust if it is the best solution among all solutions that are feasible for all parameter realizations [11].

Graph Theory and Network Planning

Graph Theory is the study of graphs which are defined by a set of vertices and a set of edges, where each edge connects two vertices. An edge can have a direction. These graphs may represent physical networks, such as electric circuits, or less tangible interactions, such as supply chains. One area of application is the critical path method, which is used to determine the longest path in an activity network to schedule activities and to minimize the total cost of a project [12, p. 2, 43, 53].

Game Theory

Game Theory is a mathematical theory that deals with the general features of competitive situations, i.e., situations where the final outcome depends primarily upon the combination of strategies selected by the adversaries, in a formal, abstract way [9].

Dynamic Programming

Dynamic Programming is a mathematical technique for making a sequence of interrelated decisions. It provides a systematic procedure for determining the optimal combination of decisions. The problem is divided into stages with a decision required at every stage [9, p. 440, 445].

Queueing Theory

Queueing Theory describes the behavior of queuing systems. It includes the (stochastic) arrival process of requests, the (stochastic) service process of customers and, consequently, the departure process of customers, rejected/waiting customers, servers, etc. [13]. We will learn more about this area in the section Queuing Theory [14].

Simulation

Simulation is dealing with testing different scenarios or decisions of a problem without implementing them in the real world. To execute these virtual experiments quickly simulations are implemented as computer programs. Simulation is especially attractive if a problem is too complex to build a mathematical model and to solve it to optimality. We will learn more about this area in the section Simulation [15, 16].

7.3   Solution Methods

In Operations Research, two main possibilities for solving the mathematically formulated problems exist: they can either be solved exactly or heuristically. Whereas an exact solution procedure aims at finding an optimal solution, a heuristic can in general only provide a feasible solution that is often of "good quality", i.e., within a certain range around the optimum. For determining exact solutions (commercial) solvers are often used. One of them, IBM ILOG CPLEX together with its modeling language OPL is used in this chapter for solving the examples and therefore now briefly described.

7.3.1   Exact Solutions

The easiest way to get an optimal solution to an optimization problem is to solve it with an optimization software package like the IBM ILOG CPLEX Optimization Studio. The language to implement the formulation in is called OPL, the solver that determines the optimal solution CPLEX. It can solve MILPs, ILPs and Quadratic Problems. In addition, the IBM ILOG CPLEX Optimization Studio offers with CP another solver that can solve Nonlinear Problems and that is especially well-suited for Scheduling Problems. It uses solution procedures from Constraint Programming. Figure 7.3 shows the user interface of the IBM ILOG CPLEX Optimization Studio.

Besides the IBM ILOG CPLEX Optimization Studio other optimization software exists. The FICO Xpress Optimization Suite for example uses its own solvers and its modeling language Xpress-Mosel. Other tools like Aimms offer a user interface with an own modeling language and use third party solvers like CPLEX.

CPLEX offers various algorithms for solving Linear Programming problems, for example the simplex algorithm. Mixed Integer Programming problems would usually be solved by the Branch-and-Bound algorithm.

The simplex method was developed and published by Georg Dantzig in 1947 [17] and is considered one of the mostly used algorithms of this century. It finds an optimal solution to a Linear Program. Geometrically, the decision space (the set of feasible solutions) of a Linear Program can be seen as a system of linear inequalities that defines a convex polyhedron. It can be shown that there is either no optimal solution or at least one corner (extreme point) of the polyhedron is optimal. Starting from a given corner the simplex algorithm finds another corner with a higher (or equal) objective value. The simplex algorithms stops when the optimal value with an optimal (corner) solution is found [18, 19].

The Branch-and-Bound method [20] is used for solving discrete optimization problems (e.g. Integer Linear Programs) by systematically dividing (branching) the set of feasible points into subsets. Starting with the entire set at the root of the tree, the problem is solved for each subset, thus, forming nodes in an enumeration tree. Subsets are formed by dividing the sets according to the solution of the previous node, where one variable is considered and branches are formed according to its

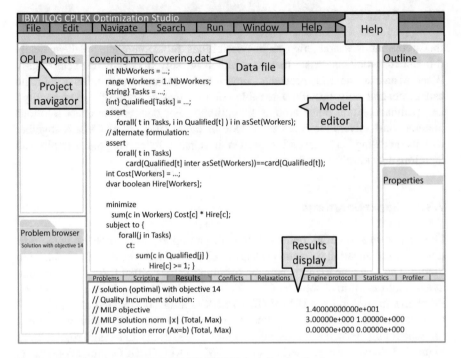

Fig. 7.3 User interface of the IBM ILOG CPLEX Optimization Studio

possible values with regard to integrality. These form new constraints for calculating
the problem in the next node. By computing upper and lower bounds through solving
a relaxed version of the original problem, i.e., without considering the integrality
restriction, the number of sub problems to be solved is reduced. Those sets having a
solution worse than the best available solution (the lower bound) at the same stage
are eliminated, since a branch will not produce any solutions with values higher than
on this stage [7, 18, 19].

Thanks to the IBM Academic Initiative it is possible for students and researchers
to get a free version of the IBM ILOG CPLEX Optimization Studio. The Studio
offers a range of examples that can be used as a starting point when implementing
a model. Using the Bin Packing problem the basic concepts of OPL are briefly
described in Sect. 7.4.

7.3.2 Heuristics

Heuristics are often used if problems cannot be solved within a reasonable amount
of time. That might for example be the case if a solution is needed in practice within
seconds, but the problem itself is NP-hard and the problem instance is big.

Heuristics can be classified using different kinds of categories. For example, there
are general heuristics like Greedy or problem specific heuristics that are especially
constructed for only one (or a small group of) problem(s). Construction heuristics

determine a first, feasible solution while improvement heuristics build on a starting solution and aim at improving it in terms of the underlying objective function

Another important group of heuristics are the metaheuristics that are described by Osman and Laporte [21] as follows:

"A metaheuristic is formally defined as an iterative generation process which guides a subordinate heuristic by combining intelligently different concepts for exploring and exploiting the search space, learning strategies are used to structure information in order to find efficiently near-optimal solutions."

Often heuristics only find local optima. A local optimum is a solution that is better than the ones in its neighbourhood but there might be another solution in the solution space that is better, i.e., has a smaller objective function value. Here, the neighborhood is defined by all solutions that can be built from the current solution through a transformation rule. In the end, a solution can be locally optimal but still not be very good overall [22]. The overall best solution is called a global optimum, but depending on the problem instance there might be more than one.

In the following, several (meta-)heuristics are presented.

Local Search

"A local search procedure operates just like a local improvement procedure except that it may not require that each new trial solution must be better than the preceding trail solution" [9, p. 615].

Local search procedures usually start with a feasible solution and move on to other solutions in the neighborhood of the current one with each iteration. Using a local search procedure means deciding how this rule is to be carried out, which solution will be used for the next iteration and in which order all the solutions of a neighborhood will be analyzed.

In the narrower sense, local search procedures are those that allow worse solutions to be chosen for the next iteration in order to overcome a local optimum. Simulated annealing and tabu search are local search procedures [23, pp. 129–130].

The algorithm terminates if there are no remaining solutions in the neighborhood or if the chosen number of iterations have been executed. The best solution found in the overall process is declared the final solution.

Challenges when using this metaheuristic include finding an initial trial solution, specifying the definition of the term "neighborhood" and implementing a procedure to randomly select a new solution [9, pp. 626–629].

Simulated Annealing

"Simulated annealing is another widely used metaheuristic that enables the search process to escape from a local optimum" [9]. A basic simulated annealing algorithm starts with an initial trial solution. The next trial solution is chosen randomly among the immediate neighbors of the current trial solution. This candidate is always accepted if it offers a better solution value than the current one. If it is worse than the current one, it is accepted with a probability of acceptance. This probability depends on how much worse the solution is, as well as on a changeable parameter T. The algorithm starts with a relatively large T. As it progresses T decreases resulting in a lower and lower probability to accept worse solutions. If a candidate is not accepted, the process is repeated with another one which is again randomly chosen from the current solution's neighborhood.

Tabu Search

"Tabu search is a widely used metaheuristic that uses some common-sense ideas to enable the search process to escape from a local optimum" [9]. Tabu search is a local search procedure in which the complete neighborhood of a solution is evaluated with the steepest ascent/mildest descent approach. In each iteration the neighborhood is searched for the solution with the best solution value which is then chosen as the new current solution for the next iteration. This is also the case if the best solution value is worse than the solution value of the current solution. To prevent coming straight back at the better solution in the next step, a tabu list is created. All chosen solutions are saved in this list and not allowed to be chosen again as a current solution.

Challenges of this metaheuristic include the definition of a neighborhood, the representation of a solution on the tabu list and a stopping rule [9, pp. 615–617].

Genetic Algorithms

Genetic algorithms are based on an analogy to the "theory of evolution" by Charles Darwin. The notion of the "fittest solution" surviving to the next generation is used by this metaheuristic. A genetic algorithm uses a population (a set of feasible solutions) which evolves with each iteration. Some of the best solutions—the ones with the highest or lowest solution value—are kept for the next iteration. This is called "selection". Two solutions can be used to create a new one with features of both parents ("crossover"). "Mutation" occurs on a single solution when a small part of the solution is changed. This accounts for features that have never been possessed before by any of the previous members of the population.

Challenges when using this metaheuristic include deciding on a population size, implementation of the three steps to obtain a new generation of the population and finding a suitable stopping rule ([9, pp. 635–637]).

Greedy

Opening procedures are called "greedy" if they always choose the solution with the biggest gain in objective function value for the next step. They are unforesightful [23, p. 129]. On the other side, they are often quite easy to implement.

In the following, some important problems for service planning are presented. For Bin Packing and Routing problems also specific heuristics are presented.

7.4   Bin Packing

In a Bin Packing problem objects of different sizes must be packed into a number of finite bins each having the same fixed capacity. The aim is to minimize the number of bins needed to do so. In the following, the example of assigning surgeries to operating rooms is used to further explain the Bin Packing Problem.

7.4.1 Introduction

One of the hospital domains with high value creation is the surgical ward. Nevertheless, costs incurred at the surgical ward are among the highest within a hospital. A study of 100 U.S. hospitals in 2005 found out that an operating room minute is charged by an average of 62 dollars. These numbers do not even include surgeon and anesthesia provider fees [24]. Another article that investigates the operating room allocation and the case scheduling of two hospitals states that an annual excess labor cost of 2 or 1.4 millions, respectively, could have been saved in private-practice [25]. Therefore, it is crucial for the profitability of a hospital to use the resource operating room time as efficiently as possible. In the following we call an operating room open if the necessary staff and equipment to run the operating room on a given day/shift are available. Hence, the number of open operating rooms should be minimized while ensuring that the demand is met. The demand of an operating theater is given by a set of surgeries that need to be performed and that may have different durations. So the task is to allocate these surgeries in the operating rooms while minimizing the number of open rooms. Assuming the durations of the surgeries to be known in advance and calling the operating rooms bins and the surgeries items we can model the problem of assigning surgeries to operating rooms as a classical Bin Packing problem which will be explained in the following. Of course, reality is more complex since we might not have all information about the demand before the beginning of the work day, the surgery durations are usually not deterministic and we have to consider many restrictions about the allocation and sequencing of surgeries. Still, the Bin Packing model may provide some insight into the problem.

7.4.2 Theory

We consider bins with capacity b and $n \in \mathbb{N}$ items with sizes $a_1, a_2, \ldots, a_n$ with $a_i \leq b$ for all $i \in \{1, 2, \ldots, n\}$. The task is to put the items into bins where we want to minimize the number of bins used. As we have n items given, we will use at most n bins. Therefore, we assume n bins being available in the following. We formulate the Bin Packing problem as a binary integer linear programm (BILP). In order to do so, we need two binary decision variables. The variable x_{ij} equals 1 if item j is put in bin i and 0 otherwise. The variable y_i is 1 if bin i is open, i.e., there is at least one item assigned to it, and 0 otherwise. The BILP is then given by

$$\min \sum_{i=1}^{n} y_i \tag{7.1}$$

$$\text{s.t.} \sum_{j=1}^{n} a_j x_{ij} \leq b y_i, \qquad \forall i \in \{1, 2, \ldots, n\} \tag{7.2}$$

$$\sum_{i=1}^{n} x_{ij} = 1, \qquad \forall j \in \{1, 2, \ldots, n\} \tag{7.3}$$

$$y_i \in \{0, 1\}, \quad \forall i \in \{1, 2, \ldots, n\} \tag{7.4}$$

$$x_{ij} \in \{0, 1\}, \quad \forall i \in \{1, 2, \ldots, n\}, \forall j \in \{1, 2, \ldots, n\} \tag{7.5}$$

The objective (7.1) is to minimize the number of bins used. The first constraint (7.2) assures that no item is assigned to a bin that is not open and that the bin's capacity is not violated by the sum of the sizes of the assigned items. The next constraint (7.3) states that every item is put in exactly one bin. The constraints (7.4) and (7.5) are the domain constraints that ensure that the decision variables x_{ij} and y_i are binary.

7.4.3 Heuristics

The Bin Packing problem is NP-hard [26], i.e., the time to find the optimal solution of the problem increases exponentially with the size of problem instances for all currently known algorithms. Therefore, heuristics have been developed to find near optimal solutions in a reasonable amount of time. The First Fit Decreasing algorithm initially sorts the items in order of decreasing size. In this order the items are put in bins where every item is put in the first open bin, i.e., a bin to which there is at least one item already assigned, which still has enough space. If there is no such bin a new one is opened. In the worst case, the value of the objective function is 50 % higher than the optimal value [27, p. 67, 68]. Another heuristic is called Best Fit Decreasing. First, the items are also sorted in decreasing order as done by the First Fit Decreasing but then an item is put in an open bin that minimizes the residual capacity of the bin. If the allocation to an already open bin is not possible, a new bin is opened. The worst case performance is the same as for First Fit Decreasing [27, p. 67, 68]. In Fig. 7.4 a sequence of items is shown that needs three bins to be packed when applying the First Fit or Best Fit heuristic whereas the optimal packing only needs two bins.

Until now we considered the situation that every item as well as its size is known in advance of the allocation decision. In the real world this is often not the case. For example in our operating theater, emergencies might occur that should be treated on the same day. To cover this aspect, we consider the online Bin Packing problem with and without lookahead. In the online Bin Packing problem, only one item and its size are given at a time. After having put it in a bin, a new item is revealed. As we are missing the information about upcoming items in general, we will not be able to perform as well as an optimal algorithm that knows every item in advance. Two examples of heuristics solving online Bin Packing problems are First Fit and Best Fit which work similarly to First Fit Decreasing and Best Fit Decreasing with the difference that of course we do not sort the items in advance since we have to allocate one item at a time. In the worst case the heuristics could use 7/4 times as many bins as the optimal solution if the items were known in advance [27, p. 67, 68].

Sequence of items (bin capacity b=1):

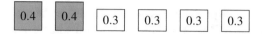

Optimal solution: First Fit and Best Fit solution:

                       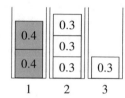

Fig. 7.4 Comparison of the optimal solution and the heuristics' solution

We may also have the situation that we know about more than one item at a time but not about every upcoming item. This additional information is called lookahead. For the Bin Packing problem, it has been shown that lookahead does not lead to a significant improvement of performance [28]. The Bin Packing problem has of course more applications besides assigning surgeries to operating rooms, for example it can be used to model the assignment of clients to servers by a cloud provider or to model the assignment of tasks to machines.

7.4.4 Example

Let us consider a day in the hospital operating theater. We need to schedule 10 surgeries with lengths 30 min, 30 min, 40 min, 60 min, 60 min, 90 min, 90 min, 120 min, 150 min, 240 min and we have 3 ORs which are operating 8 h a day. The questions are: Can we schedule all ten surgeries on 1 day and if this is the case, how many operating rooms do we need? As the time needed in total for the surgeries is 900 min = 15 h 10 min we need at least two bins (which correspond to $2 \cdot 8 \, h = 16 \, h = 960 \, min$). Two bins is optimal as we can allocate the surgeries as follows:

Operating room 1	Operating room 2
240 min, 150 min, 90 min	120 min, 90 min, 60 min, 60 min, 40 min, 30 min, 30 min

Using the First Fit heuristic we obtain the following allocation:

Operating room 1	Operating room 2	Operating room 3
30 min, 30 min, 40 min, 60 min, 60 min, 90 min, 90 min	120 min, 150 min	240 min

7.4.5 OPL Code

When writing an OPL model it is good practice to separate the model itself from the data. That means the model is written into a so-called mod-file name.mod and the data into a dat-file name.dat. Then, it is possible to run the model with different dat-files which is often very useful. For the Bin Packing example the mod-file is called BinPacking.mod and the dat-file BinPacking.dat.

When CPLEX processes the model it goes from the top to the bottom. Therefore, it is important to care for the order when declaring parameters which is usually done first. Parameters can be integers, real numbers, strings, ranges, sets or arrays. Next are the decision variables always starting with the keyword dvar. Then, the constraints block follows starting with the keyword subject to and surrounded by brackets { }.

Constraints can be named name: constraint to make them accessible in the OPL studio by their name. Comments are often useful which start by //.

In the dat-file only the names of the parameters are set equal to the values, the type declaration is only included in the mod-file.

BinPacking.mod

```
1   // parameters: n
2   int NumberOfItems = ...;
3   int NumberOfBins = ...;
4
5   range Bins = 1..NumberOfBins;
6   range Items = 1..NumberOfItems;
7
8   float ItemSizes[Items] = ...; // a_j
9   float BinSize = ...; // b
10
11  // decision variables
12  dvar boolean BinUsed[Bins];
13      // y_i = 1 if bin i is used and 0 otherwise
14
15  dvar boolean Assign[Bins][Items];
16      // x_ij = 1 if item j is put in bin i and 0 otherwise
17
18  // objective function: minimize the number of bins used
19  minimize sum(b in Bins) BinUsed[b];
20
21  // constraints
22  subject to{
23
24  ctBinCapacity:
25      forall(b in Bins)
26      // Assignment only for open bin + ok bin capacity
27      sum(i in Items) ItemSizes[i] * Assign[b][i] <= BinSize*BinUsed[b];
28
```

```
29  ctAssign:
30    forall(i in Items)
31      // every item is put in exactly one bin
32      sum(b in Bins) Assign[b][i] == 1;
33  }
```

Listing 7.1 BinPacking.mod is the mod file for the Bin Packing example

Binpacking.dat

```
1  // data
2  NumberOfItems = 10;
3  NumberOfBins = 3;
4  ItemSizes = [30, 30, 40, 60, 60, 90, 90, 120, 150, 240];
5  //a_ij in minutes; b = 8h*60 = 480 min
6  BinSize = 480;
```

Listing 7.2 BinPacking.dat is the dat-file file for the Bin Packing example

7.5 Location Problems

7.5.1 Introduction

For many services the locations of facilities are important. When buildings need to be constructed, location decisions are in general strategic, as for example schools, hospitals or ambulance bases are built to be used for several decades. That means that a poor decision can have (costly) consequences for a long time. Tactical decisions arise for example if additional warehouse space is rented for the upcoming year.

Different types of location models can be distinguished and for each type many different models exist. One main factor to distinguish location models is the definition of the set of candidate locations. The two main possibilities are that they can be anywhere in the considered space or that there exists a discrete set of candidate locations to choose from. If a location problem includes an underlying network (e.g., a street network), candidate locations must lie on the network. They can even be restricted to the set of nodes only.

Similar assumptions can be made on the set of demand locations. In addition, a time horizon can be included into the problem such that location decisions are made for a fixed number of periods. These multi-period models can for example restrict the number of locations to open in each period or they can also allow to only close locations again after a certain time limit.

An overview over the different location problems including emerging fields of research and application areas can be found for example in [29].

In the following, four different location problems are described. They belong to the two main groups of location problems, namely Coverage Problems and Average Distance models. For all models a short example for a potential application in the area of emergency services in healthcare is given.

7.5.2 Set Covering Problem

The Set Covering Problem [30] minimizes the number of facilities that are needed to cover all demand. For the formulation, first the following notation is needed. We denote by I a set of demand nodes and by J a set of candidate facility locations. The costs of locating a facility at location $j \in J$ are given by f_j. d_{ij} expresses the distances between demand node $i \in I$ and candidate location $j \in J$ and D is the coverage distance.

$$a_{ij} = \begin{cases} 1 \text{ if } d_{ij} \leq D \\ 0 \text{ else} \end{cases}$$

The variable a_{ij} therefore says if a demand node can be covered by a potential location which is only the case if the distance from $j \in J$ to $i \in I$ is below the threshold D.

The binary decision variables state if a location is opened:

$$X_j = \begin{cases} 1 \text{ if location } j \text{ is established} \\ 0 \text{ else} \end{cases}$$

Then, the formulation looks as follows:

$$\min \sum_{j \in J} f_j X_j \tag{7.6}$$

$$\text{s.t. } \sum_{j \in J} a_{ij} X_j \geq 1 \qquad \forall i \in I \tag{7.7}$$

$$X_j \in \{0, 1\} \qquad \forall j \in J \tag{7.8}$$

The objective function (7.6) minimizes the cost for opened facilities. Constraints (7.7) assure that the demand nodes are covered. Finally, constraints (7.8) are the domain constraints.

The formulation can for example be used to determine a set of ambulance bases from where ambulances can reach all the inhabitants of a region within a given maximum travel time. For many countries in the world, this maximum travel time is defined by law and therefore important to fulfil. In Germany, the maximum travel time varies for the federal states and lies between 8 and 15 min, for example.

7.5.3 Maximal Coverage Problem

The Maximal Coverage Problem [31] maximizes the number of covered demands with a fixed number of facilities. In addition to the notation for the Set Covering Problem h_i expresses the demand at demand node $i \in I$ and p states the number of facilities to locate.

The additional binary decision variables state if a demand node is covered.

$$Z_i = \begin{cases} 1 \text{ if demand node i is covered} \\ 0 \text{ else} \end{cases}$$

The Maximal Covering Model can be stated as follows:

$$\max \sum_{i \in I} h_i Z_i \tag{7.9}$$

$$\text{s.t.} \sum_{j \in J} a_{ij} X_j - Z_i \geq 0 \qquad \forall i \in I \tag{7.10}$$

$$\sum_{j \in J} X_j = p \tag{7.11}$$

$$X_j \in \{0, 1\} \qquad \forall j \in J \tag{7.12}$$

$$Z_i \in \{0, 1\} \qquad \forall i \in I \tag{7.13}$$

The objective function (7.9) maximizes the covered demand. Demand at a node i can only be covered if it is reachable by at least one location within the maximum travel time and if this location is also opened, as stated by constraints (7.10). Constraint (7.11) assures that only p facilities are located. (7.12) and (7.13) are the domain constraints.

This formulation can also be used for locating ambulance bases, for example. In that case, only a fixed number p of bases is to be located, maybe due to a cost limit. As it might be that not all demand nodes can be covered by the p locations, it is the aim to at least cover as many potential patients as possible. Therefore, each demand location gets a value for the demand assigned similar to a weight of this location. This could be the number of inhabitants for example that correspond to a demand location.

7.5.4 P-Median Problem

While Median Problems in general minimize the demand-weighted average distance to travel between all demand nodes and the respective closest facility, the P-Median Problem [32] does so by locating a fixed number of p facilities.

To be able to minimize the average distance each demand location must be assigned to a facility. This is fixed in new binary decision variables. The decision variables X_j stating if a facility is opened are also necessary.

$$Y_{ij} = \begin{cases} 1 \text{ if demand node i is assigned to a facility at candidate location j} \\ 0 \text{ else} \end{cases}$$

The P-Median Problem then looks as follows:

$$\min \sum_{j \in J} \sum_{i \in I} h_i d_{ij} Y_{ij} \tag{7.14}$$

$$\text{s.t.} \sum_{j \in J} Y_{ij} = 1 \qquad \forall i \in I \tag{7.15}$$

$$Y_{ij} - X_j \leq 0 \qquad \forall i \in I, j \in J \tag{7.16}$$

$$\sum_{j \in J} X_j = p \tag{7.17}$$

$$X_j \in \{0, 1\} \qquad \forall j \in J \tag{7.18}$$

$$Y_{ij} \in \{0, 1\} \qquad \forall i \in I, j \in J \tag{7.19}$$

The objective function (7.14) minimizes the sum over all demand-weighted shortest distances between each demand location and the assigned facility. Therefore, it minimizes the demand-weighted average distance to travel between all demand nodes and the respective closest facility. Constraints (7.15) ensure that each demand location is assigned to exactly one facility location. A demand node can only be assigned to a facility location, if this facility is opened, as stated by constraints (7.16). Constraint (7.17) assures that only p facilities are located. Constraints (7.18) and (7.19) are the domain constraints.

Besides calling for an ambulance, patients from many countries can also consult out-of-hour doctors for help if they have a medical problem during nights or on the weekends. These doctors are often working in centrally located practices that all potential patients can more or less reach in the same time. In that case the P-Median Problem can be solved to determine those locations.

7.5.5 P-Center Problem

The P-Center Problem [32] also locates p facilities but under the objective to minimize the maximum distance between any demand node and the respective closest facility. This maximum distance is expressed by the decision variable Q.

The P-Center Problem can be formulated as follows:

$$\min Q \tag{7.20}$$

$$\text{s.t.} \sum_{j \in J} Y_{ij} = 1 \qquad \forall i \in I \tag{7.21}$$

$$Y_{ij} - X_j \leq 0 \qquad \forall i \in I, j \in J \tag{7.22}$$

$$\sum_{j \in J} X_j = p \tag{7.23}$$

$$\sum_{j \in J} d_{ij} Y_{ij} - Q \leq 0 \qquad \forall i \in I \tag{7.24}$$

$$X_j \in \{0; 1\} \qquad \forall j \in J \tag{7.25}$$

$$Y_{ij} \in \{0; 1\} \qquad \forall i \in I, j \in J \tag{7.26}$$

The objective function (7.20) minimizes the value of Q. Q represents the maximum distance between any demand node and its assigned closest facility as assured by constraints (7.24). Therefore, the objective function minimizes the maximum distance. A demand node must be assigned to exactly one facility location as ensured by constraints (7.21) and it can only be assigned to a facility location, if this facility is opened, as stated by constraints (7.22). Constraint (7.23) again assures that only p facilities are located. Constraints (7.25) and (7.26) are the domain constraints.

In case of an emergency, patients are usually taken to the nearest hospital by an ambulance. Some Emergency Medical Service systems apply the so-called "scoop-and-run" process that says that a patient is to be taken to the hospital as fast as possible where the treatment of the patient starts. Therefore, when planning the location of new hospitals that contain an emergency room it could be the aim to do it in such a way that the maximum distance for all potential patients is minimal, i.e. that all potential patients can reach a hospital as fast as possible if necessary.

7.6 Routing Problems

7.6.1 Introduction

The challenge of determining routes that are optimal regarding the traveled distance or the overall needed time often arises in the service sector. For example, technicians need to visit several customers on a day, sometimes within predefined time frames and their supervisors do not want them to spend most of the time driving around instead of working and serving the customers. In general, routing problems (Vehicle Routing Problems, VRP) are defined on graphs representing a city or a region, for example. These graphs consist of a set of nodes representing for example houses or crossroads and edges connecting the nodes. The edges are usually weighted with the distance (time or "way") between nodes. In addition, the demand of the customers is expressed either at the nodes or on the edges. In the first case, each node with demand greater than zero needs to be visited (at least once). This is the case for the technicians for example. When demand is defined on the edges, than each edge with demand greater than zero needs to be traversed at least once. This problem arises for example for garbage pick-up or post delivery.

7.6.2 Traveling Salesman Problem

A Traveling Salesman Problem (TSP) is the "easiest" vehicle routing problem although it is already difficult to solve. It can be explained as follows: A traveling salesman has to visit a number of places n. He is looking for a tour including all stops n that starts and ends at his home. So he asks himself how this tour should look like in order to minimize the traveled distance [33].

This problem also arises in home health care: A nurse has a number of patients that must be visited during a day. As the traveling salesman, a nurse wants (and has) to visit all the patients. To save time as well as costs, driving times/distances shall be minimal. For each nurse, a single TSP is solved. That is, to model the problem the number and location of the patients have to be known. That is, we assume for a nurse that n patients need to be visited. We model these patients as nodes in a network and denote by $N = \{1, \ldots, n\}$ the set of all nodes. The nodes are connected by arcs if it is possible to drive from one node to the other without passing a third node. These arcs are then weighted by distance. That is, we have for each pair of nodes i and j that is connected a distance d_{ij}. The binary decision variable x_{ij} is equal to 1 if the nurse visits patient j directly after patient i and 0 else.

The model then looks as follows:

$$\min \sum_{i \in N} \sum_{j \in N} d_{ij} x_{ij} \tag{7.27}$$

$$\text{s.t.} \sum_{j \in N | i \neq j} x_{ij} = 1 \qquad \forall i \in N \tag{7.28}$$

$$\sum_{j \in N | i \neq j} x_{ji} = 1 \qquad \forall i \in N \tag{7.29}$$

$$\sum_{i \in S} \sum_{j \in S} x_{ij} \leq |S| - 1 \qquad 2 \leq |S| \leq \frac{n}{2}, S \subset N \tag{7.30}$$

$$x_{ij} \in \{0, 1\} \qquad \forall i, j \in N \tag{7.31}$$

The objective function (7.27) of the model minimizes the total traveled distance. The constraints (7.28) and (7.29) assure that each node is entered and left exactly once, i.e., visited exactly once. Constraint (7.30) must hold for all possible

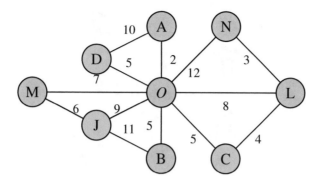

Fig. 7.5 The network with the eight patient locations and Emily's office

constructions of a set S that always contains at least 2 and at most $\frac{n}{2}$ nodes from the underlying graph. These constraints prohibits subtours by assuring that all nodes in this subset are only connected by one arc less than there are nodes in the set. Therefore, not all nodes can be connected and there cannot be a subtour containing theses nodes. This only needs to be restricted for subtours containing at most half the nodes because if there is a subtour there must be at least another one. Constraints (7.31) are the domain constraints.

Example

The home healthcare provider "FeelGood" has employed 2 nurses and serves 15 patients. They already assigned patients to nurses. Nurse Emily has to visit 8 patients per day: Anna, Ben, Chris, Donna, Julia, Lucy, Maxwell and Nicol.

In order to save fuel, she wants to find the route with the minimum distance that visits all the patients. For doing so, she has looked up all the patients' locations and all the distances between them and to/from her office where she starts and ends her tour using the network in Fig. 7.5. The distances on the edges are in km.

As a student once implemented the TSP in OPL (see Section Exact Methods) for her she can use CPLEX to solve it. As a solution, she gets the following route with a length of 66 km that can also be seen in Fig. 7.6: Office, Maxwell, Julia, Ben, Anna, Lucy, Nicol, Chris, Donna, and Office.

7.6.3 Vehicle Routing Problem with Time Windows

The Vehicle Routing Problem (VRP) is the generic term of routing problems, and therefore also includes the TSP. A VRP in general concerns the distribution of "goods" between depots and final users [34] whereas "goods" can mean basically everything including workforce of personnel. The Vehicle Routing Problem with Time Windows (VRPTW) is in its easiest form a TSP where customers need to be visited within (soft or hard) time windows. In general, it involves finding a set of

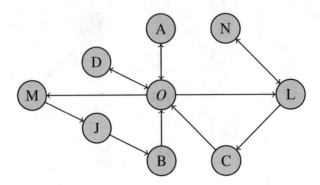

Fig. 7.6 Emily's route

routes, starting and ending at a depot, that cover a set of customers. Often, a set of (homogeneous) vehicles is available for serving the customers.

The next formulation is based on the one published by Dantzig and Ramser [35].

The variables are defined as follows: There are a fleet of vehicles K, a set of customers/users C and a directed graph G. The starting depot (0), the returning depot $(n + 1)$ and the set of customers form the set of vertices N. All direct connections between vertices are represented in the set of arcs A. There is a cost c_{ij} assigned to each arc as well as a time t_{ij} that is needed to traverse arc (i, j). Examples for the cost of an arc could also be the time needed to traverse it or it could be the distance between the two nodes similar to the TSP. The service time at customer i is denoted by s_i.

q is the capacity of a vehicle. Since they are homogeneous, there is no index. Every customer's demand is denoted by d_i. Additionally there exists a time window $[a_i, b_i]$ during which a vehicle must arrive at customer i.

The decision variable $x_{ijk} \in \{0, 1\}$ takes a value of 1, if vehicle k drives directly from vertex i to j, otherwise 0. Additionally, y_{ik} denotes the time vehicle k starts to service customer i [35].

$$\min \sum_{k \in K} \sum_{i \in N} \sum_{j \in N} c_{ij} x_{ijk} \tag{7.32}$$

$$\text{s.t.} \sum_{k \in K} \sum_{j \in N} x_{ijk} = 1 \qquad \forall i \in C \tag{7.33}$$

$$\sum_{i \in C} d_i \sum_{j \in N} x_{ijk} \leq q \qquad \forall k \in K \tag{7.34}$$

$$\sum_{j \in N} x_{0jk} = 1 \qquad \forall k \in K \tag{7.35}$$

$$\sum_{i \in N} x_{i,n+1,k} = 1 \qquad \forall k \in K \tag{7.36}$$

$$\sum_{i \in N} x_{ihk} - \sum_{j \in N} x_{hjk} = 0 \qquad \forall h \in C, k \in K \qquad (7.37)$$

$$x_{ijk}(y_{ik} + t_{ij} + s_i - y_{jk}) \leq 0 \qquad \forall i, j \in N, k \in K \qquad (7.38)$$

$$a_i \leq y_{ik} \leq b_i \qquad \forall i \in N, k \in K \qquad (7.39)$$

$$x_{ijk} \in \{0, 1\} \qquad \forall i, j \in N, k \in K \qquad (7.40)$$

The objective function (7.32) minimizes the overall traveled distance. Constraints (7.33) assure that each customer is visited exactly once. The capacity of a vehicle cannot be exceeded (7.34). Constraints (7.35) and (7.36) state that each route starts and ends at the depot (7.37) are the flow conservation constraints. Constraints (7.38) set the times when the vehicles start service at the customer locations and constraints (7.39) ensure that the defined time windows for the starting service are kept. Constraints (7.40) are the domain constraints.

Example

Nurse Emily realizes that it is not that easy to order her patients as actually they need to be visited during specific time windows. Some of the patients need help in the morning for getting dressed. Others need their medication at lunch or just need their blood pressure to be measured sometime during the day. When Emily tries to incorporate the time windows into her tour, she does not get a feasible solution but realizes that she cannot serve all her patients in time. Therefore, she approaches her boss. He decides to reorganize all patient-to-nurse assignments and to additionally hire a third nurse. That is, he now has to solve a Vehicle Routing Problem with Time Windows. He has to reassign the 15 patients to his 3 nurses in order to assure that the patients are visited within their time windows while still minimizing the overall traveled distance. The nurses are all going to start and end their routes from the little office building their boss has rented for all the paper work and for storing medicine and other materials. The underlying network is represented in Fig. 7.7.

Table 7.1 gives for all 15 patients A to P the service times (s_i) in minutes and the earliest and latest arrival times (a_i and b_i) as time of day.

Emily's boss implements the VRPTW in OPL, builds a data file using the data that the nurses collected and solves the problem with CPLEX. The three resulting routes are displayed in Fig. 7.8. The route lengths are 41, 27, and 36 km.

Table 7.1 Service times and earliest and latest arrival times for the 15 patients

i	A	B	C	D	E	F	G	H	I	J	K	L	M	N	P
s_i	30	20	90	40	60	50	80	70	80	20	90	50	40	30	70
a_i	14	8	16	12	16	16	8	14	12	14	12	9	8	9	9
b_i	18	10	18	14	18	18	10	18	14	18	14	13	10	13	13

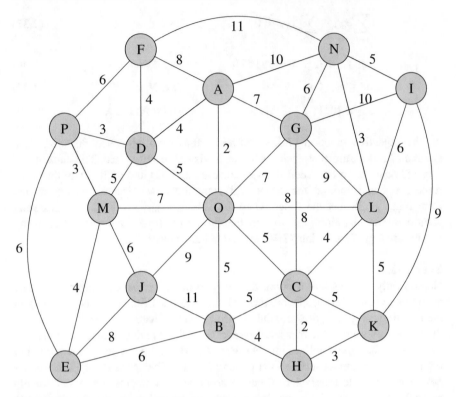

Fig. 7.7 The network with the 15 patient locations and the office

7.6.4 Heuristics

Savings

The savings heuristic was developed by Clarke and Wright in 1964 [36] to solve the Vehicle Routing Problem. Until today it is the most widely used heuristic in this field. It can also be used to obtain a first solution for the symmetric Traveling Salesman Problem.

Starting point of this heuristic are tours from the depot to each node and back to the depot. The procedure then tries to combine tours thereby shortening the overall length of the tours. Therefore, the saving S_{ij} when combining to tours is calculated as: $S_{ij} = c_{i0} + c_{j0} - c_{ij}$. Here, c_{ij} denotes the costs of arc ij as presented in the description of the VRPTW. Two tours are combined if the saving generated by their combination is positive and larger than any other possible saving. This is done repeatedly until no further saving is possible when combining two routes Savings can only be calculated between the first and the last nodes of tours and not within the same tour.

The Saving heuristic is based on the triangle inequality therefore only problems complying with this can be reasonably solved by this heuristic [37, pp. 343–344].

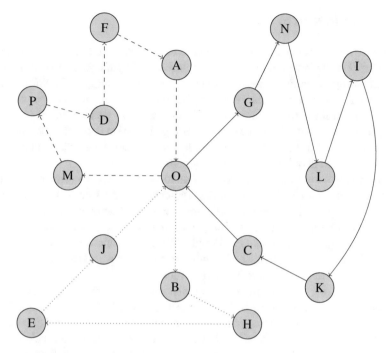

Fig. 7.8 The routes of the three nurses

Insertion Heuristics

The insertion heuristic is used to solve a classic Traveling Salesman Problem, but it can also be used to solve a VRPTW. It is an iterative procedure which adds nodes to a tour until all nodes are served.

The heuristic starts with a subtour that consists only of one node. Additional nodes are added using different criteria ("nearest, farthest, cheapest, random insertion"). The position of the node in the tour is determined by calculating the cost of an insertion at this point generates. The node is inserted at the one with the cheapest cost. In case of a VRPTW this insertion also needs to be feasible regarding the time windows.

"Nearest" and "cheapest" insertion can be shown to produce tours which are at most twice as long as the optimal tour if the triangle inequality holds for the problem. Even though "farthest" and "random" insertion can produce tours up to 6.5 times as long as the optimal solution under the same conditions, they tend to get better results in practice [37, pp. 341–342].

In the following, we shortly present two additional planning problems namely appointment planning and territory design.

7.7   Appointment Planning

If a service requires provider and costumer to be physically present matching supply and demand with respect to time is a main problem. To gain planning certainty and to avoid costumer waiting time, appointments are often arranged. Traditionally, the appointment assignment is mainly done by the provider, e.g., the costumer calls and is assigned a point in time or a time slot. Sometimes also preferences of costumers are taken into account. Given the service setting, assigning appointments can be an easy or a difficult task. In the following, let us consider appointment planning in health care which is often a non trivial problem.

The already mentioned complexity is due to the fact that we often have to deal with stakeholder with different objectives. Typical provider objectives are maximization of throughput, minimization of idle time and minimization of over time. Patient objectives can be timely access to care, short waiting times, consideration of their preferences (e.g., time and personnel) and sufficient consultation times. Obviously, some of those objectives are in conflict with each other (e.g., low idle time and short waiting times). Hence, a trade-off has to be found.

Considering the waiting time of patients we distinguish between two types, indirect waiting time/lead time and direct waiting time. The indirect waiting time is the time span between request and actual appointment/treatment date. High indirect waiting times may lead to deterioration of the patient's health. The patient might also change the provider. The direct waiting time is the time the patient spends in the waiting room. High direct waiting times (for non-urgent patients) are mainly a source of frustration for patients and might therefore also lead to a loss of patients for the provider. Thus, the provider should consider the patients' objectives significantly when establishing a trade-off.

An additional reason for complexity within appointment planning in health care are the different types of uncertainty a health care system is often confronted with. For example, patients with urgent problems show up and have to be treated right away disrupting the schedule or scheduled patients arrive late or even not at all. Often the proportion of no-shows (patients not showing up for their appointment) is higher in settings with longer indirect waiting times. A further source of uncertainty might be non-urgent walk-ins as well as the length of the treatment/consultation. The treatment time is often not known in advance and may vary strongly depending on the patient, treatment and provider.

Based on the setting, a service provider should first decide if he or she wants to use appointments and if yes to which extent, i.e., he or she has to decide on an appointment policy. When no appointments are assigned we speak of a walk-in policy. For example an emergency room operates under the walk-in policy. In the traditional policy the schedule is filled with appointments (also walk-ins might occur). The carve-out policy assigns appointments to patients but reserves some capacity for same day demand (urgent cases or walk-ins). Recently, a new policy has gained a lot of attention which is the open access policy. Patients call in

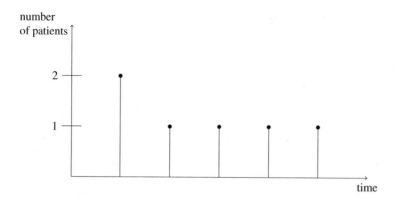

Fig. 7.9 Bailey-Welch rule

the beginning of the day and are assigned a same day appointment, if possible. Appointments for future days are not allowed regardless of the patient's problem.

If a policy is chosen where appointments are assigned (traditional, carve-out) appointment systems [38] can be used to formalize the schedule. An appointment system consists of an appointment rule, patient classification and adjustment rules.

An appointment rule determines how many patients are scheduled to which appointment times. The time between two appointment times is called appointment interval and the number of patients scheduled to the beginning of such an interval is called block size. We can now construct different appointment rules. The individual-block/fixed interval appointment rule is the most common one. At the beginning of each interval one patient is scheduled and all appointment intervals have the same length. Another common appointment rule is the Bailey-Welch rule which differs from the individual-block/fixed interval rule only by the fact that two patients are assigned to the beginning of the first interval of the day (see Fig. 7.9). This first block of the day is called the initial block. We can also construct more complex rules with variables block sizes and variable intervals.

Further, patients can be classified into different categories if needed. This can been done for example based on the expected service duration or on the specific problem/illness of the patient. Then, the provider decides about when to allow the different patient categories to be scheduled. Last but not least, adjustment rules have to be defined that determine how to react if reality deviates from the planned schedule.

A lot of research has been done in order to support appointment decisions of health care providers starting from the 50s. To decide about admission/access of patients Markov decision processes are often applied. To determine a schedule for a certain day (stochastic) optimization models are commonly used. Due to the complexity of the problem, simulation is another frequently used method. Further, queuing theory can help to gain insight into a service system.

7.8 Territory Design

Territory Design is the problem of grouping small geographic areas (so called basic areas) into larger clusters (so called districts or territories), in a way that the latter are acceptable according to relevant planning criteria. Typical examples for basic areas are cities, counties, zip code areas, streets etc. There are several different applications of territory design, for example Political Districting, School Districting, Winter Services Districting or Sales Territory Design.

The task of designing sales territories, for example, is to divide the market area in regions of responsibility for every salesman or office. Every salesman should have (approximately) the same workload. To minimize the (expensive and nonproductive) travel time, the regions should be contiguous and compact. Other planning criteria could require the same sales potential to every region or a good accessibility (e.g. highways, public traffic) within the territory. Typical basic areas in this case are cities or zip code areas, but also smaller sales territories or single costumers. Often the desired number of regions and the locations of the salesman are given by the company, but both could also be part of the planning process. Especially for sales companies, profit maximization is another important criterion for the planning process.

In Territory Design, different planning criteria exist that depend on the application and can be placed under the three general headings: demographic, geographic and political.

Balance Every territory should have (approximately) the same "size" or "weight" with respect to one (or more) activity measure(s), for example number of inhabitants, sales potential, workload etc.

Capacity Limitations The sum of all activity measure of one territory has to respect some capacity limitations, such as the capacity of a school is limited by the number of existing rooms.

Compactness Figuratively a territory is said to be compact if it is nearly round-shaped and undistorted. This criterion is useful to reduce the travel time inside the territory. In the case of political districting it helps to prevent "Gerrymandering".

Contiguity The territory should be continuous, due to administrative reasons and especially in the context of political districting to complicate "Gerrymandering".

Accessibility Inside the territory there should be a good accessibility of the central point (for example the school) or between the basic areas. Depending on the application a good accessibility by bus, train, car is desired.

Exclusive and Total Assignment Every basic area is assigned to exactly one territory.

Number of Territories Often the desired number of territories is given, but it could also be part of the planning process.

Location Often the central location is given (e.g., existing schools), but it could also be part of the planning process (e.g., location for a new office).

Fig. 7.10 A possible
reclassification of German
post code areas into 100
health care districts made
with Lizard (http://lizard.ior.
kit.edu/english/index.php)

Profit Maximization Especially for sales companies, profit maximization is another important criterion for the planning process. The territories should be chosen in a way that the estimated profit is as big as possible.

Some countries have a centralized health care system. Instead of freely choosing a doctor a patient gets assigned to a health center. Often, all inhabitants of one region are assigned to the same health center The problem of designing those health care districts can be modeled and solved using territory design. For example, Fig. 7.10 shows one possibility how Germany could be divided into 100 health care districts using the post code regions as basic areas.

In the following, we take a closer look at two important areas of Operations Research namely Queuing Theory and simulation.

7.9   Queueing Theory

Queuing Theory is the mathematical study of waiting lines (queues). It is considered as a part of Operations Research because the results are often used when making business decisions about the resources needed to provide a service.

In the following an introduction into Queuing Theory is presented and an example from the area of healthcare (a doctor's practice) is given.

7.9.1 Introduction

According to an article of the New York Times Sunday Review from 2012 American citizens spend 27 billion hours waiting in queues yearly. This is about the time 20 million people work in 1 year [39]. Besides wasting work and free time of people, queue waiting also leads to frustration. By better understanding and planning, this enormous waiting time could be decreased, people could spend their time more efficiently and hence would endure less frustration due to waiting.

Why do queues form anyway? On one side there are entities that require some kind of service. On the other side this service is provided by a limited amount of service providers. Hence, if at some point there are more entities requiring service than there are service providers available, entities will have to wait and form a queue. Even if on average the service providers work faster than entities arrive queues from due to the variability of inter arrival times and service times [14]. This is a key finding of Queueing Theory.

Queueing systems can be found in a lot of settings. Entities and service providers can be people, e.g., patients are waiting in the waiting room to see their doctor or they can be things, e.g., items waiting in a production line or they can be both, e.g., clients are waiting to draw money from ATMs in a bank.

Of course we can also imagine settings where we have several queues in parallel or sequentially, e.g., queues in front of checkstands in a supermarket or patients waiting to be seen first by a nurse and then again waiting to see the doctor. Using Queueing Theory those different settings can be grouped together by certain characteristics and then analyzed abstractly with regard to interesting performance indicators. Therefore, Queueing Theory is a helpful tool to understand the behavior of queueing systems and also to design queueing systems. In order to design a new queuing system it is important to weight the costs of operating the service providers and the costs for waiting of the entities. Especially, when people are involved waiting times are perceived as an important diminishment of the overall service quality. Here, Queueing Theory provides helpful information in order to find a good trade-off.

7.9.2 Underlying Theory

In the following we will focus on the case where we have one queue. In Queueing Theory such a queueing system is characterized by several parameters: the arrival process (inter-arrival time distribution) of the entities A, the service time distribution S, the number of service providers c, the capacity of the queue K, the size of the population N of entities to be served and the queueing discipline D. Usually, the inter-arrival times and service times are assumed to be randomly distributed with probability distributions that do not change over time. Often we have $A \sim M$ or $S \sim M$ where M stand for Markovian, i.e., exponentially distributed inter-arrival times (which means a poisson arrival process) or service times. We may also have $A, S \sim D$ or $A, S \sim G$ where D stands for a deterministic distribution and G stands

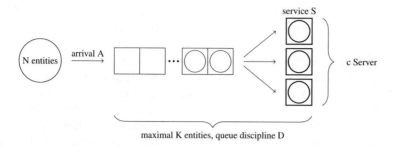

Fig. 7.11 A queueing system

for a general distribution. In Queueing Theory the arrival rate (corresponding to A), i.e., the average number of entities arriving per time unit, is often denoted by λ whereas the service rate (corresponding to S), i.e., the average number of serviced entities per time unit is denoted by μ. Queues can have a maximum queue capacity $K < \infty$ (where the entities being served are included), e.g. in an environment where a limited waiting area is available. If $N < \infty$ we assume that we have a finite population of entities that will potentially join the queue. Queues are typically processed on a first come first serve basis (first in first out-FIFO) but there are also different queue disciplines e.g. last come first served (last in first out-LIFO) or priority based. Based on the parameters presented Kendall's notation $A/S/c/K/N/D$ is used in Queueing Theory to describe a certain setting. If K, N and D are not given they are set to $K = N = \infty$ and D =FIFO by default. In Fig. 7.11 a schematic representation of a queuing system including the parameters of Kendall's notation is shown.

Queuing Theory strives to give analytical statements about queueing systems. Special interest is devoted to the state of the queuing system which we define as the number of entities in the system, i.e., the length of the queue plus the number of entities being served. In Queueing Theory queueing systems are seen as a special case of a Markov processes. Using the theory of Markov processes and Markov chains a steady state with a stationary distribution no matter what initial state we started in is often deducible based on assumptions that are easy to verify. If this is the case we can determine interesting indicators of our queuing system such as the average number of entities L in the system, the average queue length L_q, the average time of an entity spend in the system W and the average waiting time W_q given that our queueing system is in a stationary state. Sometimes using Queueing Theory we can also deduce transient results, i.e., determine how the state distribution changes over time. But in this short introduction we will focus on stationary considerations.

A first important relationship is Little's Law: $L = \tilde{\lambda}W$. Here $\tilde{\lambda}$ is the effective arrival rate of the queueing system, i.e., the arrival rate of the entities that really enter the system. This rate may differ from the arrival rate λ because if $K < \infty$ we have to reject entities if the capacity of the queue is reached. Until time T on average $\tilde{\lambda}T$ entities enter the system. Entities that entered the system before time $T - W$ on average will have left the system at time T. These are $\tilde{\lambda}(T - W)$ entities. Therefore, we have an average number of $L = \tilde{\lambda}T - \tilde{\lambda}(T - W) = \tilde{\lambda}W$ entities in our queueing system. Similarly, we can show: $L_q = \tilde{\lambda}W_q$.

Let us now investigate the $M/M/1/K$ queuing model. In this case there exists a stationary distribution to which our system converges regardless of the initial state. Our goal is to determine L, L_q, W and W_q for the stationary distribution of the queue where we focus on the derivation of L and W and only state the results for L_q and W_q. Let λ and μ be the arrival rate and the service rate, respectively and let $p_i, i \in \{0, \ldots, K\}$ be the probability that there are i entities in the system. Of course we then have $L = \sum_{i=0}^{K} ip_i$. If the arriving entities follow a poisson process and are accepted or rejected with a certain probability, here $1 - p_K$ and p_K, respectively then one can derive that the resulting effective arrival process is also a poisson process here with rate $\tilde{\lambda} = \lambda(1 - p_K)$. Hence, by Little's Law we have $W = \frac{1}{\lambda(1-p_K)} \sum_{i=0}^{K} ip_i$. Hence, we are left with determining $p_i, i \in \{0, \ldots, K\}$. Our queueing system shows an especially easy structure as a Markov process: It is a birth-death process, i.e., being in one state (for example system length $i \neq 0, K$) the system can at the most change to a state one higher or lower as the current state (here system length $i - 1$ if an entity leaves the system or $i + 1$ if a new entity arrives).

Due to the memoryless characteristic of the exponential distribution the rates to change from one state to the other do not change with the time already spend in a state. In Fig. 7.12 the different states of the considered queuing system and the transition rates between them are depicted. The Markov process theory tells us that we can determine the stationary distribution of the system by making sure that the rate flows cancel out for each state, i.e.,

rate flow cancelation for state 0 : $\lambda p_0 = \mu p_1$

rate flow cancelation for state 1 : $\lambda p_1 = \mu p_2 + \lambda p_0 - \mu p_1 = \mu p_2$

rate flow cancelation for state 2 : $\lambda p_2 = \mu p_3 + \lambda p_1 - \mu p_2 = \mu p_3$

$$\ldots$$

rate flow cancelation for state K : $\lambda p_{K-1} = \mu p_K$

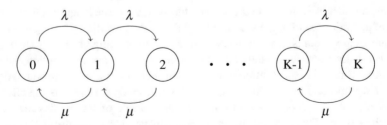

Fig. 7.12 Transition rates between states

Let $\rho = \lambda/\mu$ be the so called traffic intensity. For $i \in \{0, \ldots, K\}$ and $\rho \neq 1$ after some calculations we obtain

$$p_i = \frac{(1 - \rho)\rho^i}{1 - \rho^{K+1}}$$

Plugging the formula for p_i into the formulas for L and W and doing some calculations leads to

$$L = \frac{\rho}{1 - \rho} - \frac{(K + 1)\rho^{K+1}}{1 - \rho^{K+1}}$$

and

$$W = \frac{1}{\lambda(1 - \frac{(1-\rho)\rho^K}{1-\rho^{K+1}})}\left(\frac{\rho}{1 - \rho} - \frac{(K + 1)\rho^{K+1}}{1 - \rho^{K+1}}\right)$$

In the case of $\rho = 1$ we have

$$p_i = \frac{1}{K + 1}$$

for $i \in \{0, \ldots, K\}$ and therefore

$$L = \frac{K}{2}$$

and

$$W = \frac{1}{\lambda(1 - \frac{1}{K+1})}\frac{K}{2} = \frac{K + 1}{2\lambda}$$

The formulas for L_q and W_q can be derived using $L_q = \sum_{i=1}^{K}(i - 1)p_i$ and Little's Law.

7.9.3 Example

Let us consider a doctor's practice which operates under the walk-in policy. This means the practice does not assign appointments but patients just walk in. For the sake of simplicity, let us assume that the practice is open 24 h a day. Patients come in according to a poisson process with rate $\lambda = 3$ per hour which means exponentially distributed inter-arrival times with mean $1/\lambda = 1/3$ h and the doctor is able to treat patients at a rate of $\mu = 4$ per hour where his service time is exponentially distributed with mean $1/\mu = 1/4$ h. We assume a limited waiting space of $K - 1 = 5$

places and further suppose that patients are called up in order of their arrival. We are therefore dealing with an $M/M/1/K$ queueing model as presented in the last section. Using the derived formulas we can calculate the average number of patients in the system L, the average queue length L_q, the average time spend in the system W and the average waiting time W_q of a patient in the waiting room. First we see that $\rho = \frac{3}{4} \neq 1$. Plugging ρ into the presented formulas leads to $L = 1.92$ and $W = 0.67\,h$.

7.10 Simulation

Imagine being responsible for designing a new complex service environment such as a hospital or an airport. These are very complicated strategic tasks as you have to consider many stakeholders, many of restrictions and future trends. To minimize costs and to secure smooth work flows, the service environment should be build according to the processes that are going to take place in it. Given the first architectural design how can you be sure that it fulfils all the requirements? In such a situation simulation can be a helpful tool. You could build an abstract model of the main processes in the service environment, implement it in a simulation program on your computer and then test the architectural design. Using simulation you are able to test different scenarios and to control the design performance by keeping track of important performance indicators. To evaluate a layout design, important indicators could be congestions on corridors, waiting time and walking distances of costumers and many more. Given the values of these indicators for different layouts and scenarios you should be able to take justified decisions.

7.10.1 Underlying Theory

In this short introduction to simulation we will focus on computer-based simulations of real world dynamics. In this sense, simulation is a methodology to investigate complex dynamic systems in order to gain insight and to support decisions. Simulations are often used if analytical considerations are too complicated due to complexity or if real world experiments on the system are impossible, dangerous or too costly. The idea of simulation is to imitate the most important real world processes of a system. To do so the first difficult task is to identify involved processes and to build an abstract model with all the important and influencing processes being formalized. These processes can be modeled as deterministic, e.g. laws of nature or stochastic, e.g. throwing dice. For ease of use, this model then can be implemented, e.g. with help of a simulation software. The next step should be the verification and validation of the model to evaluate if the model is build correctly and if it is working properly. Finally, one runs the simulation under different parameter variations, i.e., one performs simulation experiments. The simulation output should include statistics of important indicators of the considered system. Based on those statistics, the simulation user should be able to understand the impact of parameter changes on the system and to take reasonable decisions in the real world.

We consider the following types of dynamic simulation:

- Continuous simulation.
- Discrete simulation.
- Hybrid simulation.

Continuous simulations model continuous processes, i.e., changes of the system happen continuously at any point in time. This simulation method is often applied to physical phenomena for example to model the weather using a lot of differential equations. In contrast, discrete simulations model discrete processes, i.e., changes of the system happen at discrete time points. An example would be to model a queueing system in a service environment. The system changes its state, i.e., the number of entities in the system at discrete time points when someone arrives or leaves. A hybrid simulation combines characteristics of continuous and discrete simulations.

Next, we will explain three main modeling paradigms which are:

- System dynamics.
- Agent based modeling.
- Discrete event modeling.

In continuous simulation, system dynamics is the modeling method mainly used. System dynamics models the behavior of complex dynamic systems which may exhibit non-linear behavior. It considers dynamics on an aggregated level. Distinguished elements are stocks, i.e., sets of entities/things in the same state; flows, i.e., rates that indicate the flow from one stock to another, and feedback loops, i.e., positively or negatively self-enforcing effects, which may lead to non-linear behavior. Consider, for example the introduction of a new product or service to the market in marketing. Your stocks could be the users and nonusers. There is a flow from the nonuser stock to the user stock for example due to word of mouth effects. Here, it seems plausible that the rate of converting nonusers to users is depending on the number of users (positive feedback loop).

The agent based simulation is a decentralized simulation method where the behavior of the hole system is the result of the simulation of the behavior of individual entities so called agents. For example, if we want to model a group of people interacting with each other agent based simulation is especially suitable. Consider the same marketing example as above. Applying agent based simulation allows to model different reactions of people with different characteristics to publicity and to word of mouth recommendation. The modeling often leads to an discrete or hybrid simulation.

In discrete simulation we can have a time-discrete or an event-discrete modeling. In time-discrete modeling we update the state of our system in time intervals of fixed length. In contrary, in the more popular event-discrete modeling the changes of our system state are triggered by events. Events in turn happen after a certain residence time in a state. The residence time can be deterministic or stochastic.

Here one could think of a queue where the arrival and the departure of an entity are deterministic or stochastic events that change the state of our system, i.e., the number of entities in the queueing system. Often, queues are an important part of service systems especially if we focus on service quality for clients which also includes waiting times. Therefore, discrete event simulation is a particularly important tool to investigate services.

7.10.2 Example

As a simple example we compare two queueing systems. Consider a small supermarket with two checkstands. In the first system people line up in one queue in order to pay. In the second system we have two separate queues, one for each checkstand. We assume the following: people arrive according to a poisson process (exponential inter-arrival times) with rate $\lambda = 2$ per minute and service times are exponentially distributed with rate $\mu = 1.1$ per minute. Further, the queue capacity is not limited. The two systems can be implemented with different tools. We used AnyLogic 7 which is a multi-method simulation software covering all the three modeling paradigms explained. The AnyLogic process modeling library covers the following necessary elements for our simulation: source, service, resource pool and sink. In the source the entities (here costumers) are generated. Hence, in our case the source models the entrance of the supermarket. The service element brings together queue and service. In our simulation the service elements model the checkstands and their queues. The resource pool indicates the kind and number of service stations. In our case the resource pool models the cashiers. Finally, entities are destroyed in the sink which is our exit of the supermarket. We link the elements together as can bee seen in Fig. 7.13 and enter the given specifications where we also enable statistics for the service element. Now we can use elements of the analysis palette such as the bar chart or the histogram to depict the statistics of the simulation graphically. We run the simulation as long as necessary to reach approximately the steady state. Therefore, we can stop the simulation when the distributions for the length of the queue only change marginally with more time. Being in steady state, the two systems give different results. If there is only one waiting line on average 8.7 costumers are waiting whereas in the case of two waiting lines there are 9.3 people waiting on average. Concerning the mean waiting time people have to wait 4.3 min on average in the system with one queue and 4.6 min in the system with two queues. In Fig. 7.13 a screenshot of the one queue simulation in AnyLogic is shown.

We conclude that in this case it is preferable to install one waiting line for the two checkstands. We also could have used Queueing Theory in order to treat this problem. In fact, it has been shown by Queueing Theory that it is always preferable to use one joined queue if there are several servers. Simulation can not produce general results of this kind. But remember in Queueing Theory exact analytical results are only available for some specific distributions as for example for the exponential distribution. Further, these results are only valid in the stationary case.

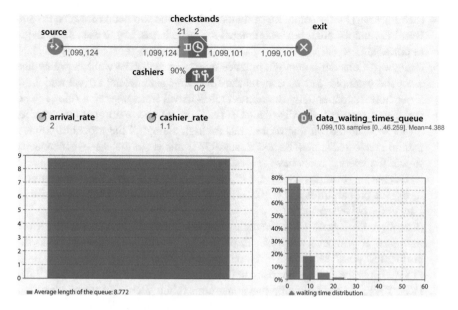

Fig. 7.13 AnyLogic screenshot of the one queue simulation

Using simulation we have the advantage to implement very easily any distribution and time varying parameter and get approximate results for this specific case.

7.11 Conclusions

In this chapter an introduction into Operations Research for Service Science is given. A selection of planning problems is presented that can be used to implement or improve different aspects of service delivery. Especially in the area of healthcare the use of Operations Research in practice to improve underlying processes and logistics is important as well as promising. The Government Operational Research Service (GORS) is another good example for the use of OR to improve services in practice. Besides the application itself this is also an interesting field for research.

Review Section

1. (Foundations) Explain the idealized planning process in your own words and use an example to illustrate the steps.
2. (Foundations) Give a generic formulation for a linear and a mixed integer linear program.
3. (Foundations) Explain the difference between an exact approach and a heuristic and give examples for both.

4. (Bin Packing) Find a sequence of items such that the two heuristics First Fit and Best Fit yield different bin assignments for those items. Try to use as few items as possible.

5. (Queuing) Consider a doctor's practice operating under the walk-in policy just as in the example. Let us assume the following parameters: arrival rate $\lambda = 5$ per hour (exponentially distributed inter-arrival times), service rate $\mu = 6$ per hour (exponentially distributed service times) and waiting room capacity $K - 1 = 4$. Is the waiting room capacity high enough if the probability that a patient is rejected should be less than 0.05? If this is not the case what capacity should the waiting room have at least?

   Derive the formulas for L_q and W_q in the $M/M/1/K$ case. Hint: To compute L_q use the probabilities $p_i, i \in \{0, \ldots, K\}$ already calculated. Then apply Little's Law to derive the formula for W_q.

6. (Location Problems) Find examples for the location problems either from literature or your everyday life. Explain why you think the model fits to the problem. If possible, choose different service domains.

7. (TSP) Apply the savings heuristic to the home healthcare example in Sect. 7.6.2.

8. (VRPTW) Add the following two constraints to the VRPTW formulation:

   - Not more than P customers with $P \geq \frac{|N|}{|K|}$ shall be assigned to each vehicle $k \in K$.
   - Each route should end at the returning depot before the closing time l_{n+1}.

9. (OPL) Implement all the formulations of this chapter using either the data given in the examples or come up with new examples. Separate the data from the model by using a .mod-file for the model and a .dat-file for the data.

10. (Simulation) Implement a simple queueing system in AnyLogic with one server and a limited queue capacity. Use the following parameters: exponential inter-arrival times with rate $\lambda = 1$ per minute, exponential service times with rate $\mu = 1.2$ per minute and a queue capacity of 3. Collect statistics on the average queue length and the average waiting time over a long period of time. Compare these values to the results you obtain using the formulas from the section Queueing Theory.

Key Terms

Operations Research   Operations Research is the discipline of applying advanced analytical methods, i.e., optimization methods, to help make better decisions.

Linear Programming   Linear Programming deals with solving linear programs, i.e, optimization problems where decision variables take real values and the objective function and the constraints are linear.

Integer Programming Integer Programming is concerned with solving integer and mixed integer programs, i.e., optimization models where some or all of the decision variables are restricted to integer values.

Simplex Algorithm The simplex algorithm is one of the most important algorithms to determine an optimal solution to a linear program.

Branch-and-Bound Algorithm The Branch-and-Bound algorithm is one of the most important algorithms to determine an optimal solution to an integer (linear) program.

Heuristic A heuristic is an algorithm that finds a solution to an optimization problem which is in general not optimal.

Simulation Simulation is a methodology to imitate the most important real world processes of a system in order to investigate complex dynamic systems and to support decisions.

Further Reading

George Nemhauser and Laurence Wolsey. *Integer and Combinatorial Optimization.* Wiley, 1999.

Frederick Hillier and Gerald Lieberman. *Introduction to Operations Research.* McGraw Hill, 2001.

Andrei Borshchev. *The Big Book of Simulation Modeling: Multimethod Modeling with AnyLogic6.* AnyLogic North America, 2013.

References

1. Butchers R et al (2001) Optimized crew scheduling at air New Zealand. Interfaces 31(1):30–56
2. Justesen T (2015) Check-in counter allocation. http://www.gurobi.com/pdf/copenhagen-case-study-counter-low-res.pdf. Accessed on 12 Jan 2015
3. Justesen T (2015) Stand and gate allocation. http://www.gurobi.com/pdf/copenhagen-case-study-aircraft-low-res.pdf. Accessed on 12 Jan 2015
4. Cook T (2015) Presidential portrait. Accessed on 12 Jan 2015
5. OR-Champions (2015) Operational research and the science of better. Accessed on 12 Jan 2015
6. Daskin M (2010) Service science: service operations for managers and engineers. Wiley-Blackwell, Chichester. ISBN:978-0-470-52588-3; 0-470-52588-6
7. Dantzig G (1963) Linear programming and extensions. Rand Corporation, Santa Monica, pp 94–104
8. Schrijver A (2000) Theory of linear and integer programming. Wiley-Interscience series in discrete mathematics and optimization. Wiley, Chichester. ISBN:0-471-98232-6; 978-0-471-98232-6
9. Hillier F (2010) In: Lieberman G (ed) Introduction to operations research, vol 9. McGraw-Hill, New York. ISBN:978-0-07-337629-5; 0-07-337629-9; 0-07-126767-0; 978-0-07-126767-0
10. Birge JR (2011) Introduction to stochastic programming. In: Louveaux F (ed) Springer series in operations research and financial engineering. Springer, New York. ISBN:978-1-461-40237-4

11. Ben-Tal A, El Ghaoui L, Nemirovskij A (2009) Robust optimization. Princeton series in applied mathematics. Princeton University Press, Princeton. ISBN:978-0-691-14368-2; 0-691-14368-4
12. Gross J (ed) (2004) Handbook of graph theory. Discrete mathematics and its applications. CRC Press, Boca Raton. ISBN:1-58488-090-2
13. Lakatos L, Szeidl L, Telek M (2012) Introduction to queueing systems with telecommunication applications. Springer, Berlin
14. Haviv M (2013) Queues: a course in queueing theory. International series in operations research and management science. Springer, New York. ISBN:978-1-461-46765-6
15. Law A (2015) Simulation modeling and analysis. McGraw-Hill Education, New York. ISBN: 1-259-25438-0
16. Borshchev A (2013) The big book of simulation modeling: multimethod modeling with AnyLogic 6. AnyLogic North America, Lisle. ISBN:978-0-9895731-7-7
17. Dantzig G (1951) Maximization of a linear function of variables subject to linear inequalities. Cowles Commission Monograph No. 13, pp 339–347
18. Gass S, Fu M (2013) Encyclopedia of operations research and management science. Springer, New York, p 131
19. Vanderbei R (2001) Linear programming. In: Foundations and extensions. International series in operations research and management science, vol 37. Springer, New York
20. Land AH, Doig AG (1960) An automatic method of solving discrete programming problems. Econometrica J Eco Soc 28:497–520
21. Osman IH, Laporte G (1996) Metaheuristics: a bibliography. Ann Oper Res 63:513–623
22. Nelson B (2013) Foundations and methods of stochastic simulation: a first course. International series in operations research and management science. Springer, Boston. ISBN:978-1-461-46160-9
23. Domschke W, Drexl A (2007) Einfuhrung in Operations Research: mit 63 Tabellen. Springer-Lehrbuch. Springer, Berlin. ISBN:978-3-540-70948-0; 978-3-540-23431-9
24. Shippert R (2005) A study of time-dependent operating room fees and how to save $ 100,000 by using time-saving products. Am J Cosmet Surg 22(1):25–34
25. Abouleish A et al (2003) Labor costs incurred by Anesthesiology groups because of operating rooms not being allocated and cases not being scheduled to maximize operating room efficiency. Anesth Analg 96(4):1109–1113
26. Garey M, Johnson D (2008) Computers and intractability: a guide to the theory of NP-completeness. Freeman, New York. ISBN:0-7167-1045-5; 978-0-7167-1044-8
27. Bramel J, Simchi-Levi D (1997) The logic of logistics. Springer, New York. ISBN:978-1-4684-9311-5
28. Dunke F (2014) Online optimization with lookahead. Ph.D. thesis, Karlsruhe, KIT, Diss.,
29. Laporte G, Nickel S, da Gama FS (eds) (2015) Location science, vol 145. Springer, New York. ISBN:978-331-91311-1-5
30. Toregas C et al (1971) The location of emergency service facilities. Oper Res 19(6):1363–1373
31. Church R, Velle C (1974) The maximal covering location problem. Pap Reg Sci 32(1):101–118
32. Hakimi S (1964) Optimum location of switching centers and the absolute centers and medians of a graph. Oper Res 12:450–459
33. Menger K (1932) Das Botenproblem. In: Menger K (ed) Ergebnisse eines Mathematischen Kolloquiums, vol 2. Teubner, Leipzig, pp 11–12
34. Toth P, Vigo D (2001) The vehicle routing problem. SIAM, Philadelphia. ISBN:0-89871-498-2; 0-89871-579-2
35. Dantzig G, Ramser J (1959) The truck dispatching problem. Manag Sci 6(1):80–91
36. Clarke GU, Wright JW (1964) Scheduling of vehicles from a central depot to a number of delivery points. Oper Res 12(4):568–581
37. Grunert T, Irnich S (2005) Optimierung im Transport. Wege und Touren, vol 2. Shaker, Aachen. ISBN:3-8322-4515-4
38. Cayirli T, Veral E (2009) Outpatient scheduling in health care: a review of literature. Prod Oper Manag 12(4):519–549
39. Stone A (2012) Why waiting is torture. The New York Times, Sunday Review

Service Co-creation

8

Johannes Kunze von Bischhoffshausen, Peter Hottum, and Tim Straub

Summary

This chapter provides an overview on different aspects of co-creation in a service context. The first section introduces the concept of value co-creation in service systems and elaborates on the relationship of co-creation to service value propositions, service encounters, service quality, and service productivity. Furthermore, it introduces the concept of customer relationships, as well as concepts and methods that can be applied in order to manage these relationships for co-creation with customers. The third section elaborates on the different roles a customer can play within service co-creation, and its managerial implications.

Learning Objectives
1. Identify the relationship between co-creation of value in service systems, service encounters, service quality, and service productivity.
2. Analyze the nature of relationships in a service co-creation context and get an overview of concepts and methods to manage customer relationships.
3. Understand the concept of customer participation, different customer roles and be able to manage customer participation.

▶ **Opening Case** My coke rewards

J.K. von Bischhoffshausen (✉) • P. Hottum • T. Straub
Karlsruhe Service Research Institute (KSRI), Karlsruhe Institute
of Technology (KIT), Karlsruhe, Germany
e-mail: johannes kunze@kit edu; peter hottum@kit edu; tim.straub@kit.edu

© Springer International Publishing Switzerland 2015
J. Cardoso et al. (eds.), *Fundamentals of Service Systems*, Service Science: Research and Innovations in the Service Economy, DOI 10.1007/978-3-319-23195-2_8

Coca Cola Co-creates Value Through Electronic Services

My Coke Rewards is Coca-Cola's customer loyalty marketing program, launched in 2006 in the United States as the largest program in Coca-Cola's history. Later, it has been implemented in several countries all over the world. Customers enter codes printed on Coca-Cola brand products using their individual profile on the My Coke Rewards website. These codes are converted into virtual loyalty points. These points can be converted into various rewards (giveaways, magazine subscriptions, movie tickets, sweepstakes, and coupons) which are offered by Coca-Cola and several program partners (including McDonald's, Amazon, Nike, and Delta). For some partners, the collaboration between Coca-Cola and its partners is bi-directional and partners integrated My Coke Rewards in their promotion activities. For example, in the 2009 McDonald's Monopoly game, the player received My Coke Rewards points for landing on the community chest field.

With more than 14 million members, My Coke Rewards is one of the most successful marketing programs in the United States. Coca-Cola increased customer interaction with its My Coke Rewards program by switching to highly personalized and segmented emails. The average clickthrough rate increased by 46 % and member activity increased by 57 %. Every month, the My Coke Rewards web site receives approximately six million visits. According to comScore, the website became a top 500 visited site, with over four million unique monthly visitors.

Subsequently, the program has been extended by leveraging additional technologies such as QR codes, which are printed on Coca-Cola products to scan information on the My Coke Rewards website about brand products and prizes. Furthermore (Fig. 8.1), Coca-Cola vending machines were equipped with facilities to read plastic cards (My Coke Rewards Card) which can be picked up directly at the vending machines and linked to the My Coke Rewards profile. With the rise of near field communication (NFC) and contactless payment systems using smartphones, Coca-Cola vending machines started to support virtual cards held in mobile wallets.

Several concepts which are discussed in this chapter can be observed from the My Coke Rewards program case. Coca-Cola, the program partners and the consumers form a service system: different parties interact in a dynamic network which requires taking a system perspective rather than focusing on bilateral interaction. My Coke Rewards yields advantages for all involved partners: Coca-Cola, customers and program partners. Coca-Cola benefits from an increased interaction with their customers, additional attention through social media, and an indisputably valuable access to consumption data and user profiles from their consumers. Consumers gain value through a highly customized experience and access to their rewards. Partners benefit from additional attention through the My Coke Rewards website, access to program members, as well as access to consumer profiles.

All partners are involved in the value creation process and actively participate in co-production (e.g., typing in codes) which subsequently results in value creation. Furthermore, the classical roles of providers and customers are blurring. In the context of My Coke Rewards, the role of the customer changes from a pure consumer

Fig. 8.1 Coca Cola vending machines, equipped with modern technologies, facilitate customer interaction and customization

of softdrinks to a co-marketer who receives loyalty points for referring the program to friends. The case illustrates how long-term relationships are profitable for all involved parties. This also demonstrates that even non-contractual transactional settings can turn into a long-term relationship.

▶ **Opening Case**

8.1   Key Concepts

In order to understand how value is co-created in a service context, a closer look at several highly relevant concepts is required. These concepts are service systems, service value propositions, service encounters, service quality, and service productivity. They may differ from their related concepts in the product world. An understanding of their service-specific characteristics is, therefore, required.

8.1.1   Co-creation

In a service context, the involvement and contribution of all participants has an influence on the result of the service transformation process. This joint value creation between multiple participants will be explored from a conceptual viewpoint in this section.

R Service co-creation requires the involvement and contribution of all participants.

Providing a service is rarely a process between two persons only. The service provider and the customer are both part of further networks. In case of a service provider these networks may be a department, company or other business networks. In case of the customer, these can be social networks, such as friends and family for consumers.

▶ **Definition (Co-creation)** Co-creation is about joint creation of value by the company and the customer.

Both partners are involved in further systems, where a successful service provision will have a direct influence. For example, the service of private lessons for students and an improvement in school will also have an influence on the students' social system, such as their families. The service of business consulting may have an influence on the performance of a department and, therefore, on the relationship to other parts of the company as well.

If we see the involved parties as parts of interlinked relationships, this chapter can adopt the idea of systems. We all belong to systems that are interlinked based on relationships—a class of students is a system, a sports club is a system, the family is a system as well. Even virtual environments, such as Facebook groups or online gaming communities form a system.

This chapter follows the concept of a service system introduced in Chap. 1. A service system is *a dynamic value-cocreation configuration* of [25] *people, technology, other internal and external service systems and shared information* [26]. This means, the common objective of involved parties is to generate value for each of the parties or at least for the system they are part of. Based on this definition we can see a service system as a special type of an open and dynamic system in which further service systems are interacting by applying various resources to co-create value for achieving certain objectives. In contrast to the separated roles of consumer and provider, more and more service systems are consisting of equal partners that interact in symmetric relationships (see Fig. 8.2).

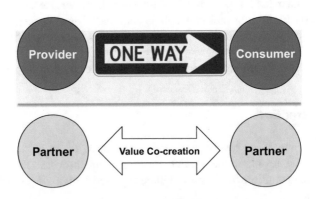

Fig. 8.2 Provider and consumer roles are blurred in co-creation

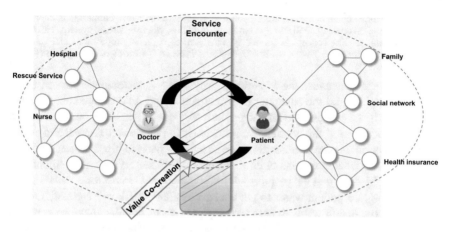

Fig. 8.3 The healthcare system is an example for a service system

What kind of resources are applied to create a certain value? Resources are contributions of each party, which can be physical aspects that are necessary to provide the service. For example, in a self service gas station, a customer needs to bring in a car and the provider provides the necessary infrastructure to fuel the car. It is equally important to also integrate resources that are intangible, such as information, knowledge and skills. The customer has to provide information on the destination to a taxi driver; a provider has to apply practical knowledge to consult a customer. These kinds of resources are called *operand resources*.

Service systems, as described above, could be parties in further service systems. This can be easily illustrated using a case from healthcare: The smallest conceivable service system is a single person e.g. a patient or a doctor. They are part of further systems—such as the family or peer support groups in case of patients; hospitals in case of medical staff (see Fig. 8.3).

Those larger service systems emerge through interactions among the system. Furthermore, all kinds of enterprises and organizations, as players in the economy, can be perceived as service systems. A huge difference when examining services in contrast to products is the relationship between providers and customers.

Furthermore, instead of one-way and one-time transactions providers and customers even build bilateral continuous relationships. In these relationships, the involved parties can be seen more and more as value partners.

A related, yet different, concept to service systems are supply chains. Supply chains consist "of all parties involved, directly or indirectly, in fulfilling a customer request. These supply chain does not only include the manufacturer and suppliers, but also transporters, warehouses, retailers, and customers themselves. Within each organization, such as a manufacturer, the supply chain includes all functions involved in receiving and filling a customer request. These functions include, but are not limited to, new product development, marketing, operations, distribution, finance, and customer service." [1]. According to Lusch [2] the obvious remarkable difference is the chain view instead of a network view.

Hence, a supply chain can be regarded as nested in a service network. Furthermore, supply chains are often characterized through strong or rigid ties, whereas service systems can be loosely coupled. The concept of service systems focuses on value propositions and value co-creation of involved parties, while supply chains focus on delivering or adding value [2].

The distinction between the two roles of providers and customers is blurred, since both the provider and the customer jointly create value. As described above value co-creation is the process that characterizes a service. To stress the continuous and joint creation of value, the producer and consumer can be viewed as equal and nearly symmetric partners whose interactions are based on a partnership. The benefit of the performed service interactions often times manifests itself in the achievement of a composite objective that the partners have and the service strives for.

For example, a patient wants to get the best available medical treatment. On the other hand, the doctor wants to help as many patients as possible, but also wants to earn some money and enjoy his end of work each day. These are two contrasting objectives and only by meeting both of them to a certain extent a service system can succeed on the long run.

The customer roles differ as well. For products like a car, a relationship between a car manufacturer and a customer is not really necessary. Once the car is bought, the product is transferred to the customer and the value could be applied or used. The roles of provider and customer are quite clear. Services are different: Services can only be generated with a contribution from both, the provider and the customer. It is not possible in a useful manner that a service can be provided without an initial contribution of the provider and the customer. Both of them have to contribute and they are both responsible for the initiation of the value creation. Also because of that, services are related to the concept of value co-creation—commonly performed by a customer and a provider.

8.1.2 Service Value Proposition

In the past, value propositions for service offerings were created by the service provider in order to convince customers that they will receive a certain value at certain cost. Value can be very complex and may involve intertwined value dimensions based on the stakeholders' culture, location in a particular geographical region, educational background, religious beliefs, etc. [3]. Kwan and Müller-Gorchs [4] suggested a value proposition as a set of vectors offered by a service provider $VP = \{SE, B, C, P, Q, Sc, R, M, FR\}$, where,

SE—Service Experience offered by Service Provider (SP)
B—Benefits to be received by the customer
C—Costs of service
P—Probability of successfully performing the service
Q—Quality of service
Sc—Schema of data exchange between service provider and customer
R—Rules of behavior for service provider and customer

M—Metric with which the service is to be evaluated
FR—Failure Recovery

Example (Value proposition)

Our service will provide such and such experience which will result in certain benefits to you. It will cost x. We have a good reputation and will be capable to perform the service successfully and with high quality. We will exchange data about each other in a particular format. We will perform the service based on the agreeable upon criteria and you will also be expected to perform in a certain manner in order to co-create value as intended. You will be able to measure our performance and vice versa. In case of service failure, we will perform certain procedures to restore service [3].

However, service providers need to be aware of the system view when formulating the value proposition. This includes considering the partner network of the provider as well as the business or social network of the customer service system. Even if a system wide view is hard to obtain, looking one step beyond current borders can be helpful. Therefore, Kwan and Hottum [3] proposed moving from the notion of B2B and B2C to B2X2Y that enables understanding a value system (service provider, customer, and the customer's customer). This is illustrated in Fig. 8.4. While service providers in a B2C setting might focus on how they enable value co-creation with their customers, they need to take into account the role of their business partners. Therefore, a shift from a narrow (B2C) to a wider (*B2*B2C) focus is required (row 1). The same applies for companies that integrate

	Relationship	Example	Narrow view	B2X2Y view
1	B2C → *B2*B2C	IBM (partner role) runs IT of Deutsche Bank, in order to enable Deutsche Bank to offer their services to their consumer costumers.	Provider ⇒ Customer	Partner Customer Provider
2	B2C → B2*B2*C	IBM (provider role) uses partners to sell their offering, especially to small businesses.	Provider ⇒ Customer	Provider Customer Partner
3	B2C → B2C2S	Deutsche Bank offers a hypothecary credit to a family man to buy a house for his family.	Provider ⇒ Customer	Provider Social System Customer
4	B2B → B2B2*B*	IBM runs IT of Deutsche Bank, in order to enable Deutsche Bank to offer their services to their business costumers.	Provider ⇒ Customer	Provider Customer's Customer Customer

Fig. 8.4 The B2X2Y view (based on Kwan and Hottum [3])

their business partners into service encounters (from B2C to B2*B*2C) (row 2). Furthermore, companies that are offering services to consumers (B2C) need to take the social system of the consumer into account (B2C2*S*) (row 3). Companies offering services to companies (B2B) should be aware of the customer's customers (B2B2*B*) (row 4).

8.1.3 Service Encounters

A typical difference between selling and buying a product and providing and consuming a service is the increased interaction between the provider and the customer. This becomes clear by comparing the process of visiting a doctor (service) to buying medicine at the pharmacy (product). The process of visiting the doctor starts with scheduling an appointment, either by using a web portal or calling the doctor's receptionist. Registering at the reception and spending time in the waiting room are also steps within the process before actually meeting the doctor in the consultation. A consultation is highly interactive as well, the doctor typically asks the patient about symptoms, habits and previous diseases. This interaction needs to be driven by all involved parties which is discussed in Sects. 8.2.2 and 8.3. Buying medicine in the pharmacy is far less interactive: handing the prescription to the pharmacist and receiving the medication might even work without any verbal communication.

These different steps in the service process where the provider and the customer meet are called service encounters. Service encounters can be physical or remote. Even finding a parking lot at a medical practice can be considered as a service encounter, as the customer approaches the sphere of the provider. Service encounters are crucial for service management due to two implications: First, service encounters facilitate co-creation. Second, as discussed in the following, service encounters can turn into moments of truths.

Types of Encounters

The potential for co-creation is implied by the nature of a service encounter as parties exchange resources as well as collaborative practices in which the provider and the customer jointly perform value-creating activities. According to Payne [5], there are basically three broad *types of encounters* which facilitate value co-creation: communication encounters, usage encounters, and service encounters.

- *Communication encounters* are mainly performed in order to connect with customers, for example a doctor's website containing information on the opening hours.
- *Usage encounters* are encounters where customers use the core service, for example the consultation with the doctor.
- *Service encounters* consist of customer interactions with customer service personnel, however remote, or interaction with electronic services. Examples are scheduling an appointment by calling the receptionist or using the doctor's webpage.

Moments of Truth

The perspective of service encounters as *moments of truth* and its implications for management were advocated by Jan Carlzon. A moment of truth is an opportunity to form an impression anytime a customer comes into contact with any aspect of a business, however remote [6].

> "Last year, each of our ten million customers came in contact with approximately five SAS employees, and this contact lasted an average of 15 s each time. Thus, SAS is created 50 million times a year, 15 s at a time. These 50 million moments of truth are the moments that ultimately determine whether SAS will succeed or fails as a company. They are the moments when we must prove to our customers that SAS is their best alternative."
>
> Jan Carlzon (former CEO of SAS Airlines)

The focus of the concept of moments of truth expresses that every interaction with the customer can determine his perception of service quality and therefore his likelihood to further co-create with the provider. Managing these moments of truth is crucial for the provider, otherwise the customer might not return. Furthermore, moments of truth provide opportunities to further co-create and generate additional business for the provider. Section 8.2.3 discusses the challenges for the provider in managing these moments of truth along different customer touchpoints.

▶ **Definition (Moment of Truth)** An opportunity to form an impression anytime a customer comes into contact with any aspect of a business, however remote [6].

Typically, providers and customers take a different perspective on value creation (illustrated in Fig. 8.5). Many providers consider the interaction in service encounters less important than the encounter where the actual usage of the "core" service takes place. However, for a customer, communication encounters and service encounters may be first chance to perceive service quality. Negative experiences in these encounters can eventually determine the customer's likelihood to stay in the relationship before he actually is involved in a usage encounter. For example, a patient encounters a doctor's webpage with outdated information on the opening hours or he experiences an unfriendly doctor's receptionist. Both could lead to his decision of switching the doctor before he actually meets him.

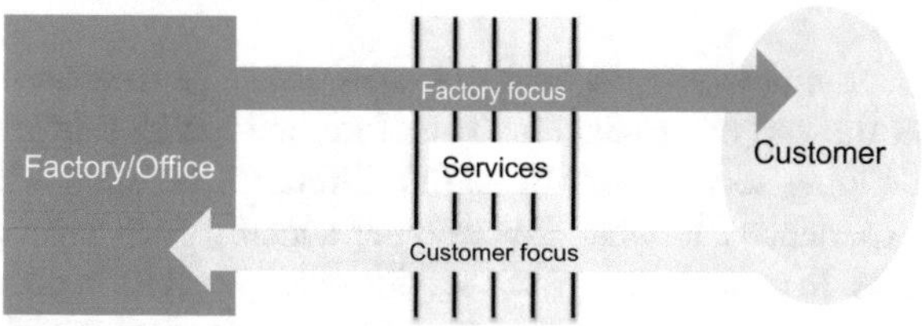

Fig. 8.5 Factory vs. service perspective (adapted from Grönroos [7])

The customer's first perception of the service was rendered negatively during the first service encounters, even though the doctor could be an excellent doctor. Therefore, it is crucial for a service business to also consider the customer perspective—and vice versa—for a successful co-creation.

8.1.4 Service Quality

In some product environments, quality is relatively easy to determine. Quality in a product environment can be related to the performance of a product, its features, its reliability, etc. Although the concept of quality might vary, depending on the context of a product, they usually have in common that the compliance to certain quality standards can be measured. For example, a car component manufacturer can measure quality of its components within the production process before the customer actually encounters the product.

The situation is different in a service setting. The process perspective on services implies that the production and the consumption of the service cannot completely be separated. Consumption and at least some production take place during the service encounter. This nature of a service implies the major challenge for managing service quality: it is determined within the service encounters—that's why they can turn into moments of truth.

▶ **Definition (Service Quality)** A measure of how well the service level delivered matches customer expectations [8].

Of course, the quality of the resources needed within the service process can often be determined beforehand. However, good quality of resources does not always result in good service quality. This can be demonstrated using the doctoral surgery example: All the medical devices and consumables may comply to a certain quality standard. However, if the doctor is not able to handle the devices appropriately or uses the wrong ones, service experience would be negatively influenced. Therefore, service quality needs to be regarded differently from quality in the product world.

R Service quality is determined during the service encounter and cannot be determined upfront.

It is obvious that quality cannot easily be measured as in the case of a product at the end of production. Therefore, marketing scholars came up with the idea of defining service quality as the difference between what the customer expects to experience and what the customer actually does experience during the service process. In general, decreased service quality results in decreased customer satisfaction. A challenge of managing customer satisfaction (which is in the following further detailed as a *gap* between customer's expectation and perception) is that customers simply do not always tell the provider if they were satisfied or not, particularly when the service process is a more standardized and anonymous process such as the airline industry or in the context of an electronic service.

The average business only hears from 4 % of their customers who are dissatisfied with their products or services. Of the 96 % who do not bother to complain, 25 % of the customers have serious problems [9].

As a consequence, measuring customer satisfaction is crucial, but how can we define and explore customer satisfaction? Parasuraman et al. [8] defined different service quality dimensions which, if fulfilled, may lead to customer satisfaction. The service quality dimensions are:

Reliability   Perform promised service dependably and accurately. Example: Doctor identifies the right diagnosis corresponding to the patients symptoms.
Assurance   Ability to convey trust and confidence. For example, a doctor is polite and shows respect for the patient.
Tangibles   Physical facilities and facilitating goods. For example, the cleanliness and nice atmosphere of a medical practice.
Empathy   Ability to be approachable. For example, a doctor is a good listener.
Responsiveness   Willingness to help customers promptly. For example, the direct treatment of a patient in case of an emergency and after consultation and inquiries.

Parasuraman et al. [10] furthermore developed SERVQUAL, a questionnaire for measuring service quality according to these quality dimensions. SERVQUAL contains 44 questions which are rated using a Likert-scale where customers rate their agreement with statements using a scale from 1 (I totally disagree) to 7 (I fully agree).

An alternative approach suggested by Fred Reichheld is the Net Promoter Score. It is based on a single question: How likely are you to recommend our company/product/service to your friends and colleagues? Customers are regularly asked to answer this question based on a 0 (not likely) to 10 (very likely) scale. The underlying idea is that customers who are satisfied would be more likely to recommend the service to their friends or colleagues.

Apart from choosing the right scale (way of measurement), it is also a challenge to measure customer satisfaction at the right point of time. Measuring too early would lead to meaningless results because the customer has not collected enough experience, measuring too late could result in not reaching unsatisfied customers.

Even when companies are able to measure service quality, it is not always trivial to find the causes for the gap between customer expectation and customer perception. Parasuraman et al. [8] developed a model which breaks down the different reasons for such a gap. They identified four gaps which can be the reason for a difference between customer expectation and customer perception (see Fig. 8.6). Those gaps are: *market research gap*, *design gap*, *conformance gap*, and *communication gap*.

The *market research gap* is caused by a different understanding of customer expectations by the management. For example, in an IT service environment, the management might think that 99 % reliability per month is acceptable for the

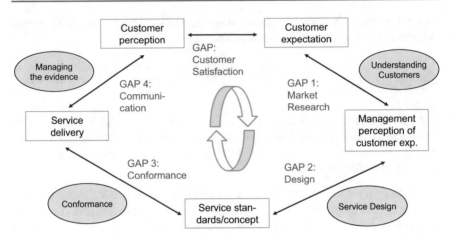

Fig. 8.6 The service quality GAP model (adapted from Parasuraman et al. [8])

customer. However, the customer may not expect any outages, when deciding to utilize a distinct IT service.

The second gap (*design gap*) is related to designing the service standards appropriate to the management's perception of customer expectations. For example, if the management wants to achieve 99.9 % reliability according to the customer requirements, a management decision to minimize redundancy systems might result in a setup which does not meet customer's requirements.

The third gap is the *conformance gap*, which is caused by a difference between the defined service concept and the actual implementation for service delivery. An example would be a delivery team that does not implement a required redundancy system.

The final gap is the *communication gap* which may be caused by a different customer perception of what has been actually delivered. For example, a reliability of 99.9 % means a potential outage of more than 7 h per month. If the outage causes an online shop to go offline for a few hours before Christmas, this may result in a highly biased customer perception of what has actually been delivered.

All these gaps can negatively influence customer experience. However, once identified, actions can be taken in order to reduce the gaps.

8.1.5 Service Productivity

In general, productivity is defined as the ratio between output and input. In a production context, input and output are relatively clear and in most cases easy to assess. Inputs are the raw materials, working hours, production machines, etc. The outputs on the other hand are the number of produced goods. Increasing productivity

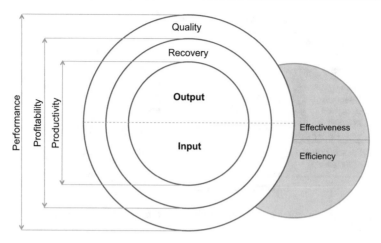

Fig. 8.7 The triple P-model (adapted from Tangen [11])

can, therefore, be either achieved by increasing the output or reducing the input (and keeping the other constant) or both, e.g. through an optimization of the production process.

Very often the terms productivity, performance, profitability, effectiveness and efficiency are confused or used simultaneously. The triple P-model of Tangen [11] (also illustrated in Fig. 8.7) clarifies the relationship between those concepts. The model considers productivity as defined within this section. Profitability is also the ratio of output and input, but in contrast to productivity it is concerned with a monetary ratio in which price factors (for example recovery costs) are included. Performance is the overall concept that includes profitability and productivity and other non-cost factors such as quality, speed, delivery and flexibility. Effectiveness and efficiency are terms that can be applied to all the three P's. Effectiveness is the degree to which a desired result is achieved, for example if a certain patient is healed after a medical surgery. Efficiency is concerned with how well the input is utilized, for example how much medication was needed.

In contrast to production, productivity of services, however, is a more complex issue. In the beginning of Adam Smith's modern economics, services were considered as supporting activities which negatively influence productivity. With the rise of service economies and the increasing importance of services, also for manufacturers (see Chap. 3 on Service Innovation), the situation changed. When it comes to productivity however, there are several shortcomings when applying the traditional productivity concept in a service context. Indeed, the concept of productivity has been developed for the production process in a closed system. In a product context, production and consumption are often separated and in particular the customer is not involved in the production process.

In a service context, the customer actively participates in different roles (see Sect. 8.3) and brings in his resources. Furthermore, the definition of productivity as

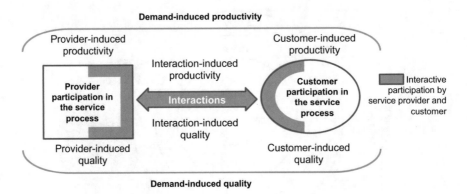

Fig. 8.8 Productivity, quality, and relationship marketing in service operations (adapted from Grönroos [7])

the ratio of output and input includes the assumption that the output has a constant quality (see Eq. (8.1) proposed by Grönroos [7]). This is rarely the case in a service context and therefore service productivity cannot be regarded isolated from service quality.

$$Productivity = \frac{output}{input}(constant\ quality) \qquad (8.1)$$

Figure 8.8 illustrates this and proposes service productivity as a construct of provider-induced productivity, interactive productivity and customer-induced productivity which cannot be regarded isolated from quality. The crucial managerial implication is that managers need to take into account those different perspectives when deciding about actions which impact productivity. Sometimes, an action which increases the productivity of the provider decreases the productivity of the customer. For example, an interactive voice response system in a call center might increase the productivity of the call center, but may tremendously reduce the productivity of the customer when he has to navigate through a menu of voice commands or put on hold.

Figure 8.8 furthermore illustrates, that quality and productivity can be influenced by external factors, in particular demand. A system perspective is also considered in Eq. (8.2).

$$Productivity = \frac{result\ of\ a\ service\ to\ the\ beneficiary}{use\ of\ assets\ of\ the\ service\ system} \qquad (8.2)$$

8.2 Customer Relationships

Managing customer relationships becomes very important for service providers and companies that strive to enrich their business with services. Why is that? Providers need to interact much more with their customers in a service context. Furthermore, as discussed in the beginning of this chapter, services are at least to some extent co-created by the customer (details are provided in the following Sect. 8.3). This requires a different view on the relationship, compared to a product business where companies offer their pre-manufactured products to customers.

8.2.1 Service Context

Companies that are in the service business or target at becoming a service business need to change the perspective and focus on relationships rather than on single transactions. This shift has an impact on the way companies regard their customer relationships along several dimensions. Table 8.1 reflects the major differences between a business that is focused on selling single products (Transaction View) and a company that strives to maximize the long-term value of customer relationships.

There are a number of differences along several dimensions that can be observed in this context [12]. First, the structure of the cooperation with the customer is different. While a company focuses on each individual transaction, a relational view is focused on a close mutual relationship. For example, within a transactional setup the contractual settings are negotiated for every transaction separately. This can create tremendous negotiation costs for both parties. In a close mutual relationship,

Table 8.1 Comparison between transactional and relational view based on Donaldson and O'Toole [12]

Strategic dimension	Transaction view	Relational view
Structure	Based on each individual transaction	Close mutual relationship
Strategy formulation	Firm induced—firm as independent actor	A two-party dyad or network interconnection
Organization-environment	Firm has control over choices	Embedded in a social system
Study of the customer relationship	Customer as external passive respondents to a firm's marketing effort	Customer as active/interactive participants in a firm's marketing
Resource allocation	Control of resources and risk of sharing are major concerns	Allocation and effect of resources on the relationship
Coordination mechanism	Power is advantage and gives control	Parties trust each other and act equitably
Nature of exchange	Short-term view minimizes investment in the relationship	Long-term view permits committed action

parties agree on a (formal or informal) strategic framework for their cooperation and minimize the effort for each individual transaction.

Second, the strategy formulation is different. Taking the transaction view, a firm will induce its strategy as an independent actor. That means one firm will define its strategy and the customer can only choose to cooperate with the firm or not. A firm taking the relational view will define a strategy at least as a two-party dyad. Even better, the company will consider itself as a partner within a network. As we will explore in Sect. 8.3, the customer is an active participant, rather than an external passive respondent, in the relational view. While in a transactional setup one party can own resources and use them for dominating the relationship, resources are allocated between partners in a relational view. Furthermore, a relational view implies that the coordination is based on trust between the two partners. Finally, the exchange is long-term oriented in a relational view.

Maximizing the long-term value of customer relationships requires understanding customer loyalty and its link to profitability. Customer loyalty is not a specific concept of service co-creation. However, the relational nature of services increases the importance of customer loyalty for managers and academia. When modern economies became service-dominated, many companies put effort into creating profitable long-term relationships with their customers.

In 1990, Reichheld and Sasser [13] drew attention from managers and academics by stating a simple, yet impactful, message: every company should strive to keep every customer the firm could profitably serve. Within this movement, many companies started focusing on building long-term relationships with their profitable customers. It is claimed that customer defections have a strong impact on the bottom line: by retaining just 5 % more of their customers, companies could boost profit by almost 100 % [13]. Several benefits of long-term customer retention lead to increasing profit. This is also called the *loyalty effect*. The loyalty effect is an umbrella term for a set of effects that come into play when customers are successfully retained over a period of time (see Fig. 8.9).

While customers can be unprofitable in the first period, profits can increase over time through the following effects:

Acquisition Cost Acquisition costs are those costs spent on acquiring new customers. These costs include: advertising targeting new customers, commissions on sales for new customers, and sales force expenses for acquiring new customers. By reducing acquisition costs through retaining their existing customer base, companies are able to increase their profit.

Per-Customer Revenue Growth Customer spendings tend to increase over time. This revenue growth can be composed of revenue from cross-selling (selling additional services) and the revenue from upselling (selling more or a higher-quality version of products or services that a customer already bought or intended to buy).

Operating Costs Communication with existing customers is regularly more efficient. On the one hand, customers get to know a business and get familiar with their products and services. On the other hand, the provider company learns more

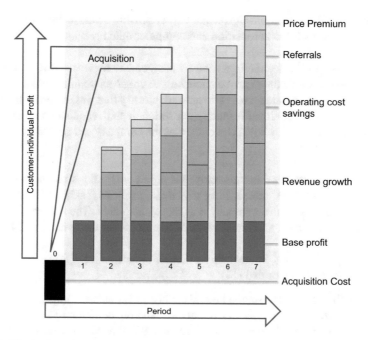

Fig. 8.9 The *loyalty effect* (based on Reichheld and Sasser [13])

about the customer's preferences and needs. This collaborative learning could lead to enormous productivity advantages that could be translated into lower costs.

Referrals Another important advantage of retaining customers is that satisfied long-term customers recommend providers to other customers (see also customer role co-marketer). Furthermore, customers that get in contact with a provider through a recommendation tend to be more profitable and stay in the relationship for longer. Additionally, chances are good that referred customers fit well with the products and services the provider offers, since people tend to associate with people like themselves.

Price Premium Existing customers often pay higher prices than new customers. This could be the results of individual trial discounts at the beginning of the relationship or self-selection. Therefore, long-term customers tend to be less price sensitive on individual items than new customers.

8.2.2 Customer Relationship Management

The term *customer relationship management* (CRM) emerged in the software vendor and management practitioner communities in the mid-1990s. Software vendors (such as Oracle, SAP, and Microsoft) use the term to describe software for managing customer relationships. Other terms focusing on the technological aspects of CRM are sales force automation and computer aided selling, rarely used today however.

In contrast to the technology focus, management regards CRM as a holistic approach to managing customer relationships to create shareholder value. The term was coined by the movement in academia and industry that was driven by the finding that keeping customers loyal is much more valuable than acquiring new customers. Therefore, keeping every loyal customer that the company can profitably serve was the new imperative.

▶ **Definition (Customer Relationship Management)** The strategic process of selecting customers that a firm can most profitably serve and of shaping interactions between a company and these customers. The ultimate goal is to optimize the current and future value of customers for the company. [14]

Breaking down this strategically-oriented definition of CRM, the following components can be identified [14]:

Strategic Process CRM should be holistically and constantly implemented within the organization, across all functional units and on all hierarchy levels.

Selection The value of the customers (see Sect. 8.2.4) needs to be the decision basis for resource allocation.

Interactions Interacting in a bi-directional dialog should be the normative goal, especially in a service context. Managing customer interaction is called Operational CRM (Sect. 8.2.3).

Customers Customers can be consumers (B2C) and businesses (B2B). Whenever possible and profitable, individualization for each customer should be realized.

Current and Future Value of the Customer Instead of focusing on the value of single transactions, current and future customer lifetime value should be optimized.

R   In fact, CRM is not a new concept, but brings back the relationship orientation which was common in the pre-industrial era (however, very inefficient without IT support) and lost through the anonymous mass-production in the industrial era.

The different perspectives on CRM have often led to confusion in the past and many CRM projects failed because the where focused too much on technology rather than implementing CRM in processes and organization which is supported by technology.

A closely related concept is the more academically coined term relationship marketing. Relationship marketing aims at integrating customers, suppliers and other infrastructural partners into a firm's developmental and marketing activities [15]. This integration leads to close interactive relationships with suppliers, customers or other value chain partners of the firm.

In the academic community, the terms *relationship marketing* and CRM are often used interchangeably; sometimes CRM is also labeled as *information-enabled relationship marketing*.

CRM and relationship marketing are crucial concepts for scholars and practitioners of services marketing. As services are typically produced and delivered by the same institution, service providers are usually involved in the production and delivery of their services (that's why it is preferable to use the term co-creation in the service context).

8.2.3 Operational CRM

Operational CRM, sometimes also called Front-Office CRM, is concerned with managing the different customer touchpoints and providing a holistic service experience to the customer (see also Chap. 4 on Service Design). These different touchpoints (sometimes also called interaction channels) facilitate service encounters. Managing the co-creation of value in customer experiences involves determining which channels should be used for customer touchpoints in which service encounter occurs. The decision the provider has to take related to customer touchpoints is twofold: on the one hand, the provider needs to decide which customer touchpoints will be used for initiating interaction with the customer, e.g., the media for advertisement (TV advertising). On the other hand the service provider needs to decide which interaction channels can be used by the customer for initiating interaction with the provider, e.g. through a service hotline or a web portal (Fig. 8.10).

The managerial complexity is not only induced by different customer touchpoints but also by a set of challenges which is discussed in the following.

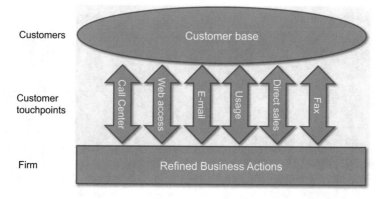

Fig. 8.10 Managing customer touchpoints (based on Dyche [16])

Challenge 1: Managing Interaction in a Service System Network

Typically a service process is concerned with a cascade of service encounters. It is not always the case that this interaction happens along the same touchpoints. Very often, cascades of service encounters happen along different customer touchpoints. For example, a medical surgery starts with calling the doctor's assistant, then registering at the welcome desk before actually facing the doctor. The challenge is not only managing the different channels (phone and face to face), but also managing different people involved. In this simple scenario, there can be up to three different employees (assistant receiving the call, assistant at welcome desk, doctor) of the service provider which contribute to the experience of the customer.

A lack of consistency and alignment of their actions with previous customer interaction could negatively influence customer experience. Unavailability of the doctor because the assistant on the phone has not scheduled an appointment in the doctor's calendar is not satisfying for the patient. Even more complexity is added in a B2B context. Here, not only the service provider is a system of employees, even the customer organization consists of multiple employees which interact with the provider. Typically, employees of the customer organization have different roles, needs and authorizations. Therefore, a customer which is an organization is also called many-headed (see Fig. 8.11) [17].

For managing this network of interaction in order to ensure aligned actions, a careful documentation of previous customer encounters is required. IT, in particular CRM systems, fulfill this requirement by providing the possibility for employees and IT systems to make their previous customer interaction visible to the whole organization. Figure 8.12 shows an example of the CRM system called CAS genesisWorld. Anybody in the provider organization can get an overview on previous customer interactions by listing the records from the database and viewing its details. However, implementing a CRM system does not automatically lead to an

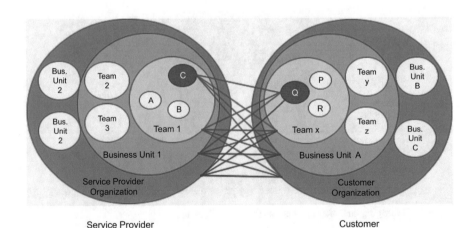

Fig. 8.11 Service encounters in a B2B setting

Fig. 8.12 The CRM system CAS genesisWorld (courtesy of CAS Software AG)

efficient and effective management of customer relationships. Carefully designed processes of managing customer relationships can be supported by CRM systems, but a CRM system not integrated in processes will not provide additional value.

Challenge 2: Managing Part Time Marketing
The second challenge refers to the concept of part time marketing which is a typical scenario in service firms. Employees of product firms can typically be categorized into front-office employees (employees with customer contact) and back-office employees (employees without customer contact). Front-office employees are typically sales and marketing employees, while back-office employees are programmers, engineers, administrative staff, etc. However, in a service environment there are virtually no employees which are not involved in customer interaction. Although their job is not focused on customer interaction full-time, they become part-time marketers. For example, IT architects for IT services need to directly interact with the customer as well. The managerial implication of part-time marketing is the appropriate training and alignment of the part-time marketers is required.

Challenge 3: Managing the Balance of Empowerment and Control
The third challenge is concerned with finding the right balance between employee empowerment and control. Employee empowerment means giving the employees which interact with the customer the right to decide what the best action in a specific setup is. On the other hand, a specific degree of standardization and control over

the service process is required by the organization. For example, in some countries paramedics are not allowed to utilize all medication by themselves without a doctor. Although it might be helpful in some scenarios, in those countries the doctors should keep control about this part of the service process and, therefore, paramedics are not empowered to do so. Managing the balance of empowerment and control is a tradeoff between empowerment and need to be adapted to the specific service scenario.

8.2.4   Analytical CRM

While operational CRM focuses on managing customer interaction, analytical CRM applies methods discussed in Chap. 6 on Service Analytics in order to understand this interaction to conduct implications for business actions.

▶ **Definition (Analytical CRM)** The purpose of analytical CRM is to systematically manage and analyze customer data conducted in operational CRM.

Analytical CRM can support relationship management over the whole customer lifecycle: from targeting the right customers to engage, to tracking activities during the service relationship and to predicting which customers are likely to churn. A related important area of analytical CRM is the determination of the Customer Lifetime Value (see Sect. 8.2.4). The methods and techniques used in analytical CRM are extensively discussed in Chap. 6. Operational CRM and analytical CRM can be considered as a closed loop: Customer data is collected during operational CRM processes, while analytical CRM analyzes the data and provides insights that can be used to manage and improve operational CRM processes. An important field of application of analytical CRM is determining the value of a customer, which will be discussed in the following.

Knowing the importance of long-term relationships, metrics needed to be found in order to measure and monitor the success of marketing programs. This led to the notion of Customer Lifetime Value (CLV) and Customer Equity (CE). CLV is the value of a customer over the entire relationship with a company. CE is the total aggregated CLV of all customers of a company. There are several reasons why these two metrics became more and more important. First, marketing departments need to be accountable to show the return of marketing programs and the value of a customer base. Second, traditional financial metrics such as the stock price have limited capability to express the success of marketing programs. Third, classical product profitability measures are not applicable in service firms. Finally, although long-term customers are more profitable in general, not all long-term customers are profitable.

▶ **Definition (Customer Lifetime Value (CLV))** The value of a customer over the entire relationship with a company. Customer Equity (CE) is the total aggregated CLV of all customers of a company.

By determining the CLV of all customers, companies can distinguish their customers and treat them according to their CLV. Looking at the CLV, it may be profitable in the long term to offer a product or service cost-neutral, while it could be profitable to terminate the relationship with loyal customers which will be unprofitable in the future. Amazon is an example for both strategies. Amazon's first Kindle Fire was sold at $199 in 2011, which most likely means losses at first—but the company was taking a long-term view:

> "When you think about the economics of the Kindle business, we think about it in totality. We think of the lifetime value of those devices. So we're not just thinking about the economics of the device and the accessories; we're thinking about the content. We are selling quite a bit of special offers devices, which include ads, so we're thinking about the advertisement and those special offers and those lifetime values. [...] And we look at the total economics, which include the device, the accessories, the content, as well as any ad-based revenue and special offers. So those are the things that we're looking at as we think about the lifetime value of a device, and we like what we see."

> Tom Szkutak (CFO Amazon.com)

On the other hand, Amazon closes accounts of unprofitable German customers extensively using returns, which is a cost-intensive issue of retailers in Germany. Consumer protection laws guarantee that a consumer can return an item at the retailer's expense. When a consumer abuses this and turns Amazon into their at-home showroom, the costs can add up quickly.

Many quantitative approaches exist to express the lifetime value of each customer in a number as a basis for marketing decisions. One example for a financial model for determining the CLV is the model of Kumar and Reinertz [14]:

$$CLV = \sum_{t=0}^{T} \frac{(p_t - c_t)r_t}{(1 + i)^t} - AC \qquad (8.3)$$

where

p_t = price paid by a consumer at time t,
c_t = direct cost of servicing the customer at time t,
i = discount rate or cost of capital for the firm,
r_t = probability of customer repeat buying or being "alive" at time t,
AC = acquisition cost, and
T = time horizon for estimating CLV.

This model can be illustrated using an example from the IT service domain. Assume a scenario where you could allocate our marketing budget to either acquire customer 1 (medium sized IT company) or customer 2 (start up). Customer 1 might generate a high gross profit $(p_t - c_t)$ in period 1, but generates only small gross profit in the following periods. Customer 2 might generate small gross profit $(p_t - c_t)$ in period 1, but increasingly generates gross profit in the following periods which, summed up and discounted may result in a higher customer lifetime value than customer 1. A detailed calculation is illustrated in the following.

Year from acquisition	Service Fee	Service Costs	Gross Contribution	Marketing Costs	Actual Retention Rate in period	Total Survival Rate	Expected number of remaining customers	Profit per customer per period	Discounted profit per customer per period	Total discounted profits per period
0	$100	$50	$50	$10	0.10	0.10	100	$40	$40	$4,000
1	$100	$50	$50	$10	0.50	0.05	50	$40	$36	$1,818
2	$100	$50	$50	$10	0.50	0.03	25	$40	$33	$826
3	$100	$50	$50	$10	0.50	0.01	13	$40	$30	$376
4	$100	$50	$50	$10	0.50	0.01	6	$40	$27	$171
									Total customer equity	$7,191

i=	0.10
I =	1000
T =	5

Fig. 8.13 Example of total customer equity

Example

The IT service provider IT Gump currently has a customer base of 1000 customers. In the following, customer equity for a period of 3 years (including the current year) is calculated:

- Gross contribution (GC) of each customer is $2000 (each year).
- Marketing and service costs (MSC) are estimated $1000 per customer (each year).
- Interest rate is 10 % p.a.
- Predicted retention rate in the current year is 0.5 and will increase to 0.8 in the following year. No customers are expected to leave during the last year.
- Acquisition costs are not part of the calculation.

The example illustrates the importance of taking long term relationships and long term customer value into account. Even with a very low customer retention rate and a high interest rate, the value of the customer base in year 0 is much bigger when comparing total lifetime value with first year profit ($7191 vs. $4000) (Fig. 8.13).

8.3   Customer Participation

The adoption of service co-creation involves the joint value creation between multiple participants, in particular between customers and providers. Customer participation is the concept of integrating the customer in the processes of the company. Many tasks usually done within the company are partly or fully outsourced to the customer. But what is the advantage of getting the customer more involved? Customer participation can lead to cost savings opportunities, besides many other advantages such as giving customers the feeling of being part of the whole process. While customer participation has been used in services for a long time, the advent of modern ICT technologies helps this concept to take off in recent years.

▶ **Definition (Customer Participation)** The concept of integrating the customer in the processes of the company.

As discussed in Sect. 8.1, the customer more and more becomes an active partner in service co-creation. This section discusses several practical concepts about how the customer can participate (so called customer roles [18]) and how customer participation can be managed.

8.3.1 Customer Roles

This section presents different customer roles, which can be used as a framework to better understand how the customer can be involved in co-creation [18]. An overview of the different customer roles is given in Table 8.2. When is it best to use which customer role? Customers can not only participate in running services but

Table 8.2 Overview of customer roles (based on Straub et al. [18])

Customer role	Description	Examples
Co-designer	The customer helps as an 'organizational consultant' during decision making and design processes	McDonald's burger design contest, Lego Digital Designer
Service-specifier	The customer triggers the service delivery through his specification	Expedia (online travel agency) build your own package, mi adidas (customize shoe), Dell (customize laptop)
Co-marketer	The customer supports the marketing of a service, particularly through word-of-mouth	Refer a friend bonus programs (e.g. Barclaycard), facebook company pages
Quality-controller	The customer assists in assuring the quality of production and delivery through open testing and complaints	Google Mail (beta phase), honestly.com (Feedback via smartphones)
Co-producer	The customer provides input in form of production factors, such as work, know-how, information, money, etc.	YouTube, Wikipedia
Substitute for leadership	Customers' wishes and orders determine the tasks of the employees	Customer in a restaurant, call center agents
Helper	The customers help each other without interaction of the company	Stack Overflow (web forum for programming problems), student association

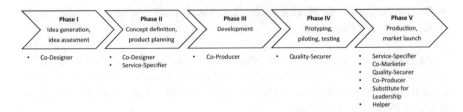

Fig. 8.14 Customer roles mapped to steps in the innovation development process (adapted from Herstatt [19])

in its development as well, as already discussed in the chapters on service innovation and service design. An exemplary overview on different customer roles aligned to a service development process [19] is given in Fig. 8.14.

Co-designer

A Co-designer is an organizational consultant who assists the company in decision and design processes [20]. The customer playing this role contributes his knowledge to the creation of new services and products. Through this process, the customer's view and insights are integrated early in service creation processes (Phase I, Phase II). Using the creativity of customers, providers can partially outsource service development and get early feedback to prevent failure in service development. An example is the McDonald's burger design contest. The earlier customer feedback is integrated in service design, the more likely it will suit the customers' preferences. McDonald's did this in Germany with a design contest. Customers designed over 300,000 burgers from which five winners were produced based on customer votes.

▶ **Definition (Co-designer)** An organizational consultant who assists the company in decision and design processes.

Service-Specifier

Service-specifiers are customers who define the characteristics and properties of a service before the service delivery. Through the actions of a service-specifier the company gets informed about the details of the service which needs to be delivered (Phase II) or developed (Phase V). This specification triggers service delivery [21]. For services like booking a flight or going to the doctor's office it is a common concept. A specification of the customer about where to travel to or a definition of the symptoms is needed to trigger service delivery. Modern ICT technologies have pushed the concept. Nowadays custom made PCs can be ordered from Dell through the use of a web interface. Customers specify the configuration to their own preferences. This is also known as mass customization.

▶ **Definition (Service-Specifiers)** Customers who define the characteristics and properties of a service before the service delivery.

Co-marketer

Co-marketers play an important role in advertising services. They support the company's marketing mainly through word-of-mouth recommendations. For example, one customer needs to go to the doctor's office and seeks advice as to which doctor to go to. He either asks his friends or searches online for recommendations resulting in a positive or negative marketing effect [22]. Recommendations by customers are heavily influenced by their own experiences, hence promotion mainly starts after their own purchase (Phase V). This shows the importance of a good CRM as well, as already discussed in Sect. 8.2.2.

▶ **Definition (Co-marketers)** Customers who are advertising services.

Quality-Controller

Customers can assist in assuring the quality of a service through their actions. This role mainly covers two types of customers. The Quality-Controller who is directly integrated in testing phases (Phase IV) and the Quality-Controller who gives feedback about his service experience (Phase V). Besides in-house testing, open test phases outside the company like open beta tests exist (e.g. software development). Many of those test phases incorporate target groups–their customers. Projects like Google's e-mail service Gmail used an open beta phase (April 1, 2004), where thousands of customers used their service before official release on July 7, 2009.

▶ **Definition (Quality-Controllers)** Customers assisting in assuring the quality of a service through their actions.

Co-producer

A *co-producer* is a customer who provides production factors for the company– work, information, money, know-how, etc. [23]. During participation a co-producer can be seen as part-time employee of the company (Schneider and Bowen 1995). Through self-service concepts work is delegated to customers. For example, customers are using self-service gas stations, vending machines or are filling out forms about their medical history when going to the doctor's office instead of getting served by an employee (Phase V). Through Web 2.0 concepts the development of content is outsourced to the customers. Main parts of the development are outsourced to Co-producers who draft Wikipedia articles or produce YouTube videos (Phase III).

▶ **Definition (Co-producer)** A customer who provides production factors for the company.

Substitute for Leadership

In services it is often the case that the customer has control over the employees' tasks. In such cases the customer adopts the role of the *substitute for leadership*. The customers wishes and orders determine the tasks of the employees, for instance in a restaurant. Customers have control over the tasks which a waitress has to fulfill through their orders. The boss of the waitress may just state the waitress' tasks as to fulfill the customers wishes. In many cases the employee sees the customers as his direct supervisor instead of his actual boss. The employee's motivation to give his best is thereby directly influenced by the interaction with the customer.

▶ **Definition (Substitute for Leadership)** A customer who has control over the employees tasks and, thereby, acts as a supervisor and evaluator.

Helper

In many cases customers help each other without interaction with the company. This role is known as *helper*. Customers help each other to find directions in a hospital or a customer's service experience is heavily influenced by another customer's behavior, e.g., in a waiting room (Phase V). Companies can outsource easy problem solving tasks to their customers using for instance web forums. A prominent example is Stack Overflow. On this website, programming problems can be stated and are solved by other customers serving as helpers.

▶ **Definition (Helper)** A customer helping another customer without participation of the company.

8.3.2 Managing Customer Participation

As outlined in the previous section, customer participation was used in many prominent examples. But is this concept really used by the broad audience? An exploratory study by Straub et al. [18] identified the five most important roles for German service companies. Fifty three practitioners in the field of service innovation and open innovation filled out a questionnaire about their experiences with different customer roles. Results indicate the Service-Specifier as the most used customer role in practice, as depicted in Fig. 8.15. Since their sample consisted of companies who are either service companies or have a significant service share in their business, the application of the Service-Specifier role is not surprising. Furthermore all five roles are applied by industry. This underlines the importance of this concept.

In order to achieve certain goals, a companies' management has to consider the implications of customer participation. Customer integration mainly influences customer satisfaction, the company's market share, and the costs of projects. The effects of customer participation are, however, not solely positive. Positive effects might be the main motivation behind such projects, but there are potential risks as well. In order to fully evaluate the decision of integrating customers in a project, companies have to look at both sides of the coin. In the following section we will discuss these positive and negative implications. A short overview is given in Table 8.3.

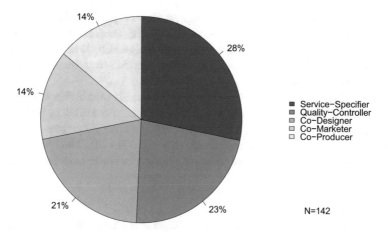

Fig. 8.15 Application of customer roles [18]

Table 8.3 Comparison between positive and negative implications from customer participation

Positive implications	Negative implications
Increased customer satisfaction	Coordination overhead
Increased market shares	Missing know-how of the customer
Decreased costs	Increased costs
Other	Misunderstandings
	Loss of know-how
	Lack of motivation
	Idea rejection
	Other

Positive Implications

Through customer participation, a variety of positive effects might be possible. Service quality, customization, innovation success, market orientation, and marketing of services are just a few factors which potentially can be positively influenced. The three main factors usually considered are decreased costs, increased customer satisfaction and increased market shares [24]. Hence, we will look in detail at these three main implications:

Decreased Costs Customers take over tasks which are usually performed by employees of the company, hence costs are saved. Co-producers work for free when they, for example, fill out a form in a doctor's practice. Through word-of-mouth marketing of co-marketers less money needs to be spent on the promotion of services. New service development gets cheaper through outsourced work to co-designers. Quality-controllers save costs by testing new services for free.

Increased Customer Satisfaction Through customer participation a feeling of association with the company is achieved. Quality-controllers might complain about problems of a service. If the customer's feels that he is taken seriously and that the problem's solution takes all his critical feedback into account, it will give him a sense of satisfaction.

Increased Market Shares Customer participation can lead to higher market shares. Satisfied and loyal customers may purchase services more often or buy different services of the same company. Co-marketers recruit more customers to purchase the companies' services through positive word-of-mouth. New service development who integrates co-designers may have a better market success chance leading to higher market shares.

Negative Implications

Besides positive implications, there are potential risks as well. This should be considered when realizing projects integrating customers to minimize their potential negative implications. While it is hard to identify universal risks of customer participation, since they depend on the industry, company, and project the customer participates in. The most common risks are coordination overhead, missing know-how of the customer, misunderstandings between the customer and the employee, costs, loss of know-how, lack of motivation of the customer, and rejection of customer ideas by the employees of the company. We will now look in detail at these negative implications:

Coordination Overhead Through the participation of the customer new challenging tasks may arise. The customer's input has to be integrated in corporate structures. Hence, complexity and a reduction of flexibility have to be faced by the company. This is known as coordination overhead.

Missing Know-How of the Customer It is not clear from the beginning of the participation, if a customer has the needed knowledge for a successful participation. This is known as missing know-how. Take for example a diabetic patient who should inject his insulin but does not know how to use a syringe. Therefore, in some cases trainings for customers are required.

Increased Costs Customer participation often needs one or several employees guiding the customers throughout their participation. New employees are only one reason why costs can increase. This risk is closely related to coordination overhead.

Misunderstandings Customers often have good advice for companies, but it is misunderstood by the employee or vice versa. On the one hand, customers may not know the right terms to communicate with an expert of the company. On the other hand, the customers' feedback may not be transported from the corresponding customer relations person to someone within who could use this vital information.

Loss of Know-How The more the customer participates the more he knows about the company's know-how. Some customers learn to accomplish the service result on their own. Moreover customers who had access to intellectual property (IP) (e.g., co-designers participating in new service development) likely learn

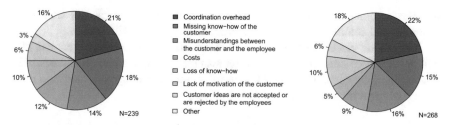

Fig. 8.16 Comparison of reservations (*left*) and negative experiences (*right*) [18]

facts about the company's future plans, which could be made public or sold to competing companies. As a consequence, NDAs (non-disclosure agreements) are common practice to avoid these problems.

Lack of Motivation Often customers start participating but tend to drop out, because they lose interest. One challenge for the company is therefore to keep the customers motivated throughout the participation process.

Idea Rejection Narrow-minded employees with a great expertise often reject customer ideas, based on their attitude to be always better informed than a 'simple' customer. Accepting new opinions from people whose expertise is not proven is not easy. This will not only lead to the rejection of a potentially successful idea, but to unsatisfied customers as well.

Is striving towards more customer participation a good idea for every service? This question can not be answered easily. In the end it depends on many factors like the company's structures, the project in mind, the experience with customer participation, the company's customers, and many more. Interestingly, there are substantial differences between reservations against customer participation and negative experiences with customer participation, as depicted in Fig. 8.16. For instance, many companies fear of losing their own know-how or intellectual property (IP) via the participation of the customer and his potential to spread the information. On the other hand, companies who gained experience with customer participation see this potential risk less important. This indicates, that a lot of companies have a different opinion about the risks of customer participation before implementing it and should carefully evaluate the decision on how to integrate customers.

8.4   Conclusions

This chapter provided an overview on selected topics of co-creation in a service context. It introduced the concept of value co-creation in service systems. As presented in the opening case, a service system view requires taking all participants into account, rather than focusing on bilateral interaction.

This chapter introduced several concepts that are of importance for co-creation, such as service value propositions, service encounters, service quality, and service productivity. This chapter furthermore presented several concepts for managing customer relationships. As providers need to interact much more with their customers in a service context, managing customer relationships is a critical task for service providers and companies that strive to enrich their business with services.

This chapter closed with an overview on the different roles a customer can play within service co-creation, as well as its managerial implications. Since both, the provider and the customer, jointly create value, understanding and managing these roles is of great importance for service providers.

Review Section

Review Questions

1. Why are service encounters important?
2. What is unique about quality and productivity in a service context?
3. What is the difference between transactional and relationship marketing?
4. What is customer relationship management and what are its components?
5. Why is customer loyalty important?
6. What are the different customer roles customers can play in service co-creation?
7. What are the advantages and disadvantages of customer participation for the service provider?

Project

CumuTools is a young start-up founded by two computer science students at a technical university. The software-as-a-service solution Cloud Management Center enables companies to holistically integrate, manage, and monitor different software and infrastructure cloud services provided by different vendors. Their business mentors acknowledged that there is a big market for the Cloud Management Center in the future. On the other hand, Cloud Management Center is still in beta status and further development is required within the next years in order to enter into broader markets. Furthermore, integrating services from multiple cloud providers is still in its infancy in many companies. As a consequence, the customer base is expected to grow slowly in the beginning. To accelerate the growth of the customer base, CumuTools plans to follow an aggressive pricing strategy. Customers should be attracted by offering a free one-year testing phase and customers could cancel their subscriptions at any time within this testing phase. After the one year testing phase, customers have to pay a fixed service fee of $1000 per customer firm per year.

CumuTools has developed and extensively tested their software using the university's infrastructure in the past. However, for entering public cloud markets, CumuTools needs a dedicated infrastructure to host the Cloud Management Center. Relying on public cloud offerings for hosting the Cloud Management Center is not an option, since it has specific performance requirements that can't be fulfilled in a virtualized environment. Therefore, CumuTools negotiates with TMC, a global firm providing IT hardware, software and services. TMC offers CumuTools two different options for providing the required infrastructure: they could either use standard infrastructure (Option 1) or they could decide to run their applications on a high performance and scalable infrastructure (Option 2). According to TMC, both options come with a guaranteed availability of 99.9 %, but Option 2 is assumed to be much more reliable.

CumuTools estimated the service costs for both options. Option 1 results in $200 service costs per customer, Option 2 results in $400 service costs per customer. Due to cost reasons, CumuTools decided to choose Option 1. CumuTools is a start-up just established with limited financial resources. As the liability of CumuTools includes private capital, the founders are highly risk averse and want to minimize liabilities. They estimated the 99.9 % monthly availability to be sufficient and were confident that the pricing was attractive enough for customers to tolerate minor variations in service quality. Furthermore, they are currently implementing an offline function for the Cloud Management Center which could serve as a buffer in case of short unavailability. CumuTools implemented the Cloud Management Center using TMCs infrastructure and started promoting their software-as-a-service solution. The average marketing costs for each customer are determined to be $100.

As expected, the customer base grew slowly in the beginning until a renowned CIO journal reported about the start-up company and its new Cloud Management Center. Suddenly, there was a dramatic increase in the new subscriptions and CumuTools was finally able to acquire 20,000 subscribers in their first year. However, a few weeks later there was an unexplained large drop in customer satisfaction accompanied by a slow-down in the rate of new subscriptions. The small and improvised Service Desk was overwhelmed by calls from angry customers. The top three complaints were (1) unavailability of Cloud Management Center (2) slow web interface of Cloud Management Center (3) missing interim-saving option for form settings. When asking for specifications about their problems however, most of the customers were unable to provide technical details.

After extensive research, CumuTools recognized that their infrastructure was not sufficient. The unavailability of the infrastructure was spread over peak times and the missing scalability intensively slowed down the web interface of Cloud Management Center. Furthermore, the developers were not able to implement the offline function for the Cloud Management Center as planned. CumuTools considers building a more stable and scalable new infrastructure using Option 2, but already subscribed customers stayed on the old infrastructure. As a consequence, only 5 % of the customers remained after the first year. By setting up a special marketing program ($150 marketing costs), CumuTools was able to decrease customer defects to 50 % in the following years.

Exercise 1

You have been brought in as a management consultant to solve the problem of CumuTools. You immediately remember the Service Quality Gap Model to evaluate the problem and communicate it to the firm's management.

- Explain the concept of the GAP model and explain its components.
- Explain why the GAP model is an appropriate tool in this situation.
- Identify the types of gaps that derive from the given case and map them to the corresponding GAP.
- Specify for each gap which kind of action is adequate to reduce it.

Exercise 2

You attend the meeting in order to support CumuTools in negotiating the conditions for the provision of the required infrastructure by TMC. However, after a 3 h meeting, both parties were not able to determine a fee which is acceptable for both. CumuTools is a start-up just established with limited financial resources. As the liability of CumuTools includes private capital, the founders are highly risk averse. TMC on the other hand is willing to engage in risky contracts due to high market pressure. Do you see any possibility for co-creation between TMC and CumuTools? Brainstorm scenarios how the parties could work together.

Exercise 3

Calculate the Customer Equity (CE) over 5 years for the given case. Assume an interest rate of 10 %.

Exercise 4

Calculate the CE over 5 years in case CumuTools had chosen Option 2. Due to higher customer satisfaction, assume a customer retention rate of 10 % in the first period and 80 % in the following periods. Assume a decrease of marketing costs to $20 after the first period.

Exercise 5

Identify the roles the customers of CumuTools could play in this case. Specify how CumuTools could benefit from this customer participation.

Key Terms

Service Systems are value-cocreation configuration of people, technology, other internal and external service systems and information

Service Encounters are different steps in the service process where the provider and the customer meet.

Customer Relationship Management is a holistic approach to managing customer relationships to create shareholder value.

Operational CRM is concerned with managing the different customer touchpoints.

Analytical CRM involves understanding the customer activities that occurred in the front office

Customer Lifetime Value is the value of a customer over the entire relationship with a company

Customer Equity is the total aggregated Customer Lifetime Value of all customers of a company.

Customer Participation is the concept of integrating the customer in the processes of the company.

Further Reading

Christian Grönroos. *Service Management and Marketing: Customer Management in Service Competition.* John Wiley & Sons, 2007.

Christopher Lovelock, Paul Patterson, and Jochen Wirtz. *Services Marketing.* Pearson, 2014.

Vineet Kumar. *Customer Relationship Management.* John Wiley & Sons, 2010.

Alan Wilson, Valarie Zeithaml, Mary Jo Bitner, and Dwayne Gremler. *Services Marketing: Integrating Customer Focus Across the Firm.* Mcgraw-Hill, 2006.

References

1. Chopra S, Meindl P (2016) Supply chain management: strategy, planning, and operation. Prentice Hall. http://www.pearsonhighered.com/educator/product/Supply-Chain-Management-Strategy-Planning-and-Operation/9780133800203.page
2. Lusch RF (2011) Reframing supply-chain management: a service-dominant logic perspective. J Supply Chain Manag 47(1):14–18. ISSN: 15232409
3. Kwan SK, Hottum P (2014) Maintaining consistent customer experience in service system networks. Serv Sci 6(2):136–147
4. Kwan SK, Müller-Gorchs M (2011) Constructing effective value propositions for stakeholders in service system networks. In: Proceedings of SIGSVC workshop. Sprouts: Working Papers on Information Systems, vol 11, pp 1–23
5. Payne AF, Storbacka K, Frow P (2007) Managing the co-creation of value. J Acad Mark Sci 36(1):83–96. ISSN: 00920703
6. Carlzon J (1989) Moments of truth. HarperBusiness, New York, pp 160
7. Grönroos C (2007) Servie management and marketing, 3rd edn. Wiley, Chichester
8. Parasuraman A, Zeithaml VA, Berry LL (1985) A conceptual model of service quality and its implications for future research. J Mark 49(4):41. ISSN: 00222429
9. Fitzsimmons J, Fitzsimmons M (2007) Service management: operations, strategy, information technology w/student CD. McGraw-Hill/Irwin, New York, pp 537
10. Parasuraman A, Zeithaml VA, Berry LL (1988) SERVQUAL: a multiple-item scale for measuring consumer perceptions of service quality. J Retail 64:12–40

11. Tangen S (2005) Demystifying productivity and performance. Int J Product Perform Manag 54(1):34–46. ISSN: 1741-0401
12. Donaldson B, O'Toole T (2003) Strategic market relationships: from strategy to implementation. Wiley, New York
13. Reichheld FF, Sasser W (1990) Zero defections: quality comes to services. Harv Bus Rev 105:289
14. Kumar V, Reinartz W (2012) Customer relationship management: concept, strategy, and tools. Springer texts in business and economics. Springer, Berlin
15. Sheth J, Parvatiyar A (2000) Handbook of relationship marketing. Sage, Thousand Oaks
16. Dyché J (2002) The CRM handbook: a business guide to customer relationship management. Addison-Wesley, Boston
17. Gummesson E (2008) Total relationship marketing. Butterworth-Heinemann, Oxford
18. Straub T et al (2013) Customer integration in service innovation: an exploratory study. J Technol Manag Innov 8:25–33
19. Herstatt C (1991) Anwender als Quelle für die Produktinnovation. Dissertation, ETH Zürich
20. Schneider B et al (2005) Understanding organization-customer links in service settings. Acad Manag J 48:1017–1032
21. Lengnick-Hall CA (1996) Customer contributions to quality: a different view of the customer-oriented firm. Acad Manag Rev 21(3):791–824. ISSN: 0363-7425
22. Swan JE, Oliver RL (1989) Postpurchase communications by consumers. J Retail 65(4):516–533. ISSN: 00224359
23. Büttgen M (2009) Erscheinungsformen der Kundenintegration und Ansätze eines Integrationsmanagements. In: Stauss B (ed) Aktuelle Forschungsfragen im Dienstleistungsmarketing. Gabler, Wiesbaden, pp 105–132
24. Bettencourt L (1997) Customer voluntary performance: customers as partners in service - delivery. J Retail 73(3):383–406
25. Spohrer J et al (2008) The Service System Is the Basic Abstraction of Service Science. In Proceedings of the 41st Annual Hawaii International Conference on System Sciences. IEEE, pp 104–113
26. Spohrer J et al (2007) Steps Toward a Science of Service Systems. IEEE Computer Society, 40:71–77

Service Markets

9

Simon Caton, Christian Haas, Wibke Michalk,
and Christof Weinhardt

Summary

A key aspect of service systems is exploring and studying their economic
and business components. Services are commonly part of an ecosystem that
consists of other services (potentially competitors), service consumers, and
further aspects such as underlying laws and regulations. This chapter focuses
on the design and analysis of service markets, which define how services are
purchased and exchanged. In particular, market engineering is discussed as a
structured approach to study service markets. This chapter should be regarded as
an entry point into this domain, and assumes no prior knowledge. Therefore, a
key focal point is on establishing the fundamental aspects of service markets from
an economic point of view along with a methodology (agent-based computational
economics) for their study and analysis.

Learning Objectives
1. Apply the basics of microeconomic systems to the context of services.
2. Create business and pricing models for service markets.
3. Understand the key challenges in addressing economic questions with an
   implicit understanding of their core assumptions.
4. Analyse economic settings using multi-agent systems as a methodological
   framework for addressing economic questions.

▶ **Opening Case** Amongst the blind, the one-eyed man is King.

S. Caton • C. Haas • W. Michalk • C. Weinhardt (✉)
Karlsruhe Service Research Institute (KSRI), Karlsruhe Institute
of Technology (KIT), Karlsruhe, Germany
e-mail: christof.weinhardt@kit.edu

© Springer International Publishing Switzerland 2015
J. Cardoso et al. (eds.), *Fundamentals of Service Systems*, Service Science: Research
and Innovations in the Service Economy, DOI 10.1007/978-3-319-23195-2_9

Fig. 9.1 A motivating
example of service economics

In everyday life even slightly better knowledge of how humans make decisions
can have an impact. Understanding the basic economic principles and decision
metrics of a given situation can drastically change the outcome. See Fig. 9.1 (a real
photo) as a motivating example of how even a basic understanding of economic
metrics can influence a given situation. Here, Caroline is clearly being outbid by
an unknown rival, who has more information about the context than she does: they
know that there is an iPod touch missing, and that someone is willing to pay $50 to
get it back. The rival's strategy is simple: outbid Caroline and (hopefully) receive
an iPod touch at a reduced price.

Although this example is over exaggerating the need for a knowledge of
economics, there are some fundamental messages that are of importance:

1. Economic settings of this type can be modelled as a strategic setting (referred to
   as game).[1] In this case, Caroline moved first and her rival second.
2. Such settings can be one-shot or involve multiple moves or interactions. Caroline
   could return and remove the other bid, increase her own bid, or never realise that
   she has been outbid and lose her iPod touch.
3. Information concerning economic context, and the moves of others are important. The rival could not have made their move without having first observed
   Caroline's.

---

[1]This is the focus of the economic discipline Game Theory, which studies such (economic)
interactions from a strategic perspective, see [1].

4. If in the future Caroline lost her phone, and had she seen the rival's move, this could change her own behaviour based upon this experience. This could be manifested by using a message like: "Lost iPhone: a reward will be given upon return". In this case, she has changed the rules of the game to better suit her first mover situation.

5. There are other actors in the game that affect its outcome; namely the person who finds the iPod touch (assuming it is found). Neither player knows for certain how this actor will behave, and therefore mechanisms are used to guide the third party to the desired result. In this case, incentivise the return/sale of the iPod touch through a tangible increase in utility: a monetary reward.

Although this example may seem a little far fetched, there are countless similar examples. Perhaps the two most well known, and illustrative, examples are the Amazon bot bidding war of 2011 that caused a little known book to be sticker priced at $23.7 million (see [2]). The cause? Two repricing algorithms of well-established sellers observing and reacting to each other's price changes as a proxy for demand. The source of the problem, as Micheal Eisen notes in his blog [3], seemed to be that the sellers' pricing strategies were coupled with each other in a way that suggests that seller A tried to undercut seller B, whereas seller B inflated seller A's price presumably because they did not own a copy of the book and would consequently have to purchase it themselves if a sale took place. What started as a fairly common business strategy, turned into a 10 day pricing battle of the bots, as neither seller thought to add an upper bound in their pricing model.

The second well-known phenomenon that is particularly relevant for the consideration of pricing, and economic modelling, is the fact that humans sometimes make questionable purchasing decisions that deviate from the expected, rational behaviour. Consider, for example, buying gift certificates on platforms like eBay. It is clear that the maximum bid price should be at most the face value of the certificate (plus potentially service or shipping fees). However, studies (e.g., [4, 5]) of certificate purchasing on eBay have illustrated bidders spending more than the reported face value. Why does this happen? Well there are many schools of thought, but most research suggests that the joy of winning overrides the (dis)utility of winning (by paying slightly more than the value of the good).

From the perspective of services, the understanding of the economic setting (such as the position within a service market) is of crucial importance for its success, irrespective of aspects of innovation, design, implementation, and optimisation. Therefore, this chapter will present the basic foundations of microeconomics and associated computational methods that can be used to assess the economic context of services within a service market.

► **Opening Case**

9.1 Microeconomics

As seen in the opening examples, an understanding and correct assessment of the
(economic) environment and relevant principles therein is necessary for both the
participants and the designer of service markets. This section, therefore, introduces
the necessary foundations that are required to analyse this setting. There are several
economic theories that try to explain the behaviour of markets and their participants,
where the neo-classical theory is probably the best-known.

▶ **Definition (Microeconomics)** The study of individual and small business economic decisions, and their effect, when aggregated, on the demand and supply of
goods and services throughout the entire economy.

However, despite being a model that offers various insights into markets and
their dynamics, some of its underlying assumptions are not representative of many
existing markets. Thus, the next sections elaborate on institution-based economics
that focus on designing the structure and the rules of markets in light of certain
market goals.

9.1.1 Running Use Case

As unifying use case, the service market AppExchange[2] will be used in this
chapter. AppExchange is a market for third-party services that are centred around a
main service: a Customer-Relationship-Management (CRM) software provided by
Salesforce.[3]

On AppExchange third party providers can offer complementary services to
the main product and advertise them to customers. Examples are billing and
payment services, and email and messaging services. For a provider of such a third-
party service several questions are relevant: How do I position my service on the
marketplace, e.g., by setting price and quality levels? How do competitive services
affect my own service? What are good strategies to act in such a service market?

Figure 9.2 displays the conceptual structure of the service marketplace AppExchange. Structured around a central service offering, the CRM tool Salesforce,
services and applications of different third-party providers are offered on the
marketplace and can be purchased by customers. This use case is applied throughout
the chapter to explain important concepts and definitions.

---

[2]https://appexchange.salesforce.com/.

[3]http://www.salesforce.com.

Fig. 9.2 A conceptual overview of the service market AppExchange

9.1.2   Neo-classical Economics and its Limitations

In neo-classical economics, markets are mechanisms that match supply and demand. The price at which goods or services are exchanged evolves on the basis of interaction between supply and demand, resulting in one specific price for which the goods are traded.

For a long time, a general view of economists on the underlying processes for how the individual actions of single users lead to the aggregated behaviour of the market (i.e., the resulting price in this case) was that "the market will take care if permitted to do so", which is often not a satisfactory explanation of the real processes [6].

There are several other assumptions that limit the expressiveness of this model for the practical design of markets. The following issues are to be taken into consideration in the context of service markets.

Utility Maximisation of Consumers
It is assumed that consumers select the good or service that yields the highest utility value for them, which is measured through a function that determines a utility value of the good/service given its specific attributes. Thus, utility functions embody the preferences that users have for certain goods/services and their characteristics. For example, if a service consumer's utility function contains the price and the quality of a service as attributes, a utility maximising user selects the service which yields the highest value for the price and quality combination. Aspects which are not considered in the utility function (e.g., previous experience with a given service provider), yet might influence the actual user decision, cannot be captured by this approach unless it can be specified as part of the utility function.

Profit Maximisation of Suppliers

(Service) providers are assumed to pursue the goal of profit maximisation. Other aspects, e.g., reputation effects, are not considered in the decision process for (service) providers.

Homogeneous Goods

A market is characterised by the assumption that goods/services are homogeneous, thus allowing them to be completely interchangeable. However, in reality services are often only homogeneous with respect to certain aspects (such as the price), yet might have different properties other than their main functionality. Two services with the same functionality, e.g., payment services, might be homogeneous in aspects like certain functionalities, yet can have different (quality) attributes such as guaranteed availability, fault handling, etc.

No Personal or Time Preferences

Participants in a neo-classical market base their decision solely on the maximisation of utility (consumers) or profit (providers), and do not consider additional aspects such as personal experience with a given (service) provider.

Perfect Transparency of Markets

In order to make their decision, market participants are assumed to have complete knowledge of the available goods and services on the market, i.e., knowing each available alternative and its properties, thus allowing the participants to select the best option. However, in reality not all potential alternatives might be known (especially when no centralised market places exist), and participants might lack information about all the relevant service properties (such as the actual availability). In the AppExchange example, perfect transparency would imply that the participant has knowledge of over 1000 applications as well as their attributes.

No Transaction Costs

The absence of transaction costs means that participants do not consider aspects such as the necessary time to search for available alternatives in their decision procedure. However, especially when many different services exist, participants might face a trade-off between investing more time to continue the search for other alternatives, and the additional expected gain from finding more alternatives, thereby limiting the number of actual services that a participant has information about.

Immediate Response of Market Participants

If supply and demand are matched and the goods are exchanged at the market price, it is assumed that all involved transactions (payments, exchange of goods, consumption of services, etc.) are happening immediately.

Clearly, some of these assumptions do not reflect the reality of a service market such as AppExchange. For example, the missing consideration of transaction costs is unrealistic, or as Stigler puts it, "[t]he world of zero transaction costs turns out to be as strange as the physical world would be with zero friction" [7, p.12]. When services are provided, requested, and exchanged, participants have a variety of costs connected to their participation in the given market.

Service consumers have search costs to get information about existing service offers and their properties, coordination costs to come to an agreement with service providers, and so on. This aspect is neglected in neo-classical theory. Institution-based economics, as presented in the next section, is an approach that addresses some of these limitations.

9.1.3   Institution-Based Economics

Practically all interactions that people experience in today's world are governed by institutions.

▶ **Definition (Institution)** Institutions are humanly devised constraints that structure political, economic, and social interaction [8].

There are numerous examples of institutions, ranging from governments and laws to traffic lights that structure traffic flow. Institutions are also relevant for economics. The field of institution-based economics considers (service) markets as institutions that govern the exchange of goods and services based on given or designed constraints. One of the main goals of markets as institutions is to reduce the transaction costs of the market participants. For example, by specifying on which basis service providers are matched to consumers, the need of costly individual agreement processes is reduced. Similarly, in a market where users can efficiently search through the available offers and requests, the costs for extensive search becomes lower.

As stated in the definition, institutions aim to provide a structure to the economic interactions of market participants. Hence, they represent rules how participants interact with each other and the market, how allocations are determined, which business model is used for the market, the specifics of the used infrastructure to host a market, etc.

By relaxing some of the assumptions of neo-classical economics, such as acknowledging the existence of transaction costs, it is a more suitable approach for the design of markets. Hence, the next section introduces the concept of market engineering as a structured methodology to analyse, assess, and design markets as institutions.

9.2   Market Engineering

When considering a service from an economic perspective there are several aspects (e.g., pricing and business models, marketing, and differentiated notions of quality) that one must consider, as well as the aims and objectives for the service within

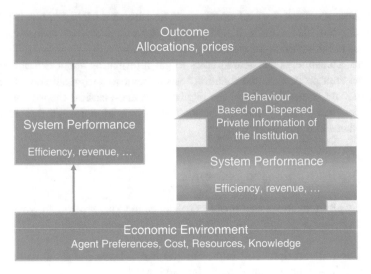

Fig. 9.3 Smith's microeconomic system (adapted from [9])

its economic setting such as a service market. However, before deliberating in this manner and designing the business and economic axioms of a service, it is important to understand the general economic system in which one will position a service.

To model the economic environment and resulting market constructs, Smith's definition of a microeconomic system [9], as well as the notion of market engineering as defined by Weinhardt et al. [10] and Neumann et al. [11], are used to frame the economic scenario, objectives, classify performance, and define key terms.

9.2.1 Smith's Microeconomic System

In his seminal work, Smith [9] defined the basic components of a microeconomic system: the economic environment, institution, behaviour of system actors, the outcome of the system, and notions of performance (see Fig. 9.3). This definition is of key importance as it provides the first frame of reference for discussing an economic setting.

Economic Environment
The *economic environment* constitutes the collection of all actors (agents) that participate in or interact with the considered system. Specifically, this includes their individual parameters, for example, their preferences (for resources, outcomes, etc.), their cost functions (e.g., for producing/providing resources), and their knowledge about the environment as well as other actors. The available resources, their initial distribution as well as other (exogenous) factors that affect the microeconomic system are also part of the environment. Hurwicz defines the environment as "the set of circumstances that have an impact on the performance of the institution,

but are outside the control of the mechanism designer" [12]. In other words, the environment is input to the institution design challenge, and necessary for any subsequent performance evaluation of an institution.

In a service market setting, the economic environment would include the service providers with their internal cost and quality functions (i.e., how expensive is it for a particular provider to offer a service of a given quality), and the service consumers with their preferences (e.g., how they rank the importance of certain quality attributes in their utility function). In the AppExchange example, the economic environment comprises the other service providers with their characteristics, and the consumers interacting with the platform to purchase additional services (as well as the maximum amount they are willing to pay for the requested services).

Institution

The *institution* is the formalisation of (distributed) resource allocation that is governed by a set of predefined rules. In abstract terms, the institution defines humanly devised constraints that are imposed upon system actors in order to achieve a certain outcome. The institution defines all rules that affect how interaction and trading takes place. This includes the definition of a market language (for example, placing bids in an auction), communication protocols (e.g., how bids are submitted), constraints that affect when trading state transitions occur (e.g., opening, closing, clearing, payment of an auction etc.), and how allocations are determined.

A service market is an example for such an institution. In particular, the institution defines the allocation mechanism used to match supply and demand (e.g., using auctions to sell service offers), and the interaction between service providers and consumers. On AppExchange, consumers can purchase additional applications and services that are offered on the market.

Behaviour

Behaviour relates to the (decision) processes of system actors that connect environmental conditions with the institution to result in valid actions and ultimately yield one or more outcomes. Simply speaking, given a certain environment the institution prescribes a certain behaviour on the actors, which then results in a specific market outcome. In the simple example of an auction, the institution determines how bids are placed, how the winner and price is determined, and other contractual issues. Given their individual parameters (such as valuations for the auctioned good), the institutional rules lead to a certain behaviour, for example a particular bidding behaviour in auctions.

Outcome

The *outcome* of the system is the confluence of supply and demand resulting in one or more artefact allocations, which in turn correspond to a price determined by the institution. The outcome is the result of the behaviour of actors participating through an institution.

System Performance Properties

To evaluate the quality of a market outcome, certain *system performance metrics* are used to determine how the observed outcome performs compared to a desired outcome (e.g., the theoretical optimum). Note that information about the environment (such as initial resource endowments) is needed to determine system performance, as the market outcome fundamentally depends on the given environment. When it comes to measuring system performance, there are many performance metrics that can be considered. However, note that it might not be possible to achieve good performance in all considered performance metrics, as some might be contradictory and others incompatible with one another.

The literature presents and discusses many different performance measures as well as their compatibilities with one another. Therefore in this chapter, we discuss these metrics only at a glance for completeness (the reader is referred to [13–15] for more information). Also note, that the objective of the system should first be considered before the means to assess its performance. However, from the perspectives of game theory and mechanism design, an overview of the standard performance properties is provided in Table 9.1.

In the setting of AppExchange, the behaviour of consumers can be indirectly observed by their purchasing decisions, e.g., which services are purchased most often by users. The observation of system performance in practice is harder, as some of the information needed to make this assessment are most likely not available. On the other hand, the mechanism used to allocate resources has certain theoretical

Table 9.1 List of system performance metrics

Metric	Description
Pareto optimality	No change in allocation can improve the payoff for one actor without a detrimental effect on at least one other actor.
Allocative efficiency	The allocation maximises the total utility across all actors.
Informational efficiency	The degree to which prices reflect the information available in the market.
Individual rationality	Actors are not worse off by participating, e.g., no payment of upfront fees without receiving something in return.
Incentive compatibility	When the best strategy an actor can employ is to reveal relevant private information truthfully.
Privacy preservation	The guarantee that other actors are not able to learn private information.
Revenue maximisation	Select the outcome that maximises the revenue to the seller.
Fairness	Fairness corresponds to the variance in utilities among actors; the lower the variance the fairer the mechanism.
Budget balance	The system does not have to be externally subsidised.
Computational costs	The computational effort required to reach an equilibrium and calculate one or more allocations.
Equilibrium	No agent has an incentive to deviate from the outcome state.
Convergence	The trend (and speed) in which all taken actions lead to an expected system state.

properties with respect to the mentioned metrics, hence the characteristics of the applied mechanism (in AppExchange, a posted price allocation) can be inferred by theoretical considerations.

9.2.2 Market Engineering Framework

There have been many extensions to Smith's definition, however of key interest to this chapter is the definition of the *market engineering object* by [10,11]. The market engineering approach concentrates on a market-based view of institutions and is an ideal framework for designing and analysing service markets. Its main objective is, given a socio-economic and legal environment (similar to the environment definition in Smith's model), to achieve a certain market outcome through the design of a market structure. The components of the market engineering object are illustrated in Fig. 9.4.

Transaction Object

When reflecting on the constitution of the market engineering object, it is clear that one of the key aspects that differentiates this approach to Smith's microeconomic system is the transaction object: the artefact, and its corresponding properties that are traded. In the context of services, the representation of the *transaction object* can

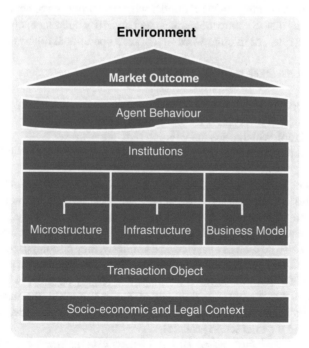

Fig. 9.4 The market engineering object (adapted from [10,11])

quickly become complicated. This is due to reasons of customisability, the transitive nature of a service and the temporal constraints this implies, and the inclusion of non-functional properties that are potentially not well defined. It is not the objective of this chapter to discuss how to define a transaction object for service systems, rather to raise the issue that this is a challenge.

From the perspective of a service market, an unambiguously defined transaction object is required, ideally using a standardised (domain-specific) term language. Smith's notion of the economic environment is also slightly augmented to capture general actor demographics, social norms, and legal constraints that are outside the control of the institution and therefore considered as exogenous properties.

Institutions

An important refinement of the market engineering process, compared to the Smith's model, is that the *institutions* component is further detailed into three sub-components. The *microstructure* component defines all the previously mentioned micro-economic aspects, i.e., the market rules. Usually, there are four types of rules captured by the institution as a form of trading protocol:

1. Message rules specifying how participants interact with the market.
2. Allocation rules determining how the instances of the trading object are allocated to agents (market participants).
3. Payment rules defining what the participants have to pay in the market, how payment is made, and potentially under what constraints payment is necessary.
4. Control rules that structure the market mechanism by defining opening, transition and closing rules, or in other words a market's operational timeframe.

For a service market, examples for these rules are:

1. The placing of bids in an auction for services.
2. The allocation of a service offer to the highest bidder.
3. The calculation which price the winning bidder has to pay.
4. The start and end times of the auction.

The second part of the market structure, the (IT) *infrastructure*, defines the implementation of the market, for example the technical platforms that are used to provide the functionality described in the other components (e.g., specifying how an online auction platform is implemented). The implementation of the market structure may also be seen as a service, and similarly, may be composed of electronic services. Thinking back to the computational costs performance metric mentioned earlier, it is clear that this performance metric is largely considered in this part of the institution. An example for this part of the institution is the implementation of the AppExchange market, specifically, the access to the service, the payment procedures, and the interaction protocols.

The final part of the market structure, the *business structure*, considers the business model of the market, for example how revenue is intended to be generated,

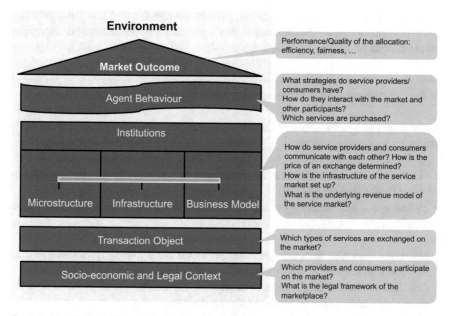

Fig. 9.5 The market engineering object applied to service markets

who pays for the infrastructure, and who owns the platform. In the AppExchange example, the business structure determines how the platform is financed (e.g., through payment-based access to additional services, or advertisements), who the underlying data belongs to, and so on. To exemplify the application of the market engineering process in the context of service markets such as AppExchange, Fig. 9.5 shows sample questions that are addressed by this approach.

Market Outcome

As Smith's microeconomic system is encapsulated as a component of a market structure, it becomes apparent that actor behaviour, previously included in the microstructure, now transcends the structure to yield the *market outcome*. In Smith's system behaviour acted as a mediating component that connected the environment to the outcome. This change implies that in the market engineering approach, there is no cause-effect relationship between the market structure and agent behaviour (as in Fig. 9.3), i.e., the designed institution does not imply a certain behaviour, but behaviour is influenced by the implemented institution.

Agent Behaviour

Agent behaviour directly determines the market outcome. Or put differently the macro outcome of the market is a result of one or more actions at the market's micro layer. It is for this reason, that emphasis is placed on the microeconomic perspective of service economics, as it is the actions of agents at the micro layer that direct

the macro level outcome(s). Therefore, in Sect. 9.3 agent-based computational economics is presented as the methodological approach for modelling and simulating
micro actions as a multi-agent system.

9.3   Testbedding Service Markets

In the beginning of the chapter, several questions were raised that are important for
the study of service markets:

- How should a service market be implemented, and what mechanisms should be
  used to allocate the services?
- What is a good strategy for service providers and consumers to act on these
  markets?

Whereas the first question is particularly relevant in the design phase of a market,
i.e., when the designer of a service market decides the mechanisms that are applied
in the market, the latter question is interesting for market participants both in the
design phase and in case of already existing markets.

Independent of the actual scenario, i.e., whether a service market is designed or
an existing market adjusted, the potential design choices need to be evaluated to
test their effects on the market and the participating users. For example, a change
in the applied allocation mechanism can have complex effects on the supply and
demand of the market as well as the behaviour of participants in the market. In
practice, it is not always feasible to introduce changes (potentially only to a subset
of participants) and then observe the effects to determine the consequences. Hence,
as the effects have to be nevertheless predicted, another methodological approach is
necessary to study complex systems such as service markets.

Several approaches to tackle this challenge have been proposed and are consistently used in practice. If feasible, changes in the market (e.g., market interfaces)
are introduced to only a small set of selected participants to study the effects
of such changes. Laboratory experiments are often used to study the economic
effects of different policies, e.g., the behaviour of participants under different
allocation mechanisms. This chapter focuses on a complementary approach to these
approaches: agent-based computational economics, which models the system at
hand as computer simulation and studies the dynamic effects of changes in service
markets, both from a system level (e.g., performance) and individual level (e.g.,
change in strategies). This methodology has emerged over the past years as useful
tool to model complex (service) systems and the effects therein as the result of the
aggregated actions and interactions by actors in an environment.

9.3.1 Agent-Based Computational Economics

Agent-based Computational Economics (ACE) is the computational study of economies modeled as evolving systems of autonomous interacting agents [16, 17]. In other words, agent-based computational economics is a methodological approach to study dynamic economic systems of numerous independent components, where system behaviour results from the interaction of these components. Before introducing ACE as a methodology for posing and answering questions in service markets, it makes sense to first introduce a few key terms:

► **Definition (Multi Agent System (MAS))** The totality of agents and their virtual economic world, where the latter is typically referred to as the environment. A MAS consists of two or more agents that act in an environment.

Many definitions of an agent exist, and often differ slightly depending on the application domain. For the purposes of this chapter, an agent is defined as follows:

► **Definition (Agent)** An autonomous program situated within and part of an environment, which it can sense, socialise in, move around and intelligently act upon over time in pursuit of its own agenda and realisation of goals and so to affect any actions it may take in the future.

A key term that is raised here, and disambiguated from previous contexts, is environment.

► **Definition (Environment)** The totality of software or human agents as well as their characteristics, environmental rules of other system related components, endowment (e.g., underlying hardware), system rules, and other entities such as artefacts, sensors, and actuators.

Based on these definitions, ACE allows economies and markets to be understood as study of phenomena emerging from interactions among intelligent, self-interested individuals [18]. Tesfatsion proposed the analogy of a culture dish for how the modeller constructs and executes an ACE study in [19]. The culture dish analogy identifies three simple steps that constitute the research process:

1. Create a virtual economic world (environment), and populate it with one or more agent types.
2. Set the initial world conditions, parameters, constraints, and rules.
3. Take a step back and observe (without any further intervention) how the world evolves over time.

It is clear that based upon this analogy, there are two key factors that define how a multi agent system serves the purposes of the researcher. Firstly, that it is assumed the result of the study is the consequence of emergent behaviour. This is noted in step 3, as the modeller may not intervene with the virtual world. Secondly, that all world events and outcomes are driven and triggered by the parameterisation of the agents, and their interactions. This aligns with the notion of agent behaviour determining a market outcome.

In terms of characterising an agent, Jennings and Woolridge [20] identified four hallmarks, each of which refers to or influences an agent's ability to make decisions namely: autonomy, social ability, responsiveness, and proactiveness, which are defined as follows:

Autonomy The ability to act independently (i.e., without human intervention). Autonomy requires the ability to interpret and understand the environment, and the (basic) ability to make decisions.

Social Ability The ability to communicate implicitly and/or explicitly. Here, explicit social actions refer to the use of a typically standardised communication protocol between two or more agents for forms of message passing: where the prominent example is the agent communication language (see: [21]). Implicit social actions refer to agent actions that cause a "change" in the environment, and the consequential perception of cause and effect by other agents.

Responsiveness The ability of an agent to respond in a timely fashion to observed environmental changes.

Proactiveness The opportunistic, self-interested, and potentially adaptive actions that facilitate goal-orientated behaviour. Here proactivity may also imply the ability of an agent to determine the probability of goal achievability, and deviate its course(s) of action as appropriate. Therefore, when a goal is perceived as unachievable, a change in behaviour may ensue.

9.3.2   ACE Software: NetLogo

Before introducing some example models in detail, a quick note on the implementation of agent-based models, as many different software frameworks exist.[4] However, for the purposes of this chapter and its projects, NetLogo[5] is recommended for reasons of power, ease of learning, and its excellent documentation. Many example models also exist that can be used to study markets as well as the market engineering process.

NetLogo as a multi-agent programmable modelling environment for simulating natural and social phenomena is particularly well suited for modelling complex systems that develop over time [22]. In comparison to other programming languages, it is surprisingly easy to learn and natural language-like. It is not the intention of this chapter to teach NetLogo (there are many books dedicated to this—see the further reading section).

---

[4]Leigh Tesfatsion keeps an up-to-date list on her website, which is well worth visiting for general information regarding agent-based computational economics: http://www2.econ.iastate.edu/tesfatsi/ace.htm—last accessed February 2014.

[5]http://ccl.northwestern.edu/netlogo/—last accessed February 2014.

For the purposes of market engineering, NetLogo provides an easy to use framework rich with example economic models from the computational economics community. Using NetLogo, students and scholars alike can easily build and extend complex microeconomic models. Agents (or turtles in NetLogo terminology) can be endowed with a wide variety of capabilities to foster the study of markets as well as the aspects of their engineering. Examples include but are not limited to bidding strategies, direct as well as indirect communication, and differing levels of intelligence.

Direct communication here refers to explicit social behaviour such as message passing and Indirect communication, here, refers to observing the actions of other agents individually or collectively.

Similarly, the economic environment (or institutionalisation of the environment) can be modified and experimented with, for example, to observe potential changes in agent behaviour and the effect(s) of different parametrisations of the microeconomic, infrastructure or business components of an institution. Finally, as a simulation environment, NetLogo provides the capabilities to control the volume of agents that participate in a given model. Thus allowing for small-scale studies (ten or fewer agents) as well as large-scale studies (with tens to hundreds of thousands of agents).

Figure 9.6 shows the NetLogo interface and highlights its key aspects.

UI Components NetLogo programs are typically controlled via a UI, and contain a number of simple UI components, such as buttons, sliders, switches, and plots to control runtime variables as well as display specific results.

Ticks NetLogo is a discrete simulation environment where simulation time is represented as ticks. In each tick, it is common practice for all agents (turtles in NetLogo terminology) to have the option to perform one or more actions.

Tabs There are three basic tabs that constitute the NetLogo interface. The Interface tab (shown in Fig. 9.6), the information tab, which contains the program's documentation, and the code tab, which contains the program code.

World The world (environment) is a discrete grid of cells (called patches). Programmers can define specific parameters of the world, where wrapping (the feature where edges cells are considered neighbours) is of key significance.

Settings The model settings.

Command Centre A control point for issuing commands to NetLogo entities.

9.3.3 A Short Overview of ACE Models

To demonstrate each of the Jennings' and Woolridge's hallmarks in practical settings, the interested reader is referred to three studies from the literature: Schelling's segregation model [23], Epstein and Axtell's sugarscape [24], and Arthur's El Farol bar problem [25].

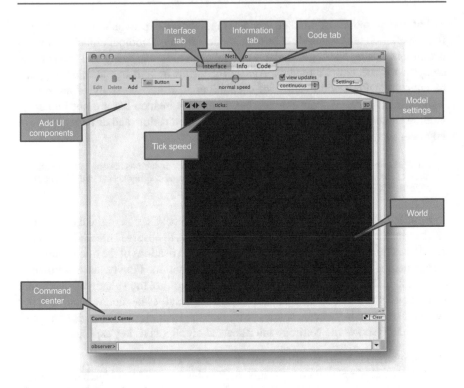

Fig. 9.6 The NetLogo interface

Each of these models, whilst simple, demonstrates the power and usefulness of simulation-based approach in subtly different ways, and thus highlights key methodological aspects that are important in the study of service markets. This is despite the fact that on the outset, they may not appear to address economic questions.

Segregation Model

Schelling's *segregation model* is one of the first known applications of multi-agent systems to social science problems, and therefore this model is naturally very simple. This should not however, cloud its significance: it shows how even in the presence of simple preferences and one common threshold value, a specific community of agents can collectively make individual decisions based upon local information that have system-wide implications.

Figure 9.7 shows how a small preference for one's neighbours to be of the same colour can lead to total segregation.

Sugarscape

Epstein's and Axtell's *sugarscape* lends itself very nicely to basic notions of an economy, and the exploration of a resource space. It is also anecdotally referred to as being a similar approach to how Starbucks chooses its store locations, however, this is not confirmed.

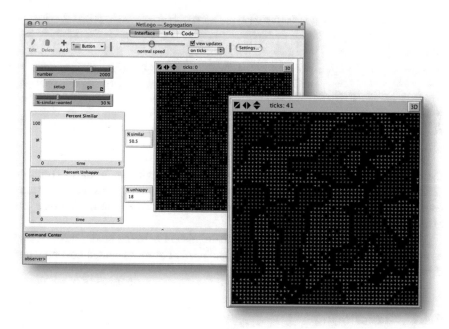

Fig. 9.7 Simulation of the segregation model in NetLogo

Bar Problem

Arthur's El Farol *bar problem* provides a basic framework to study how agents can use multiple hypotheses for the basis of a simple decision (in this case whether to attend or not attend a bar). This model clearly illustrates a (simple) method for modelling boundedly rational agents as well as their decision processes.

Each model has a corresponding open source NetLogo implementation (see [26–28]). Although the detailed explanation of these models is outside the scope of this chapter, detailed explanations as well as ready-to-use implementations can be found in the literature provided at the end of the chapter.

9.4   Case Study 1: Pricing Strategies

The marketplace AppExchange is an example of a service market where complementary services to a central CRM tool are offered. It is a sound assumption that most of these services can be purchased for a certain price, i.e., the respective providers charge a fee for service usage. At the same time, consumers can be assumed to have a certain willingness to pay for services that they request, i.e., they have an internal threshold above which they won't purchase the service any more. For the designer of a service market in general, and AppExchange in particular,

Table 9.2 Classification of pricing strategies

Strategy	Description
Static pricing	Price of the service is the same for all customers.
Flexible pricing	Price of the service depends on either the willingness to pay, the combination (bundle) of purchased services, or the group that a customer belongs to.
Dynamic pricing	Price of the service is determined dynamically through auctions or negotiations.

the question is how the offered services are matched with the requests from the consumers, and how the price for the purchases is determined. This first case study exemplifies different pricing strategies that can be applied by the market designer and/or service providers.

In general, pricing strategies can be distinguished between static, flexible, and dynamic pricing strategies, as shown in Table 9.2. For an extended coverage and discussion the reader is referred to [29, 30].

9.4.1 Static Pricing

Static pricing represents the simplest form of pricing strategy. In this case, the price of a service is set to one amount and is the same for all potential buyers. Consequently, consumers that have an equal or higher valuation for the service will purchase it. Consumers with a lower valuation for the service will not purchase it. The total revenue is defined by the number of consumers that purchase the service times the fixed price.

The most important question in this case is how the price is actually determined. In static pricing, this question depends on the existence of competitive services on the market. If the service provider offers an application with unique properties for which no complementary service exists, it has a monopoly for this service and can charge the revenue-maximising price. However, if complementary services exist, competition must be considered.

Two examples for models in this case are the (stylised) Bertrand competition and monopolistic competition, which both consider the pricing of a service when multiple provider offer the same homogeneous good (Bertrand) or a complementary product with similar yet slightly different characteristics (monopolistic competition). These competitions lead to prices that equal the production costs of the service (Bertrand) or above (monopolistic) and hence yield a zero (Bertrand) or positive (monopolistic) profit for the service provider.

The disadvantage of such static pricing models is that on the one hand, they are inflexible towards heterogeneous users which might have a different willingness to pay for the service. On the other hand the application of simple price finding

Fig. 9.8 Dimensions in
which service offers can be
varied (based on [29, 30])

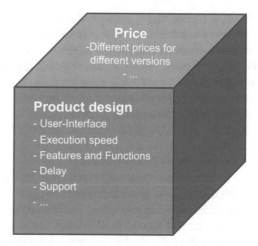

models such as a Bertrand competition can lead to prices which are, in the long-run,
not sustainable for the providers unless providers collusively (and thus potentially
illegally) fix prices above the marginal production costs.

9.4.2 Flexible Pricing

Flexible pricing, in contrast to static pricing, allows the specification of different
prices for a service depending on certain circumstances, like user types (e.g.,
professional vs. private users) and service versions (e.g., gold-level with best quality
vs. silver-level with lower quality levels and reduced price). Figure 9.8 shows a
representation of the dimensions in which services can be varied.

In general, three different models of flexible pricing are distinguished.

First Degree Price Differentiation
In models of *first degree price differentiation*, also called personalised pricing, each
consumer is charged their maximal willingness to pay. This assumes that a provider
is somehow able to determine the maximum willingness to pay or able to extract
this from the consumer, which is an assumption that is not given in many real-
life settings. For example, on AppExchange the providers most likely do not have
information about the willingness to pay from (potential) consumers.

Second Degree Price Differentiation
In *second degree price differentiation* models, referred to as self-selection models,
the provider offers services in different versions or bundles. This can relate to
different functions of a service, whereas more or extended functions lead to a higher
price. Or, a service bundle can be offered at a lower price than buying each service
individually. A prominent example of such service bundling is the combination of
word-processing software with spreadsheet and email programs into a bundle which

is offered at a price that is lower than the combined individual prices. This type of model gives the consumers the flexibility to choose the version or bundle that best fits their needs and willingness to pay, but requires complex valuation schemes in place. In an optimal case, the consumer is able to express their willingness to pay for each available service version and each bundle. This type of price differentiation can also be seen on service markets such as AppExchange, where services are offered in different quality settings for different prices, and the consumer is free to choose which quality-price combination is best for them.

Third Degree Price Differentiation

Finally, in *third degree price differentiation* models, services can be priced differently for different user groups. For example, the service can be offered at a lower price for student or academic users. The revenue in flexible pricing is determined in a more complex way than in static pricing: for each price, the number of consumers is determined and multiplied by the price. Afterwards, the sum over all the per-price-revenues is calculated. This pricing type can often be seen when services are sold in special versions or prices for academic/student users, or to private users compared to professional users.

9.4.3   Dynamic Pricing

Whereas the static and flexible pricing specify the price of the service in advance, in *dynamic pricing* models the actual price is determined dynamically, potentially resulting in different prices over time. Two examples for such dynamic pricing models are *negotiations* and *auctions*. In negotiations, the price of the service is determined via a bilateral exchange between the provider and consumer. An exchange can occur either digitally, or in an over the counter-like format.

Even though the applications and services on AppExchange are sold using (predominantly) flexible pricing strategies, auctions are widely used for electronic services in general, such as auctioning the position of advertisements in search results with the GoogleAds[6] auction. Standard auction formats for single services are English, Dutch, First-Price Sealed Bid (FPSB), and Second-Price Sealed Bid (Vickrey) auctions. For all of the auctions, the highest bidder is the winner. However, the price that the winner needs to pay is determined differently.

The English and Dutch auctions, also known as "open-outcry" auctions, are mechanisms where bidders announce their bid in public. English auctions require increasing bids to be placed by all bidders. As soon as there is no bidder willing to place a higher bid, the highest bidder is announced the winner and has to pay their bid. In a Dutch auction, the auctioneer starts with a high price and decreases the price in pre-determined steps. The first bidder to accept a price is the winner and pays the price that they accepted.

---

[6]http://www.google.com/ads/—last accessed February 2014.

The FPSB and Vickrey auctions are carried out with private bids that only the auctioneer can see. In FPSB auctions, each bidder privately submits a bid to the auctioneer, who determines the highest bidder, i.e., the winner. The winner pays their bid. In a Vickrey auction, the winner is determined in the same manner, but has to pay the second-highest bid. Each of these auction formats can lead to different outcomes for the offering party and incurs different strategies on the bidder side. As soon as more than one service or even bundles are auctioned, the formats become more complex and hence, require more complex strategies on the buyer side.

Overall, it can be seen that the pricing strategies for services on service markets are as varied as the markets themselves. Finding the best pricing strategy is a complex task, and depends on the type of service market (i.e., if the pricing type is given or freely selectable), the types of offered services (e.g., whether quality differentiation is possible to enable different service levels), and the number of competitors on the market.

9.5   Case Study 2: Complex Service Networks

The first case study considered different pricing strategies for service providers who want to offer their services on a marketplace such as AppExchange. Whereas the purchase of single applications and services is certainly a common application, consumers are often interested in purchasing a bundle of complementary services. For example, a consumer might want to enhance the standard functionality of an application with additional payment and billing services, which can be purchased from a set of different providers. In such a setting, several interesting questions can be asked: Which combination of services should the consumer choose? How is the price determined in such a setting?

This second case study aims to show how an agent-based approach can be leveraged to address these questions in the context of service markets. For the case study, following scenario is considered, which is based on [31].

On an online service marketplace such as AppExchange, multiple service providers offer modular services with different functionality. For example, providers can offer billing services for online transactions, or database services to store information about transactions or consumers. This simple example is pictured in Fig. 9.9. In addition to the single, modular services, the marketplace offers a functionality to purchase complex services that are composed of multiple single services. In the previous example, this could be the combination of a billing and storage service. Such service networks are also called service value networks [32] as they create value through the composition of single services to complex services. Consumers of the marketplace can either buy single or composite services. In case several providers offer services of the same functionality, an economic mechanism determines which offer (combinations) fits best to the request of a consumer, and determines the prices of these offers [32].

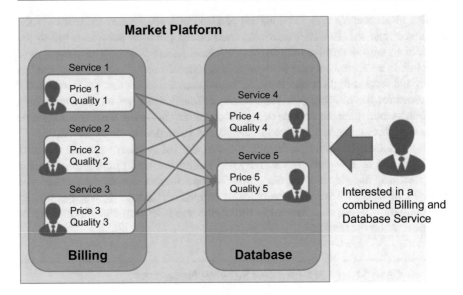

Fig. 9.9 Simplified example of a service network

From the perspective of a service provider who offers one or multiple services on such a marketplace, the question is which service configuration and price it has to offer in order to be allocated to consumer requests. This is a complex problem, as it not only depends on the specifics of the requests, but also on the offers and configurations of competitors. Hence, an interesting question is how the providers can learn which service offer configurations are promising and maximise their revenue.

Using the previously introduced terminology, the service providers and the consumers of the marketplace constitute the economic environment. The institution is defined by the marketplace, its allocation and pricing rules, and its technical infrastructure and business models (e.g., providers have to pay a fee to participate in the market). Given the marketplace and the institution, the goal of the service providers, in this case, is to learn profitable service offer configurations. The resulting behaviour is the potential adjustment of the service offers to consumer requests and/or competitors' offers. Finally, the observable outcomes are the actual service offers and their configurations which are offered on the marketplace.

Coming back to the question how a service provider can learn a profitable service offer configuration, an analytical approach is most likely infeasible, depending on the number of competitors and the general market complexity. In contrast, an agent-based computational economics approach seems to be a promising option as it is able to handle this complexity.

Modelling this system with the tool set of ACE, the service providers and consumers constitute the agents of the model. Each service provider can be modelled as having a certain capability of learning, i.e., the ability to determine the profitability of the own service offer and to adjust its configuration. In case multiple service providers have such learning capability, the resulting dynamics, i.e., which service offer configurations are learned and how they match the consumer requests, are interesting questions that can be studied with such an ACE approach. For example, if consumers can be segmented into distinct market segments with certain requirements, simulation-based experiments have shown that service providers are able to segment the market by differentiating their service offers (and thus potentially avoid competition if each provider concentrates on a segment, see [31]).

This case study serves as an example how an ACE approach can help to model complex scenarios in a service network and to predict dynamic effects. Further questions which might be interesting are the dependency of the results on the number of providers, the number and segmentation of consumer, and the applied market rules. Additionally, questions like the emergence of collusive behaviour between providers (e.g., if they charge prices higher than predicted in a competitive environment) can be studied as well.

9.6 Conclusions

This chapter has discussed some of the fundamental aspects of studying service markets, with the aim of providing a basic understanding of how to construct, model, and analyse economic settings. It is an introductory chapter, and as such has only scratched the surface of economic methods and concepts. It has presented the Smith's microeconomic system as well as Weinhardt et al's, and Neumann's notion of market engineering to provide an economic framework for service markets. In doing so, the unravelling of the economic context for service markets is approached as the emergent product of individual actions that simulates human behaviour. Agent-based computational economics was presented as a methodology to simulate a specific economic scenario, and endow agents with human-like properties.

Subsequently, two case studies were presented to foster the introduced concepts through their application in the context of a sample service market, AppExchange. The first case study considered different pricing strategies how service providers can determine the prices of their offers. In the second case study, the setting of a service value network was presented to illustrate how agent-based computational economics can be applied to complex scenarios.

Review Section

Review Questions

1. What assumptions do neo-classical markets impose, and how realistic are they?
2. What are the main components of the microeconomic framework of Smith and the market engineering framework of Weinhardt et al., respectively? What are their differences?

3. Explain the differences between the presented types of price differentiation and illustrate pros and cons by means of examples.
4. Imagine you want to sell a web service and determine its price. What kind of pricing mechanism would you as a service provider prefer? What kind of pricing scheme would you prefer if you were a consumer?
5. Describe in your own words the goals of agent-based computational economics? Provide examples of questions that can be studied using an ACE approach.

Projects

1. Imagine you are starting a company that sells web-based services that support healthcare services. Please describe how you can apply the market engineering methodology to assess your company's situation. The revenue model is an essential component for your company's success and should include the pricing for your service. Please argue how you would choose a pricing strategy, and why the chosen strategy is right for your given situation.
2. Take the three NetLogo models presented in this chapter and extend each one with at least two new features of scientific interest.[7]

Further Reading

David Easley and Jon Kleinburg. *Networks, Crowds and Markets: Reasoning about a Highly Connected World.* Cambridge, 2010.

Nicholas Jennings and Michael Wooldridge. *Agent Technology: Foundations, Applications, and Markets.* Springer, 1998.

Leigh Tesfatsion and Kenneth Judd. *Handbook of Computational Economics: Agent-based computational economics.* North Holland, 2006.

Steven Railsback and Volker Grimm. *Agent-Based and Individual-Based Modeling: A Practical Introduction.* Princeton University Press, 2011.

References

1. Fudenberg D, Tirole J (2000) Game theory. MIT Press, Cambridge
2. Lawrence PA (1992) The making of a fly: the genetics of animal design. Blackwell, London
3. Eisen M (2011) Amazon's $23,698,655.93 book about flies. http://michaeleisen.org/blog/?p=358

---

[7]Students not familiar with NetLogo are recommended to first work through at least the first five chapters of Railsback and Grimm's textbook on agent-based models mentioned below in further reading.

4. Jones M (2011) Bidding fever in eBay auctions of Amazon.com gift certificates. Econ Lett 113(1):5–7
5. Wolf J, Arkes H, Muhanna W (2006) Do auction bidders really want to win the item, or do they simply want to win? Available at SSRN 764785
6. McAfee P (1998) Four issues in auctions and market design. Revista Anal Econ Revista de Economía 13(1):7–24
7. Stigler G (1972) Law and economics of public policy: a plea to the scholars. J Legal Stud 1:1–12
8. North D (1991) Institutions. J Econ Perspect 5(1):97–112. doi:10.1257/jep.5.1.97. http://www.aeaweb.org/articles.php?doi=10.1257/jep.5.1.97
9. Smith V (1982) Microeconomic systems as an experimental science. Am Econ Rev 72(5):923–955
10. Weinhardt C, Holtmann C, Neumann D (2003) Market-engineering. Wirtschaftsinformatik 45(6):635–640
11. Neumann D (2004) Market engineering - a structured design process for electronic markets. Karlsruhe Scientific Publishing, Karlsruhe
12. Hurwicz L (1973) The design of mechanisms for resource allocation. Am Econ Rev 63(2):1–30
13. Campbell D (1987) Resource allocation mechanisms. Cambridge University Press, Cambridge, MA, pp 17–38
14. Wurman P (2000) Market structure and multidimensional auction design for computational economics. 15–20
15. Fama E (1970) Efficient capital markets: a review of theory and empirical work. J Financ 25(2):383–417
16. Tesfatsion L (2002) Agent-based computational economics: growing economies from the bottom up. Artif Life 8(1):55–82
17. Tesfatsion L, Judd K (2006) Agent-based computational economics. Elsevier, Amsterdam
18. Krugman P (1996) What economists can learn from evolutionary theorists. In: A talk given to the European Association for Evolutionary Political Economy
19. Tesfatsion L (2006) Agent-based computational economics: a constructive approach to economic theory. Handb Comput Econ 2:831–880
20. Jennings N, Wooldridge M (1998) Agent technology: foundations, applications, and markets. Springer, Berlin
21. ACL Fipa (2002) Fipa ACL message structure specification. Technical report. Foundation for Intelligent Physical Agents. URL:http://www.fipa.org/specs/fipa00061/SC00061G.html
22. Wilensky U (1999) Netlogo. Center for connected learning and computer-based modeling. Northwestern University, Evanston, IL. http://ccl.northwestern.edu/netlogo/
23. Schelling T (1978) Micromotives and macrobehavior. Norton, New York
24. Epstein J, Axtell R (1996) Growing artificial societies: social science from the bottom up. Brookings Institution Press, Washington, DC
25. Arthur W (1994) Inductive reasoning and bounded rationality (The El Farol Problem). Am Econ Rev 84:406–411
26. Wilensky U (1997) Netlogo segregation model. Center for connected learning and computer-based modeling. Northwestern University, Evanston, IL. http://ccl.northwestern.edu/netlogo/models/Segregation
27. Li J, Wilensky U (1999) Netlogo sugarscape 1 immediate growback model. Center for connected learning and computer-based modeling. Northwestern University, Evanston, IL. http://ccl.northwestern.edu/netlogo/models/Sugarscape1ImmediateGrowback
28. Rand W, Wilensky U (2007) Netlogo El Farol mode. Center for connected learning and computer-based modeling, Northwestern University, Evanston, IL. http://ccl.northwestern.edu/netlogo/models/ElFarol

29. Varian H, Repcheck J (2010) Intermediate microeconomics: a modern approach, vol 6. WW Norton & Company, New York
30. Shapiro C, Varian H (2013) Information rules: a strategic guide to the network economy. Harvard Business Press, Watertown, MA
31. Haas C, Kimbrough SO, van Dinther C (2013) Strategic learning by e-service suppliers in service value networks. J Serv Res 16(3):259–276
32. Blau B et al (2009) Service value networks. In: IEEE conference on commerce and enterprise computing, 2009. IEEE, New York, pp 194–201

Service Research

10

Jorge Cardoso, Björn Schmitz, and Axel Kieninger

Summary

This chapter provides an outlook on two recent research streams from the field of services: service network analysis and service level engineering. Service network research seeks to understand what factors explain the topology and dynamic nature of service networks. Service level engineering proposes to improve service level management by considering customers' business objectives rather than to focus on the IT infrastructure that provides the service. These streams look beyond the boundaries of services and focus on systems of services represented as networks and bring customers to take part of service systems.

Learning Objectives
1. Describe the elements that form a service network and contrast service networks with other types of networks.
2. Explain how service networks can be reconstructed using the web as a large-scale database.
3. Identify the application domains of service network analysis.

(continued)

J. Cardoso (✉)
Department of Informatics Engineering, Universidade de Coimbra,
Coimbra, Portugal

Huawei European Research Center (ERC), Munich, Germany
e-mail: jcardoso@dei.uc.pt; jorge.cardoso@huawei.com

B. Schmitz • A. Kieninger
Karlsruhe Service Research Institute (KSRI), Karlsruhe Institute
of Technology (KIT), Karlsruhe, Germany

© Springer International Publishing Switzerland 2015
J. Cardoso et al. (eds.), *Fundamentals of Service Systems*, Service Science: Research
and Innovations in the Service Economy, DOI 10.1007/978-3-319-23195-2_10

4. Understand the importance of defining service level objectives.
5. Be able to explain how optimal and efficient service level objectives can be defined using service level engineering.

► **Opening Case**   The emergence of networks

A TWITTER USER IS WORTH $110; FACEBOOK'S $98; LINKEDIN'S $93
Forbes, Nov. 7, 2013

What do Twitter, Facebook, and LinkedIn have in common? They are all social networking sites, which rely on the notion of relationships to create large scale networks connecting people spread all over the world.

Figure 10.1 shows Jorge Cardoso's LinkedIn network. Relationships connect nodes representing people, which are clustered according to shared affiliations. Hubs emerge as larger set of nodes, which connect to other clusters. Each cluster, illustrated with a different color, aggregates people that are related according to common characteristics such as the company they work for.

The orange cluster includes researchers working on process management; the green one shows professionals that have worked at the software company SAP; the yellow cluster includes professionals from the Madeira Island; and the light blue cluster shows a group of scholars and researchers from the Karlsruhe Institute of Technology (KIT).

The analysis of such a structure, using network theory, can provide interesting insights. For example, the node marked in the figure with an arrow (→) fills a so-called *structural hole* because it bridges three large groups: the yellow, the green, and the orange clusters. The importance of this node is significant. It indicates that the people on either side circulate in different flows of information, i.e., different groups exchange different types of information. Therefore, anyone filling this structural hole will have access to a large pool of non-overlapping information coming from three different contexts. It has been proven that people in such positions have access to complementary information and show, as a consequence, a higher probability to innovate (see Chap. 3).

The applicability of network theory is not limited to social networking and it is gaining a significant importance in many other fields, such as service science, ecology, economics, and energy grids. In fact, understanding how services operate as part of large-scale global networks, as well as the related risks and gains of different network structures and their dynamics, is becoming increasingly critical for society. Many research questions and challenges remain to be answered:

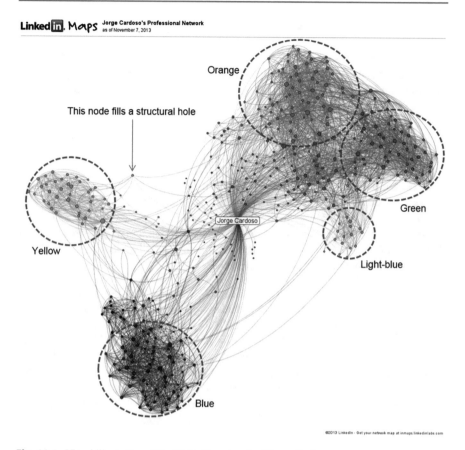

Fig. 10.1 Visual illustration of the LinkedIn network of Jorge Cardoso

Ecological Networks Understanding the networks which capture the relationships between species may help predict how ecosystems respond to change.

Economic Networks Economic crises illustrate a critical need for a new and fundamental understanding of the structure and dynamics of economic networks.

Energy Networks Investigate why well-structured networks, like the US power grid, have more critical nodes that increase vulnerability, compared to randomly structured networks.

Supply chain networks are another field of interest for network theory. Deutsche Post DHL understands their importance and redesigns supply chain networks to improve performance. The use of state-of-the-art network optimization tools, such as the software application Supply Chain Guru, enables the visualization and optimization of supply chains for major improvements in criteria such as cost, service level, risk, and carbon footprint.

▶ **Opening Case**

10.1   Advanced Topics

This section provides an introduction to two emerging research fields which will contribute to a better understanding of services as interconnected nodes forming networks and service levels as strong commitments which bind providers and customers. The fields are termed:

1. Service networks analysis.
2. Service level engineering.

Service networks are acquiring a particular importance because the study and analysis of their behavior can provide new scientific insights on how service-based economies operate at a global scale. Service level engineering supports the management of service quality in outsourcing agreements. It investigates the definition of appropriate target values for service quality measures to achieve economically beneficial outsourcing agreements.

Service Networks Analysis Understanding how networks that interconnect services evolve over time, and the risks and potential benefits of different network topologies, is becoming increasingly critical for society [1]. Service network analysis can be seen as the next logical step after studying individual services. Service networks promise to change our understanding of service-based systems. It tackles an important societal challenge because understanding what factors influence the evolution of global service networks can lead to the edification of more efficient economies. The long-term goal of service network theory is to understand, analyze, predict, and control the evolution of global service networks.

▶ **Definition (Service Networks Analysis)**   The use of techniques and algorithms to study service networks. In contrast to the analysis of other types of networks, service networks analysis places emphasis on service systems (see Chap. 1), service relationships which form well-defined structures (e.g., delivery networks or supply chain networks), behavior (possibly described as interorganizational business processes), and a purpose.

Service network analysis can break new grounds scientifically with two main achievements: (1) reconstructing global service networks—something that has never been achieved before—and (2) providing algorithms that will help to understand the fundamental properties of service networks. While algorithms have been developed for social network analysis, no research has been conducted so far to develop algorithms for large-scale service network analysis.

Service Level Engineering In outsourcing agreements, the management of service quality constitutes a major challenge for service providers and their customers [2, 3]. Organizations and customers often have difficulties to agree on meaningful metrics to measure service quality and there is still a lack of understanding with regard to the impact that reductions in service quality have on a customer's business. In this context, the definition of adequate service level objectives has the potential of achieving considerable gains in efficiency, which could realize additional economic benefits for providers and customers.

▶ **Definition (Service Level Engineering)** Service Level Engineering (SLE) is a systematic engineering approach to determine business-relevant Service Level Indicators (SLI) and efficient Service Level Objectives (SLO) for Service Level Agreements (SLA).

Service level engineering provides a structured approach to (1) define service quality metrics that are relevant from a business point of view and to (2) determine efficient target values for these metrics which consider the business impact of reductions in service quality.

10.2   Service Network Analysis

Societies are becoming increasingly service-oriented [4]. Service revenues from companies, such as Rolls Royce, Caterpillar, and ThyssenKrupp, often reach more than 35 % of total sales [5]. In the field of information technology, the global spending on cloud services is expected to grow 40 % over the next 7 years. Despite these facts, services are still the least studied part of the economy [6].

The observation that the power of service-based economies is no longer restricted to individual organizations, but spans across networks, is the main driver for conducting service network research. Networks play an important role in many application areas such as energy grid distribution and smart city planning. Service networks are a class of networks of emerging interest since worldwide economies are becoming increasingly connected. Nonetheless, while the economies of many countries are becoming service-oriented, very few studies on service networks exist. Understanding when, why, where, and how service networks function best is fundamental for the future because their analysis can provide an "x-ray" of service-based economies.

10.2.1 Motivation

The last decade has seen an growing interest in the study of networks in many fields of science. Examples are numerous, from the Internet, the world wide web, linked data, social networks, financial networks, railway networks, food chain networks, and innovation networks, to physical systems, such as power grids. However, the field of service networks has received less attention. Figure 10.2 shows some types

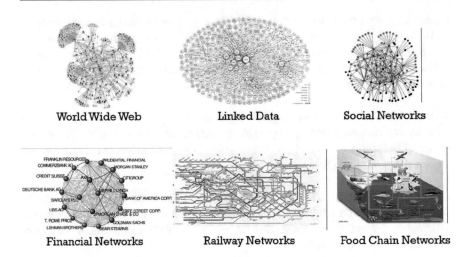

Fig. 10.2 Examples of networks from various fields [8–10]

of networks that are already established objects of studies. Understanding these various types of networks is part of a broader field of research, termed *network science* [7].

▶ **Definition (Service Network)** A *service network* is defined as a mathematical graph structure composed of service systems, which are composed by nodes connected by one or more specific types of *service relationship*, the edges. A *service system* is a functional unit with a boundary through which interactions occur with the environment, and, especially, with other service systems.

The theories and tools to be developed by researchers to analyze networks can have applications in many fields. To obtain more tangible and practical results it is convenient to follow the Occam's razor principle, and to focus on a particular use case or domain, such as cloud services. The idea is to reconstruct cloud service networks showing how these services are becoming interdependent and related world wide. When service network analysis is applied to cloud services, reasoning about software-based services and the technical and business relationships established between services requires a totally different approach for modeling and analysis when compared to other types of networks, such as the ones illustrated in Fig. 10.2.

Figure 10.3 shows (on the left side) a relatively small service network manually reconstructed from information found on the web. The network identifies consumer, competitor, supplier, and complementor relationships between cloud services, such as Amazon EC2, SugarCRM, Heroku, Microsoft Azure, Oracle CRM On Demand, and web-based self-services, such as Twitter or LinkedIn. It also shows (on the

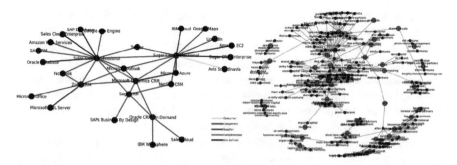

Fig. 10.3 Examples of a simplified cloud service network manually reconstructed (*on the left*) and of a large service network automatically reconstructed (*on the right*), from information available on the web

right side), a large service network which captures the relationships between cloud service providers in the field of Big Data. The red circles represent startups and the blue circles represent venture capital firms that have invested in those startups.

Service networks are decentralized and, thus, do not have a centralized control. Their behavior emerges as a result of the interactions among and between their nodes through relationships. What makes them fundamentally different are the characteristics of the nodes and relationships. For example, social networks are mainly composed of people and human relationships. On the other hand, service networks involve service systems which are composed of people, technology, and processes. Also, the relationships are characterized by a very different nature since they take the form of associations, memberships, dependencies, and other aspects of business relations [11].

10.2.2 Research Questions

The rapid adoption of cloud computing places a huge responsibility on service providers because society is becoming more and more dependent on cloud services. Understanding how services are being organized as (global) networks, the dependencies between them, and the robustness of the global infrastructure to failures is fundamental. On April 20, 2011, parts of Amazon AWS and its Elastic Block Store (EBS) service suffered a major outage. It took two days for service to be fully restored. Well-known failures of Amazon AWS have impacted hundreds of companies, such as Netflix, Instagram, and Heroku [12]. The dependencies between services are becoming increasingly complex and pervasive. For example, the NY Times relies on Amazon EC2, NASDAQ stock market depends on Amazon S3, and Business Objects (an SAP company) uses Amazon EC2. This brings increased importance to the analysis of service networks.

The problem is not limited to cloud computing. It also applies to other types of service networks, such as financial and supply chain networks. While network science has shown its relevance in the fields of energy, transport, and computer networks [7], studies on the field of service networks are still scarce (c.f. [11, 13–17]). Society has accepted and enjoyed the benefits of interconnected services, but it has not rigorously asked if it has answers to solve the accompanying second-order effects or more unwelcome consequences (e.g., butterfly effect), as well as the business opportunities, which underline specific network structures.

Service network analysis can offer a systematic, automated, and scientific study of large-scale cloud service networks. Service network analysis, similarly to link analysis and social network analysis, provides new theories and methods to discover knowledge in service domains. A central research statement, which still needs to be explored, is given as follows:

> Organizations are increasingly adopting cloud computing – however, it is not clear how cloud services depend on each other and which network structures are being formed. The analysis of large-scale cloud service networks will provide an understanding of their risks, robustness, and underlying business opportunities.

More precisely, relevant research questions are:

1. To what extent can service networks be reconstructed based on the information available on the web (c.f. [15])? This requires accessing and retrieving cloud service descriptions using the web as a comprehensive distributed database.
2. How can service network properties be measured and analyzed (c.f. [18])? Many important algorithms for network analysis developed in other fields (e.g., social networks) need to be exploited and adapted to study service networks.
3. How can service network analysis results be used to evaluate and improve existing infrastructures (c.f. [14, 19])? It is necessary to obtain an in-depth understanding of the factors that underlie the formation of cloud service networks, and service networks in general, by developing suitable theories, methods, and tools.

10.2.3 Existing Approaches

So far, previous work and tools to analyze service networks have tackled conceptual, small-scale, and manually designed networks (e.g. [20–27]). Approaches are restricted to the manual construction of networks from the information available in firms' surveys, teardown reports, on-site analysis, and tracing flows firm to firm (e.g., [28, 29]). For example, Guide and Wassenhove [30] have manually studied closed-loop supply chains by tracing products from supplier to consumers and vice-versa (e.g., Dell and Apple supply chains [28, 31]). This type of approach can also be used to reconstruct service networks, but it is often too costly because extensive manual labor is required to identify each service and their relationships. As a result, only networks of a small size can be reconstructed.

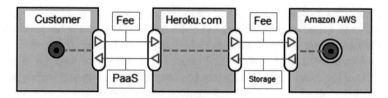

Fig. 10.4 Example of an e^3value model representing a network involving three services interacting via their interfaces

Other approaches, such as the e^3value and e^3service [21], provide a conceptual and graphical notation, and tools for the modeling of service networks. Figure 10.4 shows a simple example on how a network of services can be constructed using e^3 modeling. Unfortunately, these types of approaches are also impractical for reconstructing global service networks because they only work for small-scale networks. They still require manual reconstructing and analysis of networks.

10.2.4 Contributing Fields

Recent developments in the fields of information and communication technologies (ICT), and service management, design, and engineering have reached a maturity stage which enables to analyze service networks on a large scale. As observed by Chesbrough and Spohrer [32], "the abundance of information about people, technological artifacts and organizations has never been greater, nor the opportunity to configure them meaningfully into service relationships that create new value". This analysis requires to access information about services to reconstruct and model networks.

Open movements, such as open source, open data, and open innovation, provide the initiative to share information on services; service-dominant logic place emphasis on service trading rather than product exchange; linked data bring the technology to interlink data globally; network science sets the theoretical stage for service network analysis; semantic web technologies provide the global platform for information integration; business models contribute with theories to understand the structure of service models.

From these contributing fields, three can be highlighted because they provide critical foundations which make the analysis of service networks possible: network science, service-dominant logic, and linked data.

Network Science   Network science [7] can provide important discoveries on how the structure of networks (small world, random, scale free, etc.) affect their robustness and efficiency. For example, the world-wide web forms a large directed graph with an apparent random character. Nonetheless, the topology of the graph has evolved to a so-called scale-free network [33] by preferential attachment [34], i.e. when establishing hyperlinks, documents prefer the popularity of certain documents (of popular sites) which over time become hubs.

Service-Dominant Logic   Vargo and Lusch [4] introduce the concept of service-dominant logic and show that society has been gradually moving from a product-based orientation to a service-orientation, where the elements of economical exchange are services, rather than products. This places services at the center of society and economies.

Linked Data   Linked data [8] brings a different paradigm for data integration from computer science. It enables the easy integrating of distributed information at a global scale using semantic web principles (see Chap. 5). The use of background information in the form of linked data can enrich service descriptions and service networks to levels never seen before. This is essential for bringing information on distributed services together. In the context of Linked Data, it has been proved that companies and governments are willing to share data for the benefit of society. The same paradigm can be followed for sharing service systems descriptions.

10.2.5 Large-Scale Service Networks

One approach to study service networks is to use the information publicly available on services on the web which can be exploited for many scientific and exploratory purposes. This rich and diverse knowledge can be put to various uses ranging from service network optimization and analysis to identify under-explored service markets. To accomplish this, it is a fundamental requirement to create service networks, which translates into the discovery of relationships between the various services that are provided by distinct organizations, globally distributed across industry sectors and countries. Therefore, developing a mechanism to analyze large-scale service networks entails:

- Discovery. The discovery of information on services and relationships available on the web.
- Formalization. The formalization of the information found using service and relationship models which can be processed automatically by computers.
- Reconstruction. The reconstruction of service networks by aligning services and relationship models.
- Analysis. The development of algorithms to analyze the reconstructed networks.

The computer supported analysis of large-scale service networks and automated reconstruction, in opposition to manual approaches based on direct observations, can provide a bird's-eye view on service-driven societies. This has not been possible until now.

Information Sources

One interesting idea is to access, retrieve, enrich, and integrate service descriptions and service relationships from the web to automatically reconstruct service networks. Once services and relationships are integrated, suitable algorithms will enable analyzing and studying networks.

Information on services and relationships can be acquired using manual or automated methods. Automated methods, e.g., by using web scraping and wrappers, can crawl unstructured service sources from the web, such as corporate web sites, marketplaces (e.g., homeadvisor.com, Sears' servicelive.com, servicealley.com, and redbeacon.com), and other distributed information sources (e.g., companies reports, LinkedIn pages, twits, and blogs), and create instances on-the-fly. Explicit and implicit relationships can also be identified by inferring or deriving similarities between services.

Service Network Formalization

The formalization of service networks requires giving structure to unstructured service descriptions and relationships found on the web. Recent developments in formal service and relationship descriptions, such as the Unified Service Description Language (USDL) [35], Linked USDL [36], and Open Semantic Service Relationship (OSSR) [11], can be used as shared models to represent service networks. Linked USDL relies on a shared vocabulary for the creation of service models and includes concepts such as pricing, service level, availability, and roles. The family of languages termed *-USDL can be used to model and provide computer-understandable descriptions for services. These languages[1] allow formalizing business services and service systems in such a way that they can be used effectively for dynamic service outsourcing, efficient software-as-a-service trading, and automatic service contract negotiation.

For service relationship modeling, the OSSR model can be used to capture the dependencies that exist between cloud services. The model considers that service systems are represented using Linked USDL and derives a rich, multi-level relationship model. Service relationships are very different from the temporal and control-flow relations found in business process models. They relate service systems, accounting for various perspectives such as roles, associations, dependencies, and comparisons.

Example

The various relationship types shown in Fig. 10.3 are prescribed by the OSSN model. Four relationship types are displayed: customer, supplier, complementor, and competitor.

---

[1]Linked-USDL = http://linked-usdl.org/.

Network Reconstruction

To integrate service descriptions from multiple sources into comprehensive models is a complex task. Semantic technologies, from the field of Linked Data [8] (e.g., DBpedia [37] and Alchemy [38]), can be used to provide background knowledge to facilitate the establishment of connections between formal service descriptions to reconstruct networks. This is a fundamental step because keyword-based technology does not take meaning and context into account.

A major benefit of using the web as a large database is the ability to deeply mine data and discover patterns between services. Entity extraction, concept analysis, and text mining are all required approaches to develop suitable algorithms to assist in the reconstruction of service networks.

Service Network Analysis

A wide spectrum of techniques and algorithms can be developed to study service networks. For example, reasoning techniques can explore the notion of relationships as bonds. By discovering strong cliques (i.e., services connected to many services), it can be hypothesized that the stronger the relationships, the stronger the unification and the greater the commonality of fates (i.e., what happens to one service will also happen to the other services). As a result, it would be possible to infer that a tightly coupled service network will sink or swim together. Other fundamental algorithms, which are valuable to implement, come from the field of network science. For example, algorithms to detect if a service network is *scale-free* [18]. This property strongly correlates with the robustness of a network to failures. This can prove to be important in financial markets. As another example, the *preferential attachment* [34] can be explored to forecast the structural evolution of service networks. Other properties from the field of social networks can also be explored, such as network centrality, density, reachability, and connectivity [10]. The analysis requires efficient algorithms from graph theory since service networks are large-scale and developing polynomial-time algorithms is typically difficult.

Among the many theories that network analysis proposes, the notion of centrality measures the (relative) importance of a node with respect to the remaining nodes of a network. Applications of this metrics include evaluating how influential a person is within a social network. Figure 10.5 shows a social network (a) and a service network (b). The centrality degree of node A, which is defined as the number of links incident on a node, of network (a) is 6. Node A in the service network (b) has the same centrality degree, 6. Nonetheless, network (b) has characteristics which can be used to better estimate the importance of node A. In fact, it would be more intuitive that the centrality degree of a node (service) increases as its number of partners, complementors, and customers increases, and the degree decreases as the number of competitors increases. In other words, service centrality can be expressed as:

$$centrality = +w_s G + w_s F + w_c E + w_o D \tag{10.1}$$

$$-w_p B - w_p C \tag{10.2}$$

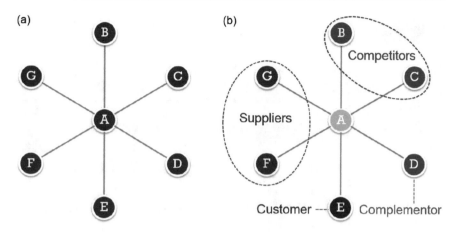

Fig. 10.5 Degree centrality can be used to study the relative importance of services within a service network

If such a service centrality function holds with actual service networks and the weights w_s, w_c, w_o, w_p can be determined, its application can help evaluate and rank the importance of services that engage in business transactions with other services in networks.

10.2.6 Research and Business Challenges

Since information about services publicly available on organizations' web sites (e.g., customer references,[2] technology[3] and alliance partners lists,[4] and business reports[5]) or in academic studies (e.g., [28, 31]) is mainly expressed in natural language it is nowadays extremely difficult to identify anything substantial and significant about service networks directly from this data. As an example, Fig. 10.6 shows the Amazon AWS partner network, which contains information indispensable for reconstructing part of the service network. The information available is unstructured, it does not comply to any common semantics, and is often not easily accessible (see for example [39]).

Existing approaches, e.g., e^3value and e^3service, are only suitable for manually modeling small-scale service networks (c.f. [20, 21]). Conceptually speaking, it would theoretically be possible to manually reconstruct networks by interweaving

---

[2]http://smepartnerfinder.sap.com/en.

[3]http://www.ontotext.com/partners.

[4]http://www.aws-partner-directory.com.

[5]http://www.itif.org/files/KraemerValueReport.pdf.

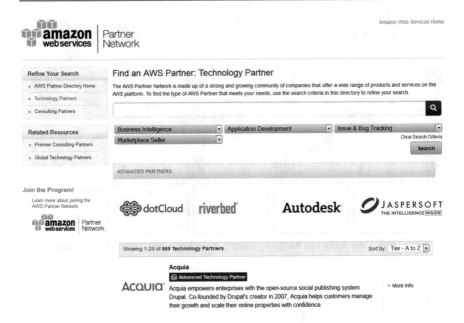

Fig. 10.6 Amazon AWS partner network

services as explained. From a practical side, however, this is almost impossible due to the considerable amount of time and effort required to do this manually.

Up to now, analyzing large-scale networks to identify patterns (e.g., the Bullwhip effect—a phenomenon which shows larger and larger swings in inventory in the back end of product supply chains) and to undertake optimizations has not been possible.

It is necessary to develop models, methods, and tools, which relieve experts from most of the burden of this manual effort. Specifically, it is necessary to provide enough automation, so that service network analysis becomes realizable with a reasonable workforce. It is clear that only automated approaches can enable the large-scale analysis of service networks and that manual techniques only work with very small networks with up to 10 or 20 services since it is time consuming and costly to read long reports and make surveys.

From the perspective of using reconstructed service networks from web data, the biggest difference with past approaches stems from the fact that they have implicitly or explicitly relied on the closed world assumption. This assumption is valid when service networks are designed with the goal of studying a specific, known service provider and its relationships with its customers, others providers, and its competitors (similar to an ego-network analysis [40] or a supply chain analysis [41]). At the global scale there is no choice but to use the open world approach as consistency and completeness cannot be assumed [42]. Furthermore, the amount and level of heterogeneity being captured on the web of services is next to that of the World Wide Web itself. This will require new algorithms that can handle large-scale networks working under uncertainty constraints and can recognize multi-level service relationships [11].

10.2.7 Application Domains

The use of theories developed in the context of service network research is not limited to the cloud service domain, and extends to financial, educational, healthcare, and governmental service networks. Understanding how services operate as part of a large-scale global network, the related risks and gains of different network structures and their dynamics finds many application domains in society.

Cloud Computing

The dependencies between infrastructure- and platform-as-a-service, software-as-a-service, as well as with technology-mediated services (e.g., bank ATMs, online banking, and distance learning) and technology-generated services (e.g., ITIL Service Desk and healthcare emergency units) make the resulting networks highly nonlinear. As a result, a small disturbance in a platform-as-a-service, such as Amazon AWS, can lead to catastrophic outcomes (a propagation problem studied in chaos theory and related to the butterfly effect) in other services (e.g., Netflix, Pinterest, and Instagram). Service network research can help in the design of cloud service infrastructures to minimize the propagation and acceleration of instability throughout networks, and design systems more adaptable and resilient.

Governments and Regulatory Bodies

Governments can rely on scientific data to pass more informed legislations. Understanding the dynamics and laws governing service networks can provide, e.g., authoritative insights on why and how financial service systems fail. It can explain how the 2007–2012 global financial crisis propagated throughout global service networks. Analysis can provide scientific grounds for the engineering of efficient and robust service network topologies to resist adverse environments.

Regulatory bodies can analyze service networks to detect topological patterns, such as oligopolies, monopolies, or 'cartels' in service markets. For example, a power-law distribution pattern can be used to identify oligopolies because it implies that only a few large service providers exist, whereas the occurrence of small providers is extremely common. Using service network research, the European Commission can, e.g., survey service markets more effectively. In fact, the type of study done by Ilzkovitz et al. [43] on the possible causes of service sector malfunctioning in the EU can benefit from using service network algorithms to automatically identify competitive pressures by using structural hole and ego theory [10]. These theories enable studying the strategic importance of certain services in networks.

Financial Networks

Financial service networks are another application domain. Today's financial networks are highly interrelated and interdependent. Any disturbances that occur in one service of a network may create consequences in other services. For example, in 2008, the economic problems initiated a chain reaction that started in the US and caused problems in European markets and almost took Iceland to bankruptcy. Leading financial service businesses closed (e.g., Lehman Brothers investment bank), others merged, and yet new services were created. The configuration and topology of financial service networks changed as a reaction mechanism. The disaster was a surprise for most people, but local information to each financial institution and financial services was available and could have been utilized to anticipate and minimize the catastrophe. Unfortunately, the information was not accessible to regulators.

10.3 Service Level Engineering

Information and communication technology is ubiquitous and society heavily depends on its functionality and availability. IT services ensure that laptops, smart phones and tablets are working and are key for almost every technology-related product, service or solution. Many products or services are nowadays either developed, produced, delivered or consumed via information technology.

To ensure that IT services are provided at the required level of quality, service providers and their customers set up contractual agreements—so called service level agreements (SLA)—to stipulate quality objectives for services. As the perception of quality is usually subjective, technical metrics—so called service level indicators (SLI)—are used to define service quality and to establish a common understanding of it. For each of these service level indicators a target value—denoted as service level objective (SLO)—is defined.

The concept of SLI and SLO will be illustrated by an example from IT outsourcing. It is assumed that a company wants to outsource part of its IT infrastructure to an external service provider. The company can purchase a particular IT service at two different levels of quality, for example, with an availability of 99.95 % or of 99.99 %. Both measures refer to a monitoring period of one week. Referring to this example, the service level indicator used to define service quality is "service availability". Service level objectives that customers can purchase are 99.95 % (option 1) or 99.99 % (option 2).

Depending on service and customer requirements considered, service quality may also be described by other service level indicators, such as response time, throughput or security related quality requirements.

10.3.1 Motivation

Nowadays, people constantly interact with smart phones and tablets, they browse the web, watch TV, etc. If one of these services is not delivered at the required level of quality this may be inconvenient, the impact may not be significant, however. If one listens to music over the internet and the connection breaks down, people may retry after a couple of minutes, they may change to an analog radio or they may simply do something else. In such a case, though inconvenient, consequences of a low level of quality (e.g., an unavailable service) may be low.[6]

Failures of services that are used in a business context, i.e., to support value creating activities of companies, may be much more severe. If a company's business processes rely on the availability of underlying supporting services, the situation outlined above will change. This is illustrated by looking at an example from the automotive industry. Production processes in the automotive industry are complex, yet well organized. Production is organized according to the just in time principle and follows an orchestration of streamlined activities, many of which are supported by underlying IT services. Assuming that one or more of these services experience a significant loss in quality (e.g., they are unavailable), consequences are not restricted to a mere "feeling of inconvenience" any longer. If a disruption of service is severe or too long, the assembly line may be stopped, mechanics may have to work overtime to achieve given lot sizes, etc. In this case, service disruptions result in a financial impact. Thus, companies will try to make sure that services are delivered at appropriate quality levels, which they stipulate in service level agreements.

There are even more extreme cases for which service downtime or reductions in service quality will lead to immediate losses in revenue. One example is high-frequency trading of banks. In high-frequency trading, algorithms and underlying IT services are used to trade stocks in quasi real time. If these services are unavailable financial consequences may be severe. According to [44],[7] 1 min of downtime in brokerage operations may lead to approximate downtime cost of \$107,500 for a financial institution. Though such figures should be treated with caution, the financial impact of service downtime in high frequency trading is obviously much more severe than a disruptive internet connection of someone listening to an internet radio station.

Downtime cost have been studied in a variety of industries. Besides the case of the banking industry there are other examples that got a lot of media attention, like a major outage of Amazon's e-commerce platform in 2013 [45], or a breakdown of Virgin Blue's (airline) ticketing system in 2010, which lead to losses in the

---

[6]Of course, there are exceptional cases in a B2C context as well. For instance, if someone is not able to make an emergency call with his cellphone because of a service disruption, the impact on someone's life might be severe.

[7]In order to provide readers with a rough idea of costs of downtime, this article uses numbers that are based on a study by Gartner Dataquest.

amount of several million dollars [46]. These examples underpin that service level objectives should be defined with care and that decision makers should be aware of the monetary impact that service disruptions have on their and others' business.

10.3.2 Problem Statement

The cases presented above show that requirements for quality of service—and, thus, stipulated service level objectives—will differ depending on the service and the environment, and that they will be influenced by a service's criticality to a great extent. While the individual listening to music may live with a streaming service being unavailable for half an hour over the day, such an availability objective may lead to serious problems in an automotive production process. For a high-frequency trader, such a service level objective would most likely be intolerable.

Looking at the three examples, the high-frequency trader would probably need the highest availability of service, followed by a production manager in the automotive industry and the person streaming music. However, asking all three people whether they need a service availability of 99.95 % or of 99.99 % (see the example in Sect. 10.3), they may have difficulties in agreeing on one objective or the other. As an increase in service quality usually entails an increase in cost or service prices, decision makers have to weigh the additional cost for increasing service levels against the additional benefit they gain from higher quality of service (or damage caused by low service quality).

If the price difference between option 1 and option 2 in the example was €5000, the high-frequency trader and production manager would probably choose the higher service level (option 2), as otherwise resulting losses in profit (trading) or additional cost of production downtime may justify the additional investment. A user of a music streaming service may not be willing to pay such a price for an increase of service availability. Still, the question remains how decisions would change if the price difference between both service levels was higher or lower. What if criticality of a service was higher or lower, or if business processes were affected differently?

Often, decision makers have difficulties in understanding the tradeoff between investing in higher service levels and the way that business is affected, if such an investment is withheld [3]. As a result, service levels are often stipulated according to "best guesses" of experts, which frequently result in suboptimal solutions [47]. As Kieninger et al. [48] put it:

> [...] in practice and academia, up to now there is no commonly accepted engineering approach [...] to precisely define [cost-efficient] service quality.

The problem of determining appropriate service level objectives can be studied from different angles. Depending on how services are delivered—i.e., by an internal IT department or by external service providers—SLO may be optimized by the service customer or by its provider. Moreover, from a societal perspective, one might aim to find a service level that optimizes the benefit of the entire service system (see Chap. 1). If one of the involved parties unilaterally optimizes, this relates to *optimal* service level objectives. If social welfare is maximized, this relates to *efficient* SLO. Thus, when trying to determine optimal or efficient service levels, the perspective taken needs to be considered.

10.3.3 Existing Approaches

In practice and academia, a variety of approaches exist that deal with the determination of service level objectives. Many contributions to this topic originate from research on the design and negotiation of service level agreements, especially in the IT outsourcing domain. Approaches are manifold and differ with regard to objectives pursued, perspectives taken (e.g., customer, provider, and service system) and methods applied. The following sections describe a selection of these approaches.

The simplest way to determine service level objectives is to make a good estimate of the level of service quality required. Service customers may ask internal experts that have a deep knowledge of respective services and business processes to make a best guess of the level of service quality required. Experts may assess the criticality of a service for the business and they may consider the price of a service at particular levels of quality to finally evaluate different offers by internal or external service providers. Service providers, on the other hand, may follow a similar approach by asking internal experts how reliable their systems are, how often they fail, and which service levels objectives they can guarantee to achieve.

The second type of approaches analyzes past performance data to derive optimal service level objectives. Such approaches (see [49]) assume that future service behavior can be predicted—at least to a certain extent—from historic performance data, for instance, by means of analytics (see Chap. 6). Service providers can use the insights they gain from these analyses to offer service level objectives that are realistic (e.g., SLO which have been achieved in past contract periods) and which they will most likely be able to meet in future contract periods. Service customers may pursue a similar approach to determine criticality of a service, for instance, by analyzing load patterns of similar services and by analyzing whether provided service levels were sufficient. Approaches usually allow weighting data based on their period of observation. Providers or customers may attach higher importance to more recent data, they may take account of seasonal trends, etc.

The approaches introduced above have in common that service level objectives are mainly determined on the basis of past performance data and by assessing criticality of a service. However, measuring criticality of a service is difficult. Referring back to the example of high-frequency trading and the automotive production process (see Sect. 10.3), one would probably argue that services supporting these activities are highly critical. Yet, the financial impact of service downtime or reductions in quality of service may differ significantly in both cases. Thus, it would obviously be valuable to take cost of downtime into account when quality of service is defined.

Respective approaches have inter alia evolved in the domain of Business-driven IT Management (BDIM) (see [47,50–52]). Authors in this domain—namely a group of academics around Sauvé et al.—have suggested to define service level objectives for IT services on the basis of financial considerations. The general idea is to derive optimal SLOs by trading off two types of cost: On the one hand, there are cost for the IT-infrastructure that is used to provide a service at a given level of quality. On the other hand, there is *business financial loss* (e.g., losses in revenue) that is caused by performance degradations. By assessing infrastructure cost and business financial losses for different configurations of IT-infrastructure, optimal service level objectives can be derived that minimize total cost. In another article by Sauvé et al. [47], this approach is for example applied to determine optimal SLO for an e-commerce website.

In this chapter, only a limited number of approaches could be discussed. Certainly, there are other contributions to this field which may analyze other issues of the problem addressed. The various approaches introduced differ significantly in their complexity. To conclude that more complex approaches are better is misleading, however. Depending on the setting considered—e.g., business requirements, criticality of service, service price, and cost of downtime—any of the approaches outlined above may be suitable for defining target values for quality of service. Taking the music streaming service as an example, users may intuitively know quite well how much they are willing to pay for a service at a given level of quality. For such a setting, a complex analysis of downtime cost or an assessment of past performance data might be excessive.

When applying the introduced approaches, one should be aware of the following shortcomings: Asking experts to determine optimal service level objectives may lead to suboptimal solutions. Experts might not be available, they may exhibit significant errors in judgment and different experts might come up with different recommendations. This implies that the outcome of such an approach may be random to some extent. Furthermore, approaches that depend on the analysis of historic performance data can usually not be applied for newly developed services and thus for innovative service offerings. In addition, such approaches assume that service behavior and consequences of service disruptions do not abruptly change in the future. Finally, except for the BDIM papers, proposed methods do not take account of cost of downtime when service level objectives are defined. As already noted, however, cost of downtime may have a significant impact on someone's decision to purchase a service at one quality level or the other.

10.3.4 Service Level Engineering

The definition of service quality is far from trivial. The importance of stipulating optimal or efficient service level objectives is usually affected by three factors: By the amount of cost of providing particular service levels, by the amount of financial impact caused by service incidents, and, third, by the duration of contracts.

A scenario in which all three factors are usually high is IT-outsourcing. In IT outsourcing, companies source out parts of their internal IT infrastructure to one or several external service providers. In such a setting the definition of optimal service levels is highly important for service customers, as they cannot easily adjust service levels once an outsourcing agreement has been established. In this domain (though not limited to it), another promising approach to determine optimal or efficient service levels has been developed, which is service level engineering [48].

The concept of service level engineering addresses two main issues in the definition of service quality. First, quality of service should be described by meaningful indicators that are understandable from a business point of view. Second, the determination of efficient service level objectives should be driven by the impact that degradations of service quality have on the business—i.e., the cost of downtime should be considered. As the focus of this chapter is on the definition of SLO, it will not elaborate on the identification of meaningful service level indicators in more detail.

In contrast to some of the presented approaches above (e.g., "best estimation", analysis of past performance data), Kieninger et al. [48] argue that the determination of SLO should be driven by financial considerations. The advantage of such an approach is that the decision which quality level to purchase is reproducible and thereby more transparent. In principle, service level engineering suggests to define SLO by measuring the cost of quality (e.g., the service price or internal cost for providing a particular level of quality) and by trading these off against the adverse impact that reductions in service quality have on the customer's business. In the generic approach, two dimensions of cost are defined: Variable service cost to measure the cost of quality, and business opportunity cost to measure the financial impact of quality reductions on the business (cf. [48]).

▶ **Definition (Variable Service Cost)** The cost that a provider incurs for providing the service. It includes all direct and indirect costs that are variable with respect to the SLO, i.e., which depend on the decision which quality of service to provide.

Variable service cost may mainly comprise cost for operating the IT-infrastructure used to provide a service at a specific level of quality. This may comprise cost for hardware, software, support personnel, etc. Intuitively, variable service cost will rise with increasing service levels. For instance, if the availability of a service is increased from 99.95 % to 99.99 % (see example in Sect. 10.3.4), providers need to spend more money on resources, e.g., more reliable servers, better trained support personnel, etc., leading to higher variable service cost.

▶ **Definition (Business Opportunity Cost)** The cost for the customer that is incurred due to an imperfect service compared to the cost of a perfect service.

In contrast to variable service cost, business opportunity cost are a measure to monetarily quantify the impact of quality degradations on business. If the production line of automotive manufacturers or IT services of banks break down (see Sect. 10.3) companies will incur opportunity cost such as losses in revenue, additional expenses like cost of labor, or intangible cost components like customer dissatisfaction, losses in reputation, etc. For business opportunity cost, the relation to a certain quality level will most likely be contrary to variable service cost. That is, for higher SLO, business opportunity cost will usually decrease. If the availability of IT services in high-frequency trading is increased, the total length of service downtime will decrease which will potentially lead to lower losses in revenue as more trades can be made.

Based on these two cost dimensions the service level engineering approach now suggests to define a quantitative optimization problem to find the particular service level objective that minimizes the sum of both cost dimensions, i.e., the total cost. Figure 10.7 provides an idealized illustration of this optimization problem for two continuous cost functions considering the target values of one service level indicator only. As explained before, it can be seen that variable service cost increase with increasing service level objectives whereas business opportunity cost behave contrary and decrease with increasing SLO. By adding up variable service cost and business opportunity cost, a third function can be derived, indicating the total cost of stipulating specific service level objectives.

The total cost function can finally be used to determine the particular service level objective SLO_{opt} that minimizes total cost. As service level engineering is considered to be a generic engineering approach, the optimization problem can be defined and solved for various perspectives. That is, it might aim to identify an *optimal* service level, where either service provider or service customer unilaterally optimize their benefit, or it might aim for the identification of *efficient* service level objectives, which maximize the benefit of the service system that is jointly formed by the service provider and the customer. Depending on the perspectives taken,

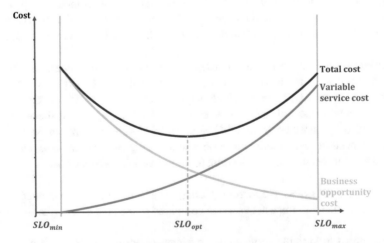

Fig. 10.7 Idealized graphical representation of the quantitative optimization problem for the determination of optimal service level objectives

different functions have to be considered [48]. If a service customer purchases a service from an external service provider (IT-outsourcing) and a customer perspective is taken when optimizing, it is obviously not the variable service cost, but the service price that matters for the optimization problem of the customer. If service quality is defined by more than one service level indicator the optimization problem becomes multidimensional and usually more complex to solve.

Non-linear Business Opportunity Cost

Service level engineering currently experiences a second stream of research which originates from the observation that business opportunity cost might develop non-linearly with regard to single service incidents. This is illustrated by looking at an example of the e-commerce platform amazon.com. It is assumed that the internal IT department of Amazon can guarantee that the platform will be available 99 % during a fictive reference period of 1,440 min (1 day). The one percent that the service is unavailable accounts for a total of 14.4 min. Assuming that in each reference period the web site goes down once, for the entire 14.4 min (cf. the provided example at the end of Sect. 10.3), consequences would most likely be severe. Not all visitors will be willing to postpone their shopping activities and might go to other e-commerce web sites instead. Now, assuming that the 14.4 min of total outage time are caused by many very short outages (e.g., around one second) visitors of the web site might not care (Fig. 10.8). In this case, the effect of a service disruption might be very small compared to one long outage.

The (aggregated) service availability is 99 % in both examples. The consequence of this finding is that it is not enough to determine variable service cost and business opportunity cost on basis of (aggregated) service level indicators. The business opportunity cost caused are obviously not the same in both examples. Kieninger et al. [53] speak of non-linear business opportunity cost functions (with regard to single service incidents) in this context. Due to this observation they have extended their initial approach by describing service quality not only on basis of aggregating service level indicators like service availability which conceal outages' individual durations, but also with regard to the distributions of service incidents constituting

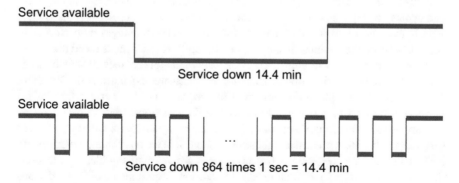

Service available

Service down 14.4 min

Service available

Service down 864 times 1 sec = 14.4 min

Fig. 10.8 Exemplary service incident patterns resulting in equal service downtime

the (aggregated) service level. With regard to the example provided, they would not only specify that service availability is 99 %, but also, that it was caused by one outage incident of 14.4 min or by 864 service outages of one second each. Interested readers find additional information on the extension of the approach in [53, 54].

10.3.5 Research and Business Challenges

Though the definition of optimal or efficient service level objectives has received increasing attention, both, in academia and in practice, there are still many challenges to address, especially with regard to the following issues: The impact of imperfect service quality, or rather reductions in service quality, need to be translated into financial measures. Furthermore, service providers need to be able measure and forecast, which service levels they are likely to achieve and at which cost. Moreover, whenever service provider and customer are two legally independent companies (e.g., in IT-outsourcing settings), there is a problem of information asymmetry (see Chap. 1) between both parties.

The measurement and forecast of service quality is still a challenge for service providers. In order to measure the impact of reductions in quality of service (e.g., service outages), providers and customers would need to agree on an end-to-end measurement of service quality. That is, service level indicators would need to be defined in such a way that they are directly relevant from an end-user perspective [48]. Today, most service level indicators are defined for single components of the IT-infrastructure and not for the application that is used by an end-user. Moreover, most approaches in this domain assume that providers are able to attach cost to the delivery of particular service levels. In order to derive a variable service cost curve in the service level engineering approach, providers need to be able to measure, determine and forecast how different service levels can be achieved through different configurations of IT-infrastructure, related processes, etc. Such data is usually not available today. Service quality is often subject to fluctuation and service delivery environments are unstable. The more unstable service quality is, however, the more difficult is the determination of optimal service level objectives.

Regarding the quantification of business impact, it is still a challenge for companies to determine or even consider the cost of imperfect service quality. This is mainly due to the fact that the impact of service outages or performance degradations on the business is not sufficiently understood. This is owed partly to a missing business and IT alignment (service level indicators are technical metrics and sometimes not well understood by stakeholders of business departments), but it also results from the complexity of assessing the consequences of service failures [2]. Assessing the cost of downtime requires people to analyze how value is created in companies and complex networks. There are many interdependencies between services and business processes, and assessing these in terms of monetary measures is difficult. This holds especially for consequences that are intangible, i.e., customer dissatisfaction, losses in reputation, etc. In addition, requirements of industries and even individual companies are highly heterogeneous, which implies that estimates of business cost for outage or performance degradations in specific industries may not simply be generalized. Instead, each case requires a thorough analysis and service levels have to be defined accordingly.

The last challenge is limited to settings in which services are outsourced, i.e., service customers outsource part of their services to an external provider. Outsourcing settings are usually governed by means of service level agreements that specify mutual rights and obligations. As such contracts are incomplete by nature, providers or customers may have an incentive not to disclose private information about their internal variable service cost or business opportunity cost or they might strive to make untruthful statements about their cost on purpose. In such cases, optimal or efficient service level objectives are more difficult do determine.

Challenges that have been described in this section are the main reasons preventing more complex approaches from being applied in practice and from stipulating optimal or efficient service level objectives. Thus, advanced methods have to be developed that allow overcoming the problems of today's approaches.

10.3.6 Contributing Fields

Contributing fields with regard to service level engineering are manifold. Service providers require adequate methods from statistics and analytics to monitor, measure and forecast service quality levels and to determine variable service cost. The more complex the approaches get, the more advanced methods are needed to derive such cost. This is particularly the case if distributions of service incidents shall be considered (see explanations provided in Sect. 10.3.4).

The determination of business opportunity cost functions requires service customers to gain a deep knowledge of their processes and the interdependencies between business and IT. Contributing fields in this context are business process modeling and simulation that support customers in developing this knowledge and making it explicit (see e.g., methods proposed in [54] for the determination of business opportunity cost functions). Once both cost functions are established, methods from operations research may help to solve the quantitative optimization problem of determining optimal service level objectives. Again, problem complexity increases with increasing number of service level indicators and, additionally, if distributions of service incidents are considered.

Contributing fields are not limited to the ones presented. If services are provided in an outsourcing relationship, providers will have to think about which service levels they still offer without taking too much risk of violating service level agreements. In this context, methods from decision and insurance theory are needed to make sound decisions (see [55]). From a customer's point of view, approaches from auction theory and mechanism design can realize benefits when services are offered by multiple external providers and an optimal service price shall be achieved (see [53]).

10.3.7 Application Domains

Most of the approaches that have been introduced in this chapter are applied in the field of information technology—especially in service level management. Though the definition of service level objectives is of great importance in this context, the application of the presented methods is not limited to the domain of IT services.

The consideration of expert opinions and the analysis of past data are established methods which are applied in a variety of fields and industrial contexts. In Chap. 6, a number of examples have been presented to illustrate how companies use algorithms and statistics to generate insights from analyzing data.

The principle to trade-off different types of cost against one another—as suggested in service level engineering—has been applied in other disciplines as well. As service level engineering is considered to be a generic engineering approach, it is well suited for defining optimal or efficient target variables in other application domains. An adoption of the approach requires decision makers to model the interplay between the cost needed to raise a target variable (variable service cost) and the adverse monetary impact resulting from this particular target variable (business opportunity cost). For example, in the manufacturing industry, the approach may be used to determine optimal lot sizes for production processes, and to define target values for the optimal availability of spare parts.

To conclude, service level engineering provides a structured approach to define meaningful service level indicators and to determine efficient or optimal service level objectives. Despite the progress that has been made in this field, there are still many challenges that need to be addressed in the future.

10.4 Conclusions

The network-based nature of businesses was made evident in the global financial crisis that unfolded in 2008. The collapse of a few banks in the US resulted in catastrophic problems around the world as a demonstration of the butterfly, ripple, and domino effects of interconnected systems. Service network analysis can provide many new insights into how service-based economies are structured since little is known about how service providers establish relationships. Reconstructing and analyzing large-scale service networks is a hard undertaking that has never been tackled before. Currently, the most modern approaches and tools only provide manual solutions to deal with conceptual and small-scale networks. The development of new methods and techniques is required.

The second part of this chapter elaborated on approaches to determine appropriate service quality levels for (IT-)services. First, service level engineering was introduced as a systematic engineering approach to define business-relevant service level indicators and corresponding cost-efficient (or cost-optimal) service level objectives. Building on this, related research and business challenges, contributing fields of research as well as potential application domains were discussed.

Concluding it can be said that, despite the progress that has been made in this field, there are still many challenges that need to be addressed in future research.

Review Section

Review Questions

1. Contrast the characteristics of the nodes and relationships that are part of the www, linked data, social networks, financial networks, railway networks, and food chain networks.
2. Choose a web site that operates as a registry for services, such as findthebest for cloud computing.[8] With the information available from the registry, manually reconstruct a service networks with 10–15 services similar to the one shown in Fig. 10.3.
3. Using the notion of co-occurrence, use Google's search engine to determine the "strength" or support from the web for the relationships identified in the previous exercise. Each edge will have a weight to express its strength.
4. Apply the metrics size, density, centrality, and distance from the field of social networking to the service network created. What can be learned? How could the metrics benefit from an adaptation to deal specifically with service networks?
5. Using NetworkX (NX),[9] a Python package for the study of complex networks, develop a software program to visualize the network created.
6. Explain the role of service level indicators and service level objectives in measuring and defining service quality.
7. Which approaches are there to define service level objectives? What are their advantages and disadvantages?
8. Explain in more detail how service level engineering can be applied to define service level objectives. Elaborate on the trade-off between the two cost types considered in service level engineering.
9. What are the challenges of defining and measuring service quality in practice?

Project

Service Network Analysis
Service networks take many forms. They can represent and relate services with a strong human component, such as the ones publicized at homeadvisor.com or servicelive.com, or with a strong ICT component, such as the ones advertised at programambleweb.com.

---

[8]http://cloud-computing.findthebest.com/.
[9]http://networkx.github.io/.

This projects looks into the reconstruction of networks of services with a strong ICT component. The objective is to use the information available at programambleweb.com on Web API. Each Web API can be seen as a service implemented using web services (see Chap. 5) and described by their features, tags, providers, protocols, popularity, etc. Relationships can be extracted from the information that relates similar Web API. For example, the Twitter Web API is related to the Facebook Web API since they both provide access to social networking services.

Using a scrapping tool, such as scrapy.org, extract the information on individual Web API and their relationships. The information can be stored in a relational database to be used to reconstruct a large-scale network. Afterwards, the network can be analyzed. Interesting insights can be gathered by calculating the degree centrality of Web API and, then, use the notion of eigenvector centrality to measure the influence of an Web API in other Web API.

Once the analysis has been conducted, write a short report that describes the settings of the environment (e.g., how was the scraping tool used, how was the extracted information stored in the database, and how was the network represented and reconstructed) and the results obtained from the analysis. Discuss the findings and explain how they might contribute to a better understanding of the topology of service networks.

Service Level Engineering

The definition of appropriate service level indicators and optimal service level objectives is key when negotiating service level agreements for outsourcing relationships. The examples of Virgin Blue's ticketing system and Amazon's e-commerce platform have shown that service outages may have a significant adverse impact on business. In this project you will slip into the role of an IT manager who is responsible to purchase an IT service from several external IT outsourcing providers.

Your company, EnergyComp, is a leading provider of energy services in Europe. Among others, the company offers to analyze and optimize their clients' energy consumption patterns in order to increase energy efficiency and to optimize cost. The provision of EnergyComp's services heavily depends on the availability of underlying IT infrastructure, as energy consumption data from customers is constantly transferred to and analyzed by EnergyComp's servers.

As EnergyComp's current outsourcing agreement with an external IT service provider will expire at the end of the year, you are responsible for negotiating a new outsourcing contract. Knowing that service availability is key you have analyzed the influence of service outages on EnergyComp's business operations. The analysis resulted in the following business opportunity cost function [EUR per minute of outage]: $f_{outage}(x) = 0.5999x^2 + 0.3028x$.

In order to identify a cost-optimal service solution, you have invited several IT service providers to respond to a request for proposal. As you intend to apply a service level engineering approach you have stated that each offer needs to consist of a tuple of an incident distribution (including a specification of the total outage time) and a service price. The incident distribution shall be characterized as a generalized

Table 10.1 Providers' service offers

Provider	Incident distribution	Total outage time (min)	Service price
Provider A	B(5;30)	420	€ 1550
Provider B	B(5;15)	405	€ 1700
Provider C	B(5;5)	425	€ 1250
Provider D	B(15;5)	390	€ 1900
Provider E	B(30;5)	430	€ 1200

beta distribution $B(\alpha; \beta)$ with parameter values α and β. The monitoring period is one week, the maximum duration of a single outage allowed is 30 min (i.e. the generalized beta density function is restricted to an interval of 0 to 30 min).

You have received the following bids by service providers (see Table 10.1):

Exercise 1

As an experienced IT manager you are asked to make an optimal purchasing decision. Recently you have heard of service level engineering, a novel approach to determine optimal service level objectives for outsourcing contracts.

- Explain the concept of service level engineering as well as its objectives and elaborate on the two types of costs considered.
- Why is service level engineering an appropriate method to solve the problem at hand? Elaborate on the advantages of service level engineering compared to the approaches introduced in Sect. 10.3.3.

Exercise 2

One of your colleagues in the IT department suggests to simply purchase the service offer with the highest guaranteed level of (aggregated) service availability instead of applying service level engineering.

- Calculate the (aggregated) level of service availability for each of the service offers defined in Table 10.1.
- Based on the obtained results, explain why the suggested method of your colleague is inappropriate to identify the cost-optimal service offer. Elaborate on the consequences of non-linear business opportunity cost functions.

Exercise 3

Having convinced the management that service level engineering is a suitable method to apply, you are asked to identify the cost-optimal service offer to purchase.

- Calculate the business opportunity cost for each service offer defined in Table 10.1. Name and explain the parameters that are needed to calculate business opportunity cost and explain how they influence the calculation. (Hint: See [53] for further information on how to calculate the business impact of service outages based on distributions of service incidents.)

- Which of the service offer(s) would you recommend to purchase? Explain your choice.

Exercise 4

Now assume that business opportunity cost develop linearly, for instance, with a business opportunity cost function of $f_{outages}(x) = 2x$.

- Explain how the results obtained in Exercise 3 change if business opportunity cost develop linearly. Which service offer would you suggest to purchase and why?
- Having the prior suggestion of your colleague in mind: How could the calculation of optimal service offers be simplified in case of linear business opportunity cost?

Key Terms

Network Science   A research field which studies complex networks such as telecommunication networks, computer networks, biological networks, and social networks. It builds from contributions on graph theory, statistics, data mining, and sociology.

Social Network   A network view of social relationships in terms of network theory consisting of individual and relationships between the individuals (e.g., friendship, kinship, and organizations).

Service Network   A network view of service interactions in terms of network theory consisting of services and relationships between the services (e.g., provider, customer, and competitor).

Service Network Analysis   The use of theories and methods to facilitate the quantitative or qualitative analysis of service networks by describing features of a network either through a numerical or visual representations.

Web Crawler   A software program that visits web sites and reads their pages and other information to create entries for a search engine index. They can be used to crawl for information on services and their relationships.

Service Level Indicator   An indicator to quantitatively measure service quality.

Service Level Objective   A target value for a service level indicator.

Service Level Engineering   An engineering approach to define business-relevant service level indicators and associated efficient service level objectives.

Business Opportunity Cost   The adverse monetary impact on business that is incurred by a service at imperfect service quality compared to a service at perfect quality.

Further Reading

David Easley and Jon Kleinberg. *Networks, Crowds, and Markets: Reasoning About a Highly Connected World.* Cambridge University Press, 2010.

Ronald S. Burt. *Brokerage and Closure: An Introduction to Social Capital.* Oxford University Press, 2007.

Rick Sturm, Morris Wayne and Mary Jander. *Foundations of Service Level Management.* Sams Publishing, 2000.

Office of Government Commerce. *ITIL Service Design.* The Stationery Office, 2011.

References

1. Spohrer J, Maglio PP (2010) Service science: toward a smarter planet. In: Introduction to service engineering. Wiley, New York, pp 1–30. ISBN: 9780470569627. doi:10.1002/9780470569627.ch1
2. Unterharnscheidt P, Kieninger A (2010) Service level management – challenges and their relevance from the customers' point of view. In: 16th Americas conference on information systems (AMCIS)
3. Taylor R, Tofts C (2005) Death by a thousand SLAs: a short study of commercial suicide pacts. Technical report. Hewlett-Packard Labs
4. Vargo S, Lusch R (2004) The four service marketing myths: remnants of a goods-based, manufacturing model. J Serv Res 6(4):324–335
5. Teeri T, Hirst L (2009) Making service science mainstream white paper. Technical report. Aalto University and IBM
6. Spohrer J et al (2007) Steps toward a science of service systems. Computer 40(1):71–77
7. Börner K, Sanyal S, Vespignani A (2007) Network science. Annu Rev Inf Sci Technol 41(1):537–607
8. Bizer C, Heath T, Berners-Lee T (2009) Linked data - the story so far. Int J Semantic Web Inf Syst 5(3):1–22
9. Schweitzer F et al (2009) Economic networks: the new challenges. Science 325(5939):422–425 doi:10.1126/science.1173644. http://www.sciencemag.org/content/325/5939/422.abstract
10. Easley D, Kleinberg J (2010) Networks, crowds, and markets: reasoning about a highly connected world. Cambridge University Press, Cambridge
11. Cardoso J (2013) Modeling service relationships for service networks. In: 4th international conference on exploring service science (IESS 1.3). Lecture notes in business information processing. Springer, Heidelberg, pp 114–128
12. Armbrust M et al (2010) A view of cloud computing. Commun ACM 53(4):50–58
13. Cardoso J et al (2012) Open semantic service networks. In: The international symposium on services science (ISSS 2012), Leipzig, 2012, pp 1–15
14. Cardoso J, Pedrinaci C, De Leenheer P (2013) Open semantic service networks: modeling and analysis. In: 4th international conference on exploring service science (IESS 1.3). Lecture notes in business information processing, vol 143. Springer, Heidelberg, pp 141–154
15. Cardoso J et al (2013) Foundations of open semantic service setworks. Int J Serv Sci Manag Eng Technol 4(2):1–16
16. De Leenheer P, Cardoso J, Pedrinaci C (2013) Ontological representation and governance of business semantics in compliant service networks. In: 4th international conference on exploring service science (IESS 1.3). Lecture notes in business information processing, vol 143. Springer, Heidelberg, pp 155–169

17. J. Cardoso (2013) Open service networks: research directions. In: 6th international C* conference on computer science & software engineering. ACM, New York, pp 2–3
18. Mislove A et al (2007) Measurement and analysis of online social networks. In: 7th ACM SIGCOMM conference on internet measurement. ACM, New York, pp 29–42
19. Leskovec J et al (2008) Microscopic evolution of social networks. In: 14th ACM SIGKDD international conference on knowledge discovery and data mining. ACM, New York, pp 462–470
20. Gordijn J, Yu E, van der Raadt B (2006) e-service design using i* and e3value modeling. IEEE Softw 23:26–33
21. Akkermans H et al (2004) Value webs: using ontologies to bundle real-world services. IEEE Intell Syst 19(4):57–66
22. Allee V (2000) Reconfiguring the value network. J Bus Strategy 21(4):36–39
23. Weill P, Vitale M (2001) Place to space: migrating to eBusiness models. Harvard Business School Press, Boston
24. Bitsaki M et al (2008) An architecture for managing the lifecycle of business goals for partners in a service network. In: Mähönen P, Pohl, K, Priol, T (eds) Towards a service-based internet. Lecture notes in computer science, vol 5377. Springer, Berlin/Heidelberg, pp 196–207. ISBN: 978-3-540-89896-2
25. Applegate L (2001) Emerging e-business models: lessons from de field. Harv Bus Rev 9:801
26. Parolini C (1999) The value net: a tool for competitive strategy. Wiley, Heidelberg
27. Osterwalder A, Pigneur Y (2010) Business model generation. Wiley, New York, p 281
28. Linden G, Kraemer KL, Dedrick J (2009) Who captures value in a global innovation network?: the case of Apple's iPod. Commun ACM 52(3):140–144
29. Barboza D (2010) Supply chain for iPhone highlights costs in China, New York Times, 5 July, 2010.
30. Guide D, Van Wassenhove L (2009) The evolution of closed-loop supply chain research. Oper Res 57:10–18
31. Kapuscinski R et al (2004) Inventory decisions in Dell's supply chain. Interfaces 34(3):191–205
32. Chesbrough H, Spohrer J (2006) A research manifesto for services science. Commun ACM 49:35–40
33. Wang XF, Chen G (2003) Complex networks: small-world, scale-free and beyond. IEEE Circuits Syst Mag 3(1):6–20
34. Yule U (1925) A mathematical theory of evolution based on the conclusions of Dr. J. C. Willis. Philos Trans R Soc Lond 213(2):21–87
35. Cardoso J et al (2010) Towards a unified service description language for the internet of services: requirements and first developments. In: IEEE international conference on services computing (SCC), Florida, 2010, pp 602–609
36. Cardoso J et al (2013) Cloud computing automation: integrating USDL and TOSCA. In: 25th conference on advanced information systems engineering (CAiSE). Lecture notes in computer science, vol 7908. Springer, Heidelberg, pp 1–16
37. Mendes PN et al (2011) Dbpedia spotlight: shedding light on the web of documents. In: 7th international conference on semantic systems (I-Semantics)
38. AlchemyAPI (2013). http://www.alchemyapi.com/. Accessed 29 July 2013
39. Frei F (2008) The four things a service business must get right. Harv Bus Rev 86(4):70–80, 136
40. Kleinberg J et al (2008) Strategic network formation with structural holes. In: 9th ACM conference on electronic commerce. ACM, New York, pp 284–293
41. Harland C (1996) Supply chain management: relationships, chains and networks. Br J Manag 7(s1):S63–S80
42. Krötzsch M et al (2011) A better uncle for OWL: nominal schemas for integrating rules and ontologies. In: 20th international conference on world wide web. ACM, New York, pp 645–654

43. Ilzkovitz F, Dierx A, Sousa N (2008) An analysis of the possible causes of product market malfunctioning in the EU: first results for manufacturing and service sectors. Technical report, Directorate General Economic and Monetary Affairs (DG ECFIN), European Commission

44. Marquis H (2006) In: itSM Solutions DITY Newsletter, vol 2. http://www.itsmsolutions.com/newsletters/DITYvol2iss47.pdf. Dec 2006

45. Skariachan D (2013). http://www.reuters.com/article/2013/08/19/net-us-amazon-website-idUSBRE97I0UT20130819. Published by Reuters on August 19th, 2013. Accessed 19 Sep 2013

46. O'Sullivan M (2011). http://www.theage.com.au/business/navitaire-and-virgin-blue-settle-20110404-1cyla.html. Published by TheAge on April 5th, 2013. Accessed 9 Sep 2013

47. Sauvé JP et al (2005) SLA design from a business perspective. In: 16th IFIP/IEEE international workshop on distributed systems: operations and management (DSOM), pp 72–83

48. Kieninger A, Westernhagen J, Satzger G (2011) The economics of service level engineering. In: 44th annual Hawaii international conference on system sciences (HICSS). IEEE Computer Society, Kauai

49. Ludwig A, Kowalkiewicz M (2009) Supporting service level agreement creation with past service behavior data. In: Business information systems workshops. Springer, Heidelberg, pp 375–385

50. Sauvé J et al (2006) Optimal design of e-commerce site infrastructure from a business perspective. In: 39th annual Hawaii international conference on system sciences (HICSS), vol 8. IEEE, Kauia, p 178

51. Marques FT, Sauvé JP, Moura JAB (2007) Service level agreement design and service provisioning for outsourced services. In: Network operations and management symposium, 2007. IEEE, Rio de Janeiro, pp 106–113

52. Marques F, Sauvé J, Moura A (2009) SLA design and service provisioning for outsourced services. J Netw Syst Manag 17(1):73–90

53. Kieninger A et al (2013) Leveraging service incident analytics to determine cost-optimal service offers. In: 11th international conference on Wirtschaftsinformatik, vol 2, pp 1015–1029

54. Kieninger A et al (2013) Simulation-based quantification of business impacts caused by service incidents. In: 3rd international conference on exploring service science. Lecture notes in business information processing, vol 143. Springer, Heidelberg, pp 170–185

55. Schmitz B et al (2014) Towards the consideration of performance risks for the design of service offers. In: 4th international conference on exploring services science. Lecture notes in business information processing, vol 169. Springer, Heidelberg, pp 108–123

Index

© Springer International Publishing Switzerland 2015
J. Cardoso et al. (eds.), *Fundamentals of Service Systems*, Service Science: Research and Innovations in the Service Economy, DOI 10.1007/978-3-319-23195-2

Printed in the United States
By Bookmasters